Jesus Is The One

Michael S. Syslo

*I dedicate this book to my children
and their families.*

*I would like to thank Bill Soucie and Deacon Jerry Szostak
for their reviews and comments.*

Books by Michael S. Syslo
"Lord, Lord"
Vincentian Spirituality
Return to Him
It's All About Love
For Your Love Alone
What Would Jesus Do?
Wisdom Across the Ages
Hope: My Advent Calendar
One-Liners to Guide Our Lives

ISBN 979-8-218-60287-1

The Prophecy Fulfilled?
Can the Story be Believed?

For thousands of years, in the words and writings of the Jewish prophets, prophecies were made that the Messiah would come. These prophecies were spread out through the sacred scriptures. Throughout these thousands of years, the descendants of Abraham experienced both prosperity and slavery. And to be completely honest about this, I would think that, during the time of prosperity, the descendants of Abraham were little concerned about the Messiah or even the need for a Messiah. We humans tend to look for a savior only in adversity. And there was plenty of adversity throughout the history of the Jewish people, the Chosen People.

History shows that the God of the Jewish people, Yahweh, had come to the aid of His chosen race many times. He had established covenant after covenant with His people and they failed to keep their end of the bargain over and over again. Yet, Yahweh was faithful to His covenants. Why would anyone, especially Almighty God, put up with such betrayal over and over again?! Only one thing can account for this – LOVE. It was out of love that God created humanity and out of love that He tolerates all of our abuses. Then after thousands of years, the prophecy was fulfilled – or was it?

It was about two thousand years ago that this story begins. It was one of those times of adversity. The Jewish people were under the control of the Roman empire. A young woman, a virgin, was pregnant and gave birth to a boychild in a small town in Judea, Bethlehem. This had been one of the prophecies. She, Mary, and her husband, Joseph, named this boy Jesus.

Hearing of the birth of the long-awaited Messiah, Herod, the then king of the Jewish people, wanting to ensure his own kingship and control over Israel, ordered the death of all children in that area who were two years old or younger. This way, Herod was sure to eliminate any competition to his power and authority. Fortunately, Joseph was warned in a dream of what was to occur; he and Mary took the child and escaped to Egypt to avoid the massacre. After Herod's death, they returned to their home in the town of Nazareth. And Jesus lived a life in obscurity for 30 years.

The time had come for Jesus to make Himself known and start to fulfill His mission. But the prophecies had called for someone to prepare the way. This was John, known as the Baptist, who was actually a distant relative of Jesus. John went about Judea calling for people to repent of their sins and seek the forgiveness of God. As a means to show they sought forgiveness, John baptized people, thus the name Baptist. It was John who recognized Jesus as the one who was to come and recommended to his followers to follow Jesus. It was from this time on that Jesus' ministry had begun.

Jesus' ministry took Him throughout Judea and Galilee. He preached, He taught, He healed, He raised people from the dead. He did all of the things the Messiah should do; but not the things the people thought He would do; He did not free them from the control and authority of Rome. He was a spiritual leader, not a political one.

And then, to top everything off, He allowed Himself to be surrendered into the hands of the Jewish leadership to be tried and crucified as a criminal. How could He be the Messiah?! The Messiah was supposed to bring order and peace, to free the Jewish people from the control of the pagan world. He did not lead His people to victory over the Romans.

He was killed by the Jewish leadership and the Romans openly in Jerusalem. Some of His followers say He rose from the dead, and He was seen by various groups; but this is denied by both the Jewish leadership and the Romans. Who was to be believed?

For anyone but the true Messiah, the Son of the living God, the story would end here. It is not over. It is through Jesus' life, His teachings, His works, His passion, death, and resurrection that He brings life to all of us. It is this that is the basis of the following pages. Jesus is the one. Be happy, smile, know it. Let us see what that means.

Introduction

Father ... this is eternal life, that they may know You, the only true God, and Jesus Christ whom you have sent. (John 17:3) This is the opening line of the *Catechism of the Catholic Church.* I chose to use this opening because I truly believe that Jesus Christ is the only Son of God and that knowing Him and following His example and teachings is the only key to eternal life. I have also stated this in lectures and in my writings. God sent us His only begotten Son to redeem us and to show us how He expects us to live. Jesus' life is a clear example that the way God, our Father, expects us to live is possible.

A few years ago, I came across the following prayer from St. Teresa of Calcutta (Mother Teresa). She titled it *He is the One.*

> *He is the Word made Flesh. Jesus is the Bread of Life.*
> *Jesus is the Victim offered for our sins on the Cross.*
> *Jesus is the Sacrifice offered at the Holy Mass for the sins of the world and mine.*
> *Jesus is the Word – to be spoken.*
> *Jesus is the Truth – to be told.*
> *Jesus is the Way – to be walked.*
> *Jesus is the Light – to be lit.*
> *Jesus is the Life – to be lived.*
> *Jesus is the Love – to be loved.*
> *Jesus is the Joy – to be shared.*
> *Jesus is the Sacrifice – to be offered.*
> *Jesus is the Peace – to be given.*
> *Jesus is the Bread of Life – to be eaten.*
> *Jesus is the Hungry – to be fed.*
> *Jesus is the Thirsty – to be satiated.*
> *Jesus is the Naked – to be clothed.*
> *Jesus is the Homeless – to be taken in.*

Jesus is the Sick – to be healed.
Jesus is the Lonely – to be loved.
(Jesus is the Hope – to be realized.
Eternal Father, help me to imitate Your Son in my
daily life. Amen.)

I say this prayer every morning. The last three lines in parentheses are my own addition. It was this prayer that inspired the title of this book. Jesus is our everything. It is Jesus whom we should imitate in all we say and do. To repeat an important point, it is Jesus' lived example and His teachings that show that the life God expects of us is possible.

Socrates was one of the great philosophers. Not having known Jesus, he wrote, "If we could but see God, we would know how we ought to live." Socrates lived more than 400 years before Christ was born. If Socrates had known Jesus, he would have had his example to live by.

On January 27, 2001, Bishop J. Peter Sartain, Diocese of Little Rock, wrote, "An end to abortion on demand will not be secure if we do not examine our individual and collective consciences and let God teach us how to live and how to submit every facet of life and society to His sovereign wisdom." In this particular instance, Bishop Sartain was addressing the serious problem of abortion. However, the key part of the statement begins with the "if". He emphasizes the need for us to form our consciences with the guidance of God and live as He leads us.

I have read the Gospels. For over 40 years of attending daily Mass, I have read and heard the Gospel stories many times. I have read a number of books about the life of Christ. And, yes, I have watched the movies depicting His life. But, sad to say, I have never undertaken a serious study of His life. For the last 40 years of my life, a portion of it has been dedicated to the Society of St. Vincent de Paul. And one of the things that has been clearly shown is that St. Vincent based his ministries and his teaching on the life and teachings of Jesus. That could very well be what influenced this drive in me to know my savior better.

I have written several books before this, and I have spoken to many groups. One message that is common among my writings and presentations is that our Lord is the one we should model our lives on. We should be imitating His life and following His teachings. That is what you do when you truly love and respect someone. The finest example of love and respect for someone is imitation. Below is a picture of my son-in-law, Jeff, and my grandson, Evan.

Talk about imitating someone you love! I actually picture myself walking next to Jesus, imitating His words and actions. In this picture, I would be on His left. If we turned around, I would be on His right. But in all reality, I would be with Him constantly. Better yet, He would be with me constantly. And He is. If I truly love our Lord, if I truly want to walk like Him, talk like Him, do things in the way He would do them, then I must study Him, how He lived, what he taught. Then and only then could I answer the question: what *would* Jesus do?

In this book, I will be reflecting on Jesus' life and teachings. I will attempt to follow His life as presented to us in the four Gospels. I am not going to present historical clarity. That is not my purpose. Many authors, more qualified than I am, have done so. This attempt is comparable to a personal journal. I will present His life as one story, combining all four Gospels, as one flowing story. The reflections on each passage are mine. They are thoughts I had at the time of the writing. There may be multiple reflections on certain passages; but the reader must remember they are my personal thoughts.

Our Lord speaks to each of us differently, so the reader may not agree with my interpretation of what I have read. In fact, the next time I read one of the passages, I may reflect on it differently. But that is the magic of the Word of God. He speaks to each of us in a way that we need it when we need it. Although all of His words are truth, that truth may have a special meaning for us at particular times in our lives.

From a structure and sequencing point of view, I have based my reflections on "John and the Synoptic Gospels Comparison Chart" and then, "The Synoptic Gospel Parallels with John Continued" which can be found at GospelParallels.com. My Scripture Source is the New American Bible Revised Edition which can be found on the internet.

It is my hope that the reader will find this to be worthwhile reading and a consideration for his/her own reflections.

From Our Lord's Prayer:
Thy Will be Done!
(Fiat Voluntas Tua!)

Part 1
Jesus' Birth and
Early Years

Prologue

<u>Matthew, Chapter 1</u> *[1] The book of the genealogy of Jesus Christ, the son of David, the son of Abraham.*

<u>Mark, Chapter 1</u> *[1] The beginning of the gospel of Jesus Christ [the Son of God].*

<u>Luke, Chapter 1</u> *[1] Since many have undertaken to compile a narrative of the events that have been fulfilled among us, [2] just as those who were eyewitnesses from the beginning and ministers of the word have handed them down to us, [3] I too have decided, after investigating everything accurately anew, to write it down in an orderly sequence for you, most excellent Theophilus, [4] so that you may realize the certainty of the teachings you have received.*

<u>John, Chapter 1</u> *[1] In the beginning was the Word, and the Word was with God, and the Word was God. [2] He was in the beginning with God. [3] All things came to be through him, and without him nothing came to be. What came to be [4] through him was life, and this life was the light of the human race; [5] the light shines in the darkness, and the darkness has not overcome it. [6] A man named John was sent from God. [7] He came for testimony, to testify to the light, so that all might believe through him. [8] He was not the light but came to testify to the light. [9] The true light, which enlightens everyone, was coming into the world. [10] He was in the world, and the world came to be through him, but the world did not know him. [11] He came to what was his own, but his own people[g] did not accept him. [12] But to those who did accept him he gave power to become children of God, to those who believe in his name, [13] who were born not by natural generation nor by human choice nor by a man's decision but of God. [14] And the Word became flesh and made his dwelling among us, and we saw his glory, the glory as of the Father's only Son, full of grace and truth. [15] John testified to him and cried out, saying, "This was he of whom I said, 'The one who is coming after me*

ranks ahead of me because he existed before me.'" [16] *From his fullness we have all received, grace in place of grace,* [17] *because while the law was given through Moses, grace and truth came through Jesus Christ.* [18] *No one has ever seen God. The only Son, God, who is at the Father's side, has revealed him.*

All of the Gospels have an introductory statement. It only makes sense that they would. Matthew starts his gospel with the genealogy of Jesus, proof that Jesus is a descendent of Abraham and specifically in the line of David – one of the Messianic predictions.

Mark opens with the coming of John the Baptist, the precursor of the Messiah. The opening is simple and straightforward.

Luke is writing directly to Theophilus, telling the story of Jesus, based on eyewitness testimony. There is no indication that Luke actually knew and spoke to Jesus. His eyewitness testimony came from Jesus' Mother and from the Apostles. Luke also spent a great amount of time specifically with Peter and Paul. This is a practical approach similar to the one he used for the Acts of the Apostles. As will be seen in the next chapter, Luke also leads with John the Baptist.

Of all the Gospels, John's is the most challenging because he is focused on our Lord's divinity. Like Mark and Luke, he introduces John the Baptist who is the witness to the light coming into the world. But again, John emphasizes Jesus' divinity and that is his purpose throughout the Gospel as well as the letters he wrote that are included in the New Testament.

All four Gospel writers approach the life and teachings of our Lord from a different perspective as well as toward a different target audience.

In Luke's introduction, he indicates something that I never really considered: "Since many have undertaken to compile a narrative of the events ..." I am not naïve. I just have not considered that there were "many" who had undertaken the task of recording things about Jesus' life and teachings before Luke wrote his story around 85 A.D. (C.E. for the politically correct). I have to concede that, for 50 or so years after Jesus ascended, there were many so taken by our Lord and all He did and taught that they wanted to record what they knew so it could be passed down. I have to keep in mind that is exactly what I am doing. Luke was not an eyewitness to Jesus' life and teachings; but he believes (as well as the Church) that his sources were accurate and reliable.

John introduces Jesus as the second person of the Trinity without actually saying it. Even though John lived longer than the other Apostles, I do not believe he had a better grasp of the Triune God. He was still formulating a basic understanding. That is not criticism. The concept of the Trinity is a mystery. Even though we have been pondering this for 2,000 years, the Church still views it as a mystery.

Jesus is the Word of God. John tells us: *"All things came to be through Him, and without Him nothing came to be."* To repeat an important point for all believers: without Him nothing came to be. Here is another concept that we humans cannot fathom. It is the idea of nothingness. Every aspect of our being is dependent on the existence of something. Genesis describes this nothingness as an abyss. When a painter creates a picture, he starts with a canvass and some ideas based on the world around him of what to create. When an author writes a book, he starts with paper and, again, some ideas based on the world around him of what to write. God had the abyss, nothingness, before Him and His own imagination. And God created something out of nothing.

And the Word became flesh. God took on a human body. God's Word brought life into the world and then took on a fully human body to reconcile humanity to the Father for having committed the original sin. The Word was fully human and fully divine. Only God can reconcile with God.

John, like Mark, opens his Gospel with John the Baptist. The Baptist was the precursor of the Messiah. Moses foretold the coming of the Messiah and John the Baptist was the final prophet preparing His way.

So much of what is written in the Gospels is meaningful to the point of almost taking any statement or part of a statement and reflecting on it alone. However, that is not my purpose. My purpose is to study my Lord and God, Jesus the Christ, to learn as much as I can from what He did and said. I will start with John 1:18, *"No one has ever seen God. The only Son, God, who is at the Father's side, has revealed Him."* Jesus' earthly mission was not only to reconcile mankind to the Father but to also reveal the Father to mankind, to let us know who the Father truly is and that living according to the Will of God is not only possible and meaningful, it is necessary to gain eternal life. This is what I have come to believe and what I hope to develop in this study.

Like me, all the Gospel writers were not eye witnesses of Jesus life. However, like me they all believed that Jesus was both human and divine.

Lord, open my mind and my heart to what it is that You would have me learn. Your life and teachings are the goal of my study. Help me to filter my way through all that is presented in the Gospel stories. Help me to grow in love of You. Amen.

Birth and Childhood

The Promise of the Birth of John the Baptist

<u>Luke 1:5-25:</u> *⁵ In the days of Herod, king of Judea, there was a priest named Zechariah, of the division of Abijah. And he had a wife from the daughters of Aaron, and her name was Elizabeth. ⁶ And they were both righteous before God, walking blamelessly in all the commandments and statutes of the Lord. ⁷ But they had no child, because Elizabeth was barren, and both were advanced in years. ⁸ Now while he was serving as priest before God when his division was on duty, ⁹ according to the custom of the priesthood, he was chosen by lot to enter the temple of the Lord and burn incense. ¹⁰ And the whole multitude of the people were praying outside at the hour of incense. ¹¹ And there appeared to him an angel of the Lord standing on the right side of the altar of incense. ¹² And Zechariah was troubled when he saw him, and fear fell upon him. ¹³ But the angel said to him, "Do not be afraid, Zechariah, for your prayer has been heard, and your wife Elizabeth will bear you a son, and you shall call his name John. ¹⁴ And you will have joy and gladness, and many will rejoice at his birth, ¹⁵ for he will be great before the Lord. And he must not drink wine or strong drink; and he will be filled with the Holy Spirit, even from his mother's womb. ¹⁶ And he will turn many of the children of Israel to the Lord their God, ¹⁷ and he will go before him in the spirit and power of Elijah, to turn the hearts of the fathers to the children, and the disobedient to the wisdom of the just, to make ready for the Lord a people prepared." ¹⁸ And Zechariah said to the angel, "How shall I know this? For I am an old man,*

15

and my wife is advanced in years." [19] And the angel answered him, "I am Gabriel. I stand in the presence of God, and I was sent to speak to you and to bring you this good news. [20] And behold, you will be silent and unable to speak until the day that these things take place, because you did not believe my words, which will be fulfilled in their time." [21] And the people were waiting for Zechariah, and they were wondering at his delay in the temple. [22] And when he came out, he was unable to speak to them, and they realized that he had seen a vision in the temple. And he kept making signs to them and remained mute. [23] And when his time of service was ended, he went to his home. [24] After these days his wife Elizabeth conceived, and for five months she kept herself hidden, saying, [25] "Thus the Lord has done for me in the days when he looked on me, to take away my reproach among people."

Luke continues his presentation with the announcement and conception of John the Baptist. John is the precursor of the Son of God. He is filled with the spirit of Elijah. It was prophesied that Elijah would return and prepare the world for the coming of the Messiah. John is the fulfillment of that prophecy.

Throughout the New Testament, reference is made to the many prophecies that foretold the coming of the Messiah. The importance of this cannot be diminished. How else would we know that the Messiah has arrived, if not through the fulfillment of the prophecies that had come over more than a thousand years?

Zechariah is the focus in this passage. He will father a son! It is hard to believe since he and Elizabeth are considered to be beyond childbearing. But he gets the message and is reluctant to believe what he hears. Is this simply a dream or is this a real visit from an angel with a real message from God? Zechariah learns quickly that this is the real thing. The angel Gabriel tells him he will be speechless till the baby is born. Sometimes it is hard to believe, even when the prediction is of a spectacular nature.

The story, as presented, does not say that Zechariah actually consented to this. The angel Gabriel explained it to him and how he would know this was happening. Sometimes faith has to be drawn out of us by physical means such as we will see later. In this case, Zechariah's faith was aided by his lack of speech.

The stage is set. The coming of the precursor is not a miracle but is manifested by the unexpected conception, pregnancy, and birth of a child to an elderly couple. God has a way of doing amazing things with little or no fanfare. John the Baptist, son of Zechariah and Elizabeth, from a small town in the hill country of Judah, would prepare the way of our Lord. And the life of the world is about to change.

Lord, prepare me. Prepare my mind and my heart for what is to come. Help me to not take these stories for granted, simply because I have heard and read them many times. Help me to believe when You send me a message. Amen.

The Annunciation

Luke 1:26-38: *²⁶ In the sixth month the angel Gabriel was sent from God to a city of Galilee named Nazareth, ²⁷ to a virgin betrothed to a man whose name was Joseph, of the house of David. And the virgin's name was Mary. ²⁸ And he came to her and said, "Greetings, O favored one, the Lord is with you!" ²⁹ But she was greatly troubled at the saying, and tried to discern what sort of greeting this might be. ³⁰ And the angel said to her, "Do not be afraid, Mary, for you have found favor with God. ³¹ And behold, you will conceive in your womb and* *bear a son, and you shall call his name Jesus. ³² He will be great and will be called the Son of the Most High. And the Lord God will give to him the throne of his father David, ³³ and he will reign over the house of Jacob forever, and of his kingdom there will be no end." ³⁴ And Mary said to the angel, "How will this be, since I am a virgin?" ³⁵ And the angel answered her, "The Holy Spirit will come upon you, and the power of the Most High will overshadow you; therefore, the child to be born will be called holy—the Son of God. ³⁶ And behold, your relative Elizabeth in her old age has also conceived a son, and this is the sixth month with her who was called barren. ³⁷ For nothing will be impossible with God." ³⁸ And Mary said, "Behold, I am the servant of the Lord; let it be to me according to your word." And the angel departed from her.*

The birth of the precursor, the one who will come before, has been set in place. The announcement has been made to the father. Now is the time for the announcement to be made to the chosen mother of the Messiah. The virgin birth of the Messiah, as prophesied, is being announced in this passage from Luke.

Let us begin with the angel's greeting. *"And the angel said to her, 'Do not be afraid, Mary,...'"* Do not be afraid. This is the same greeting that can be found throughout the bible, but it is especially used by our Lord in these Gospels. God knows how our human nature works. There has to be a way to bring peace to those who have just witnessed something extraordinary – the appearance of an angel, the entry of Jesus into a locked room after His crucifixion and death. There is no indication in the Gospels that Mary was afraid. Her response shows more curiosity than fear.

The Word of God is about to become the Word Incarnate. The moment young Mary says, "Yes," the moment she gives her "fiat" (may it be done according to Your word), the baby Jesus begins to form in her womb. The importance of this moment in time should never be overlooked. It is the moment that God became man and began His dwelling among us.

God has taken His first step toward reconciling man to Himself. Man could never accomplish this reconciliation on his own. Only God can reconcile with God.

"Let it be done to me according to your word." This is Mary's "fiat," her agreement to do the Will of God. It is not a sign of reluctance. She does not understand fully how this is going to happen; however, she believes in God and trusts Him. It is this confidence and trust that rings true. Next to Jesus, Mary is set before us as a true example of a life to be followed and imitated. Her willingness to do God's Will, like Jesus' willingness to do the Will of His Father in heaven, is the key to gaining eternal life. Jesus, told us that only those who do the Will of His Father in heaven will enter the gates of heaven. Mary is willing to take on the first of her two missions: to bring Jesus to us and to bring us to Jesus.

Lord, You chose the Blessed Virgin Mary over the myriad women before her to be Your Mother. And she offered her "fiat" in response. She has true faith and trust in You. Help my faith and trust to grow as I learn more about You and what You are asking of mankind. Amen.

Mary Visits Elizabeth

Luke 1:39-45: *[39] In those days Mary arose and went with haste into the hill country, to a town in Judah, [40] and she entered the house of Zechariah and greeted Elizabeth. [41] And when*

Elizabeth heard the greeting of Mary, the baby leaped in her womb. And Elizabeth was filled with the Holy Spirit, [42] and she exclaimed with a loud cry, "Blessed are you among women, and blessed is the fruit of your womb! [43] And why is this granted to me that the mother of my Lord should come to me? [44] For behold, when the sound of your greeting came to my ears, the baby in my womb leaped for joy. [45] And blessed is she who believed that there would be a fulfillment of what was spoken to her from the Lord."

Learning that her cousin Elizabeth was pregnant, especially at an advanced age, Mary arranged with her parents, Joachim and Ann, for her to spend time with Elizabeth and Zechariah, aiding her until the baby is born. This was not uncommon at that time. Family was expected to help family in their time of need. In her advanced age, Elizabeth would need help, especially as she was getting closer to the birth of her baby.

The baby John in the womb of Elizabeth recognized the spirit of the God-man in the womb of Mary as she came closer, and the joy of that encounter was felt by Elizabeth.

The angel of the Lord did not visit Elizabeth in advance to tell her Mary was coming or that Mary was pregnant. The Holy Spirit inspired Elizabeth, and she immediately recognized that Mary was also pregnant; but it was more than just that. The Holy Spirit revealed to her that Mary was pregnant with the baby to become the Messiah. And Elizabeth rejoiced with Mary.

The bond between Elizabeth and Mary was strengthened and the bond between John and Jesus was established. The Gospels do not tell us if Jesus and John ever met after birth in their childhoods. One can only speculate that there were occasions when cousins probably got together during the following thirty years.

Lord, Your presence and Mary's condition were revealed to the baby John and to Elizabeth his mother by the Holy Spirit. Please help me to recognize You in my life as I should. Amen.

Mary's Song of Praise: The Magnificat

<u>Luke 1:46-56:</u> *[46] And Mary said, "My soul magnifies the Lord, [47] and my spirit rejoices in God my Savior, [48] for he has looked on the humble estate of his servant. For behold, from now on all generations will call me blessed; [49] for he who is mighty has done great things for me, and holy is his name. [50] And his mercy is for those who fear him from generation to generation. [51] He has shown strength with his arm; he has scattered the proud in the thoughts of their hearts; [52] he has brought down the mighty from their thrones and exalted those of humble estate; [53] he has filled the hungry with good things, and the rich he has sent away empty. [54] He has helped his servant Israel, in remembrance of his mercy, [55] as he spoke to our fathers, to Abraham and to his offspring forever." [56] And Mary remained with her about three months and returned to her home.*

Here Luke records that, after Elizabeth acknowledged Mary's special condition and gift from God, Mary proclaimed praise and thanksgiving for His blessings on her and her nation. Praise and thanksgiving should be our regular greetings to God for all of the blessings He showers on us.

Mary remained with Elizabeth for about three months. Mary stayed and helped Elizabeth until the baby John was born. I believe it is safe to assume that Mary stayed after his birth a sufficient time to aid Elizabeth until she was ready to manage her day to day on her own. If we pray for Mary's intercession on our behalf for our special needs, I believe she would stay with us till we no longer need her. After all, she is our mother.

Lord, Your Mother stayed with Elizabeth in her time of need. Help me to seek the Blessed Mother's assistance in my time of need as well. As the prayer goes, "never was it known that anyone who fled to thy protection was left unaided." Remind me to seek her help in my time of need. Amen.

The Birth of John the Baptist

Luke 1:57-66: *⁵⁷ Now the time came for Elizabeth to give birth, and she bore a son. ⁵⁸ And her neighbors and relatives heard that the Lord had shown great mercy to her, and they rejoiced with her. ⁵⁹ And on the eighth day they came to circumcise the child. And they would have called him Zechariah after his father, ⁶⁰ but his mother answered, "No; he shall be called John." ⁶¹ And they said to her, "None of your relatives is called by this name." ⁶² And they made signs to his father, inquiring what he wanted him to be called. ⁶³ And he asked for a writing tablet and wrote, "His name is John." And they all wondered. ⁶⁴ And immediately his mouth was opened and his tongue loosed, and he spoke, blessing God. ⁶⁵ And fear came on all their neighbors. And all these things were talked about through all the hill country of Judea, ⁶⁶ and all who heard them laid them up in their hearts, saying, "What then will this child be?" For the hand of the Lord was with him.*

The birth of John is now a reality. The long-awaited precursor, the one with the spirit, the passion, and the zeal of Elijah has come, although there are still another thirty years before his work truly begins.

What's in a name? There seems to be much ado about the choice of name. Would he not have been effective as the precursor if his name was Zechariah the Baptist? The answer is very simple. That was the name given by the angel Gabriel: "you shall call his name John." God chose the name. God has a reason for everything He does, even if we may not understand it. Just as He chose the name for Jesus.

Does this mean that Zechariah and Elizabeth are now out of the picture? How about Mary? How long will she remain with Elizabeth? Actually, these are inconsequential questions for this episode. John the Baptist, the precursor, was born. Yes, Mary probably stayed for a short period after his birth, helping Elizabeth in whatever way she could. Then it was up to Zechariah and Elizabeth to raise the child, preparing him, in the ways they could, to take on his role as prophet. The episode may be over, but the task was not completed.

Lord, help me to recognize Your will in the missions You place before me. Give me the strength to follow Your will and the fortitude to persevere to the end. Amen.

Zechariah's Prophecy

Luke 1:67-80: *⁶⁷ And his father Zechariah was filled with the Holy Spirit and prophesied, saying, ⁶⁸ "Blessed be the Lord God of Israel, for he has visited and redeemed his people ⁶⁹ and has raised up a horn of salvation for us in the house of his servant David, ⁷⁰ as he spoke by the mouth of his holy prophets from of old, ⁷¹ that we should be saved from our enemies and from the hand of all who hate us; ⁷² to show the mercy promised to our fathers and to remember his holy covenant, ⁷³ the oath that he swore to our father Abraham, to grant us ⁷⁴ that we, being delivered from the hand* *of our enemies, might serve him without fear, [75] in holiness and righteousness before him all our days. [76] And you, child, will be called the prophet of the Most High; for you will go before the Lord to prepare his ways, [77] to give knowledge of salvation to his people in the forgiveness of their sins, [78] because of the tender mercy of our God, whereby the sunrise shall visit us from on high [79] to give light to those who sit in darkness and in the shadow of death, to guide our feet into the way of peace." [80] And the child grew and became strong in spirit, and he was in the wilderness until the day of his public appearance to Israel.*

Zechariah's prophecy is better known to many Catholics as the Canticle of Zechariah. It is part of the morning prayer of many. It not only anticipates the role that his son is going to have in the redemption of mankind, but it is a regular reminder of the true expectation of God's covenants with us: *that we, being delivered from the hand of our enemies, might serve him without fear, in holiness and righteousness before him all our days.* It was the Jewish people who failed to fulfill their part of the covenant. It is all of mankind (all who call themselves believers in the one true God) who are failing to fulfill our part of the covenants. There is no secret here, there is no finger-pointing, we are not fulfilling God's expectation of us.

Lord, daily I recite the Canticle of Zechariah. While doing so, allow me to recommit myself to fulfilling the covenant. Help me to not put my will in place of Your expectation of me. Amen.

The Genealogy of Jesus

<u>Matthew 1:2-17:</u> *² Abraham became the father of Isaac, Isaac the father of Jacob, Jacob the father of Judah and his brothers. ³ Judah became the father of Perez and Zerah, whose mother was Tamar. Perez became the father of Hezron, Hezron the father of Ram, ⁴ Ram the father of Amminadab. Amminadab became the father of Nahshon, Nahshon the father of Salmon, ⁵ Salmon the father of Boaz, whose mother was Rahab. Boaz became the father of Obed, whose mother was Ruth. Obed became the father of Jesse, ⁶ Jesse the father of David the king. David became the father of Solomon, whose mother had been the wife of Uriah. ⁷ Solomon became the father of Rehoboam, Rehoboam the father of Abijah, Abijah the father of Asaph. ⁸ Asaph became the father of Jehoshaphat, Jehoshaphat the father of Joram, Joram the father of Uzziah. ⁹ Uzziah became the father of Jotham, Jotham the father of Ahaz, Ahaz the father of Hezekiah. ¹⁰ Hezekiah became the father of Manasseh, Manasseh the father of Amos, Amos the father of Josiah. ¹¹ Josiah became the father of Jechoniah and his brothers at the time of the Babylonian exile. ¹² After the Babylonian exile, Jechoniah became the father of Shealtiel, Shealtiel the father of Zerubbabel, ¹³ Zerubbabel the father of Abiud. Abiud became the father of Eliakim, Eliakim the father of Azor, ¹⁴ Azor the father of Zadok. Zadok became the father of Achim, Achim the father of Eliud, ¹⁵ Eliud the father of Eleazar. Eleazar became the father of Matthan, Matthan the father of Jacob, ¹⁶ Jacob the father of Joseph, the husband of Mary. Of her was born Jesus who is called the Messiah. ¹⁷ Thus the total number of generations from Abraham to David is fourteen generations; from David to the Babylonian exile, fourteen generations; from the Babylonian exile to the Messiah, fourteen generations.*

Luke 3:23-38: [23] *When Jesus began his ministry, he was about thirty years of age. He was the son, as was thought, of Joseph, the son of Heli,* [24] *the son of Matthat, the son of Levi, the son of Melchi, the son of Jannai, the son of Joseph,* [25] *the son of Mattathias, the son of Amos, the son of Nahum, the son of Esli, the son of Naggai,* [26] *the son of Maath, the son of Mattathias, the son of Semein, the son of Josech, the son of Joda,* [27] *the son of Joanan, the son of Rhesa, the son of Zerubbabel, the son of Shealtiel, the son of Neri,* [28] *the son of Melchi, the son of Addi, the son of Cosam, the son of Elmadam, the son of Er,* [29] *the son of Joshua, the son of Eliezer, the son of Jorim, the son of Matthat, the son of Levi,* [30] *the son of Simeon, the son of Judah, the son of Joseph, the son of Jonam, the son of Eliakim,* [31] *the son of Melea, the son of Menna, the son of Mattatha, the son of Nathan, the son of David,* [32] *the son of Jesse, the son of Obed, the son of Boaz, the son of Sala, the son of Nahshon,* [33] *the son of Amminadab, the son of Admin, the son of Arni, the son of Hezron, the son of Perez, the son of Judah,* [34] *the son of Jacob, the son of Isaac, the son of Abraham, the son of Terah, the son of Nahor,* [35] *the son of Serug, the son of Reu, the son of Peleg, the son of Eber, the son of Shelah,* [36] *the son of Cainan, the son of Arphaxad, the son of Shem, the son of Noah, the son of Lamech,* [37] *the son of Methuselah, the son of Enoch, the son of Jared, the son of Mahalaleel, the son of Cainan,* [38] *the son of Enos, the son of Seth, the son of Adam, the son of God.*

As a lector, I always dreaded the times that I was scheduled to read the genealogy. Actually, dreaded is not the right word. I was more uncomfortable. I have always made it my habit to learn how to pronounce someone's name properly, as they would have it pronounced. I ask them to be sure. With the names in the Bible, I cannot ask the person how to pronounce his or her name. So, I have to choose from the way I have heard the name pronounced by others or simply try to pronounce it based on various rules of pronunciation and accentuation. A name is not just a name, it is important to the bearer of the name.

The primary reason that both Matthew and Luke include a genealogy of Jesus in their Gospels is to show that Jesus is a descendent of King David. They go back farther than David, but that is not pertinent here. I have not taken the time to compare lists, but I am sure others have. That is not my purpose. Jesus is a descendent of David and so that matches one of the prophecies related to the Messiah. Establishing that Jesus is the Messiah is reflected in all of the Gospels.

A question has occurred to me. I understand that Joseph was accepted by the Israelite community as the father of Jesus, although His true Father was of divine nature. I have not studied all of the Bible closely enough to know if any of the others in the genealogy were fostered rather than children by blood. It has no significant bearing on this study, but a curiosity.

Delving into the life of Jesus, understanding how He lived, and understanding what He taught are my primary focus. The fact that Jesus is the Christ adds credentials to what I want to learn.

Lord, Your genealogy is important to understanding who You truly are. I have never looked at my own descendance as being anything of importance. But maybe I should. I am the result of many who have gone before me. I am also the result of all that I have experienced in life. Help me to know myself better and, in doing so, serve You better. Amen.

The Birth of Jesus

Matthew 1:18-25: *[18] Now this is how the birth of Jesus Christ came about. When his mother Mary was betrothed to Joseph, but before they lived together, she was found with child through the holy Spirit. [19] Joseph her husband, since he was a righteous man, yet unwilling to expose her to shame, decided to divorce her quietly. [20] Such was his intention when, behold, the angel of the Lord appeared to him in a dream and said, "Joseph, son of David, do not be afraid to take Mary your wife into your home. For it is through the holy Spirit that this child has been conceived in her. [21] She will bear a son and you are to name him Jesus, because he will save his people from their sins." [22] All this took place to fulfill what the Lord had said through the prophet: [23] "Behold, the virgin shall be with child and bear a son, and they shall name him Emmanuel," which means "God is with us." [24] When Joseph awoke, he did as the angel of the Lord had commanded him and took his wife into his home. [25] He had no relations with her until she bore a son, and he named him Jesus.*

Throughout all of the thousands of years that mankind has occupied the earth, I am sure that Joseph was not the first and only man who took for his wife a woman who was pregnant by someone else. But this was a most unique circumstance, especially in light of the law of the Israelite community. There is no doubt in my mind that Joesph was the loving husband to Mary and the loving father that Jesus needed as he was growing.

I am also sure that Joseph struggled with what was revealed to him by the angel in his dream. But he accepted it as God knew he would. God chose the right man to be the caring, loving, and understanding husband that Mary needed. God chose the right man to be the caring, loving,

and understanding father for our Lord Jesus. And so, the earthly life of Jesus begins with love and a "fiat" to the Will of God.

Lord, I have always believed that You chose Martha to be my wife, my companion for life. You also planned for our three children. I hope I have been the loving, caring, and understanding husband and father You expected me to be. Amen.

It Took Place in Bethlehem

Luke 2:1-7: *[1] In those days a decree went out from Caesar Augustus that the whole world should be enrolled. [2] This was the first enrollment, when Quirinius was governor of Syria. [3] So all went to be enrolled, each to his own town. [4] And Joseph too went up from Galilee from the town of Nazareth to Judea, to the city of David that is called Bethlehem, because he was of the house and family of David, [5] to be enrolled with Mary, his betrothed, who was with child. [6] While they were there, the time came for her to have her child, [7] and she gave birth to her firstborn son. She wrapped him in swaddling clothes and laid him in a manger, because there was no room for them in the inn.*

And so, Jesus was born. We live during an amazing time. This is more than two thousand years after Jesus' birth, and we probably know more about His birth than people who lived ages before us. Much of what we know comes from tradition, from the writings of early fathers of the Church, from speculation based on the Israelite culture, from the writings and words of visionaries. The only eye witnesses of His birth have long passed away.

But what remains to be a truly amazing fact is that the Son of God became man and lived among us, regardless of whether or not we know all of the fine details of Jesus' birth. Out of love for us, God sent His only begotten Son to live among us, to live a truly human life, to grow as a human, to experience life with its joys and sorrows, to show us how we should live, to show us how to live as His Father in heaven wants us to live, to show that it is possible to live that way, to suffer and die for the sins that mankind has committed from the beginning of time and will commit throughout the future, to reconcile all mankind to His Father for the sin for Adam and Eve, and to open the gates of heaven so that we could have eternal life with God in heaven. That is no simple mission. That is a mission that could only be fulfilled by God.

Lord, I do not know if You had a specific mission for me to fulfill during my life. I tend to believe that You have many small missions that have filled my life and some still left to be accomplished. Help me to understand Your will for me and follow it as You expect. Amen.

The Adoration of the Infant Jesus

Luke 2:8-20: *[8] Now there were shepherds in that region living in the fields and keeping the night-watch over their flock. [9] The angel of the Lord appeared to them, and the glory of the Lord shone around them, and they were struck with great fear. [10] The angel said to them, "Do not be afraid; for behold, I proclaim to you good news of great joy that will be for all the people. [11] For today in the city of David a savior has been born for you who is Messiah and Lord. [12] And this will be a sign for you: you will find an infant wrapped in swaddling clothes and lying in a manger." [13] And suddenly there was a multitude of*

30

the heavenly host with the angel, praising God and saying:
[14]"Glory to God in the highest and on earth peace to those on
whom his favor rests." The Visit of the Shepherds. [15] When the
angels went away from them to heaven, the shepherds said to
one another, "Let us go, then, to Bethlehem to see this thing
that has taken place, which the Lord has made known to
us." [16] So they went in haste and found Mary and Joseph, and
the infant lying in the manger. [17] When they saw this, they
made known the message that had been told them about this
child. [18] All who heard it were amazed by what had been told
them by the shepherds. [19] And Mary kept all these things,
reflecting on them in her heart. [20] Then the shepherds
returned, glorifying and praising God for all they had heard
and seen, just as it had been told to them.

Based on the words of this passage in Luke's Gospel, the shepherds in the nearby fields may have been the first to be informed of the amazing birth. They also may have been the first to be in visitation and adoration of our Lord. Whether they were the first or not does not really make a difference. Our Lord was making sure that the local residents were made aware of this special event. And He did it in a spectacular way.

First there was the angel who made the initial announcement while cautioning them not to be afraid. Then a host of angels appeared with the first. We must face reality. They had to be frightened; unless, of course, they had seen angels before. Frightened or not, our Lord had His first visitors, and they were filled with joy to see the new baby. The sight of a newly born child will grab the hearts of most people.

Jesus was born in humility, humbled by the surroundings, humbled by the people who visited Him. We know that Joseph was a carpenter, but we also know he was

not wealthy. Jesus was born to humble parents. Jesus came as a humble servant of His Father in heaven.

Lord, help me to appreciate what You sacrificed to become human and live among us. Even though it was simply a moment in Your everlasting life, it was the beginning of an eternity for us. Amen.

The Circumcision and Presentation in the Temple

Luke 2:21-38: *[21] When eight days were completed for his circumcision, he was named Jesus, the name given him by the angel before he was conceived in the womb. [22] When the days were completed for their purification according to the law of Moses, they took him up to Jerusalem to present him to the Lord, [23] just as it is written in the law of the Lord, "Every male that opens the womb shall be consecrated to the Lord," [24] and to offer the sacrifice of "a pair of turtledoves or two young pigeons," in accordance with the dictate in the law of the Lord. [25] Now there was a man in Jerusalem whose name was Simeon. This man was righteous and devout, awaiting the consolation of Israel, and the holy Spirit was upon him. [26] It had been revealed to him by the holy Spirit that he should not see death before he had seen the Messiah of the Lord. [27] He came in the Spirit into the temple; and when the parents brought in the child Jesus to perform the custom of the law in regard to him, [28] he took him into his arms and blessed God, saying: [29] "Now, Master, you may let your servant go in peace, according to your word, [30] for my eyes have seen your salvation, [31] which you prepared in sight of all the peoples, [32] a light for revelation to the Gentiles, and glory for your people Israel." [33] The child's father and mother were amazed at what*

was said about him; [34] and Simeon blessed them and said to Mary his mother, "Behold, this child is destined for the fall and rise of many in Israel, and to be a sign that will be contradicted [35] (and you yourself a sword will pierce) so that the thoughts of many hearts may be revealed." [36] There was also a prophetess, Anna, the daughter of Phanuel, of the tribe of Asher. She was advanced in years, having lived seven years with her husband after her marriage, [37]and then as a widow until she was eighty-four. She never left the temple, but worshiped night and day with fasting and prayer. [38] And coming forward at that very time, she gave thanks to God and spoke about the child to all who were awaiting the redemption of Jerusalem.

Not much is said about the circumcision of our Lord. It is mentioned here as part of the emphasis that Jesus was not only human, but He was also subject to Jewish law. The circumcision was expected to be performed on every Jewish male. It was during this procedure that He was given the name foretold by the angel Gabriel.

Forty days was the time of purification. It is not specifically mentioned here; but the assumption is that they were still living in Bethlehem when this time had arrived. So once again, fulfillment of the law was important: the presentation of the male child to be consecrated to the Lord.

Simeon's role in this story was not to pronounce the fulfillment of prophecy. That was not his life's mission or his role in the temple. Simeon had received a grace from Holy Spirit that he would see the promised Messiah of the Lord. Simeon knew that the child he was holding was the long-awaited Messiah. This was an instant revelation.

Anna did not receive the same grace about seeing the Messiah as Simeon did, but she did respect and trust Simeon. So, when Simeon recognized the child as the long-awaited

Messiah, she accepted this as truth and was not afraid to pronounce it to "all who were awaiting the redemption of Jerusalem."

I do not want to overlook the importance of Simeon's prophecy of Jesus as the sign of contradiction and the piercing of Mary's heart. Since our Lord gave us Mary as our mother as well, we must be cognizant of all that made her the best person whose life we need to imitate (next to Jesus, that is).

The most important lesson gained from this passage is that following the law and fulfilling it was important in the earthly life of Jesus. Should that not also be important in our lives as well if we are going to imitate the life of Jesus?

Lord, guide me to what I need to do in fulfilling the law in my life. This is part of the expectation You have of me. So, once again, give me the will and the strength to follow through. Amen.

The Adoration Continues

Matthew 2:1-12: *¹ When Jesus was born in Bethlehem of Judea, in the days of King Herod, behold, magi from the east arrived in Jerusalem, ² saying, "Where is the newborn king of the Jews? We saw his star at its rising and have come to do him homage." ³ When King Herod heard this, he was greatly troubled, and all Jerusalem with him. ⁴ Assembling all the chief priests and the scribes of the people, he inquired of them where the Messiah was to be born. ⁵ They said to him, "In Bethlehem of Judea, for thus it has been written through the prophet: ⁶ 'And you, Bethlehem, land of Judah, are by no means least among the rulers of Judah; since from you shall come a ruler, who is to shepherd my people Israel.'" ⁷ Then Herod called the magi secretly and ascertained from them the*

time of the star's appearance. [8] He sent them to Bethlehem and said, "Go and search diligently for the child. When you have found him, bring me word, that I too may go and do him homage." [9] After their audience with the king they set out. And behold, the star that they had seen at its rising preceded them, until it came and stopped over the place where the child was. [10] They were overjoyed at seeing the star, [11]and on entering the house they saw the child with Mary his mother. They prostrated themselves and did him homage. Then they opened their treasures and offered him gifts of gold, frankincense, and myrrh. [12] And having been warned in a dream not to return to Herod, they departed for their country by another way.

I have just a few thoughts on this passage. The first obvious one is that the announcement of the birth of Jesus was not restricted only to the shepherds. The stargazing and studies by the magi brought them to the conclusion that they needed to investigate this special occurrence in the sky. They needed to follow the stars to find this newborn king. They did the right thing, but it unfortunately led to the killing of children.

There never has been a specific time frame associated with the arrival of the magi. I find it interesting that Matthew says the magi found the Holy Family in a house – not in the stable or cave that is linked to Jesus' birth. The house was probably where they lived after the baby's birth, so ultimately there was room at the inn or a house in Bethlehem. It makes sense that their plan was to return to Nazareth after Mary had recovered and the baby was ready for travel.

The magi, believing they found the true King of Israel, humbled themselves before the child, presenting gifts fit for a king. The gifts most likely provided the Holy Family with

a means to sustain them on the journey they were about to take.

So, as the story goes on, sorrow and death are associated with the birth of the Messiah.

Lord, I have had many opportunities to visit You and spend time with You over the years; and I failed to make the effort to be with You. Help me to make the time to do so. Amen.

The Flight into Egypt and Return

Matthew 2:13-21: *[13] When they had departed, behold, the angel of the Lord appeared to Joseph in a dream and said, "Rise, take the child and his mother, flee to Egypt, and stay there until I tell you. Herod is going to search for the child to destroy him." [14] Joseph rose and took the child and his mother by night and departed for Egypt. [15] He stayed there until the death of Herod, that what the Lord had said through the prophet might be fulfilled, "Out of Egypt I called my son." [16] When Herod realized that he had been deceived by the magi, he became furious. He ordered the massacre of all the boys in Bethlehem and its vicinity two years old and under, in accordance with the time he had ascertained from the magi. [17] Then was fulfilled what had been said through Jeremiah the prophet: [18] "A voice was heard in Ramah, sobbing and loud lamentation; Rachel weeping for her children, and she would not be consoled, since they were no more." [19] When Herod had died, behold, the angel of the Lord appeared in a dream to Joseph in Egypt [20] and said, "Rise, take the child and his mother and go to the land of Israel, for those who sought the child's life are dead." [21] He rose, took the child and his mother, and went to the land of Israel.*

In reading the Gospels and comparing them, we realize that timing is not precise. It would seem to make sense that the circumcision and the presentation took place before the visit of the magi. At the beginning of this passage, Joseph rose, took the child and His mother, and fled to Egypt for an unspecified period of time. They had to still be living in Bethlehem at the time of the magi visit.

After the magi departed, Joseph had a second dream in which he was warned of Herod's treachery and told to flee to Egypt. And Joseph obeyed. There is no indication that, this time, Joseph had trouble believing it was the angel giving him this warning. A caring and loving husband and father, Joseph's uppermost concern had to be for the safety of his family. The life of the newborn Son of God had to be preserved.

During the flight into Egypt, they were fleeing for their lives. They had to leave their home (even though it was temporary) as quickly as possible with a newborn. Our Lady and Joseph were experiencing more hardships for love of our Lord Jesus.

Herod's actions are infamous. Infanticide is an inexcusable crime and sin. Although Herod probably did not realize the babe was the Son of God, he did commit a direct sin against God Himself. All to save his own token position as ruler of a nation conquered by and under the control of Rome. God intervened to protect the Holy Family.

When Herod died, the angel visited Joseph once again and gave him clearance to move the Holy Family back to Israel. The threat to Jesus' life was ended, at least until His public life began.

Lord, Joseph may not have understood everything related to the dreams that he experienced; but he was strong enough

to follow through with what You told him to do. Grant me the gift to understand when you call on me; and grant me both the courage and the strength to follow what You want me to do. Amen.

The Childhood of Jesus at Nazareth

<u>Matthew 2:22-23:</u> *[22] But when he heard that Archelaus was ruling over Judea in place of his father Herod, he was afraid to go back there. And because he had been warned in a dream, he departed for the region of Galilee. [23] He went and dwelt in a town called Nazareth, so that what had been spoken through the prophets might be fulfilled, "He shall be called a Nazorean."*

<u>Luke 2:39-40:</u> *[39] When they had fulfilled all the prescriptions of the law of the Lord, they returned to Galilee, to their own town of Nazareth. [40] The child grew and became strong, filled with wisdom; and the favor of God was upon him.*

Once again, there seems to be a difference in timing between Matthew and Luke. But the timing is not important. What is important is the fact that Joseph took Mary and Jesus to Nazareth. That is where Joseph and Mary would raise their child. The prophecy that He will be called a Nazorean would be fulfilled.

Until Jesus is the age of 12, we know nothing specific from the Gospels about Him. But to be realistic, we would have to accept that Jesus was raised as any other boy in a Jewish family. He would be exposed to adults and children of various personalities, some devoted to their faith, some not so devoted. He was raised as a normal boy except for the fact that he had Mary and Joseph for His parents. Although part of Jesus' education would come in the

38

synagogue, Joseph and Mary were His primary sources of spiritual and moral education. Our faith calls for us to believe Jesus was fully human; so, it only makes sense that He was raised fully human.

Lord, I believe You are fully human and fully divine. I believe that, if it was necessary for us to know all the fine details of Your growth from infant to adult, then You would have inspired someone to write the story. As it is, I have more than enough still to learn about You. Amen.

The Boy Jesus in the Temple

<u>Luke 2:41-52:</u> *[41] Each year his parents went to Jerusalem for the feast of Passover, [42] and when he was twelve years old, they went up according to festival custom. [43] After they had completed its days, as they were returning, the boy Jesus remained behind in Jerusalem, but his parents did not know it. [44] Thinking that he was in the caravan, they journeyed for a day and looked for him among their relatives and acquaintances, [45] but not finding him, they returned to Jerusalem to look for him. [46] After three days they found him in the temple, sitting in the midst of the teachers, listening to them, and asking them questions, [47] and all who heard him were astounded at his understanding and his answers. [48] When his parents saw him, they were astonished, and his mother said to him, "Son, why have you done this to us? Your father and I have been looking for you with great anxiety." [49] And he said to them, "Why were you looking for me? Did you not know that I must be in my Father's house?" [50] But they did not understand what he said to them. [51] He went down with them and came to Nazareth, and was obedient to them; and his mother kept all these things in her heart. [52] And Jesus advanced [in] wisdom and age and favor before God and man.*

Over the years, I have heard many comments on what had gotten into Jesus at this time. Some say He was a typical teen (or pre-teen) adjusting to His change in life, some say He was specifically called by God the Father to stay behind. I read one story of Him accidentally being left behind. We will never know the actual reason unless He chooses to reveal it to us. All we really know is what we have here.

We know Jesus stayed behind or was left behind. We know that "after three days" Joseph and Mary found Him. We know they found Him in the temple (in His "Father's house). We also know that Joseph and Mary were tired, worried, and frustrated in their search for Him. So, Mary's question was justified, "Why?" Except that the way the question was presented, it was more of an accusation that He did this purposely. Then Jesus' response seemed to be a like response to the emotion at the time. Of course, there could be translation issues related to the culture of the Jewish people. In any case, the exchange was unexpected.

I believe the important take-away here is that Jesus returned with His parents to Nazareth and was obedient to them. Jesus, the only begotten Son of God, loved His earthly parents and we can assume His obedience to them was out of love. "Jesus advanced [in] wisdom and age and favor before God and man." Jesus became a human man, grown in wisdom, and ready to fulfill His Father's will.

This reflects the end of what we know about Jesus early years. It is not much. One assumption we can make is that Joseph taught his son to be a carpenter as he was. Learning a trade takes time, so we can assume that Jesus spent many hours in learning, both at the synagogue and in Joseph's workshop. At some point in those later years, God took Joseph from them; so, it was up to Jesus to be the mainstay for His Mother and Himself. He was known as the carpenter

from Nazareth. All of us, at some point in our lives, have to take on the role of responsible adult. This was all part of preparing Jesus for His true mission.

Lord, out of love for us, You spent thirty of our human years living among us, preparing to fulfill the mission Your heavenly Father gave You. Help me to prepare myself and be ready for what it is You would have me do. Amen.

Part 2

Preparation for

and Beginnings of

Jesus' Public Life

Preparation

John the Baptist

Matthew 3:1-6: *[1] In those days John the Baptist appeared, preaching in the desert of Judea [2] [and] saying, "Repent, for the kingdom of heaven is at hand!" [3] It was of him that the prophet Isaiah had spoken when he said: "A voice of one crying out in the desert, 'Prepare the way of the Lord, make straight his paths.'" [4] John wore clothing made of camel's hair and had a leather belt around his waist. His food was locusts and wild honey. [5] At that time Jerusalem, all Judea, and the whole region around the Jordan were going out to him [6] and were being baptized by him in the Jordan River as they acknowledged their sins.*

Mark 1:2-6: *[2] As it is written in Isaiah the prophet: "Behold, I am sending my messenger ahead of you; he will prepare your way. [3] A voice of one crying out in the desert: 'Prepare the way of the Lord, make straight his paths.'" [4] John [the] Baptist appeared in the desert proclaiming a baptism of repentance for the forgiveness of sins. [5] People of the whole Judean countryside and all the inhabitants of Jerusalem were going out to him and were being baptized by him in the Jordan River as they acknowledged their sins. [6] John was clothed in camel's hair, with a leather belt around his waist. He fed on locusts and wild honey.*

Luke 3:1-6: *[1] In the fifteenth year of the reign of Tiberius Caesar, when Pontius Pilate was governor of Judea, and Herod was tetrarch of Galilee, and his brother Philip tetrarch of the region of Ituraea and Trachonitis, and Lysanias was tetrarch of Abilene, [2] during the high priesthood of Annas and*

43

Caiaphas, the word of God came to John the son of Zechariah in the desert. ³He went throughout [the] whole region of the Jordan, proclaiming a baptism of repentance for the forgiveness of sins, ⁴ as it is written in the book of the words of the prophet Isaiah: "A voice of one crying out in the desert: 'Prepare the way of the Lord, make straight his paths. ⁵ Every valley shall be filled, and every mountain and hill shall be made low. The winding roads shall be made straight, and the rough ways made smooth, ⁶ and all flesh shall see the salvation of God.'"

John 1:19-23: *¹⁹ And this is the testimony of John. When the Jews from Jerusalem sent priests and Levites [to him] to ask him, "Who are you?" ²⁰ he admitted and did not deny it, but admitted, "I am not the Messiah." ²¹ So they asked him, "What are you then? Are you Elijah?" And he said, "I am not." "Are you the Prophet?" He answered, "No." ²² So they said to him, "Who are you, so we can give an answer to those who sent us? What do you have to say for yourself?" ²³ He said: "I am 'the voice of one crying out in the desert, "Make straight the way of the Lord,"'" as Isaiah the prophet said."*

We will encounter John later on in the Gospels, but not a lot of what he said is recorded. We know of him, and we know his place in the story of Jesus' life. Here in these verses from the Gospels, we see John as preparing the way. He is "a voice crying out in the desert, 'Prepare the way of the Lord.'" But he was not preparing the way as much as he was preparing the people. He was more than the town crier announcing the presence of some important personage. He was preparing the hearts and souls of those he encountered. He was preparing the people to receive the Messiah, the Son of God. Could the mission of any of the prophets have been more important than that of John the Baptist?

St. Peter Chrysologus expressed who he believed John was. "[John the Baptist] was the school of virtues, the instructor of life, the model of sanctity, the pattern of morality, the mirror of virginity, the epitome of purity, the example of chastity, the way of penitence, the pardon of sins, the discipline of faith. John was greater than a human being, equal to the angels, the apex of the Law, the seed of the Gospel, the harbinger of the Apostles, the silence of the prophets, the lamp of the world, the herald of the Judge, the forerunner of Christ, the preparer for the Lord, the witness of God, the mediator of the whole Trinity."

If John had tried to fulfill all of what St. Peter said of him, I believe he would have failed. I dare say that no person could ever achieve all of that by consciously trying. It was by the grace of God that John accomplished what he did. And with all of that, he did not witness the glory of the Lord. He did not see the miracles, hear the teachings, witness the resurrection. He prepared the way.

Lord, help me to control my pride. Help me to understand that when I do Your will, my words and actions are not changing the world but are assisting in Your plan for me and for others. As John the Baptist says later in the Gospels: I must decrease, and You must increase. Amen.

John's Preaching of Repentance

Matthew 3:7-10: *⁷ When he saw many of the Pharisees and Sadducees coming to his baptism, he said to them, "You brood of vipers! Who warned you to flee from the coming wrath? ⁸ Produce good fruit as evidence of your repentance. ⁹ And do not presume to say to yourselves, 'We have Abraham as our father.' For I tell you, God can raise up children to Abraham from these stones. ¹⁰ Even now the ax lies*

45

at the root of the trees. Therefore, every tree that does not bear good fruit will be cut down and thrown into the fire.

Luke 3:7-9: *[7] He said to the crowds who came out to be baptized by him, "You brood of vipers! Who warned you to flee from the coming wrath? [8] Produce good fruits as evidence of your repentance; and do not begin to say to yourselves, 'We have Abraham as our father,' for I tell you, God can raise up children to Abraham from these stones. [9] Even now the ax lies at the root of the trees. Therefore, every tree that does not produce good fruit will be cut down and thrown into the fire."*

John the Baptist certainly had a way with words. I think he got that from the spirit of Elijah. The truth, the whole truth, and nothing but the truth. It is strange that the Gospel passage from Matthew is almost identical to the passage from Luke. But, I suppose, it is not so strange. When I think about it, there are times when people remember almost word for word what someone says, if it is something that is meaningful to them.

John was not afraid to challenge people not only to do the right thing, but to examine their consciences closely to see the wrong they do. This is what gets him into trouble with Herod later on. In this case, it is the Pharisees and Sadducees. Jesus confronts them later in the same way. They lay heavy burdens on the people instead of helping them to grow closer to God, which ultimately is their job.

Lord, open my heart and drive away my fear. Help me to be willing to confront evil and help me to not only strive for the truth but to call for it from others when necessary. Help me also to listen and let You guide my words. Amen.

John Preaching and
Replies to Questioners

<u>Luke 3:10-14:</u> *[10] And the crowds asked him, "What then should we do?" [11] He said to them in reply, "Whoever has two tunics should share with the person who has none. And whoever has food should do likewise." [12] Even tax collectors came to be baptized, and they said to him, "Teacher, what should we do?" [13] He answered them, "Stop collecting more than what is prescribed." [14] Soldiers also asked him, "And what is it that we should do?" He told them, "Do not practice extortion, do not falsely accuse anyone, and be satisfied with your wages."*

From what is presented here by Luke, John's message in part was essentially the Golden Rule: treat your neighbors as you would have them treat you. Again, this is the precursor to Jesus' second greatest commandment. We can see why John drew large crowds. He told them what they wanted to hear and yet he challenged them as well. He challenged them to do the right thing and told them what the right thing is.

Lord, grant me Your wisdom to know the right path and grant me Your strength to follow that path. Amen.

John's Messianic Preaching

<u>Matthew 3:11-12:</u> *[11] I am baptizing you with water, for repentance, but the one who is coming after me is mightier than I. I am not worthy to carry his sandals. He will baptize you with the holy Spirit and fire. [12] His winnowing fan is in his hand. He will clear his threshing floor and gather his wheat*

into his barn, but the chaff he will burn with unquenchable fire."

Mark 1:7-8: *[7] And this is what he proclaimed: "One mightier than I is coming after me. I am not worthy to stoop and loosen the thongs of his sandals. [8] I have baptized you with water; he will baptize you with the holy Spirit."*

Luke 3:15-18: *[15] Now the people were filled with expectation, and all were asking in their hearts whether John might be the Messiah. [16] John answered them all, saying, "I am baptizing you with water, but one mightier than I is coming. I am not worthy to loosen the thongs of his sandals. He will baptize you with the holy Spirit and fire. [17] His winnowing fan is in his hand to clear his threshing floor and to gather the wheat into his barn, but the chaff he will burn with unquenchable fire." [18] Exhorting them in many other ways, he preached good news to the people.*

John 1:24-28: *[24] Some Pharisees were also sent. [25] They asked him, "Why then do you baptize if you are not the Messiah or Elijah or the Prophet?" [26] John answered them, "I baptize with water; but there is one among you whom you do not recognize, [27] the one who is coming after me, whose sandal strap I am not worthy to untie." [28] This happened in Bethany across the Jordan, where John was baptizing.*

What does John the Baptist tell us about the Messiah? The list is not very long:

- John himself is not the Messiah.
- The Messiah is coming after him and John is unworthy of him.
- The Messiah will baptize with the holy Spirit and fire which is different from John's baptism.

48

- The Messiah will separate his followers from those who do not believe.

As the precursor, John is preparing the way before the Messiah. He is preparing the minds and hearts of the people for the one who will baptize them with the "holy" Spirit and fire. I find it interesting that, in these references to the Spirit of God, "holy" is spelled with a lower case "h." The Holy Spirit was revealed later by Jesus. The Jewish people knew of the Spirit of God but not in the same way Christians do. Christians recognize the Holy Spirit as part of the Triune God.

There is no formal statement in the Gospels indicating that John knew his cousin is the long-awaited leader of the nation of Israel. Yet we will see that he recognizes Him as such when the Messiah is approaching.

We know who Jesus is. We know He is the Messiah. But what do we do to acknowledge His existence? Do we prepare the way? Do we tell people that He did come and that He will return? We have the advantage of over two thousand years of testimony and witness about Him. And we, His believers, are only about one-fifth of the world's population. We still have a long way to go.

Lord, fill my mouth with Your words, so that Your voice may be heard in the words I speak. Help me to open the hearts and minds of those You have called. And, like John the Baptist, help me to bring souls to quench Your thirst. Amen.

The Imprisonment of John

Luke 3:19-20: *[19] Now Herod the tetrarch, who had been censured by him because of Herodias, his brother's wife, and because of all the evil deeds Herod had committed, [20] added still another to these by [also] putting John in prison.*

49

Matthew 14:3-4: *[3] Now Herod had arrested John, bound [him], and put him in prison on account of Herodias, the wife of his brother Philip, [4] for John had said to him, "It is not lawful for you to have her."*

Mark 6:17-18: *[17] Herod was the one who had John arrested and bound in prison on account of Herodias, the wife of his brother Philip, whom he had married. [18] John had said to Herod, "It is not lawful for you to have your brother's wife."*

There are a few lessons that may be learned from these verses. First, there may be consequences that have to be faced for all of the actions or words we use. Second, those consequences may be serious or mild, short-term or long-term. Third, consequences may be imposed or mercifully forgiven. Fourth, if you are to follow what you believe to be the Will of God, then you must be willing to accept the consequences, whatever they are.

John understood what he was doing. He called out both Herod and Herodias for the wrong they were doing. I am sure the imprisonment came as no surprise to him. The Will of God is more important than the potential result of his words.

Lord, help me to understand Your will, and give me the strength to follow it, in spite of what I may face as a result. Help me to place Your will above all considerations. Amen.

The Baptism of Jesus

Matthew 3:13-17: *[13] Then Jesus came from Galilee to John at the Jordan to be baptized by him. [14] John tried to prevent him, saying, "I need to be baptized by you, and yet you are coming* to me?" [15] Jesus said to him in reply, "Allow it now, for thus it is fitting for us to fulfill all righteousness." Then he allowed him. [16] After Jesus was baptized, he came up from the water and behold, the heavens were opened [for him], and he saw the Spirit of God descending like a dove [and] coming upon him. [17] And a voice came from the heavens, saying, "This is my beloved Son, with whom I am well pleased."

Mark 1:9-11: [9] It happened in those days that Jesus came from Nazareth of Galilee and was baptized in the Jordan by John. [10] On coming up out of the water he saw the heavens being torn open and the Spirit, like a dove, descending upon him. [11] And a voice came from the heavens, "You are my beloved Son; with you I am well pleased."

Luke 3:21-22: [21] After all the people had been baptized and Jesus also had been baptized and was praying, heaven was opened [22] and the holy Spirit descended upon him in bodily form like a dove. And a voice came from heaven, "You are my beloved Son; with you I am well pleased."

John 1:29-34: [29] The next day he saw Jesus coming toward him and said, "Behold, the Lamb of God, who takes away the sin of the world. [30] He is the one of whom I said, 'A man is coming after me who ranks ahead of me because he existed before me.' [31] I did not know him, but the reason why I came baptizing with water was that he might be made known to Israel." [32] John testified further, saying, "I saw the Spirit come down like a dove from the sky and remain upon him. [33] I did not know him, but the one who sent me to baptize with water told me, 'On whomever you see the Spirit come down and remain, he is the one who will baptize with the holy Spirit.' [34] Now I have seen and testified that he is the Son of God."

Technically, Jesus words in Matthew's verses are His first recorded words in His public ministry: "Allow it..." It reflects two things: first, that He is fully human and should be treated as all other humans, and second, in all humility He requests to be treated as others. Jesus is an example of humility.

Matthew, Mark, and Luke tell essentially the same story. The only difference is that, in Matthew, the voice from the heavens says, "This is my beloved Son..." where Mark and Luke say, "You are my beloved Son..." In Matthew, the voice seems to be speaking to everyone or, at least, to John and Jesus. In Mark and Luke, the voice seems to be speaking to Jesus only, but implied that John heard as well. In John's Gospel, the only voice mentioned was that of the one who sent the Baptist. The implication is the voice that spoke to the Baptist was also from the heavens. The Baptist recognized the Son of God by the descent of the dove (the Spirit). The point in all this is that there is an agreement that a voice from the heavens led John the Baptist to the realization that Jesus was the Son of God.

In Matthew's and John's accounts, the Baptist acknowledges his unworthiness before Jesus. Yet, Jesus humbles Himself in order to show that He is truly human. He must be baptized as all others are. This is typical of Jesus as will be seen throughout the gospels. In spite of His divine nature, man must see His human nature as well. He is man among men.

This is also the first of three times that the voice, God's voice, comes from heaven acknowledging Jesus as His Son. Depending on who actually heard the statement, this is huge. If the people who were there heard the voice, then it was a confirmation of what the Baptist said, "*A man is coming after me who ranks ahead of me because he existed before me. ... He is the Son of God.*" If only John and Jesus heard the voice, then it was a confirmation to John. Jesus is the Son of God.

Lord, Your humility is a great example of how we should be not only among others, but especially before You. Remind me of this often. Amen

The Temptation

<u>Matthew 4:1-11:</u> *¹ Then Jesus was led by the Spirit into the desert to be tempted by the devil. ² He fasted for forty days and forty nights, and afterwards he was hungry. ³ The tempter approached and said to him, "If you are the Son of God, command that these stones become loaves of bread." ⁴ He said in reply, "It is written: 'One does not live by bread alone, but by every word that comes forth from the mouth of God.'" ⁵ Then the devil took him to the holy city, and made him stand on the parapet of the temple, ⁶ and said to him, "If you are the Son of God, throw yourself down. For it is written: 'He will command his angels concerning you' and 'with their hands they will support you, lest you dash your foot against a stone.'" ⁷ Jesus answered him, "Again it is written, 'You shall not put the Lord, your God, to the test.'" ⁸ Then the devil took him up to a very high mountain, and showed him all the kingdoms of the world in their magnificence, ⁹ and he said to him, "All these I shall give to you, if you will prostrate yourself and worship me." ¹⁰ At this, Jesus said to him, "Get away, Satan! It is written: 'The Lord, your God, shall you worship and him alone shall you serve.'" ¹¹ Then the devil left him, and behold, angels came and ministered to him.*

<u>Mark 1:12-13:</u> *¹² At once the Spirit drove him out into the desert, ¹³ and he remained in the desert for forty days, tempted*

by Satan. He was among wild beasts, and the angels ministered to him.

Luke 4:1-13: *[1] Filled with the holy Spirit, Jesus returned from the Jordan and was led by the Spirit into the desert [2] for forty days, to be tempted by the devil. He ate nothing during those days; and when they were over, he was hungry. [3] The devil said to him, "If you are the Son of God, command this stone to become bread." [4] Jesus answered him, "It is written, 'One does not live by bread alone.'" [5] Then he took him up and showed him all the kingdoms of the world in a single instant. [6] The devil said to him, "I shall give to you all this power and their glory; for it has been handed over to me, and I may give it to whomever I wish. [7] All this will be yours, if you worship me." [8] Jesus said to him in reply, "It is written: 'You shall worship the Lord, your God, and him alone shall you serve.'" [9] Then he led him to Jerusalem, made him stand on the parapet of the temple, and said to him, "If you are the Son of God, throw yourself down from here, [10] for it is written: 'He will command his angels concerning you, to guard you,' [11] and: 'With their hands they will support you, lest you dash your foot against a stone.'" [12] Jesus said to him in reply, "It also says, 'You shall not put the Lord, your God, to the test.'" [13] When the devil had finished every temptation, he departed from him for a time.*

It is interesting that I read these passages now. It has special meaning because this was being discussed in a radio talk show that I was listening to last night. The talk show host was actually discussing Jesus' full humanity. He was attempting to prove this through temptation. His premise was that, if Jesus was not fully human and only fully divine, then He *could not* at any time sin, so temptation was meaningless. Temptation only has meaning if the recipient

54

of the temptation has the ability to say "yes" or "no" to the temptation. Our faith tells us that Jesus is fully human and always said "no" to temptation that would lead to sin.

The first temptation from the devil is not just for food because He had been fasting for 40 days, but that Jesus should perform a miracle to serve Himself. This is something Jesus would not do. The miracles that Jesus performed were to serve or help others. This is one of the first lessons to be learned from Jesus. The special gifts that we have been given are to be used in service to others – not to benefit ourselves. If the result of the service in some way benefits us as well, that does not matter as long as the intent or motivation was to help others.

In the second temptation, the devil wants Jesus to throw Himself off a high pinnacle and call out to the angels to come and save Him from the danger. And Jesus refuses to *test* His Father. Praying for help is not testing God. Intent and motivation behind the prayer again comes into play. God may or may not answer your prayer in the way you want it answered.

In the third temptation, Satan offers Jesus all the riches and power the world can provide if Jesus will bow down and worship Satan. And Jesus pushes Satan away telling him that only God shall be worshipped.

The devil is constantly tempting us. If we give in to the small things, it becomes easier to give in to the bigger things. We are the ones who control this. Not every temptation leads to a sinful act, but it is the sinful ones that we must deny. For example, the temptation to get something we like to eat is not sinful; but it is if it leads to gluttony.

Jesus is fully human, as well as fully divine. Throughout His life He shows us not only what that means, but that a truly human life can be lived as God wills it.

Lord, give me the knowledge I need to know when I am being tempted to do or say something that will lead to sin. And give me the strength to say "no" and not regret it. Amen.

Part 3

The Beginning of
Jesus' Public Ministry
(According to St. John)

The Beginning

The Call of the First Disciples

John 1:35-51: *[35] The next day John was there again with two of his disciples, [36] and as he watched Jesus walk by, he said, "Behold, the Lamb of God." [37] The two disciples heard what he said and followed Jesus. [38] Jesus turned and saw them following him and said to them, "What are you looking for?" They said to him, "Rabbi" (which translated means Teacher), "where are you staying?" [39] He said to them, "Come, and you will see." So, they went and saw where he was staying, and they stayed with him that day. It was about four in the afternoon. [40] Andrew, the brother of Simon Peter, was one of the two who heard John and followed Jesus. [41] He first found his own brother Simon and told him, "We have found the Messiah" (which is translated Anointed). [42] Then he brought him to Jesus. Jesus looked at him and said, "You are Simon the son of John; you will be called Cephas" (which is translated Peter). [43] The next day he decided to go to Galilee, and he found Philip. And Jesus said to him, "Follow me." [44] Now Philip was from Bethsaida, the town of Andrew and Peter. [45] Philip found Nathanael and told him, "We have found the one about whom Moses wrote in the law, and also the prophets, Jesus, son of Joseph, from Nazareth." [46] But Nathanael said to him, "Can anything good come from Nazareth?" Philip said to him, "Come and see." [47] Jesus saw Nathanael coming toward him and said of him, "Here is a true Israelite. There is no duplicity in him." [48] Nathanael said to him, "How do you know me?" Jesus answered and said to him, "Before Philip called you, I saw you under the fig tree." [49] Nathanael answered him, "Rabbi, you are the Son of*

God; you are the King of Israel." [50] Jesus answered and said to him, "Do you believe because I told you that I saw you under the fig tree? You will see greater things than this." [51] And he said to him, "Amen, amen, I say to you, you will see the sky opened and the angels of God ascending and descending on the Son of Man."

Jesus words here have significance from the standpoint that He repeats them many times throughout His public life in slightly different forms. Examination: "What are you looking for?" Invitation: "Come and see..." Explanation: "You believe because..." Enticement: "You will see greater things..." Jesus is always delving deep and inviting people to see what is ahead.

I will also comment on the calling of His disciples in terms of recruitment. The bottom line is that we are called in different ways. In this passage, two disciples of John the Baptist (Andrew and another unnamed) leave John to follow Jesus. Andrew invites his brother to see who the Messiah is. Nothing further is said about the other unnamed disciple of the Baptist. This other unnamed person is traditionally believed to be John, the son of Zebedee, the author of this Gospel.

Andrew entices his brother, Simon (Peter), to come and see who this long-awaited Messiah is. That is the draw. What we learn of Peter later is that he is very much a business man and would not be drawn away from his business unless it was really important. Seeing and hearing the long-awaited Messiah was that important. Simon, who is given the name "Peter" by Jesus, is being called to more than he has any concept of at this time. As we all are. When we say "yes" to Jesus, we know not where it will take us.

I believe it is safe to assume that the unnamed person, John, invited his brother James in the same way that Andrew invited Simon Peter. Like Andrew and Simon, John and James were fishermen.

In Galilee, Philip is found. We only know at this point that he was from the same town as Andrew and Simon. We have no details other than in some way Jesus called him. Since they were all from the same town, it may be that Andrew or Simon invited Philip to join them. However, we do not really know.

As for Nathanael, Philip invited him in a way similar to Andrew calling Simon. In the case of both Nathanael and Simon, the invitation came from someone who is trusted. In speaking with Jesus, it did not take much to convince him to stay with the small group.

One of the things that I have learned over the years is that the best way to recruit followers is by personal invitation from someone who is trusted. But, once recruited, the new recruit must continually be convinced that the decision to follow was right. Not everyone who sought out Jesus was convinced to stay.

This passage addresses the call of four of the Apostles. However, there may have been more disciples at this point including John and James.

Lord, I said "yes" to Your call. Help me to be continually convinced that my decision was the right one. Amen.

The Marriage at Cana

<u>John 2:1-11:</u> *¹ On the third day there was a wedding in Cana in Galilee, and the mother of Jesus was there. ² Jesus and his disciples were also invited to the wedding. ³ When the wine ran short, the mother of Jesus said to him, "They have no*

wine." [4][And] Jesus said to her, "Woman, how does your concern affect me? My hour has not yet come." [5] His mother said to the servers, "Do whatever he tells you." [6] Now there were six stone water jars there for Jewish ceremonial washings, each holding twenty to thirty gallons. [7] Jesus told them, "Fill the jars with water." So, they filled them to the brim. [8] Then he told them, "Draw some out now and take it to the headwaiter." So, they took it. [9] And when the headwaiter tasted the water that had become wine, without knowing where it came from (although the servers who had drawn the water knew), the headwaiter called the bridegroom [10] and said to him, "Everyone serves good wine first, and then when people have drunk freely, an inferior one; but you have kept the good wine until now." [11] Jesus did this as the beginning of his signs in Cana in Galilee and so revealed his glory, and his disciples began to believe in him.

I believe I have heard or read this story a couple of hundred times over the years. I should have memorized it by now, but I have not. What is this story telling us about Jesus that will help me to live my life?

We will start with who was in attendance. Mary, the mother of Jesus, Jesus, and His disciples were present. At this point we only know of a few disciples: Andrew, Simon, Philip, Nathanael, and possibly John and James from the previous passage. Jesus was just beginning His public ministry and did not have a huge crowd following Him. The wedding family must have been fairly wealthy to be able to include friends of guests, unless those friends happened to be friends of the family as well.

The words spoken by Jesus to His Mother seem a little harsh. They remind me of His response to her when Mary and Joseph found Him in the temple at the age of twelve. I wonder if the tone reflected by the words are an indication of the attitude of Jewish men toward their women. "Why would you be concerned about me?" "Woman, what business is this to me?" In both cases, I do not believe that Jesus meant to demean His Mother in any way. I believe this was more of a customary interaction learned through their lifestyle. We know from His approach to her throughout the New Testament that He loved her dearly. Regardless of the words or expressions used, there should never be a doubt that Jesus loved His Mother deeply.

I have been reading a book by Anne Rice titled "Christ the Lord." It is a novel depicting the hidden years of Jesus' childhood. This is all conjecture; however, it leads to another view. Jesus is depicted as a young Jewish boy who has a lot of questions. Joseph, Mary, and His relatives keep telling Him that He is not ready to hear the answers to His questions and that His time will come. It could be that in this passage at Cana, Jesus is challenging His Mother that His time has not come – or has it? Based on the Anne Rice story, this could have been a private joke between Mother and Son. There is a lot we do not know about His growth and His relationship with His Mother.

In spite of the fact that this was her "concern" and not His, and in spite of the fact that this was not His "hour," Jesus obeyed the implied request of Mary. Honoring His Mother by obeying her request is an important lesson here. He did not have to perform a miracle, and as it turned out, very few people actually were aware of the miracle occurring. He did this out of love for His Mother.

This must have been one huge party; but wedding feasts had been known to last several days. The family ran out of wine, and what did Jesus give them? He gave them between 120 and 180 gallons of wine – fine wine. This may have been more than they needed. This was the first of His public "signs." I believe He performed this miracle for two other reasons as well: one to show His love for the wedding family and to show a sign to His disciples "who began to believe in Him."

Lord, help me to honor and venerate Your Mother as she should be honored and venerated. It was because of Your love for her that You helped this wedding family. In the abundance of Your generosity, You provided more than they needed and better than they needed (as was the chief steward's evaluation). Help me to follow Your example where it is appropriate. Amen.

The Journey to Jerusalem

John 2:12-13: *[12] After this He went down to Capernaum, He and His mother, and His brothers and His disciples; and they stayed there a few days. [13] The Passover of the Jews was near, and Jesus went up to Jerusalem.*

This is basically a transition passage. What is important here is that the time of year was that of Passover, the faithful are called to Jerusalem for the celebration of the feast. This was the first trip of Jesus to Jerusalem in His public life.

Lord, help me to clearly see the path You want me to follow. Amen.

The First Cleansing of the Temple

John 2:14-22: *[14] He found in the temple area those who sold oxen, sheep, and doves, as well as the moneychangers seated there. [15] He made a whip out of cords and drove them all out of the temple area, with the sheep and oxen, and spilled the coins* *of the money-changers and overturned their tables, [16] and to those who sold doves he said, "Take these out of here, and stop making my Father's house a marketplace." [17] His disciples recalled the words of scripture, "Zeal for your house will consume me." [18] At this the Jews answered and said to him, "What sign can you show us for doing this?" [19] Jesus answered and said to them, "Destroy this temple and in three days I will raise it up." [20] The Jews said, "This temple has been under construction for forty-six years, and you will raise it up in three days?" [21] But he was speaking about the temple of his body. [22] Therefore, when he was raised from the dead, his disciples remembered that he had said this, and they came to believe the scripture and the word Jesus had spoken.*

The first thing to remember here is that Jesus did not act out of anger. *"Zeal for your house will consume me."* It was a passionate action to remove the merchants and moneychangers from His Father's house. And He was clear about this when He said it was His Father's house. It is a reminder of the statement He made to Mary and Joseph when they found Him in the temple. However, this is the first time in His public ministry that He claimed God as His Father.

When the Jewish people asked for a sign (as they would do later), He gave them none. Jesus did not use miracles to amuse and satisfy curiosity. His answer would not actually be proven until His resurrection, quite a long time after He made this statement. They would not believe Him (not even His disciples) here or later, not until sometime after his resurrection.

As will be seen later, the Jewish people did not get the message. He may have connected with some of the merchants and moneychangers, but not nearly all. After His departure, everything was business as usual.

64

Lord, I pray for the grace to remember I am in Your Father's
house when I enter my church. Remind me to recognize His
house and You in the tabernacle. Amen.

Jesus' Ministry in Jerusalem

<u>**John 2:23-25:**</u> *²³ While he was in Jerusalem for the feast of*
Passover, many began to believe in his name when they saw
the signs he was doing. ²⁴ But Jesus would not trust himself to
them because he knew them all, ²⁵ and did not need anyone to
testify about human nature. He himself understood it well.

Only someone truly charismatic could attract followers
as quickly as Jesus did. He not only had a message that
people wanted to hear; but He had a way of presenting it that
people could understand, except, of course, when He spoke
in parables. People want to hear the truth, and this is what
He gave them. He also performed miracles (healings), not
for show, but to sincerely help people. This was another
draw. These were the signs spoken of in the above passage.
Again, Jesus did not give these signs to entertain or amuse;
He performed them for those in need.

Lord, open my mind to hear Your words and reflect on the
signs so that I may always strive to follow You. Amen.

The Discourse with Nicodemus

<u>**John 3:1-21:**</u> *¹ Now there was a Pharisee named Nicodemus, a*
ruler of the Jews. ² He came to Jesus at night and said to him,
"Rabbi, we know that you are a teacher who has come from
God, for no one can do these signs that you are doing unless

God is with him." [3] Jesus answered and said to him, "Amen, amen, I say to you, no one can see the kingdom of God without being born from above." [4] Nicodemus said to him, "How can a person once grown old be born again? Surely, he cannot reenter his mother's womb and be born again, can he?" [5] Jesus answered, "Amen, amen, I say to you, no one can enter the kingdom of God without being born of water and Spirit. [6] What is born of flesh is flesh and what is born of spirit is spirit. [7] Do not be amazed that I told you, 'You must be born from above.' [8] The wind blows where it wills, and you can hear the sound it makes, but you do not know where it comes from or where it goes; so it is with everyone who is born of the Spirit." [9] Nicodemus answered and said to him, "How can this happen?" [10] Jesus answered and said to him, "You are the teacher of Israel and you do not understand this? [11] Amen, amen, I say to you, we speak of what we know; and we testify to what we have seen, but you people do not accept our testimony. [12] If I tell you about earthly things and you do not believe, how will you believe if I tell you about heavenly things? [13] No one has gone up to heaven except the one who has come down from heaven, the Son of Man. [14] And just as Moses lifted up the serpent in the desert, so must the Son of Man be lifted up, [15] so that everyone who believes in him may have eternal life." [16] For God so loved the world that he gave his only Son, so that everyone who believes in him might not perish but might have eternal life. [17] For God did not send his Son into the world to condemn the world, but that the world might be saved through him. [18] Whoever believes in him will not be condemned, but whoever does not believe has already been condemned, because he has not believed in the name of the only Son of God. [19] And this is the verdict, that the light came into the world, but people preferred darkness to light, because their works were evil. [20] For everyone who does wicked things hates the light and does not come toward the light, so *that his works might not be exposed. [21] But whoever lives the truth comes to the light, so that his works may be clearly seen as done in God.*

Jesus' words and actions are essential to my study. Nicodemus came to Him "at night" which means that Jesus did not keep regular office hours. He accepted people at all times. Jesus is available to those who need Him. In this case, Nicodemus needed to speak to Him, but he did not want to be seen with such a controversial person as Jesus.

In response to Nicodemus' acknowledgement that God was with Jesus, He replied that "no one can see the kingdom of God without being born from above." This led into the discussion that has been commented on for two thousand years: "born again" and what that means. The exchange between Nicodemus and Jesus could be expected because Nicodemus was a very practical man. Obviously, he was dedicated to his faith; but the far majority of the scriptures were focused more on how to live in this world and not how to get to the next. In fact, many of the Jewish people did not even believe there is an afterlife.

I remember reading a short commentary by Max Lucado about being reborn. He compares human birth to re-birth. Consider that a baby knows nothing and must be taught everything. A baby does not know how or what to eat, how to love, how to walk, how to talk, how to read, or how to make good decisions. The same holds true for human rebirth. When you are reborn, you have to learn everything as if it was new, a new way to think, a new way to love, a new way to talk, a new way to interact with people, a new way to make good decisions. Rebirth is not instantaneous. It takes a while to become a Christian, a follower of Christ.

Jesus spoke of the Spirit. Nicodemus was aware of the Spirit but not the Holy Spirit as we understand. Jesus spoke of Himself as the Son of Man. Much of what Jesus said was confusing to Nicodemus because he never read, heard of, or studied what Jesus was talking about. And, Nicodemus was considered a wise man, a teacher. How could the words of Jesus settle comfortably in his mind without a lot of explanation? Jesus then remarks to him: *"You are the teacher of Israel, and you do not understand this? Amen, amen, I say to you, we speak of what we know, and we testify to what we have seen; but you people do not accept our testimony. If I tell you about earthly things and you do not believe, how will you believe if I tell you about heavenly things?"* I do not believe that Jesus was speaking critically or in amazement. I believe this comment was an observation meant to awaken something in Nicodemus.

"And just as Moses lifted up the serpent in the desert, so must the Son of Man be lifted up, so that everyone who believes in him may have eternal life." Here, Jesus predicted His own crucifixion, and I am sure it went right over Nicodemus' head. Even Jesus' own disciples never understood or accepted this until after He rose from the dead. Had Jesus been clearer in this statement, I believe that Nicodemus would have picked up on the historical facts of how the Jewish people treated prophets. As it is, being a student of scriptures and a teacher, Nicodemus probably recognized the reference to Exodus, whether or not he related it to how Jesus would die.

Then came one of the most famous quotes from the Gospels that was ever written: *For God so loved the world that he gave His only Son, so that everyone who believes in Him might not perish but might have eternal life.* With this Jesus actually challenged Nicodemus to believe in Him. Nicodemus started things out by acknowledging that Jesus came from God. Now Jesus is challenging him to believe He is the Son of God. Nicodemus believed that God would send the Messiah. Some believed the Messiah would be the Son of God, but not everyone. Was this step a little hard to take? For Nicodemus, it was; at least at that moment.

There is nothing in this passage that indicates that Nicodemus simply accepted what Jesus said. This whole conversation would have to be mulled over. There is also no indication that Nicodemus came back to speak to Jesus, to be tutored on what all this meant. Yet Nicodemus became a follower, a disciple, in the long run.

However, I do believe there is more to this than appears. Face it. Nicodemus came out to meet with Jesus and to talk to Him. I doubt that this was merely a five-minute conversation. Just as all of the passages coming up in which our Lord is speaking about many things. I do not believe He simply made a statement and left it at that. I believe Jesus spent at least some time explaining what He meant. As a speaker and a writer, I know first-hand that you cannot simply make a statement and walk away if you want people to understand and follow, especially in Jesus' case where His Apostles were not teachers, like Nicodemus. That does not mean that He spent hours in explanation. All of these statements coming from Jesus were more like summary statements or bullet points in today's language. They all need at least a minimal explanation that would cause people to want to hear more.

Jesus spoke to him of other things as well: *"For God did not send his Son into the world to condemn the world, but that the world might be saved through him. Whoever believes in him will not be condemned, but whoever does not believe has already been condemned, because he has not believed in the name of the only Son of God."* Here was more to challenge Nicodemus' thinking. Jesus told him that He is the Son of God; but not only that, Nicodemus and all of mankind would have to believe in Jesus as the Son of God or they would be condemned. This is a challenge to all of our thinking, because if we believe it is true, we will have to live our lives based on that belief. I believe it is true and I am trying to live my life based on that belief.

I was taught that not all of mankind will have an opportunity to learn about Jesus or even about God. So, does that mean that they are condemned for their ignorance? No, what I was taught and what I believe is that, if they are ignorant of God through no fault of their own, then God will make Himself known to them in some way so they can choose to accept and acknowledge Him. God is loving and merciful, but also just.

Then the final revelation to Nicodemus in this conversation: "*And this is the verdict, that the light came into the world, but people preferred darkness to light, because their works were evil. For everyone who does wicked things hates the light and does not come toward the light, so that his works might not be exposed.*" People prefer what the world has to offer (the wicked things). And by doing the wicked things, they choose to avoid what is good for fear of being exposed for what they are. Starting with Adam, he hid when he realized he did something wrong. This is the way of humans, hiding the bad for fear of the good.

"*But whoever lives the truth comes to the light, so that his works may be clearly seen as done in God.*" We must live our lives acknowledging God, not hiding from Him. Only in living our lives this way will others see God in the way we live.

We do not know how long Nicodemus spent with our Lord, and so we also do not know if our Lord spent any time explaining all of this to him. Explanations are not included in this passage. But, as I indicated earlier, I believe there had to be some time that evening that Jesus clarified these points, at least enough to get Nicodemus to come back for more. The story of Nicodemus ends temporarily abruptly here. But we will see him later.

Lord, Nicodemus came to the light. It may have taken a while, but he believed in the Son of God. Help me to not only believe but to continue to seek You and live by Your words and example. Amen.

Jesus' Ministry in Judea

John 3:22: *After this, Jesus and his disciples went into the region of Judea, where he spent some time with them baptizing.*

One of the things that I never really appreciated until now is the fact that they "went into the region of Judea." They walked everywhere they went. Although there were horses and other animals for riding or pulling carts and wagons, I suspect that they walked everywhere, since that was the general mode of transportation. I said I did not really appreciate it because I am currently sitting in a hotel room in Hawaii on a family vacation. We came on an airplane and drove around in rented cars.

I appreciate their walking because currently walking is really difficult for me. I have arthritis in both knees and pinched nerves in my lower back; I can walk okay on a flat, smooth surface, but not very well on inclines or stairs or rocky ground. If I was one of Jesus' disciples, I would need a small miracle to keep up with them.

I envision these long journeys as great teaching times for Jesus. He could spend hours talking with His Apostles and disciples. I am sure it was not simply an elongated, outdoor classroom. I am sure there was casual talk and an

71

exchange of humor as well. Most of the pictures that I have seen portray Jesus with a serious look on His face. I prefer to picture Him with a smile and laughing on occasion. I believe being with Jesus was normally a very happy time; or else, who would want to stick around? That is also why I look forward to being with Him in heaven. I envision eternity with my Triune God to be filled with happiness; otherwise, why would I want to go.

Back to their journey. "He spent some time with them baptizing." Did Jesus do the baptizing? Did He give them the grace and power to baptize sacramentally – baptizing with the spirit, as John had said, and forgiving original sin. Or did that come later? This verse does not tell us much, but I can imagine our Lord walking and talking them through the process.

Lord, help me to stay focused and continue on this journey with you, in spite of the things that will slow me down. Amen.

John's Testimony to Christ

John 3:23-36: *²³ John was also baptizing in Aenon near Salim, because there was an abundance of water there, and people came to be baptized, ²⁴ for John had not yet been imprisoned. ²⁵ Now a dispute arose between the disciples of John and a Jew about ceremonial washings. ²⁶ So they came to John and said to him, "Rabbi, the one who was with you across the Jordan, to whom you testified, here he is baptizing; and everyone is coming to him." ²⁷ John answered and said, "No one can receive anything except what has been given him from heaven. ²⁸ You yourselves can testify that I said [that] I am not the Messiah, but that I was sent before him. ²⁹ The one who has the bride is the bridegroom; the best man, who stands and*

72

listens to him, rejoices greatly at the bridegroom's voice. So this joy of mine has been made complete. [30] *He must increase; I must decrease." * [31] *The one who comes from above is above all. The one who is of the earth is earthly and speaks of earthly things. But the one who comes from heaven [is above all].* [32] *He testifies to what he has seen and heard, but no one accepts his testimony.* [33] *Whoever does accept his testimony certifies that God is trustworthy.* [34] *For the one whom God sent speaks the words of God. He does not ration his gift of the Spirit.* [35] *The Father loves the Son and has given everything over to him.* [36] *Whoever believes in the Son has eternal life, but whoever disobeys the Son will not see life, but the wrath of God remains upon him.*

Here we have an affirmation by John the Baptist that he is not the Messiah, and Jesus is. As the precursor, his role was to prepare the way, to announce the coming of the Messiah. Now is the time for people to follow Jesus, a time for John to decrease in popularity and following; and for Jesus to increase in both. Although his role was essentially complete, John still must spread the word.

As far as verses 31-36 are concerned, there is uncertainty about whose words these are. They could be the words of John the Baptist, Jesus, or John the Evangelist (author of this gospel). There are occasions in the gospels when Jesus refers to Himself in the third person; however, the fact that it is not treated as a quote leads me to believe it is a reflection of the evangelist. It could also be a teaching that the evangelist received directly from Jesus.

Regardless of who said the words, we must consider what is being taught. Jesus is the one who comes from above, and He is the one who testifies to the truth. Jesus was sent by God and speaks the words of God, and we are expected to believe what He says. God loves His Son

73

(Jesus) and has given all authority over to Him. "Whoever believes in the Son has eternal life, but whoever disobeys the Son will not see life, but the wrath of God remains upon him." This last statement is both a great promise and a condemnation. This corresponds to what Jesus says later in the gospels: only those who do the will of His Father in heaven will enter the kingdom of heaven.

Lord, grant me the wisdom to recognize the truth in what You say and the strength to persevere in obeying the Will of Your Father in heaven. Amen.

Part 4
Jesus' Ministry
in Galilee

The Journey into Galilee

John 4:1-3: *[1] Now when Jesus learned that the Pharisees had heard that Jesus was making and baptizing more disciples than John [2] (although Jesus himself was not baptizing, just his disciples), [3] he left Judea and returned to Galilee.*

Matthew 4:12: *When he heard that John had been arrested, he withdrew to Galilee.*

Mark 1:14a: *After John had been arrested, Jesus came to Galilee ...*

Luke 4:14a: *Jesus returned to Galilee ...*

The fact that Jesus left Judea to return to Galilee after John had been arrested is not an indication of fear on His part. His hour had come, and His ministry had begun. It was time for Jesus to start the serious training of His disciples. Galilee was the home of most of His close followers, so it made sense to train them on their home turf.

John 4:2 is an indication that the training had begun since His disciples were the ones who were doing the baptizing. What is not indicated here is if the baptizing was the same as John's. Had Jesus instituted the sacrament and given His disciples the power to forgive original sin? Or was that to come later? Implied in the notes in the Bible on this verse is that they were imitating the baptism of John. They had a lot to learn, so baptism was a good starting point. Only so much can be learned from listening to the Master. At some point, the student must start practicing.

76

Lord, we all have to start somewhere in our journey to grow to love You. I have spent many years reading, learning, preaching, and writing for love of You; yet this effort of mine to study the four Gospels seems like it is the first endeavor to really get to know You. Help me to understand what it is that You want me to learn. Amen.

The Discourse with the Woman of Samaria

John 4:4-42: *[4] He had to pass through Samaria. [5] So he came to a town of Samaria called Sychar, near the plot of land that Jacob had given to his son Joseph. [6] Jacob's well was there. Jesus, tired from his journey, sat down there at the well. It was about noon. [7] A woman of Samaria came to draw water. Jesus said to her, "Give me a drink." [8] His disciples had gone into the town to buy food. [9] The Samaritan woman said to him, "How can you, a Jew, ask me, a Samaritan woman, for a drink?" (For Jews use nothing in common with Samaritans.) [10] Jesus answered and said to her, "If you knew the gift of God and who is saying to you, 'Give me a drink,' you would have asked him and he would have given you living water." [11] [The woman] said to him, "Sir, you do not even have a bucket and the well is deep; where then can you get this living water? [12] Are you greater than our father Jacob, who gave us this well and drank from it himself with his children and his flocks?" [13] Jesus answered and said to her, "Everyone who drinks this water will be thirsty again; [14] but whoever drinks the water I shall give will never thirst; the water I shall give will become in him a spring of water welling up to eternal life." [15] The woman said to him, "Sir, give me this water, so that I may not be thirsty or have to keep coming here to draw* water." *16* Jesus said to her, "Go call your husband and come back." *17* The woman answered and said to him, "I do not have a husband." Jesus answered her, "You are right in saying, 'I do not have a husband.' *18* For you have had five husbands, and the one you have now is not your husband. What you have said is true." *19* The woman said to him, "Sir, I can see that you are a prophet. *20* Our ancestors worshiped on this mountain; but you people say that the place to worship is in Jerusalem." *21* Jesus said to her, "Believe me, woman, the hour is coming when you will worship the Father neither on this mountain nor in Jerusalem. *22* You people worship what you do not understand; we worship what we understand, because salvation is from the Jews. *23* But the hour is coming, and is now here, when true worshipers will worship the Father in Spirit and truth; and indeed, the Father seeks such people to worship him. *24* God is Spirit, and those who worship him must worship in Spirit and truth." *25* The woman said to him, "I know that the Messiah is coming, the one called the Anointed; when he comes, he will tell us everything." *26* Jesus said to her, "I am he, the one who is speaking with you." *27* At that moment his disciples returned, and were amazed that he was talking with a woman, but still no one said, "What are you looking for?" or "Why are you talking with her?" *28* The woman left her water jar and went into the town and said to the people, *29* "Come see a man who told me everything I have done. Could he possibly be the Messiah?" *30* They went out of the town and came to him. *31* Meanwhile, the disciples urged him, "Rabbi, eat." *32* But he said to them, "I have food to eat of which you do not know." *33* So the disciples said to one another, "Could someone have brought him something to eat?" *34* Jesus said to them, "My food is to do the will of the one who sent me and to finish his work. *35* Do you not say, 'In four months the harvest will be here'? I tell you, look up and see the fields ripe for the harvest. *36* The reaper is already receiving his payment *and gathering crops for eternal life, so that the sower and reaper can rejoice together. [37] For here the saying is verified that 'One sows, and another reaps.' [38] I sent you to reap what you have not worked for; others have done the work, and you are sharing the fruits of their work." [39] Many of the Samaritans of that town began to believe in him because of the word of the woman who testified, "He told me everything I have done." [40] When the Samaritans came to him, they invited him to stay with them; and he stayed there two days. [41] Many more began to believe in him because of his word, [42] and they said to the woman, "We no longer believe because of your word; for we have heard for ourselves, and we know that this is truly the savior of the world."*

This is only the second significant conversation in the gospels that Jesus participated in. There is a lot here to reflect on. Nicodemus came to Jesus looking for answers. Jesus came to Samaria looking for disciples. Although the name of Jesus has started to spread and people have started to think about Him, Jesus was always looking to invite people to grow closer to Him and His Father. Jesus was here to continue His mission to fulfill the will of His Father. And so, it begins at Jacob's well.

Jesus was alone at the well because His disciples went into town to get food. The woman from Samaria approached the well, and the conversation begins with what seems to be a simple request. As we are made to know, it is not so simple because Jews and Samaritans avoid each other. It was more than avoidance. Jewish people would not use anything used by Samaritans and vice versa. So, asking for a drink would require Jesus to use a utensil or cup she had.

Jesus said, "If you knew the gift of God and Who is saying to you, 'Give me a drink,' you would have asked Him and He would have given you living water." Jesus' statement is both a declaration and an invitation, both of which are not clear to this Samaritan. The declaration is that He Himself, the one who is speaking to her, is the gift from God. The invitation is for her to drink the living water. She jumps past the declaration and seeks to understand what this living water is. She stays with her reality and the water from Jacob's well. Is Jesus' water better than that in the well given by the patriarch Jacob?

Jesus confuses her more by pointing to the well and saying, "Everyone who drinks this water will be thirsty again; but whoever drinks the water I shall give will never thirst; the water I shall give will become in him a spring of water welling up to eternal life." This is a lot for her to take in. It is a lot for anyone to take in. He is not speaking of water that you actually drink. After all, even today, in baptism, we do not drink the baptismal water. Even today, Jesus' body and blood are in the form of bread and wine, not water. So, what is this water He is speaking of? Today, we know the *living* water is the Good News, the words of eternal life. However, the Samaritan again stays grounded in her reality, wanting some of this special water that will quench her thirst forever. So, Jesus changes the subject away from the water and focuses on what He knows about her.

Showing her that He knows about her is another way of getting the Samaritan woman to want to listen to what He has to say. But still, she is cautious because of the history between the Jewish people in Jerusalem and those in Samaria. However, she is willing to hear more. Then Jesus tells her that the place of worship is not as important as understanding who it is you are worshipping. "God is spirit, and those who worship him must worship in spirit and truth." Still not sure that she understands what Jesus is telling her, she says that she is waiting for the Messiah who will explain all things. Jesus says, "I am He;" but before He is able to *explain all things*, the conversation is interrupted by the return of His disciples.

Why did Jesus choose this woman to speak to? It was probably because He knew that others in the town would listen to her. This was exceptional since witness such as she would give would come usually from a man. Obviously, the disciples understood the way of things since they mentally questioned why Jesus chose to speak to this person – both a woman and a Samaritan. The woman then does exactly what Jesus expected; she went into town to call other people to see and hear this man who says He is the Messiah.

The disciples had a mission. They had gone into town to get food. When they returned, they offered it to Jesus. The answer was not what they expected and probably confused them. I admit it probably would have confused me. "My food is to do the will of the One who sent Me and to finish His work." They knew this was a teaching moment, but were they prepared to listen and understand?

This story about those who sow and those who reap can be applied to the disciples in a few ways. At this time, Jesus is the one who sows. He is planting seeds into the minds the Samaritan woman and of His disciples, and He will reap the harvest when they are out spreading the word. The woman is already spreading the word. The disciples will at some point sow as well; however, they may or may not be the ones who reap. Sometimes, the one sowing is gone before the harvest is ready. Then, the disciples may be the reapers of what is sown by others. This applies to us as well. We are all called to spread the good news. Yet, we may not see the results of our work. Our food is also to do the will of the one who sent us and to finish His work.

The woman fulfilled her mission. The people of the town heard enough from her to draw their interest. They wanted to hear for themselves. So, they gathered around

Jesus and invited Him to stay to tell them more. He and His disciples stayed for two days. When it was time to leave, Jesus had more disciples, more believers in the Savior of the world. Jesus' purpose for entering the Samaritan town was fulfilled.

Lord, there is a lot to mull over in this encounter You had with the woman in Samaria; however, I believe the main thing for now is to reflect deeply on my own discipleship and whether I am fulfilling Your will for me. Help me to understand what You are asking of me and give me the patience and perseverance to fulfill Your will. Amen.

Ministry in Galilee

Matthew 4:13-17: *[13] He left Nazareth and went to live in Capernaum by the sea, in the region of Zebulun and Naphtali, [14] that what had been said through Isaiah the prophet might be fulfilled: [15] "Land of Zebulun and land of Naphtali, the way to the sea, beyond the Jordan, Galilee of the Gentiles, [16] the people who sit in darkness have seen a great light, on those dwelling in a land overshadowed by death light has arisen." [17] From that time on, Jesus began to preach and say, "Repent, for the kingdom of heaven is at hand."*

Mark 1:14b-15: *[14] Jesus came to Galilee proclaiming the gospel of God: [15] "This is the time of fulfillment. The kingdom of God is at hand. Repent, and believe in the gospel."*

Luke 4:14-15: *[14] Jesus returned to Galilee in the power of the Spirit, and news of him spread throughout the whole region. [15] He taught in their synagogues and was praised by all.*

John 4:43-46a: *43 After the two days, he left there for Galilee. 44 For Jesus himself testified that a prophet has no honor in his native place. 45 When he came into Galilee, the Galileans welcomed him, since they had seen all he had done in Jerusalem at the feast; for they themselves had gone to the feast. 46 Then he returned to Cana in Galilee, where he had made the water wine.*

After leaving the Samaritan town, Jesus proceeded into Galilee. There is a minor conflict between Gospel authors here; but it is reconcilable. Matthew says He settled in Capernaum, in the regions of Zebulun and Napthali. His first place to go to was Nazareth where He was raised and then to Capernaum. John says He returned to Cana in Galilee. Since many of the gospel passages refer to Capernaum as His home, Cana must have been a stop sometime during His return to Galilee – not necessarily His destination.

Jesus did not stay in Nazareth because, as He said, *a prophet has no honor in his native place.* This is described later in a passage about His visit to Nazareth.

There are two messages in these verses that are important to remember. First is that Jesus taught in their synagogues, and the Galileans praised Him. He was very popular throughout the region. He had many followers throughout Galilee. The second message was what He was preaching to the people: "The kingdom of God is at hand. Repent, and believe in the gospel." This was a little different from the message of John the Baptist, but it was along the same lines. It was a message that people realized they needed to hear. It is a message that people today still need to hear.

Lord, You were known as the Galilean, not only from Your home but also from Your followers. You are also known as Messiah, Christ, the anointed one, Savior, Redeemer, Consoler, and many other titles. Help me, Lord, to recognize You in all those titles and in Your message, but especially as Son of God and Friend. Help me to seek You with the same ease I would my closest friend. Amen.

Jesus' Preaching at Nazareth

Luke 4:16-30: [16] *He came to Nazareth, where he had grown up, and went according to his custom into the synagogue on the sabbath day. He stood up to read* [17] *and was handed a scroll of the prophet Isaiah. He unrolled the scroll and found the passage where it was written:* [18] *"The Spirit of the Lord is upon me, because he has anointed me to bring glad tidings to the poor. He has sent me to proclaim liberty to captives and recovery of sight to the blind, to let the oppressed go free,* [19] *and to proclaim a year acceptable to the Lord."* [20] *Rolling up the scroll, he handed it back to the attendant and sat down, and the eyes of all in the synagogue looked intently at him.* [21] *He said to them, "Today this scripture passage is fulfilled in your hearing."* [22] *And all spoke highly of him and were amazed at the gracious words that came from his mouth. They also asked, "Isn't this the son of Joseph?"* [23] *He said to them, "Surely you will quote me this proverb, 'Physician, cure yourself,' and say, 'Do here in your native place the things that we heard were done in Capernaum.'"* [24] *And he said, "Amen, I say to you, no prophet is accepted in his own native place.* [25] *Indeed, I tell you, there were many widows in Israel in the days of Elijah when the sky was closed for three and a half years and a severe famine spread over the entire land.* [26] *It was to none of these that Elijah was sent, but only to a widow in Zarephath in the land of Sidon.* [27] *Again, there were many lepers in Israel* *during the time of Elisha the prophet; yet not one of them was cleansed, but only Naaman the Syrian." ²⁸ When the people in the synagogue heard this, they were all filled with fury. ²⁹ They rose up, drove him out of the town, and led him to the brow of the hill on which their town had been built, to hurl him down headlong. ³⁰ But he passed through the midst of them and went away.*

<u>Matthew 13:53-58:</u> *⁵³ When Jesus finished these parables, he went away from there. ⁵⁴ He came to his native place and taught the people in their synagogue. They were astonished and said, "Where did this man get such wisdom and mighty deeds? ⁵⁵ Is he not the carpenter's son? Is not his mother named Mary and his brothers James, Joseph, Simon, and Judas? ⁵⁶ Are not his sisters all with us? Where did this man get all this?" ⁵⁷ And they took offense at him. But Jesus said to them, "A prophet is not without honor except in his native place and in his own house." ⁵⁸ And he did not work many mighty deeds there because of their lack of faith.*

<u>Mark 6:1-6a:</u> *¹ He departed from there and came to his native place, accompanied by his disciples. ² When the sabbath came he began to teach in the synagogue, and many who heard him were astonished. They said, "Where did this man get all this? What kind of wisdom has been given him? What mighty deeds are wrought by his hands! ³ Is he not the carpenter, the son of Mary, and the brother of James and Joses and Judas and Simon? And are not his sisters here with us?" And they took offense at him. ⁴ Jesus said to them, "A prophet is not without honor except in his native place and among his own kin and in his own house." ⁵ So he was not able to perform any mighty deed there, apart from curing a few sick people by laying his hands on them. ⁶ He was amazed at their lack of faith.*

Jesus returned to the place where He had spent most of His life, Nazareth in Galilee. The people there knew Him, or at least, they thought they knew Him. We know basically nothing of His years before His public life began. We know that when He spoke in the synagogue, the people were amazed at His knowledge and His speaking ability. So, what does that tell us about Jesus in Nazareth. It confirms that before His public life, Jesus did not make known who He is. He was simply another boy grown to adulthood – no one special.

"The Spirit of the Lord is upon Me because He has anointed Me to bring glad tidings to the poor. He has sent Me to proclaim liberty to captives and recovery of sight to the blind, to let the oppressed go free, and to proclaim a year acceptable to the Lord. … Today this scripture passage is fulfilled in your hearing." This is what amazed the crowd. In itself, it did not cause a problem except to make people wonder where He got all this knowledge. There was nothing in His life in Nazareth that set Him apart. But it was the next that upset the crowd.

They had heard stories of what Jesus had done in Capernaum, about His teachings and His healings. Why was He not doing the same in Nazareth? Did He not owe it to His own people? Jesus' next comments about comparing Nazareth to what happened with Elijah and Elisha set the stage for "Amen, I say to you, no prophet is accepted in his own native place." All three of these gospel writers focused on that statement.

Our Lord knew what would come next; and yet, He made the statement. Was this one of His teaching moments? It was. They had to be told the truth. The healings in Capernaum were the result of faith, which the people close to home did not have. Jesus could have remained silent, but the truth had to be revealed. Whether they accepted the truth or not, the crowd, now the mob, chose to act.

It was Luke that finished out the scenario. The crowd decided they were going to kill Him. However, He made His way out of the crowd and escaped their fury. This scene was later brought up at His trial before Pilate.

Lord, truth is important; but there is a time for silence as well. Help me to know when to be silent and when to speak. Both speaking and keeping silent may bring on the wrath of the crowd. Help me to know which is right at the time. Amen.

The Call of the Disciples

<u>Matthew 4:18-22:</u> *[18] As he was walking by the Sea of Galilee, he saw two brothers, Simon who is called Peter, and his brother Andrew, casting a net into the sea; they were fishermen. [19] He said to them, "Come after me, and I will make you fishers of men." [20] At once they left their nets and followed him. [21] He walked along from there and saw two other brothers, James, the son of Zebedee, and his brother John. They were in a boat, with their father Zebedee, mending their nets. He called them, [22] and immediately they left their boat and their father and followed him.*

<u>Mark 1:16-20:</u> *[16] As he passed by the Sea of Galilee, he saw Simon and his brother Andrew casting their nets into the sea; they were fishermen. [17] Jesus said to them, "Come after me, and I will make you fishers of men." [18] Then they abandoned their nets and followed him. [19] He walked along a little farther and saw James, the son of Zebedee, and his brother John. They too were in a boat mending their nets. [20] Then he called them.*

So they left their father Zebedee in the boat along with the hired men and followed him.

There is an immediate question that comes to mind: what is the difference between these two passages and the one described in the gospel of John we saw earlier? The difference is that the original describes the interest shown by Andrew, Peter, Philip, and Nathaneal as they discovered who they believed to be the Messiah. In these passages, Peter, Andrew, James, and John are called to follow Jesus and become "fishers of men." Jesus is handpicking His team. Here, the four actually drop everything to follow Jesus.

What does that tell us about those four? They left their businesses, their means of making a living. As fishermen, they would have to go out daily and then sell what they caught, *if* they had surplus from what they needed just to survive. In the case of Peter and Andrew, what happened to their families when they *dropped everything*? We know from later passages that Peter had a mother-in-law who depended on him. I assumed his wife was still living. We do not know if Andrew was married. We do not know if either had children. How would their families be supported? Or did their families simply go with them to follow Jesus? Remember, only adult males were counted or had status.

Similar questions can be asked about James and John. The difference is that James and John worked for their father, Zebedee. It was his fishing business, so it probably could carry on and families could be supported.

In the case of all four, it took courage to simply drop what they were doing, abandon their livelihood, and follow an itinerant preacher, even though they believed Him to be the Messiah. The passages do not indicate if they spent much time discussing what to do before leaving. It just says they followed. That is the hardest part about doing the Will of God. Once you understand what He is asking of you, you have to courageously step forward and say "yes." No matter how strong your faith is, it still takes courage to move forward.

Lord, once I know what You are asking of me, give me the courage and perseverance to move forward. Amen.

Teaching in the Synagogue at Capernaum

Mark 1:21-22: *²¹ Then they came to Capernaum, and on the sabbath he entered the synagogue and taught. ²² The people were astonished at his teaching, for he taught them as one having authority and not as the scribes.*

Luke 4:31-32: *³¹ Jesus then went down to Capernaum, a town of Galilee. He taught them on the sabbath, ³² and they were astonished at his teaching because he spoke with authority.*

Both Mark and Luke agreed on this. Jesus went to Capernaum and entered the synagogue. I believe we can assume that Peter, Andrew, James, and John were with Him since in the previous passages He called them to follow Him.

What is important here though is that He "spoke with authority." "Not as the scribes" is also important. Jesus always presented Himself as speaking the truth, confident in what He said. People could see that. They recognized his authority. It was not like the scribes, who evidently did not leave people with confidence in what the scribes said.

I have to admit that there are many people in this world who have learned to tell lies and leave people believing it is the truth. It is not always easy to recognize the difference. It takes a process of discernment to determine the truth. And even then, sometimes you are not sure. So, what was it about Jesus that gave people confidence?

I can only answer this by what gives me confidence in who is speaking. What the speaker says must be said with confidence; it must leave me with the impression that it is based on fact; if possible, it must be accompanied by facts; and finally, it must correspond to something I believe to be true (or want to be true). Over the years, I have grown to trust what I hear from Jesus.

Lord, open my mind and heart so that I will continue to believe what You say to be true. Amen.

The Healing of the Demoniac in the Synagogue

Mark 1:23-28: *²³ In their synagogue was a man with an unclean spirit; ²⁴ he cried out, "What have you to do with us, Jesus of Nazareth? Have you come to destroy us? I know who you are—the Holy One of God!" ²⁵ Jesus rebuked him and said, "Quiet! Come out of him!" ²⁶ The unclean spirit convulsed him and with a loud cry came out of him. ²⁷ All were amazed and asked one another, "What is this? A new teaching with authority. He commands even the unclean spirits, and they obey him." ²⁸ His fame spread everywhere throughout the whole region of Galilee.*

Luke 4:33-37: *³³ In the synagogue there was a man with the spirit of an unclean demon, and he cried out in a loud voice, ³⁴ "Ha! What have you to do with us, Jesus of Nazareth? Have you come to destroy us? I know who you are—the Holy*

90

One of God!" [35] *Jesus rebuked him and said, "Be quiet! Come out of him!" Then the demon threw the man down in front of them and came out of him without doing him any harm.* [36] *They were all amazed and said to one another, "What is there about his word? For with authority and power he commands the unclean spirits, and they come out."* [37] *And news of him spread everywhere in the surrounding region.*

    I find this story interesting because of the lack of details. This is a common trait of the writers of the Gospels. As a general statement, they tend to get right to the point – what happened, what was said. Obviously, there are exceptions; and some of the stories contain lots of details.

    The last we read, Jesus and His disciples had gone to Capernaum. It said He taught in the synagogue. I believe we can assume that, in this particular case, Jesus had read the scripture and gave His comments related to the reading. It was after this that the man possessed by the demon challenged not just His teaching but His purpose for being there.

    It seems obvious from the presentation that the others in the synagogue believed there was something seriously wrong with the man. How many believed he was possessed by a demon, we are not sure; however, when it was over, it was recognized as an exorcism.

    The only recorded words of Jesus were: "Be quiet! Come out of him!" And He spoke with authority. *The unclean spirit convulsed him and with a loud cry came out of him.* That was all that was needed: a simple command and an immediate response. I believe we can assume that the possessed man was unharmed as the demon left or our Lord healed him immediately if he was harmed in any way.

    Jesus amazed the people in the synagogue and the word spread throughout Capernaum and the surrounding region.

Jesus was growing in renown. He was becoming known for His authority in speaking, for His ability to cast out demons, and His ability to heal. The Messiah was becoming known.

Lord, help me to always know that I can come to you in all of my adversity and have confidence that You will provide me with what I need. Amen.

The Healing of Peter's Mother-in-Law

Matthew 8:14-15: *[14] Jesus entered the house of Peter and saw his mother-in-law lying in bed with a fever. [15] He touched her hand, the fever left her, and she rose and waited on him.*

Mark 1:29-31: *[29] On leaving the synagogue he entered the house of Simon and Andrew with James and John. [30] Simon's mother-in-law lay sick with a fever. They immediately told him about her. [31] He approached, grasped her hand, and helped her up. Then the fever left her, and she waited on them.*

Luke 4:38-39: *[38] After he left the synagogue, he entered the house of Simon. Simon's mother-in-law was afflicted with a severe fever, and they interceded with him about her. [39] He stood over her, rebuked the fever, and it left her. She got up immediately and waited on them.*

The sequence of events seems tight here. It was after they left the synagogue, after Jesus had cast out the demon. We are never really told where they were living in Capernaum, but this is the house of Simon and Andrew; so, it is likely that this is where Jesus was residing while in Capernaum.

All three of the Gospel writers agreed to the circumstance that Simon's mother-in-law had a severe fever, severe enough for her to be in bed. Having seen Jesus in action, Simon and Andrew asked Jesus to help Simon's mother-in-law. They already saw Jesus doing amazing things, but did they know He could heal her or were they hoping for the best? He did heal her.

I find the use of a phrase especially important. It may simply be the way it was translated, so it may not be of significance. Luke says, "He rebuked the fever." Later on in the Gospels, we will here of Jesus commanding to winds to cease and the sea to be calm. It is strange for humans to hear a command being given to something that we believe has no intelligence, something that would not understand a command or even obey a command. Again, this may simply be artistic license. Jesus was not a showman. I believe He simply made the fever subside. He could do it without words. However, I also believe He wanted His disciples to know He had this kind of control. He told the fever to leave so His followers could understand what was happening – no fanfare. I have been taught and I believe that God loves all of His creation. Does all of His creation understand and respond to Him? Or does God simply *use* that of His creation which we humans identify as not intelligent?

The fact is that Jesus healed Simon's mother-in-law at the request of Simon and Andrew. I believe He would have healed her even if the request had not been made.

Lord, I believe that nothing is impossible for You. Help me to not be afraid to ask, especially for a healing. Amen.

The Sick Healed at Evening

<u>Matthew 8:16-17:</u> *[16] When it was evening, they brought him many who were possessed by demons, and he drove out the*

spirits by a word and cured all the sick, ¹⁷ to fulfill what had been said by Isaiah the prophet:

Mark 1:32-34: *³² When it was evening, after sunset, they brought to him all who were ill or possessed by demons. ³³ The whole town was gathered at the door. ³⁴ He cured many who were sick with various diseases, and he drove out many demons, not permitting them to speak because they knew him.*

Luke 4:40-41: *⁴⁰ At sunset, all who had people sick with various diseases brought them to him. He laid his hands on each of them and cured them. ⁴¹ And demons also came out from many, shouting, "You are the Son of God." But he rebuked them and did not allow them to speak because they knew that he was the Messiah.*

I mentioned this earlier. Jesus was available. It was the evening. He did not keep regular office hours. He was simply available to people who came to Him seeking help. I am sure it both amazed His disciples and irritated them as well. They were amazed that he did not turn people away; and yet, they were probably irritated because they were probably tired as was Jesus.

He cast out demons. From the sound of it, demon possession must have been common. It may have simply been thought that unidentified diseases or conditions were attributed to demons. However, nothing is actually said in these passages about the words Jesus used. For demons, He would expel them, cast them out; but for illnesses, He would use different words for healing.

This is just food for thought. The numbers are not really important. What is important is that Jesus made Himself available and was willing to heal no matter what time people came to Him. Throughout the gospels, there is never any mention about healing He could not perform.

Lord, there have been many times in my life when I have not made myself available to help when people have asked, for various reasons or excuses. Open my mind and my heart and help me to be more responsive to those who need my help. Amen.

Jesus Departs from Capernaum and into Galilee

<u>Matthew 4:23:</u> *He went around all of Galilee, teaching in their synagogues, proclaiming the gospel of the kingdom, and curing every disease and illness among the people.*

<u>Mark 1:35-39:</u> *[35] Rising very early before dawn, he left and went off to a deserted place, where he prayed. [36] Simon and those who were with him pursued him [37] and on finding him said, "Everyone is looking for you." [38] He told them, "Let us go on to the nearby villages that I may preach there also. For this purpose have I come." [39] So he went into their synagogues, preaching and driving out demons throughout the whole of Galilee.*

<u>Luke 4:42-44:</u> *[42] At daybreak, Jesus left and went to a deserted place. The crowds went looking for him, and when they came to him, they tried to prevent him from leaving them. [43] But he said to them, "To the other towns also I must proclaim the good news of the kingdom of God, because for this purpose I have been sent." [44] And he was preaching in the synagogues of Judea.*

95

Rising very early before dawn, he left and went off to a deserted place, where he prayed. We are told that Jesus regularly went off to a deserted place and prayed to His Father. What "regular" means is not for us to judge; but from this statement, we can be assured that prayer time was important to Him, as it should be to us.

But the mission must go on. Jesus had to continue His mission and spread the good news throughout the area. He needed to help them understand and grow closer to His Father. It would have been easy to stay in one place for an extended period of time, but that was not His purpose. It was to follow the will of His Father.

From the few examples we have seen so far, Jesus will move from place-to-place preaching and healing. His disciples will listen and learn. And the number of His disciples will continue to grow.

Lord, I can picture myself with You among Your disciples, watching, listening, learning, wondering in amazement at what I am seeing. Please help me to keep this level of wonder, of amazement, of learning as I strive to grow closer to You. Amen.

The Miraculous Catch of Fish

<u>Luke 5:1-11:</u> *¹ While the crowd was pressing in on Jesus and listening to the word of God, he was standing by the Lake of Gennesaret. ² He saw two boats there alongside the lake; the fishermen had disembarked and were washing their nets. ³ Getting into one of the boats, the one belonging to Simon, he asked him to put out a short distance from the shore. Then he sat down and taught the crowds from the boat. ⁴ After he had finished speaking, he said to Simon, "Put out into deep water and lower your nets for a catch." ⁵ Simon said in reply,*

96

"Master, we have worked hard all night and have caught nothing, but at your command I will lower the nets." [6] *When they had done this, they caught a great number of fish and their nets were tearing.* [7] *They signaled to their partners in the other boat to come to help them. They came and filled both boats so that they were in danger of sinking.* [8] *When Simon Peter saw this, he fell at the knees of Jesus and said, "Depart from me, Lord, for I am a sinful man."* [9] *For astonishment at the catch of fish they had made seized him and all those with him,* [10] *and likewise James and John, the sons of Zebedee, who were partners of Simon. Jesus said to Simon, "Do not be afraid; from now on you will be catching men."* [11] *When they brought their boats to the shore, they left everything and followed him.*

What comes to mind after reading this passage are a couple of questions.

1. Should not this passage be included in Part 3 of this book which reflects on the calling of the first disciples? Simon, Andrew, James, and John had already been called by our Lord to follow Him. So, this sounds like a second calling to the same four.

2. Had the four disciples not really followed Jesus and had gone back to their former lives? They may have simply been investigating this man, Jesus, and had not really made the commitment to follow Him.

I do not have the answers to these questions, so I will simply follow the lead of my guide through the sequencing of the events of Christ's life.

The crowds were beginning to build up; and so, Jesus took the opportunity to preach the good news. Preaching from Simon's boat was a good call. It separated Him from the crowd and gave Him a stage from which to tell His story. And so, He did. Nothing is mentioned here of any healings;

97

but, as I have written earlier, He made Himself available. They were likely to be close to shore so He could be heard clearly by the crowd.

He probably dismissed the crowd because He asked for the two boats to go out in deeper water for the miraculous catch: "Put out into deep water and lower your nets for a catch." Jesus has never been identified in the gospels as a fisherman, but He did know of the life and ways for fishermen. After a minor protest from Simon, both boats set out to fulfill the request of Jesus. They caught so many fish that they were in danger of their boats sinking. All the fishermen were filled with astonishment.

Here is where a short dialogue takes place and two of the most important statements of Jesus are given. Simon sank to his knees and said, "Depart from me, Lord, for I am a sinful man." Jesus said in response, "Do not be afraid; from now on you will be catching men." Jesus' response was in two parts. "Do not be afraid." I do not know how many times Jesus said this or "Peace to you." The fact is that it was often. He astonished people and especially His disciples throughout His public life. He often found the need to quiet them, calm them, assure them. Then He continued: "from now on you will be catching men." This was the mission that Simon, Andrew, James, and John were being given. It is effectively the mission given to His other Apostles and disciples. Go forth and capture souls for God.

When they brought their boats to the shore, they left everything and followed him. Was this the second calling, or was it just an affirmation of the first?

Lord, astonishment fills me over and over again as I read through the pages of Your book. I know that this ability that I have for writing is a gift from You. I hope and pray that my use of this gift is in some way "catching men" for God. Amen.

The Cleansing of the Leper

<u>Matthew 8:1-4:</u> *[1] When Jesus came down from the mountain, great crowds followed him. [2] And then a leper approached, did him homage, and said, "Lord, if you wish, you can make me clean." [3] He stretched out his hand, touched him, and said, "I will do it. Be made clean." His leprosy was cleansed immediately. [4] Then Jesus said to him, "See that you tell no one, but go show yourself to the priest, and offer the gift that Moses prescribed; that will be proof for them."*

<u>Mark 1:40-45:</u> *[40] A leper came to him [and kneeling down] begged him and said, "If you wish, you can make me clean." [41] Moved with pity, he stretched out his hand, touched him, and said to him, "I do will it. Be made clean." [42] The leprosy left him immediately, and he was made clean. [43] Then, warning him sternly, he dismissed him at once. [44] Then he said to him, "See that you tell no one anything, but go, show yourself to the priest and offer for your cleansing what Moses prescribed; that will be proof for them." [45] The man went away and began to publicize the whole matter. He spread the report abroad so that it was impossible for Jesus to enter a town openly. He remained outside in deserted places, and people kept coming to him from everywhere.*

<u>Luke 5:12-16:</u> *[12] Now there was a man full of leprosy in one of the towns where he was; and when he saw Jesus, he fell prostrate, pleaded with him, and said, "Lord, if you wish, you can make me clean." [13] Jesus stretched out his hand, touched him, and said, "I do will it. Be made clean." And the leprosy left him immediately. [14] Then he ordered him not to tell anyone,*

99

but "Go, show yourself to the priest and offer for your cleansing what Moses prescribed; that will be proof for them." [15] The report about him spread all the more, and great crowds assembled to listen to him and to be cured of their ailments, [16] but he would withdraw to deserted places to pray.

We are still in Galilee and the crowds following Jesus are growing. In this encounter with the leper, a few things need reflection. The leper approached Jesus in spite of the crowd with Him and following Him. It would normally be forbidden for a leper to approach anyone. The crowd did not chase him away. I can only assume that everyone wanted to see what Jesus would do.

Jesus' response to the leper seems to have been immediate. He willed the leper to be free of his disease. It does not look like there was any hesitation. This case is different from the fever of Simon's mother-in-law. He stretched out his hand, touched him, and said, "I will do it. Be made clean." Again, words were not necessary for the cure to take place, nor the touch; however, they were important for the leper to hear and the crowd to hear, and for them to see. He did not rebuke the leprosy as He did the fever. He simply said, "Be made clean." There was no big show; again, no fanfare. He simply responded to the request.

Next came the task. Jesus did not place conditions on His healings. He loves unconditionally. However, the cured leper had to follow the prescription in the Law to be declared clean by the temple authorities. Jesus did tell the leper to keep this quiet, even though He knew the word of this cure would spread, just like the word of all His miracles spread. *And people kept coming to him from everywhere.*

Lord, You have the power to control all of Your creations. You set the laws of nature and can override those laws at will. You also love all of Your creation. Help me to not expect too much of You. Only You know what is best for us. Amen.

The Healing of the Paralytic

<u>Matthew 9:1-8:</u> *[1] He entered a boat, made the crossing, and came into his own town. [2] And there, people brought to him a paralytic lying on a stretcher. When Jesus saw their faith, he said to the paralytic, "Courage, child, your sins are forgiven." [3] At that, some of the scribes said to themselves, "This man is blaspheming." [4] Jesus knew what they were thinking, and said, "Why do you harbor evil thoughts? [5] Which is easier, to say, 'Your sins are forgiven,' or to say, 'Rise and walk'? [6] But that you may know that the Son of Man has authority on earth to forgive sins"—he then said to the paralytic, "Rise, pick up your stretcher, and go home." [7] He rose and went home. [8] When the crowds saw this they were struck with awe and glorified God who had given such authority to human beings.*

<u>Mark 2:1-12:</u> *[1] When Jesus returned to Capernaum after some days, it became known that he was at home. [2] Many gathered together so that there was no longer room for them, not even around the door, and he preached the word to them. [3] They came bringing to him a paralytic carried by four men. [4] Unable to get near Jesus because of the crowd, they opened up the roof above him. After they had broken through, they let down the mat on which the paralytic was lying. [5] When Jesus saw their faith, he said to the paralytic, "Child, your sins are forgiven." [6] Now some of the scribes were sitting there asking themselves, [7] "Why does this man speak that way? He is*

101

blaspheming. Who but God alone can forgive sins?" [8] *Jesus immediately knew in his mind what they were thinking to themselves, so he said, "Why are you thinking such things in your hearts?* [9] *Which is easier, to say to the paralytic, 'Your sins are forgiven,' or to say, 'Rise, pick up your mat and walk'?* [10] *But that you may know that the Son of Man has authority to forgive sins on earth"—* [11] *he said to the paralytic, "I say to you, rise, pick up your mat, and go home."* [12] *He rose, picked up his mat at once, and went away in the sight of everyone. They were all astounded and glorified God, saying, "We have never seen anything like this."*

Luke 5:17-26: [17] *One day as Jesus was teaching, Pharisees and teachers of the law were sitting there who had come from every village of Galilee and Judea and Jerusalem, and the power of the Lord was with him for healing.* [18] *And some men brought on a stretcher a man who was paralyzed; they were trying to bring him in and set [him] in his presence.* [19] *But not finding a way to bring him in because of the crowd, they went up on the roof and lowered him on the stretcher through the tiles into the middle in front of Jesus.* [20] *When he saw their faith, he said, "As for you, your sins are forgiven."* [21] *Then the scribes and Pharisees began to ask themselves, "Who is this who speaks blasphemies? Who but God alone can forgive sins?"* [22] *Jesus knew their thoughts and said to them in reply, "What are you thinking in your hearts?* [23] *Which is easier, to say, 'Your sins are forgiven,' or to say, 'Rise and walk'?* [24] *But that you may know that the Son of Man has authority on earth to forgive sins"—he said to the man who was paralyzed, "I say to you, rise, pick up your stretcher, and go home."* [25] *He stood up immediately before them, picked up what he had been lying on, and went home, glorifying God.* [26] *Then astonishment seized them all and they glorified God, and, struck with awe, they said, "We have seen incredible things today."*

The story is essentially the same in all three gospel renditions. The quotes from our Lord are essentially the same as well. The first quote is significant. When the four friends brought the paralytic to Jesus, He saw their faith. They believed that Jesus could provide the cure. They did not specifically ask; or, at least, the words were not presented. The request for a cure obviously was implied by their actions. Jesus had been healing people of their illnesses and injuries throughout His public life. He has been casting out demons, and He has been showing that He has control over natural phenomenon. So, what was so special about this encounter?

Everything He has been doing is something that was done by one or more of the prophets before Him. The prophets have performed miracles, not on their own, but through the power of God. There were times when Jesus performed His miracles that He challenged what people believed and were taught, such as it is alright to do good for others on the Sabbath. It is okay to question what is being taught and seek to understand the truth. He challenged the Scribes and Pharisees about what they taught and showed that sometimes they were unfair or too controlling.

Today, Jesus taught a very special lesson; one that no one had been expecting; but one that acknowledges the truth of what the Jewish leaders had learned and taught. "Who but God alone can forgive sins?" That is the truth. Only God can forgive sins. But the lesson here is that Jesus is saying, "Yes, and I am He. I am the Son of God. I have the power to say, 'your sins are forgiven.'" The people had been thinking this but were afraid to say it. They had been awaiting the Messiah and He appeared.

Jesus gave them a great gift. I say *them* because in Luke's version, it seems like Jesus is addressing the paralytic and his four friends. In the other two versions, Jesus is addressing the paralytic. Regardless, Jesus was granting something they did not ask for. In various parts of the gospels, Jesus is seen granting these blessings before they are being requested. Jesus knows what we need and, in His love for us, He grants what we need.

Then, after the challenge from the righteous Pharisees, Jesus cures the paralytic. From the description of the story, Jesus performed a lot of healings among the people who gathered around Him. So, the paralytic was not the only one receiving such a blessing. What is important here is that Jesus used His ability to cure physical illness as proof that He has the power to forgive sins as well.

There is physical proof for the healing of maladies. There is no physical proof for the forgiveness of sins. There is nothing in the three versions of this story that indicates if they really understood that their sins were forgiven and what that would mean in the long run.

The paralytic walked away doubly blessed. The Scribes and Pharisees walked away confused and angry. Many of the people walked away blessed with their healings. His disciples walked away more amazed about their master. And many walked away not knowing what to think. Jesus, the Messiah? Jesus, the Son of God?

Lord, my sins have a way of dragging me down. Give me the courage to admit them to You and seek Your forgiveness. Help me to believe the truth of who You are. Amen.

The Call of Levi (Matthew)

<u>Matthew 9:9-13:</u> *⁹ As Jesus passed on from there, he saw a man named Matthew sitting at the customs post. He said to him, "Follow me." And he got up and followed him. ¹⁰ While*

104

he was at table in his house, many tax collectors and sinners came and sat with Jesus and his disciples. [11] The Pharisees saw this and said to his disciples, "Why does your teacher eat with tax collectors and sinners?" [12] He heard this and said, "Those who are well do not need a physician, but the sick do. [13] Go and learn the meaning of the words, 'I desire mercy, not sacrifice.' I did not come to call the righteous but sinners."

Mark 2:13-17: [13] Once again he went out along the sea. All the crowd came to him, and he taught them. [14] As he passed by, he saw Levi, son of Alphaeus, sitting at the customs post. He said to him, "Follow me." And he got up and followed him. [15] While he was at table in his house, many tax collectors and sinners sat with Jesus and his disciples; for there were many who followed him. [16] Some scribes who were Pharisees saw that he was eating with sinners and tax collectors and said to his disciples, "Why does he eat with tax collectors and sinners?" [17] Jesus heard this and said to them [that], "Those who are well do not need a physician, but the sick do. I did not come to call the righteous but sinners."

Luke 5:27-32: [27] After this he went out and saw a tax collector named Levi sitting at the customs post. He said to him, "Follow me." [28] And leaving everything behind, he got up and followed him. [29] Then Levi gave a great banquet for him in his house, and a large crowd of tax collectors and others were at table with them. [30] The Pharisees and their scribes complained to his disciples, saying, "Why do you eat and drink with tax collectors and sinners?" [31] Jesus said to them in reply, "Those who are healthy do not need a physician, but the sick do. [32] I have not come to call the righteous to repentance but sinners."

Once again, we have a situation in which the story is essentially the same reported by three gospel writers. The

105

only differences are very minor. Of the twelve Apostles, Matthew is number seven, if we go in order of the callings. We have already read the stories of the callings of Simon, Andrew, James, John, Philip, and Nathaneal.

In Matthew's case, he must have been ready for something different in his life. The simple call was, "Follow Me." There was no explanation, no long dialogue between Matthew and Jesus. The call was made, and Matthew left everything and followed Jesus. I am sure there was more to it than that. But we are not given more details, not even by Matthew himself.

Jesus was constantly under the scrutiny of others, especially the Pharisees. No matter where He went, no matter what He did, the Pharisees, scribes, scholars, or other groups were watching to catch Him in some sort of impropriety or violation of the Law. Here, Jesus was dining with Matthew and some of Matthew's guests, most likely his friends. So, the accusation: "Why does He eat with tax collectors and sinners?"

Here is something we need to reflect on. We tend to jump to conclusions of black and white, good and bad. The gray areas only show up after some thought. Regardless of who Matthew was, the Jews believed that he was evil simply because he was a tax collector. Even though it was a legitimate job, and Matthew may never have abused anyone in this role, he and his friends were bad.

Actually, the Pharisees could care less. They just wanted to create a scenario in which Jesus was guilty of something, even if it was as lame as keeping the wrong company. But Jesus responded calmly and sincerely as always, "Those who are healthy do not need a physician, but the sick do. I have not come to call the righteous to repentance but sinners." Jesus' mission was to bring souls to His Father. That is His Father's will. Jesus was in no better position than this to do so.

I am sure there were some men among the Pharisees, Sanhedrin, and Scribes who were smart and shrewd. However, they were never a match for Jesus.

Lord, there are times when I am confronted by people who challenge what I am doing or saying. Please help me to know if my words and actions are appropriate and how to respond in a way that would please You. Amen.

The Question About Fasting

<u>Matthew 9:14-17:</u> *[14] Then the disciples of John approached him and said, "Why do we and the Pharisees fast [much], but your disciples do not fast?" [15] Jesus answered them, "Can the wedding guests mourn as long as the bridegroom is with them? The days will come when the bridegroom is taken away from them, and then they will fast. [16] No one patches an old cloak with a piece of unshrunken cloth, for its fullness pulls away from the cloak and the tear gets worse. [17] People do not put new wine into old wineskins. Otherwise, the skins burst, the wine spills out, and the skins are ruined. Rather, they pour new wine into fresh wineskins, and both are preserved."*

<u>Mark 2:18-22:</u> *[18] The disciples of John and of the Pharisees were accustomed to fast. People came to him and objected, "Why do the disciples of John and the disciples of the Pharisees fast, but your disciples do not fast?" [19] Jesus answered them, "Can the wedding guests fast while the bridegroom is with them? As long as they have the bridegroom with them they cannot fast. [20] But the days will come when the bridegroom is taken away from them, and then they will fast on that day. [21] No one sews a piece of unshrunken cloth on an*

old cloak. If he does, its fullness pulls away, the new from the old, and the tear gets worse. ²² Likewise, no one pours new wine into old wineskins. Otherwise, the wine will burst the skins, and both the wine and the skins are ruined. Rather, new wine is poured into fresh wineskins."

<u>**Luke 5:33-39:**</u> *³³ And they said to him, "The disciples of John fast often and offer prayers, and the disciples of the Pharisees do the same; but yours eat and drink." ³⁴ Jesus answered them, "Can you make the wedding guests fast while the bridegroom is with them? ³⁵ But the days will come, and when the bridegroom is taken away from them, then they will fast in those days." ³⁶ And he also told them a parable. "No one tears a piece from a new cloak to patch an old one. Otherwise, he will tear the new and the piece from it will not match the old cloak. ³⁷ Likewise, no one pours new wine into old wineskins. Otherwise, the new wine will burst the skins, and it will be spilled, and the skins will be ruined. ³⁸ Rather, new wine must be poured into fresh wineskins. ³⁹ [And] no one who has been drinking old wine desires new, for he says, 'The old is good.'"*

The question of the fasting was essentially the same in all three passages. Why do the disciples of John (the Baptist) and the Pharisees fast and pray, yet the disciples of Jesus do not? In answer, Jesus compares the actions of the disciples to that of people in a wedding feast. Why would anyone at a wedding feast fast while the bridegroom is still present? Not to be chauvinistic, it was common in middle eastern weddings for the bride to leave the feast early to prepare herself for the groom. So, the groom continued to celebrate. Jesus compared Himself to the groom. The celebration would not stop while the groom was present. His disciples would not fast and pray until He was taken from them. Without giving details, Jesus is predicting that He will be taken.

It is almost as if Jesus is changing the subject, but He is taking advantage of a teaching moment. Keep in mind that this is taking place during the gathering at Matthew's place, amongst the tax collectors, sinners, and Pharisees.

In this passage, the stories presented by Matthew and Mark are almost identical, but Luke spins a slightly different tale when it comes to the wine skins. It is a good bet that it all depends on the source of the story. Mark and Luke were not present when the stories were lived out. Matthew was.

As has been told many times, you cannot patch an old garment with new cloth or pour new wine into old wineskins. The new cloth will not match the old garment just as new wine will burst old wineskins. People become set in their ways. It is difficult for those set in their ways to accept new ideas. It is not impossible, but difficult.

The Pharisees who looked to trap Jesus are the people set in their ways. They are unwilling to accept the new ideas that Jesus is presenting. However, we must keep in mind that the *new ideas* that Jesus was presenting are old ideas from the Law that people have begun to forget or misinterpret. Jesus came to fulfill the Law, not change it.

Lord, help me to never be so stiff-necked that I will not listen to Your words of truth and life. Amen.

Part 5

Sermon on the Mount

And Other Sermons

Occasion of the Sermon

<u>Matthew 4:24 – 5:2:</u> *[24] His fame spread to all of Syria, and they brought to him all who were sick with various diseases and racked with pain, those who were possessed, lunatics, and paralytics, and he cured them. [25] And great crowds from Galilee, the Decapolis, Jerusalem, and Judea, and from beyond the Jordan followed him. [1] When he saw the crowds, he went up the mountain, and after he had sat down, his disciples came to him. [2] He began to teach them, saying:*

<u>Mark 3:7-13a:</u> *[7] Jesus withdrew toward the sea with his disciples. A large number of people [followed] from Galilee and from Judea. [8] Hearing what he was doing, a large number of people came to him also from Jerusalem, from Idumea, from beyond the Jordan, and from the neighborhood of Tyre and Sidon. [9] He told his disciples to have a boat ready for him because of the crowd, so that they would not crush him. [10] He had cured many and, as a result, those who had diseases were pressing upon him to touch him. [11] And whenever unclean spirits saw him they would fall down before him and shout, "You are the Son of God." [12] He warned them sternly not to make him known. [13] He went up the mountain.*

<u>Luke 6:17-20a:</u> *[17] And he came down with them and stood on a stretch of level ground. A great crowd of his disciples and a large number of the people from all Judea and Jerusalem and the coastal region of Tyre and Sidon [18] came to hear him and to be healed of their diseases; and even those who were tormented by unclean spirits were cured. [19] Everyone in the crowd sought to touch him because power came forth from him and healed them all. [20] And raising his eyes toward his disciples he said:*

Let us take a step back. In the passages related to the healings at the Sea of Galilee, it was already presented that people were coming from all over to see, hear, and be healed by Jesus. The size of the crowd is not estimated, just that it is a large crowd. The passages from Mark and Luke are actually repetitions from that chapter. The point here is that the crowds were growing and building up to the audience to what is known as the Sermon on the Mount.

Jesus was spending a lot of time healing and casting out demons. But His mission from His Father was also to teach. People had to believe, people had to know that all God had told them to do, the way He wanted them to live, was really possible. Jesus' mission was to heal, cure, cast out demons, teach and live the way God wants people to live. He had to give people an example of life as a human being according to God. Jesus is capable of all of this – and more.

Lord, if I am going to live as You lived, to follow Your example, then I must pay close attention to all You did and spoke. You have a plan for me, a mission that has not been unveiled except for bits and pieces. Help me to know each step as I need to proceed. Give me the strength to always say "yes." Amen.

The Beatitudes

Matthew 5:3-12:
³ *"Blessed are the poor in spirit,*
  for theirs is the kingdom of heaven.
⁴ *Blessed are they who mourn,*
  for they will be comforted.
⁵ *Blessed are the meek,*
  for they will inherit the land.
⁶ *Blessed are they who hunger and thirst for righteousness,*

for they will be satisfied.
⁷ Blessed are the merciful,
* for they will be shown mercy.*
⁸ Blessed are the clean of heart,
* for they will see God.*
⁹ Blessed are the peacemakers,
* for they will be called children of God.*
¹⁰ Blessed are they who are persecuted for the sake of
righteousness,
* for theirs is the kingdom of heaven.*
¹¹ Blessed are you when they insult you and persecute you and
utter every kind of evil against you [falsely] because of
me. ¹² Rejoice and be glad, for your reward will be great in
heaven. Thus they persecuted the prophets who were before
you.

Luke 6:20b-23:
²⁰ "Blessed are you who are poor,
* for the kingdom of God is yours.*
²¹ Blessed are you who are now hungry,
* for you will be satisfied.*
Blessed are you who are now weeping,
* for you will laugh.*
²² Blessed are you when people hate you,
* and when they exclude and insult you,*
* and denounce your name as evil*
* on account of the Son of Man.*
²³ Rejoice and leap for joy on that day! Behold, your reward
will be great in heaven. For their ancestors treated the prophets
in the same way.

Not too long ago, I wrote a book of reflections for the
Advent season: *Hope – My Advent Calendar*. As part of the
daily reflections, I commented on the Beatitudes as

113

presented by Matthew. I wanted to show how the Beatitudes were a promise of hope from our Lord. I used Matthew's Beatitudes as the basis for my reflections. Here are some of my thoughts about each.

Blessed are the poor in spirit, for theirs is the kingdom of heaven. Our Lord is not saying that all of the poor are blessed. This has nothing to do with poverty. It has everything to do with what is in our minds and hearts. That is why the tag "in spirit" is added to "poor." This beatitude emphasizes what is in our hearts, what we hold dear. In order to be poor in spirit, we have to develop the attitude of detachment from the things of this world. This spirit of detachment can be achieved. We have to overcome the enticements that are presented. It is this spirit that Our Lord says will bring blessings to us. If we can attain this spirit, then the kingdom of heaven will be ours.

Blessed are they who mourn, for they will be comforted. When suffering a loss of any significance, people will mourn. It may be the death of a loved one, it may be separation from someone you care about, it may be betrayal, it may be loss of a job, it may be loss of a place to live. It may be the result of something we did, it may be the result of something someone else did that affected us, it may be an absolute accident, it may be from natural causes (illness or age), and it may be simply Mother Nature. We all handle our grief differently. This is what this beatitude is about. Those who mourn will be comforted. It is like that with with every "bad" thing that happens. Every bad thing that happens is an opportunity for someone to love another. Because that is what comfort is. It is a manifestation of someone's love for another. This is the promise, the hope we are given by our Lord Jesus.

Blessed are the meek, for they will inherit the land. In Matthew 11:29, Jesus will tell us to be "meek and humble of

114

heart." Meekness means gentleness, kindness, courtesy. Humility is truth, acceptance of what is true about ourselves without giving-in to pride. Mother Teresa wrote: "If [you] are humble, not even the whole of hell can touch you. Humility is the destroyer of pride. Humility is the destroyer of the devil." We must also keep in mind that being humble means accepting humiliations. St. Paul alluded to this when he stated in 2 Corintians 12:10: "For the sake of Christ, then, I am content with weaknesses, insults, hardships, persecutions, and calamities: for when I am weak, then I am strong." This is the tough part. Our Lord did not tell us it would be easy. However, this is what He is asking of us. We must be willing to accept this. It is easier to accept accusations of wrong doing when they are true. It is harder when they are not true; but even these our Lord asks us to accept quietly. We are not to fight back because that gives-in to pride. So, in this Beatitude, our Lord offers us hope; but, again, we must be "meek and humble of heart."

Blessed are they who hunger and thirst for righteousness, for they will be satisfied. It is important for us to understand that God wants justice to prevail even more than we do. Justice is so elusive. Unfortunately, there are too many people who are so focused on what is important for themselves that they disregard what is important for others. And, so injustice prevails. In this Beatitude, righteousness refers to something more. Righteousness wants everyone to do what is right in the eyes of God. If everyone does what is right in the eyes of God, then the world will change. We are in control. We are the ones who decide what the world will be like. We can only change how we react to people and things around us. We cannot change what other people do or think, but we can influence them. God expects us to do what is right at this moment in time. Period. God is calling us to be good and just; and, in the end, our search for righteousness will be satisfied.

Blessed are the merciful, for they will be shown mercy. Forgiveness and mercy are virtues that usually go hand-in-hand. However, they are two distinct virtues. Forgiveness exists when we decide that a wrong-doing is something we will choose to overlook. We forgive the person who committed the act. We will not forget it; but we will not let it affect how we act toward that person. Mercy, however, goes beyond forgiveness. Mercy cannot exist if there is no wrong-doing. Mercy understands that the person who committed the act deserves to experience an appropriate consequence. Mercy says that, even though the person who committed the act is deserving of the consequence, we will forego the consequence and move forward in life. Our Lord is placing a lot of emphasis on mercy; so much so, that He includes it as one of eight Beatitudes. God has shown us mercy more times than we can count. He has done so throughout human history. Mercy is such that He expects us to be as merciful to others as He is to us. If we are merciful, then God will be merciful to us. Hope always requires something from us.

Blessed are the clean of heart, for they will see God. I certainly am not able to tell if someone is clean of heart, sometimes referred to as pure of heart. In Psalm 24, only a person whose heart was clean was able to participate in temple worship. And then in Psalm 42, a person had to be clean of heart in order to behold God's face. Here, in the Beatitude, those who are clean of heart will see God. How would the temple guardians (probably the Pharisees) determine someone's right to enter the temple? One of the strongest beliefs that was passed on to every generation of Israelites and then to Christians is that anyone who looks upon the face of God will die. We are not capable of taking in His beauty and majesty. And yet, Jesus tells us that, if we are clean of heart, we will see God. Our Lord has given us the way; forgiveness of our sins and living a good life is the way. Forgiveness of our sins is easy to attain, but living a good life is harder. Yet, there is hope for us.

Blessed are the peacemakers, for they will be called children of God. I do not consider myself a peacemaker, but I have learned to deal with conflict. And the key for me is acceptance. I accept conditions as they are. The point, though, of this Beatitude is very clear. Anyone who can calm a situation and bring peace to a conflict (without causing more conflict) is blessed. The peacemaker brings calm and peace not only to those in conflict but also to observers. God has given all of us skills and talents, unique to each of us. He did not intend those special gifts to be used by us selfishly. That is why those gifts are a blessing. Blessed are all of us who use our gifts to help others for we will be called children of God.

Blessed are they who are persecuted for the sake of righteousness, for theirs is the kingdom of heaven. I do not believe this has ever happened to me directly. There were times when I was criticized for things I had done, but nothing of a serious nature. And, then, this verse is about matters of faith and essentially defending the faith. I have read stories about martyrs and what they lived through and how they died. Those are obvious persecutions. Things like that are still going on today in various parts of the world. Catholics, other Christians, and Jews are being persecuted and killed. In the United States, this is happening today. Our beliefs are being ridiculed. This persecution is not because of what we individually have said or done, but for who we are and what we say we believe. Those of us who are being persecuted for righteousness sake will be welcomed into the Kingdom of Heaven. Here is another sign of hope from our Lord.

117

Blessed are you when they insult you and persecute you and utter every kind of evil against you [falsely] because of me. Rejoice and be glad, for your reward will be great in heaven. Thus, they persecuted the prophets who were before you. These final two verses of the Beatitudes from Matthew are similar to verse 10. The difference is that the persecution is based on false testimony. However, our Lord promises us the ultimate prize for what we suffer.

Then there are the Beatitudes presented by Luke. *Blessed are you who are poor, for the kingdom of God is yours.* This is similar to the first Beatitude presented by Matthew, only Luke does not say "poor in spirit." This could be because Matthew heard it directly from our Lord and Luke heard it from others. I believe my interpretation based on Matthew is the correct one.

Blessed are you who are now hungry, for you will be satisfied. Again, this is similar to one presented by Matthew, except that Matthew treats it as *hunger and thirst for righteousness* and Luke merely treats it as *hungry*. It is important that both say we will be satisfied. Again, it is the message of hope.

Blessed are you who are now weeping, for you will laugh. Instead of *mourning*, Luke says *weeping*. Instead of being *comforted*, Luke says *laughing*. In both cases, the message is about the same. Your mourning and weeping will end and all will be calm and peaceful, ready to move on with life.

Blessed are you when people hate you, and when they exclude and insult you, and denounce your name as evil on account of the Son of Man. Rejoice and leap for joy on that day! Behold, your reward will be great in heaven. For their ancestors treated the prophets in the same way. This one corresponds with the last of Matthew's Beatitudes.

The Beatitudes are an offering of hope to all of us.

However, we must keep in mind that God expects us to be always faithful to Him, because He is always faithful to us.

Lord, the Beatitudes are a message from You as to how we should live our lives. We cannot buy our way into heaven or bargain for Your good graces; however, we are developing a relationship with our Father in heaven; and our words and actions will define how that relationship building is going. Help me to be ever open to the way You would have me live. Amen

The Salt of the Earth

Mathew 5:13: *"You are the salt of the earth. But if salt loses its taste, with what can it be seasoned? It is no longer good for anything but to be thrown out and trampled underfoot.*

Mark 9:49-50: [49] *"Everyone will be salted with fire.* [50] *Salt is good, but if salt becomes insipid, with what will you restore its flavor? Keep salt in yourselves and you will have peace with one another."*

Luke 14:34-35: [34] *"Salt is good, but if salt itself loses its taste, with what can its flavor be restored?* [35] *It is fit neither for the soil nor for the manure pile; it is thrown out. Whoever has ears to hear ought to hear."*

It is a very simple message. However, my belief in God does not allow me to place any aspect of human life to be completely lost. With God anything is possible. I believe this example is intended to be applied to one's faith. A person strong in his or her faith is usually someone with a lot of zeal or passion about it. If one loses that passion about faith, it can be dead. However, this example does not

119

completely fit the reality of faith. Faith can be rebuilt. The salt can be seasoned. By the grace of God, a person who loses faith can regain it. With God, anything is possible.

I can give myself as an example. In my early years, my faith was strong, to the point that I wanted to become a priest. My faith started to cool a little when I left the seminary, but it was still fairly strong. I helped my wife strengthen her faith. Then some years into our marriage, my faith cooled almost to a point of non-existence. However, through the grace of God, He showed me the way back. Salt can be seasoned. Through God, anything is possible.

Lord, keep watch over me. Do not let me go astray again. Amen.

The Light of the World

Matthew 5:14-16: *[14] You are the light of the world. A city set on a mountain cannot be hidden. [15] Nor do they light a lamp and then put it under a bushel basket; it is set on a lampstand, where it gives light to all in the house. [16] Just so, your light must shine before others, that they may see your good deeds and glorify your heavenly Father.*

Mark 4:21: *He said to them, "Is a lamp brought in to be placed under a bushel basket or under a bed, and not to be placed on a lampstand?*

Luke 8:16: *"No one who lights a lamp conceals it with a vessel or sets it under a bed; rather, he places it on a lampstand so that those who enter may see the light.*

In the Sermon on the Mount, we will encounter a lot of short messages such as "salt" and "light." This passage relates to one of the precepts that I have believed and practiced for most of my life. My faith is not something I simply understand; I have to live by the principles of my faith, or it is simply a bunch of words. Our faith is the lamp which must be placed on the lampstand to provide light for all to see and learn from. Our faith must be lived. We must do good works and show others how God wants us to live. The letter of St. James does an excellent job of expounding on this idea.

Lord, never let me be afraid to demonstrate how my faith guides my words and actions. I look to you for guidance and strength. Amen.

On the Law and the Prophets

<u>Matthew 5:17-20:</u> *[17] "Do not think that I have come to abolish the law or the prophets. I have come not to abolish but to fulfill. [18] Amen, I say to you, until heaven and earth pass away, not the smallest letter or the smallest part of a letter will pass from the law, until all things have taken place. [19] Therefore, whoever breaks one of the least of these commandments and teaches others to do so will be called least in the kingdom of heaven. But whoever obeys and teaches these commandments will be called greatest in the kingdom of heaven. [20] I tell you, unless your righteousness surpasses that of the scribes and Pharisees, you will not enter into the kingdom of heaven.*

<u>Luke 16:16-17:</u> *[16] "The law and the prophets lasted until John; but from then on the kingdom of God is proclaimed, and everyone who enters does so with violence. [17] It is easier for heaven and earth to pass away than for the smallest part of a letter of the law to become invalid.*

This passage from Matthew is the strongest confirmation we will ever get that the Law, as presented through Moses and all of the prophets, is still active and in force until the end of time (*heaven and earth pass away*). Jesus made it clear that He did not come to change the Law but to fulfill it. The Law was designed by God and passed on to us humans through His spokespersons. The Law was designed by God in such a way to serve mankind for all time. It has no expiration date as long as heaven and earth still exist.

Our Lord made the Law livable. Everything Jesus did was in accord with the Law of God. Everything He said was in accord with the Law of God and was in fact a clarification of the Law which did not meet the interpretation of the Pharisees. After all, He was here to fulfill the Law, not change it. This is especially true as shown by the last statement in Matthew's passage: "I tell you, unless your righteousness surpasses that of the scribes and Pharisees, you will not enter into the kingdom of heaven."

Lord, help me to be open to the requirements of the Law. Grant me an understanding mind and a willing heart to live as You would have me do so. Amen.

On Murder and Anger

<u>Matthew 5:21-26:</u> *[21] "You have heard that it was said to your ancestors, 'You shall not kill; and whoever kills will be liable to judgment.' [22] But I say to you, whoever is angry with his brother will be liable to judgment, and whoever says to his brother, 'Raqa,' will be answerable to the Sanhedrin, and whoever says, 'You fool,' will be liable to fiery Gehenna. [23] Therefore, if you bring your gift to the altar, and there recall that your brother has anything against you, [24] leave*

122

your gift there at the altar, go first and be reconciled with your brother, and then come and offer your gift. [25] Settle with your opponent quickly while on the way to court with him. Otherwise, your opponent will hand you over to the judge, and the judge will hand you over to the guard, and you will be thrown into prison. [26] Amen, I say to you, you will not be released until you have paid the last penny.

<u>Luke 12:57-59:</u> *[57] "Why do you not judge for yourselves what is right? [58] If you are to go with your opponent before a magistrate, make an effort to settle the matter on the way; otherwise, your opponent will turn you over to the judge, and the judge hand you over to the constable, and the constable throw you into prison. [59] I say to you, you will not be released until you have paid the last penny."*

This teaching is a little tough. It is easy to understand that killing makes a person liable to judgment. After all, the Commandment is "Thou shalt not murder." But Jesus is saying that merely getting angry with someone is the same as killing; or at least, the consequence is the same. Anger is an emotion and is not a sin. It is what you do as a response to that anger that can get you into trouble. So, I believe that Jesus is actually referring to the reaction based on that anger. There are actions that can effectively kill someone by destroying their reputation. If this happens, then the perpetrator should be liable to judgment.

The second part of this is the advice to settle out of court related to dealing with someone when it comes to conflict. Anger of at least one party is most likely the reason for a civil suit. You never can anticipate what will happen in court, and you may end up with a judgment you had not expected or wanted.

In any case, this particular segment of the Sermon on the Mount gives us a lot to think about. And, as can be seen so far, the Sermon covers a wide range of topics.

Lord, I know that, at times, my mind wanders to considering different scenarios as a result of something I have experienced or witnessed. Help me to keep my mind in check and not wander into possibilities that are offensive to You. And especially help me to never commit actions that relate to this teaching. Amen.

On Adultery and Divorce

Matthew 5:27-32: *²⁷ "You have heard that it was said, 'You shall not commit adultery.' ²⁸ But I say to you, everyone who looks at a woman with lust has already committed adultery with her in his heart. ²⁹ If your right eye causes you to sin, tear it out and throw it away. It is better for you to lose one of your members than to have your whole body thrown into Gehenna. ³⁰ And if your right hand causes you to sin, cut it off and throw it away. It is better for you to lose one of your members than to have your whole body go into Gehenna. ³¹ "It was also said, 'Whoever divorces his wife must give her a bill of divorce.' ³² But I say to you, whoever divorces his wife (unless the marriage is unlawful) causes her to commit adultery, and whoever marries a divorced woman commits adultery.*

Mark 9:43-48: *⁴³ If your hand causes you to sin, cut it off. It is better for you to enter into life maimed than with two hands to go into Gehenna, into the unquenchable fire. [⁴⁴] ⁴⁵ And if your foot causes you to sin, cut it off. It is better for you to enter into life crippled than with two feet to be thrown into Gehenna. [⁴⁶] ⁴⁷ And if your eye causes you to sin, pluck it out.*

124

*Better for you to enter into the kingdom of God with one eye
than with two eyes to be thrown into Gehenna, [48] where 'their
worm does not die, and the fire is not quenched.'*

Luke 16:18: *"Everyone who divorces his wife and marries
another commits adultery, and the one who marries a woman
divorced from her husband commits adultery.*

I have to comment first on the missing verses in Mark's
Gospel above. Verses 44 and 46 are missing from the text.
I did not purposely remove them. The commentary from the
Bible is: *These verses, lacking in some important early
manuscripts, are here omitted as scribal additions. They
simply repeat Mk 9:48, itself a modified citation of Is 66:24.*
Let us start with the first teaching in this segment. It
was understood at that time that adultery was a serious sin,
punishable by death, at least to the woman. Somehow men
tended to get the lighter punishment. But our Lord is placing
the heavy burden of adultery on the thoughts of committing
it. Obviously, thoughts cannot be read by anyone but God;
so, the punishment will come in the afterlife. God's
punishment for sin is more equitable, both participants will
be punished as He deems appropriate.

The next part of this segment relates to divorce, and this
is something we have to be careful about. Throughout the
world, divorce is generally accepted as a way to end a
marriage. In fact, many marriages take place with the
acknowledgement that divorce may be a realistic outcome.
Even the Catholic Church accepts divorce as a reality and
promotes compassionate treatment of both parties. The
Catholic Church also acknowledges the fact that marriages
do not always work out as expected. That is why the Church
allows for separation and annulment.

125

Our Lord, however, reminds us of how God looks at things, men and women were created to come together as one, and to live together as one till death parts them. The Church requires counseling before marriage to help people understand what they are getting into and to help prepare them for life together. Many marriages break up because the partners never really understood what they were getting into. Even with counseling, there is no guarantee. The only way for a marriage to really work is for God to be part of it and for both parties to want it to work and are willing to do what it takes.

As far as the removal of body parts is concerned, I believe our Lord was stressing the importance of maintaining our purity of thought, not to actually cutting off body parts. Removal of an eye or a hand will not stop impure thoughts. It is up to us to recognize that those thoughts are wrong and to stop them. It is desire that keeps us following those thoughts, and it is desire that can stop them.

Lord, first I want to thank You for helping Martha and I to keep our marriage together until You called her home. We had many challenges, but You guided us through them. Then, I want to seek your help ongoing to set aside all the evil temptations that come my way. It is You I want to please. Amen.

On Swearing and Oaths

Matthew 5:33-37: *[33] "Again you have heard that it was said to your ancestors, 'Do not take a false oath, but make good to the Lord all that you vow.' [34] But I say to you, do not swear at all; not by heaven, for it is God's throne; [35] nor by the earth, for it is his footstool; nor by Jerusalem, for it is the city of the* *great King. [36] Do not swear by your head, for you cannot make a single hair white or black. [37] Let your 'Yes' mean 'Yes,' and your 'No' mean 'No.' Anything more is from the evil one.*

Jesus' preliminary comments on oaths are not as important as the last two statements: *Let your 'Yes' mean 'Yes,' and your 'No' mean 'No.' Anything more is from the evil one.* So many of us feel like we have to justify what we are saying. And the simple truth about this is *trust.* If people could simply trust that what is being said is true, there would be no problems in this world. However, it is so easy for people to lie.

I know there are people in this world who believe that the written word, found in books, is the absolute truth. After all, why would anyone take the time to put lies in books or magazines. The same holds true for the internet. This is because of lack of lived experience, naïveté, and the general belief that all people are good.

This morning, I read a reflection from Max Lucado. He basically reminds us that the first lie is difficult to formulate and speak. The second is easier and after that they are easier still. We are so used to telling lies that it is commonplace and very hard to trust what others say. The pronouncement by Jesus on oaths is about trust. We simply cannot trust what others say and we have to prove to others that we speak the truth: "I swear by the life of my sweet mother."

Let your "Yes" mean "Yes," and your "No" mean "No. If we would only speak the truth in all cases, there would never be a need for taking oaths. If we kept our answers to "yes," "no," and simple explanations, life would be better for everyone.

Lord, much of my life has been spent writing and telling what I believe people need to know. I try to focus on the truth at all times. Yet, there are still times when I fail and find myself telling lies. I rationalize that the lies I tell are not important. Help me to overcome this tendency. Help me always to be truthful. Amen.

The Woes

Luke 6:24-26: *[24] But woe to you who are rich, for you have received your consolation. [25] But woe to you who are filled now, for you will be hungry. Woe to you who laugh now, for you will grieve and weep. [26] Woe to you when all speak well of you, for their ancestors treated the false prophets in this way.*

This segment only shows up in Luke. However, I believe it needs to be reflected here as part of the message Jesus was presenting both in the sermon on the mount as well as other times when He taught before crowds. Although He may have used slightly different words and varied His examples, Jesus' message is always the same.

Although Luke specifically identifies the rich, those who are living the good life, this passage is intended for all who focus their lives on the here and now. Those who experience the good things in life will over time experience the opposite. That is life in this world. We will never be totally happy in this world.

Lord, here is where I and every one of us need help. We need to keep this life on earth in perspective. If we spend our lives striving for fulfillment in this world, that is the end we will receive (we will have received our consolation). Help us strive for the life only You can provide for all eternity. Amen.

On Retaliation

Matthew 5:38-42: *[38] "You have heard that it was said, 'An eye for an eye and a tooth for a tooth.' [39] But I say to you, offer no resistance to one who is evil. When someone strikes you on [your] right cheek, turn the other one to him as well. [40] If anyone wants to go to law with you over your tunic, hand him your cloak as well. [41] Should anyone press you into service for one mile, go with him for two miles. [42] Give to the one who asks of you, and do not turn your back on one who wants to borrow.*

Luke 6:29-30: *[29] To the person who strikes you on one cheek, offer the other one as well, and from the person who takes your cloak, do not withhold even your tunic. [30] Give to everyone who asks of you, and from the one who takes what is yours do not demand it back.*

I have heard it said that if everyone practiced "an eye for an eye," then the world will be filled with blind, toothless people. But our Lord is not calling for us to let ourselves be abused either. The situations presented can cause confusing thoughts. Is our Lord emphasizing the commandment: Thou shalt not murder? Or is He promoting the Beatitude about being meek? Or is the message different?

When I think of someone who is meek and humble, believe it or not, I think of Goerge McFly, a character from "Back to the Future." I am not going to go into the details of the movie, but he is pictured as someone who simply lets others walk all over him. When reading these passages, my impression is that Jesus may be calling for people to be meek and humble before others. But that is not true.

Jesus gives us examples of situations that could be serious or simply annoying. I believe that He is telling us that our reaction to those infringements on us should not be retaliation, but love. That is the message He is telling us throughout His teachings and His living example. We should not allow ourselves to be driven to the actions the devil wants us to do. They cause our spirits to be dulled and driven away from God. Jesus wants us to become more like His Father.

This was a tough message for those who are oppressed to hear. Our first emotion is usually anger and a desire to free ourselves from the oppression. Love is not the action we want to take. It is not the advice we want to hear. Jesus does not want us to be abused and He does not want us to be further abused, but He certainly does not want us to become the abuser either.

Lord, I need Your help, so I do not allow my anger at being abused to retaliate against those responsible for causing the anger. It is an emotion that is a natural human feeling but one that does not have to end in similar action. Help me to grow in love and understand how love can be used in these situations. Amen.

On Love of One's Enemies

Matthew 5:43-48: *[43] "You have heard that it was said, 'You shall love your neighbor and hate your enemy.' [44] But I say to you, love your enemies, and pray for those who persecute you, [45] that you may be children of your heavenly Father, for he makes his sun rise on the bad and the good, and causes rain to fall on the just and the unjust. [46] For if you love those who love you, what recompense will you have? Do not the tax collectors do the same? [47] And if you greet your brothers only, what is unusual about that? Do not the pagans do the same? [48] So be perfect, just as your heavenly Father is perfect.*

Luke 6:27-28: *²⁷ "But to you who hear I say, love your enemies, do good to those who hate you, ²⁸ bless those who curse you, pray for those who mistreat you.*

Luke 6:32-36: *³² For if you love those who love you, what credit is that to you? Even sinners love those who love them. ³³ And if you do good to those who do good to you, what credit is that to you? Even sinners do the same. ³⁴ If you lend money to those from whom you expect repayment, what credit [is] that to you? Even sinners lend to sinners and get back the same amount. ³⁵ But rather, love your enemies and do good to them, and lend expecting nothing back; then your reward will be great, and you will be children of the Most High, for he himself is kind to the ungrateful and the wicked. ³⁶ Be merciful, just as [also] your Father is merciful.*

There are a few things that caught my attention in these passages. First, let us consider: *But I say to you, love your enemies, and pray for those who persecute you, that you may be children of your heavenly Father.* I do not believe I have ever considered any one an enemy; however, there have been people with whom I have had conflict or disagreement. It was not until several years ago that I really learned how to deal with this. I had been in a long discussion with someone who was promoting things that were contrary to what I had been promoting for years. This conflict had been going on for some time. I finally reached a point of frustration that I walked out on the discussion and went to the chapel that was present on the campus we were on. I unloaded all my frustrations on our Lord and asked Him what I should do to change this man. The answer was immediate. I heard the words in my mind: *Love him.* Surprised, I told our Lord that I did not think he understood what I had asked. The answer came back again immediately: *Love him.* I thought for a while and finally realized that I cannot change him, I can only change myself and my approach to him. I tried to do as our Lord asked and did not argue with him any longer. After a while, he had a change of heart. So, love your enemies. It works for me.

For if you love those who love you, what credit is that to you? Even sinners love those who love them. And if you do good to those who do good to you, what credit is that to you? Even sinners do the same. This is probably just as hard as the first statement about loving your enemies. Loving those who love you or do good to you is easy. But here, we are talking about everyone. Period. This takes thought, a change in thinking, and effort. But, as always, our Lord leads us in the right direction.

On the last point, Matthew and Luke differ. Matthew writes: *So be perfect, just as your heavenly Father is perfect.* Luke writes: *Be merciful, just as [also] your Father is merciful.* Perfection is something I can strive for; but we all learn that perfection is not something we actually achieve; and to strive to be perfect as God cannot be achieved. Luke's presentation is something we can strive for. We can be and we can learn to be merciful. It is something we can get better at over time. If I try to do something that I believe cannot realistically be achieved, I soon give up on trying. I do not believe I am very different from others. However, I can do what many inspirational writers have advised: strive to be a better version of myself.

Lord, these passages are all about love. Love takes some thought and effort. Help me to be willing to put the proper thought and effort into those whom I encounter, no matter who they are. Amen.

On Almsgiving

Matthew 6:1-4: [1] *"[But] take care not to perform righteous deeds in order that people may see them; otherwise, you will have no recompense from your heavenly Father.* [2] *When you give alms, do not blow a trumpet before you, as the hypocrites do in the synagogues and in the streets to win the praise of others. Amen, I say to you, they have received their reward.* [3] *But when you give alms, do not let your left hand know what your right is doing,* [4] *so that your almsgiving may be secret. And your Father who sees in secret will repay you.*

It has often bothered me to see people do good deeds or give contributions so that they would look good to others. However, the reality is that this is commonplace. It is part of our nature to want the approval of others; so, we often do the things we do so they can be seen and approved. Here is the kicker that we need to deal with. Jesus tells us that, if we do good things to receive the approval of other people, then that is the reward we will receive: the approval of others.

If we do things for the approval of our Father in heaven, then the reward will come from our Father in heaven. Jesus tells us that the things we do to please our Father in heaven should be done in secret; however, the good deeds we do to please our Father in heaven are not always hidden. We may also receive a reward from other people, but that was not what we were looking for. The important thing is the motive behind the action. Our Lord is more interested in the motives behind the actions.

Lord, I know that there are many times when I do good deeds but do not look for approval. Sometimes I do good deeds simply because it is the right thing to do. I do not intend them to please You or to please others. I hope that, at those times, my intentions are pleasing to You. Amen.

On Prayer

Mathew 6:5-6: [5] *"When you pray, do not be like the hypocrites, who love to stand and pray in the synagogues and on street corners so that others may see them. Amen, I say to you, they have received their reward.* [6] *But when you pray, go to your inner room, close the door, and pray to your Father in secret. And your Father who sees in secret will repay you.*

When I was still a young man in high school, I learned that the reason the early authors wrote such tremendously long books was because they got paid by the word. That is why I built up negative feelings about Charles Dickens and his colleagues. Do not get me wrong, I liked the stories; but they took so long to read, especially for a slow reader like me. I also learned that our early politicians were expected to give speeches that lasted hours. In fact, Abraham Lincoln was criticized for the brevity of the Gettysburg Address. I have also listened to preachers go on and on in prayers that seemed unending.

I can truly appreciate what Jesus says in the passage from Matthew above. I really do like things brief and to the point. However, I do like explanations. I am NOT a bullet point type of guy. There has to be a midpoint where there is appropriate balance. Jesus tells us to pray quietly and on our own where only God can hear us. Then our reward will be from Him. What more could we want.

Lord, help me to keep in mind when I am praying that prayer is a conversation between me and God. It does not have to be heard and understood by those around me. Help me to keep my focus on You. Amen.

The Lord's Prayer

<u>Matthew 6:7-15:</u> *⁷In praying, do not babble like the pagans, who think that they will be heard because of their many words. ⁸Do not be like them. Your Father knows what you need before you ask him. The Lord's Prayer. ⁹ "This is how you are to pray:*
> *Our Father in heaven,*
> *hallowed be your name,*
> ¹⁰ *your kingdom come,*
> *your will be done,*
> *on earth as in heaven.*
> ¹¹ *Give us today our daily bread;*
> ¹² *and forgive us our debts,*
> *as we forgive our debtors;*
> ¹³ *and do not subject us to the final test,*
> *but deliver us from the evil one.*

¹⁴ If you forgive others their transgressions, your heavenly Father will forgive you. ¹⁵ But if you do not forgive others, neither will your Father forgive your transgressions.

<u>Mark 11:25:</u> *When you stand to pray, forgive anyone against whom you have a grievance, so that your heavenly Father may in turn forgive you your transgressions."*

<u>Luke 11:1-4:</u> *¹ He was praying in a certain place, and when he had finished, one of his disciples said to him, "Lord, teach us to pray just as John taught his disciples." ² He said to them, "When you pray, say:*
> *Father, hallowed be your name,*
> *your kingdom come.*

*³ **Give us each day our daily bread**
⁴ **and forgive us our sins**
for we ourselves forgive everyone in debt to us,
and do not subject us to the final test."*

After telling His audience that they need to keep their prayers short and to the point, Jesus gives them an example, which turns out to be a prayer that today is said more than a million times daily around the world (my estimate). The Lord's Prayer, according to Matthew, is that prayer; and it has been repeated for two thousand years.

There have been various commentaries written about this prayer and I do not want to repeat them. However, I do have my personal take on the prayer. I wrote about it in my book *It's All About Love.* Here is what I wrote: *The Lord's Prayer is important for many reasons. Here are a few thoughts:*

- *It is the first time we are encouraged to actually refer to God as "Father." Throughout the history of the Jewish nation, the Jewish people never called God by name and never referred to Him as Father.*
- *Jesus referred to Him as "His Father." He had a different relationship with the Father than we have.*
- *Jesus told us to refer to Him as "Our Father," thus making us adopted children of His Father.*
- *Through our adoption as children of Our Father, Jesus is reminding us that we should love Him above all things.*

Luke's version of Jesus' prayer is a more abbreviated version. That does not mean there is anything wrong with it. Matthew's version was adopted by the Catholic Church as the version for normal use.

If you forgive others their transgressions, your heavenly Father will forgive you. But if you do not forgive others,

neither will your Father forgive your transgressions.
Mathew's last pronouncement is effectively reinforced by
Mark in a slightly different text. However, the message is
the same; and this message will be repeated often by our
Lord in this sermon and others to come after. If we are not
willing to forgive, then we should not expect to be forgiven.
The measure with which you measure will be measured back
to you.

*Lord, I have come to recite your prayer many times during
each day. Help me to take time to reflect on what I am
saying. These are more than just words to be repeated.
They have meaning and I need to understand rather than
recite. Amen.*

On Fasting

Matthew 6:16-18: [16] *"When you fast, do not look gloomy like
the hypocrites. They neglect their appearance, so that they may
appear to others to be fasting. Amen, I say to you, they have
received their reward.* [17] *But when you fast, anoint your head
and wash your face,* [18] *so that you may not appear to others to
be fasting, except to your Father who is hidden. And your
Father who sees what is hidden will repay you.*

This counsel on fasting is similar to that on prayer. It
simply means that we should not be doing things so that we
have the admiration or pity of others. When we do, that is
our reward (the admiration or pity of others). It effectively
eliminates the spiritual aspect of what we are doing. When
we fast, if it is our goal for it to help us grow spiritually, then
dress appropriately for the day and do not put on a sad or
harried face. We will receive more reward from our
heavenly Father if only He knows we are fasting.

137

Lord, help me to keep focused on my real purpose for fasting. It is You I want to please. Amen.

On Treasures

<u>**Matthew 6:19-21:**</u> *[19] "Do not store up for yourselves treasures on earth, where moth and decay destroy, and thieves break in and steal. [20] But store up treasures in heaven, where neither moth nor decay destroys, nor thieves break in and steal. [21] For where your treasure is, there also will your heart be.*

<u>**Luke 12:33-34:**</u> *[33] Sell your belongings and give alms. Provide money bags for yourselves that do not wear out, an inexhaustible treasure in heaven that no thief can reach nor moth destroy. [34] For where your treasure is, there also will your heart be.*

The key message in these two passages is the same and both occur in the last sentence. *For where your treasure is, there also will your heart be.* The things you value most are the things that will capture your mind and heart. Maybe you will not spend every waking hour devoted to them, but a significant amount of your personal time and activity will be dedicated to them.

Jesus tells us we should spend our time and energy acquiring the things of heaven because they cannot be destroyed. This makes sense logically; however, the things of this world are certainly attractive. We have to overcome the tantalizing delights that the devil presents to us. This is practically the ultimate theme of the Book of Proverbs. King Solomon makes a concerted effort over those many chapters and verses to convince his son to disregard the temptations the devil will place before him. He advises his son to turn away from wickedness and choose what is right before God. Solomon does not use these words, but the theme is clear to see. *For where your treasure is, there also will your heart be.*

Lord, remind me time and again that it is You that I should aim for. I know the decision is mine. Give me the strength to make the right choice. Amen.

The Sound Eye

Matthew 6:22-23: *[22] "The lamp of the body is the eye. If your eye is sound, your whole body will be filled with light; [23] but if your eye is bad, your whole body will be in darkness. And if the light in you is darkness, how great will the darkness be.*

Luke 11:34-36: *[34] The lamp of the body is your eye. When your eye is sound, then your whole body is filled with light, but when it is bad, then your body is in darkness. [35] Take care, then, that the light in you not become darkness. [36] If your whole body is full of light, and no part of it is in darkness, then it will be as full of light as a lamp illuminating you with its brightness."*

The only real difference there is between the two versions presented here is that Matthew's ending emphasizes darkness and Luke's emphasizes light.

But that is not the message our Lord is presenting. It is a simple metaphor. If we spend our lives following and in search of darkness, then darkness is what we will find. Our Lord gives this same message in a lot of different guises: the eye, the other parts of the body, the treasure we strive for, the fruit from a vine, and more. The idea is simple, if our lives are devoted to a search for and a dedication to the world and what it offers, then the end result of that search, the end

139

of our journey, will be simply the darkness the world has to offer. If we devote ourselves to God and what He wants us to do, then the end of our journey will be in the light of heaven. Our choices and the rewards or consequences of those choices are the subject of a lot of Jesus's teachings.

I keep falling back on something from St. Vincent de Paul. People understand things differently, so you must say the same thing in different ways so more people will get the message. Jesus has more than one sermon; but we can see similarities in many of His stories and parables. I do not ever want to be accused of oversimplifying the teachings of our Lord; however, if one is going to study Jesus and His life, then similarities in His various teachings are going to show up.

Lord, keep me from ever being so filled with pride that I say that I know You, I figured You out, I know what You are going to say. Help me to keep things in perspective and keep me on the path to Your light. Amen.

On Serving Two Masters

Matthew 6:24: *"No one can serve two masters. He will either hate one and love the other or be devoted to one and despise the other. You cannot serve God and mammon.*

Luke 16:13: *No servant can serve two masters. He will either hate one and love the other or be devoted to one and despise the other. You cannot serve God and mammon."*

As has been seen in other cases, these two verses are essentially the same. Although it is possible to serve two masters that have basically the same objectives, this teaching is about serving two opposites: God and the world.

That is not possible. This has been shown throughout human history. During the sharing of attention, it is not possible for both sides to receive 100% of the attention (even 50% is a near impossibility). At some point, the dedication, the loyalty, moves to the one side.

Lord, it is only with Your guidance that I can keep You at the forefront of my attention. Guide my choices. Amen.

On Anxiety

<u>Matthew 6:25-34:</u> *[25] "Therefore I tell you, do not worry about your life, what you will eat [or drink], or about your body, what you will wear. Is not life more than food and the body more than clothing? [26] Look at the birds in the sky; they do not sow or reap, they gather nothing into barns, yet your heavenly Father feeds them. Are not you more important than they? [27] Can any of you by worrying add a single moment to your life-span? [28] Why are you anxious about clothes? Learn from the way the wild flowers grow. They do not work or spin. [29] But I tell you that not even Solomon in all his splendor was clothed like one of them. [30] If God so clothes the grass of the field, which grows today and is thrown into the oven tomorrow, will he not much more provide for you, O you of little faith? [31] So do not worry and say, 'What are we to eat?' or 'What are we to drink?' or 'What are we to wear?' [32] All these things the pagans seek. Your heavenly Father knows that you need them all. [33] But seek first the kingdom [of God] and his righteousness, and all these things will be given you besides. [34] Do not worry about tomorrow; tomorrow will take care of itself. Sufficient for a day is its own evil.*

<u>Luke 12:22-32:</u> *[22] He said to [his] disciples, "Therefore I tell you, do not worry about your life and what you will eat, or*

*about your body and what you will wear. *[23]* For life is more than food and the body more than clothing. *[24]* Notice the ravens: they do not sow or reap; they have neither storehouse nor barn, yet God feeds them. How much more important are you than birds! *[25]* Can any of you by worrying add a moment to your life-span? *[26]* If even the smallest things are beyond your control, why are you anxious about the rest? *[27]* Notice how the flowers grow. They do not toil or spin. But I tell you, not even Solomon in all his splendor was dressed like one of them. *[28]* If God so clothes the grass in the field that grows today and is thrown into the oven tomorrow, will he not much more provide for you, O you of little faith? *[29]* As for you, do not seek what you are to eat and what you are to drink, and do not worry anymore. *[30]* All the nations of the world seek for these things, and your Father knows that you need them. *[31]* Instead, seek his kingdom, and these other things will be given you besides. *[32]* Do not be afraid any longer, little flock, for your Father is pleased to give you the kingdom.*

Once again, we find two passages which are essentially the same. My purpose is not to analyze why or to trace the evolution of the Gospels. I will focus on the message.

Can any of you by worrying add a moment to your lifespan? If even the smallest things are beyond your control, why are you anxious about the rest? This is one of two messages in this passage on anxiety. The point is that we should especially not be concerned about the things that might happen that are not under our control. There are people in this world whose job is to anticipate crises or disasters so that plans can be put in place for the proper actions to be taken. Recovery planning and recovery planners are rare, but necessary. This passage is not about them. For the most part, our Lord wants us to be concerned with those things that are under our control and how we act or react in response to them.

But seek first the kingdom [of God] and his righteousness, and all these things will be given you besides. The message here is to place our trust in God. He knows what we need, and He will provide for those needs. This also is one of those themes that will be repeated throughout Jesus' life. *Do not worry about tomorrow; tomorrow will take care of itself.*

Lord, as much as I talk about and write about trusting in You, I still occasionally find myself worrying about things I should not be concerned with. Help me to overcome this basic human fault and keep my actions in sync with my words. Amen.

On Judging

<u>Matthew 7:1-5:</u> *[1]"Stop judging, that you may not be judged. [2] For as you judge, so will you be judged, and the measure with which you measure will be measured out to you. [3] Why do you notice the splinter in your brother's eye, but do not perceive the wooden beam in your own eye? [4] How can you say to your brother, 'Let me remove that splinter from your eye,' while the wooden beam is in your eye? [5] You hypocrite, remove the wooden beam from your eye first; then you will see clearly to remove the splinter from your brother's eye.*

<u>Mark 4:24-25:</u> *[24] He also told them, "Take care what you hear. The measure with which you measure will be measured out to you, and still more will be given to you. [25] To the one who has, more will be given; from the one who has not, even what he has will be taken away."*

143

Luke 6:37-42: [37] *"Stop judging and you will not be judged. Stop condemning and you will not be condemned. Forgive and you will be forgiven.* [38] *Give and gifts will be given to you; a good measure, packed together, shaken down, and overflowing, will be poured into your lap. For the measure with which you measure will in return be measured out to you."* [39] *And he told them a parable, "Can a blind person guide a blind person? Will not both fall into a pit?* [40] *No disciple is superior to the teacher; but when fully trained, every disciple will be like his teacher.* [41] *Why do you notice the splinter in your brother's eye, but do not perceive the wooden beam in your own?* [42] *How can you say to your brother, 'Brother, let me remove that splinter in your eye,' when you do not even notice the wooden beam in your own eye? You hypocrite! Remove the wooden beam from your eye first; then you will see clearly to remove the splinter in your brother's eye.*

The measure with which you measure will be measured out to you. All three passages have this message included. I also commented earlier about this. It is one of the common themes in Jesus' teachings. Based on the number of times this idea is presented in the Gospels, we have to realize that it is more than just a token teaching. God expects us to be good Christians and to practice what our faith calls for. If we are not willing to forgive, if we are not willing to share, if we are not willing to help, why should we expect any of that from God? God is a loving and merciful God, but He is also a God of justice.

The splinter in your brother's eye - the wooden beam in your own eye. It is so easy for us to criticize others for the things they are doing wrong. Often, we can see their faults, but they cannot. The reverse is true as well. We often cannot see our own faults; or if we do, we downplay them.

Jesus is right in saying that we should clean up our own acts before accusing others. We spend much time justifying (or trying to justify) what we do. It is easier to point to others and judge what they are doing wrong. We fool ourselves into thinking we can do no wrong. Only God is perfect; and the sooner we accept that, the better our lives will be.

To the one who has, more will be given; from the one who has not, even what he has will be taken away. This statement from Mark is not in the other two. It relates to the parable of the talents. This is not related so much to judging as it is to deciding whether to act or not act. Squandering our gifts is sinful.

Lord, help me to always consider the various possibilities before I decide to act, especially when it involves action or inaction by others. Amen.

On Profaning the Holy

Matthew 7:6: *"Do not give what is holy to dogs, or throw your pearls before swine, lest they trample them underfoot, and turn and tear you to pieces.*

At first and even second reading of this verse, I thought it to be harsh. It is contrary to evangelical thinking. Instead of spreading the good news to all of the world, it says to be selective to whom you spread the good news. History has shown that throughout all the ages of mankind since the God of Abraham was introduced to the world, there have been people who oppose that teaching to a point of violent action including killing. Martyrs are not uncommon to the Jewish nation nor to Christianity. So, this single verse provides a good warning to discern your audience. And discernment is not always easy.

Lord, discernment is not always easy especially when we are caught up in the enthusiasm of evangelism. Help me and all other followers of Your word to know when it is right to speak and when to be silent. Amen.

God's Answering of Prayer

<u>**Matthew 7:7-11:**</u> *[7] "Ask and it will be given to you; seek and you will find; knock and the door will be opened to you. [8] For everyone who asks, receives; and the one who seeks, finds; and to the one who knocks, the door will be opened. [9] Which one of you would hand his son a stone when he asks for a loaf of bread, [10] or a snake when he asks for a fish? [11] If you then, who are wicked, know how to give good gifts to your children, how much more will your heavenly Father give good things to those who ask him.*

<u>**Luke 11:9-13:**</u> *[9] "And I tell you, ask and you will receive; seek and you will find; knock and the door will be opened to you. [10] For everyone who asks, receives; and the one who seeks, finds; and to the one who knocks, the door will be opened. [11] What father among you would hand his son a snake when he asks for a fish? [12] Or hand him a scorpion when he asks for an egg? [13] If you then, who are wicked, know how to give good gifts to your children, how much more will the Father in heaven give the holy Spirit to those who ask him?"*

The key thing I come away with from these passages is that God, like any loving father, will give you only what is good for you, regardless of what it is you have asked for. As a father, I can recognize this. Over the years, my children asked for a lot. Some things I could not afford, and I had to say "no." Somethings were simply not good for them, and

146

that required another "no." But realistically, I tried to give them what they asked for. However, I have to acknowledge God's love for us. It is His love for us that prevents Him from giving us anything that would be harmful.

Recently, I read a comment from St. Pius of Pietrelcina (Padre Pio) related to this passage: "In this we are placing our trust on the promise made to us by the Divine Master: *Ask, and it will be given to you; seek, and you will find; knock, and it will be opened to you. Everything that you ask of the Father in my name will be given you.* Yes, serene in our faith and tranquil in soul let us pray and continue to pray, because intense and fervent prayer pierces the heavens and is backed up by a divine guarantee."

Lord, help me to recognize Your love for me, particularly in the times You say "no" to the things I ask for. Amen.

The Golden Rule

Matthew 7:12: *"Do to others whatever you would have them do to you. This is the law and the prophets.*

Luke 6:31: *Do to others as you would have them do to you.*

This is known as the Golden Rule. I wrote about this in my book, *One-Liners to Guide Our Lives.* Here is some of what I wrote.

We find the Golden Rule in both Matthew and Luke, which makes it about two thousand years old. Then it goes back even farther in the Hebrew Bible (or Old Testament); in Leviticus 19:18, we find "You shall love your neighbor as yourself."

The basic premise here is that we love ourselves as much if not more than anyone else. This makes sense since we are a self-centered species. We are born that way and must learn how to care about others. So, if we treat others the way we would want to be treated, then hopefully we will treat them well.

Why is this so important? After all, if God created us to be self-centered, why not just flow with it. It is important because if we all were only concerned with satisfying our own needs, this world would be in chaos.

The Golden Rule is just part of what we call our moral compass. All the laws created by mankind that ensure the health and safety of others is an outgrowth of our morality. The Ten Commandments and other rules laid down throughout human history lead us to lives of caring about others (as well as ourselves). This is more than just ethics. It is morality.

Over the thousands of years of human existence, we have learned and grown as a species. We are sharing this world with other people. We realistically need other people to feel safe and help us in our times of trouble. We need other people to share our joy. We need them and they need us. So it only makes sense to treat them as well as we want them to treat us. It would enhance the common good.

Lord, help me to overcome my drive to satisfy my needs and my desires. You taught us that, in caring about and for others, we will ultimately care about and for each other. Help me to make this a reality. Amen.

The Straight and Narrow and Wide Broad Gate

Matthew 7:13-14: [13] *"Enter through the narrow gate; for the gate is wide and the road broad that leads to destruction, and*

148

those who enter through it are many. [14] How narrow the gate and constricted the road that leads to life. And those who find it are few.

Luke 13:23-24: *[23] Someone asked him, "Lord, will only a few people be saved?" He answered them, [24] "Strive to enter through the narrow door, for many, I tell you, will attempt to enter but will not be strong enough.*

What is the broad gate *that leads to destruction*? The broad gate is the one that leads to whatever-you-want-to-do is-okay-land. Enter through that gate and you have the freedom to do whatever; there are no restrictions. There are no restrictions, but there are consequences. Sometimes, the results of your choices are not as good as you expect. Sometimes the results of your choices are only short lived. So, as long as you are willing to accept inadequate results, short term results, and the consequences of actions, then the broad gate is the one for you.

Today, we prepare our children for entrance through the broad gate. Have you ever really observed what our children have to do to "win" in a video game? In order to achieve the goal, they effectively have to eliminate the competition: stomping, crushing, exploding, killing one obstacle after another. Video games can be seriously violent activities. You try to tell your child that killing is wrong, then you turn them loose on a video game that says just the opposite. The broad gate is so entertaining! The main attraction here is that, on the other side of the broad gate, there is more – more of the same. Then, when your children grow to maturity (?), they find that life in the world is much the same.

The straight and narrow gate is the one that is limited in choices because there are restrictions on what can be done. Rules define the narrow gate. Obedience and perseverance are tickets that allow you onto the path and through the gate. All of the teachings of our Lord lead to and through the narrow gate. The main attraction here is that, on the other side of the narrow gate, there is everlasting joy. The unfortunate reality is that the I-want-it-now-generation outnumbers the narrow-gate contingent.

Lord, in spite of the numbers, help me to keep a positive view and work toward finding my way to and through the narrow gate. And help me bring as many as I can with me. Amen.

The Test of a Good Person, "By Their Fruits"

<u>Matthew 7:15-20:</u> *[15] "Beware of false prophets, who come to you in sheep's clothing, but underneath are ravenous wolves. [16] By their fruits you will know them. Do people pick grapes from thornbushes, or figs from thistles? [17] Just so, every good tree bears good fruit, and a rotten tree bears bad fruit. [18] A good tree cannot bear bad fruit, nor can a rotten tree bear good fruit. [19] Every tree that does not bear good fruit will be cut down and thrown into the fire. [20] So by their fruits you will know them.*

<u>Matthew 12:33-35:</u> *[33] "Either declare the tree good and its fruit is good or declare the tree rotten and its fruit is rotten, for a tree is known by its fruit. [34] You brood of vipers, how can you say good things when you are evil? For from the fullness of the heart the mouth speaks. [35] A good person brings forth good out of a store of goodness, but an evil person brings forth evil out of a store of evil.*

Luke 6:43-45: [43] *"A good tree does not bear rotten fruit, nor does a rotten tree bear good fruit.* [44] *For every tree is known by its own fruit. For people do not pick figs from thornbushes, nor do they gather grapes from brambles.* [45] *A good person out of the store of goodness in his heart produces good, but an evil person out of a store of evil produces evil; for from the fullness of the heart the mouth speaks.*

A few years ago, I wrote a book titled *Wisdom Across the Ages*. It is a reflection and commentary about the *Book of Proverbs*. One of the things that was clear in the proverbs of Solomon was that the thinking at that time was clear, black and white, good and evil. I wrote in more than one place that Solomon did not account for change over time. A good person can become a bad person, and a bad person can become a good person. However, at that time, and even in Jesus' time, life was pretty much still black and white. The status of a person was based on the "blessings" he or she received from God. A wealthy person (highly blessed) was good, and a poor person (cursed) was bad. However, Jesus taught us that a good person can become a bad person, and a bad person can become a good person.

My understanding of the possibility of change has helped my faith grow. And that understanding comes from what I have learned from Jesus and hope for eternal life. Change is a necessary part of growth, and growth is necessary for every human being.

In these passages from Matthew and Luke, everything sounds black and white again. Jesus is not saying that, but understand, everything is in the present tense. A good person produces good, an evil person produces evil. Every good tree bears good fruit, and a rotten tree bears bad fruit. It takes a little thought. One of Jesus' clear teachings throughout His life is that people can be better. A person

151

can change. That is why His message is such a great message of hope. God is only concerned with who we are today, no matter what we have done in the past. That is why He is so willing to forgive our sins. A bad person can become good and produce good fruit.

Lord, I have come to You many, many times over my lifetime and have asked You to forgive my sins, over and over again. But, please read what is in my heart. I truly want to be better. Help me to become and to remain the person who produces good fruit. Amen.

Not Every Person Who Says "Lord, Lord" Shall Enter into the Kingdom

Matthew 7:21-23: *[21] "Not everyone who says to me, 'Lord, Lord,' will enter the kingdom of heaven, but only the one who does the will of my Father in heaven. [22] Many will say to me on that day, 'Lord, Lord, did we not prophesy in your name? Did we not drive out demons in your name? Did we not do mighty deeds in your name?' [23] Then I will declare to them solemnly, 'I never knew you. Depart from me, you evildoers.'*

Luke 6:46: *"Why do you call me, 'Lord, Lord,' but not do what I command?*

Luke 13:25-27: *[25] After the master of the house has arisen and locked the door, then will you stand outside knocking and saying, 'Lord, open the door for us.' He will say to you in reply, 'I do not know where you are from.' [26] And you will say, 'We ate and drank in your company and you taught in our streets.' [27] Then he will say to you, 'I do not know where [you] are from. Depart from me, all you evildoers!'*

Matthew 7:21 has been an important Gospel verse for me for quite a long time. In fact, after I retired and decided to devote my time to writing, this was the theme for my first book *"Lord, Lord."* Over the years, I had wondered what would be in store for all those people who simply did good things.

But we have to be realistic. Anyone can do good works. Even the vilest person in the world will do a good deed if it gains something for him. Doing a good deed is not always what God wants done. Doing good deeds is not like building up reward points that you can cash in at the right time. Jesus tells us that the good we do must be in response to what God wants us to do. Tough call? You bet it is. To understand God's will is not easy, but He has given us plenty of coaching and guidelines to follow. However, this is not the place to go into all of that.

The point of these passages is simple. Because you do good deeds, because you are Catholic, because you are a Jew, because you profess belief in the one God, does NOT mean that you will make it through the pearly gates. Because you are a preacher, priest, rabbi, or pope does NOT mean you have an automatic ticket to get inside. The way to make it, as Jesus tells us, is to do the will of His Father in heaven. Only God knows you. So, do not take anything for granted.

Lord, open up my mind and my heart to know Your will and grant me the strength to follow it. Amen.

The House Built Upon the Rock

Matthew 7:24-27: [24] *"Everyone who listens to these words of mine and acts on them will be like a wise man who built his*

153

house on rock. *²⁵ The rain fell, the floods came, and the winds blew and buffeted the house. But it did not collapse; it had been set solidly on rock. ²⁶ And everyone who listens to these words of mine but does not act on them will be like a fool who built his house on sand. ²⁷ The rain fell, the floods came, and the winds blew and buffeted the house. And it collapsed and was completely ruined."*

Luke 6:47-49: *⁴⁷ I will show you what someone is like who comes to me, listens to my words, and acts on them. ⁴⁸ That one is like a person building a house, who dug deeply and laid the foundation on rock; when the flood came, the river burst against that house but could not shake it because it had been well built. ⁴⁹ But the one who listens and does not act is like a person who built a house on the ground without a foundation. When the river burst against it, it collapsed at once and was completely destroyed."*

There are two important points here. The first requires listening to the words of our Lord and the second is acting upon them. It is not simply acting upon them. The implication is the action is in accord with what our Lord is saying. Doing the will of His heavenly Father is implied, as in Matthew 7:21.

Listening to our Lord's words requires that today's Christians must make an effort to study His teachings. I say "make an effort" because people today have so much information being passed on to them that it is difficult to discern what should be taken seriously. Two thousand years ago, it was the opposite problem; people simply did not have access to our Lord's teachings. We cannot be concerned with the limitations that have existed over the last two thousand years. We have Jesus' teachings available to us today in many different modes.

One of the things I really like about Jesus' method of teaching is that He gave His message out in ways that the people of that day could understand. And He told His stories in different ways to allow people with different backgrounds to understand. Fortunately, the story He used as an example, a house withstanding the onslaught of heavy winds, rains, and flooding is applicable today as well.

Lord, when I read the Bible, help me to understand the lessons presented not only based on what people understood at that time but also how it applies to today's world. Amen.

The End and the Effect of the Sermon

Matthew 7:28-29: [28] ***When Jesus finished these words, the crowds were astonished at his teaching, [29] for he taught them as one having authority, and not as their scribes.***

Mark 1:21-22: [21] ***Then they came to Capernaum, and on the sabbath he entered the synagogue and taught. [22] The people were astonished at his teaching, for he taught them as one having authority and not as the scribes.***

Have you ever been in the presence of someone who you believed had a complete grasp of what he or she is talking about? It is more than knowledge of the topic. It is more like an understanding of the inner works of the topic being presented. I have had that feeling with a few of my instructors in school and a couple in the business world.

Jesus had that impact on the people who listened to Him. I believe that part of this was because they wanted to hear what He was saying. That is why not everyone felt that way. The scribes and Pharisees did not want to believe in Him.

They did not want to hear His message because, in the long run, His message was critical of them.

Jesus spoke with authority as no one else could, simply because He is the authority.

Lord, you are the authority on all aspects of this life and the life to come. Help me to never lose my desire to read and hear Your words. Help me to always look to You for answers to my questions. Amen.

Other Sermons

Luke 6:17-20: *[17] And he came down with them and stood on a stretch of level ground. A great crowd of his disciples and a large number of the people from all Judea and Jerusalem and the coastal region of Tyre and Sidon [18] came to hear him and to be healed of their diseases; and even those who were tormented by unclean spirits were cured. [19] Everyone in the crowd sought to touch him because power came forth from him and healed them all. [20] And raising his eyes toward his disciples he said.*

Matthew 4:24 – 5:2: *[24] His fame spread to all of Syria, and they brought to him all who were sick with various diseases and racked with pain, those who were possessed, lunatics, and paralytics, and he cured them. [25] And great crowds from Galilee, the Decapolis, Jerusalem, and Judea, and from beyond the Jordan followed him. [1] When he saw the crowds, he went up the mountain, and after he had sat down, his disciples came to him. [2] He began to teach them, saying:*

Mark 3:7-13: *[7] Jesus withdrew toward the sea with his disciples. A large number of people [followed] from Galilee and from Judea. [8] Hearing what he was doing, a large number*

156

of people came to him also from Jerusalem, from Idumea, from beyond the Jordan, and from the neighborhood of Tyre and Sidon. ⁹ He told his disciples to have a boat ready for him because of the crowd, so that they would not crush him. ¹⁰ He had cured many and, as a result, those who had diseases were pressing upon him to touch him. ¹¹ And whenever unclean spirits saw him, they would fall down before him and shout, "You are the Son of God." ¹² He warned them sternly not to make him known. ¹³ He went up the mountain and summoned those whom he wanted, and they came to him.

The story is repeated. Wherever He went, people gathered around. Some wanted to hear Him speak, many wanted to be cured of illness, disease, demon possession. They hoped, they knew, they believed, Jesus is the One. He spoke the words of life and healed those who needed healing. Jesus was the answer they were waiting for. From Judea, Jerusalem, Tyre, Sidon, the Decapolis, Galilee, areas beyond the Jordan, Syria, they came. And He spoke to them.

Lord, why did I spend so much of my life looking for answers in all the wrong places? You are the One. Help me to never wander off in search of things I should not be concerned with. Amen.

Part 6
Jesus' Ministry
in Galilee Continued

Healing and Cleansing of the Leper

<u>Matthew 8:1-4:</u> *[1] When Jesus came down from the mountain, great crowds followed him. [2] And then a leper approached, did him homage, and said, "Lord, if you wish, you can make me clean." [3] He stretched out his hand, touched him, and said, "I will do it. Be made clean." His leprosy was cleansed immediately. [4] Then Jesus said to him, "See that you tell no one, but go show yourself to the priest, and offer the gift that Moses prescribed; that will be proof for them."*

<u>Mark 1:40-45:</u> *[40] A leper came to him [and kneeling down] begged him and said, "If you wish, you can make me clean." [41] Moved with pity, he stretched out his hand, touched him, and said to him, "I do will it. Be made clean." [42] The leprosy left him immediately, and he was made clean. [43] Then, warning him sternly, he dismissed him at once. [44] Then he said to him, "See that you tell no one anything, but go, show yourself to the priest and offer for your cleansing what Moses prescribed; that will be proof for them." [45] The man went away and began to publicize the whole matter. He spread the report abroad so that it was impossible for Jesus to enter a town openly. He remained outside in deserted places, and people kept coming to him from everywhere.*

<u>Luke 5:12-16:</u> *[12] Now there was a man full of leprosy in one of the towns where he was; and when he saw Jesus, he fell prostrate, pleaded with him, and said, "Lord, if you wish, you can make me clean." [13] Jesus stretched out his hand, touched him, and said, "I do will it. Be made clean." And the leprosy left him immediately. [14] Then he ordered him not to tell anyone, but "Go, show yourself to the priest and offer for your cleansing what Moses prescribed; that will be proof for them." [15] The report about him spread all the more, and great*

crowds assembled to listen to him and to be cured of their ailments, [16] but he would withdraw to deserted places to pray.

There are a few lessons to be learned from this one encounter. First, Jesus did not back off and run away from the leper. That was the normal reaction of people to the presence of lepers. Either that or throwing stones to chase them away. Jesus did not fear this disease, this or any other. He was moved with compassion as the leper drew near.

He allowed the leper to not only come close but to show Him homage and plead for a healing. The leper heard the stories of the healings Jesus performed and appealed to His compassion. In answer to the leper's statement of faith, Jesus granted his request. Jesus always displayed the love of God for His creation.

Even though the leper was cautioned NOT to spread the word, that is exactly what the leper did. Who could blame him! He was filled with joy; and we all know what it is like to be filled with joy – you want to share the good news with everyone.

Then Jesus told the leper to show himself to the priests and offer the appropriate sacrifice. This was not to build up our Lord's renown. After all, Jesus did tell him not to spread the word. This certification was to help the leper to return to a normal life, to go back to his family, to get a job, to live once again as a real person.

This morning, I was reading a book by Max Lucado, *Just Like Jesus*. In it he tells this gospel story from the eyes of the leper. I would like to share a couple of segments of the story to give you the perspective of the leper. *"Five years of leprosy had left my hands gnarled. Tips of my fingers were missing as were portions of an ear and my nose. At the sight of me, fathers grabbed their children. Mothers covered their faces. Children pointed and stared. The rags*

on my body couldn't hide my sores. Nor could the wrap on my face hide the rage in my eyes. I didn't even try to hide it. How many nights did I shake my crippled fist at the silent sky? 'What did I do to deserve this?' But never a reply. ... I came to Him as a defiant man. Moved not by faith but by a desperate anger, God has wrought this calamity on my body, and He would either fix it or end it. But then I saw Him, and when I saw Him, I was changed. ... Before He spoke, I knew He cared. ... He cupped His hands on my cheeks and drew me so near I could feel the warmth of His breath and see the wetness in His eyes. ... He could have healed me with a word. But He wanted to do more than heal me. He wanted to honor me, to validate me, to christen me."
What we believe to be true in interpreting a situation may be totally different from the perspective of the subject.

So, what I learn from this encounter is that Jesus' love for us is not to satisfy the current need but to also prepare us to move forward. It is not all about this instance, it is about the whole person. Jesus' love for us has no limits.

The imitation of Jesus has shown up millions upon millions of times throughout the ages in the form of people stepping in to help people who are suffering from disease, especially contagious disease. We see it in the stories of some of the saints, but we also know it in the lives of those whose sacrifice has not resulted in formal sainthood. Most recently, we have to recognize the efforts of care providers during the Covid-19 pandemic.

Lord, let me always come to you in humility and in homage, knowing in my heart that You can provide for my need. I should come to You with both hope and belief. Amen.

The Centurion of Capernaum
and His Servant

Matthew 8:5-13: *[5] When he entered Capernaum, a centurion approached him and appealed to him, [6] saying, "Lord, my servant is lying at home paralyzed, suffering dreadfully." [7] He said to him, "I will come and cure him." [8] The centurion said in reply, "Lord, I am not worthy to have you enter under my roof; only say the word and my servant will be healed. [9] For I too am a person subject to authority, with soldiers subject to me. And I say to one, 'Go,' and he goes; and to another, 'Come here,' and he comes; and to my slave, 'Do this,' and he does it." [10] When Jesus heard this, he was amazed and said to those following him, "Amen, I say to you, in no one in Israel have I found such faith. [11] I say to you, many will come from the east and the west, and will recline with Abraham, Isaac, and Jacob at the banquet in the kingdom of heaven, [12] but the children of the kingdom will be driven out into the outer darkness, where there will be wailing and grinding of teeth." [13] And Jesus said to the centurion, "You may go; as you have believed, let it be done for you." And at that very hour [his] servant was healed.*

Mark 7:30: *When the woman went home, she found the child lying in bed and the demon gone.*

Luke 7:1-10: *[1] When he had finished all his words to the people, he entered Capernaum. [2] A centurion there had a slave who was ill and about to die, and he was valuable to him. [3] When he heard about Jesus, he sent elders of the Jews to him, asking him to come and save the life of his slave. [4] They approached Jesus and strongly urged him to come, saying, "He deserves to have you do this for him, [5] for he loves our nation and he built the synagogue for us." [6] And Jesus went with* *them, but when he was only a short distance from the house, the centurion sent friends to tell him, "Lord, do not trouble yourself, for I am not worthy to have you enter under my roof.* [7] *Therefore, I did not consider myself worthy to come to you; but say the word and let my servant be healed.* [8] *For I too am a person subject to authority, with soldiers subject to me. And I say to one, 'Go,' and he goes; and to another, 'Come here,' and he comes; and to my slave, 'Do this,' and he does it."* [9] *When Jesus heard this he was amazed at him and, turning, said to the crowd following him, "I tell you, not even in Israel have I found such faith."* [10] *When the messengers returned to the house, they found the slave in good health.*

<u>Luke 13:28-29:</u> [28] *And there will be wailing and grinding of teeth when you see Abraham, Isaac, and Jacob and all the prophets in the kingdom of God and you yourselves cast out.* [29] *And people will come from the east and the west and from the north and the south and will recline at table in the kingdom of God.*

<u>John 4:46-54:</u> [46] *Then he returned to Cana in Galilee, where he had made the water wine. Now there was a royal official whose son was ill in Capernaum.* [47] *When he heard that Jesus had arrived in Galilee from Judea, he went to him and asked him to come down and heal his son, who was near death.* [48] *Jesus said to him, "Unless you people see signs and wonders, you will not believe."* [49] *The royal official said to him, "Sir, come down before my child dies."* [50] *Jesus said to him, "You may go; your son will live." The man believed what Jesus said to him and left.* [51] *While he was on his way back, his slaves met him and told him that his boy would live.* [52] *He asked them when he began to recover. They told him, "The fever left him yesterday, about one in the afternoon."* [53] *The father realized that just at that time Jesus had said to him, "Your son will*

163

live," and he and his whole household came to believe. [54] [Now] this was the second sign Jesus did when he came to Galilee from Judea.

The stories from Matthew and Luke are almost identical while the passages from Mark and John are similar in the end result. All show faith in the one requesting the healing. All show that the confirmation of the healing came after they had left the presence of our Lord. And the reality is that faith is the key component that is stressed by our Lord.

We see this in other healings throughout the life of our Lord. Usually, Jesus does not ask the question because the person requesting the healing has shown his or her belief in the way they encounter Him or make the request. But there are times when He asks if they believe He can do this. In the cases when Jesus chooses to do the healing as a gift out of His compassion, such as the man with the withered hand, the demonstration of their faith was not required.

Going back to the passages from Matthew and Luke, the faith of the centurion is different in that he acknowledges that Jesus can heal without being physically present. Jesus can perform any and all miracles simply by saying that is what He wants. The centurion also realizes and acknowledges his unworthiness. He humbles himself before Jesus even though he himself is a person of high station. He knows his place.

But here is also an important point to remember. When Jesus was traveling, teaching, and healing, people did not believe He is God. They may have believed He was sent by God and had power given to Him by God to perform miracles. However, they had heard enough stories and/or seen Jesus heal to believe He could do the same for them.

When Jesus acknowledged the superior faith of this gentile over that of the Israelite community, He was saying

164

that many non-Jews will enter the gates of heaven and enjoy eternal life with their Jewish patriarchs. Simply being Jewish is not a ticket to eternal life.

Lord, there are times when I honestly believe my faith is strong and there are times when I know it is weak. Help me to not only grow in my faith but to also recognize that I need to continue to grow. Amen.

The Widow's Son at Nain

<u>Luke 7:11-17:</u> *[11] Soon afterward he journeyed to a city called Nain, and his disciples and a large crowd accompanied him. [12] As he drew near to the gate of the city, a man who had died was being carried out, the only son of his mother, and she was a widow. A large crowd from the city was with her. [13] When the Lord saw her, he was moved with pity for her and said to her, "Do not weep." [14] He stepped forward and touched the coffin; at this the bearers halted, and he said, "Young man, I tell you, arise!" [15] The dead man sat up and began to speak, and Jesus gave him to his mother. [16] Fear seized them all, and they glorified God, exclaiming, "A great prophet has arisen in our midst," and "God has visited his people." [17] This report about him spread through the whole of Judea and in all the surrounding region.*

Here is another case of our Lord acting out of compassion rather than being requested to grant a healing as in the previous stories. However, this is not just a healing, it is raising someone from the dead. It shows those watching that He either has the power to do so or He has been gifted by God with the authority to act in God's name.

At any rate, His compassion for the widow and her situation is shown in His act. Implied in the circumstances

165

is the fact that she was now an unsupported widow. Our Lord's act not only restored the life of her only son but restored her own security as well.

Word of this spread quickly throughout Judea.

Lord, help me to recognize Your love for us in the actions You take on our behalf. Amen.

The Healing of Peter's Mother-in-law

<u>Matthew 8:14-15:</u> *[14] Jesus entered the house of Peter and saw his mother-in-law lying in bed with a fever. [15] He touched her hand, the fever left her, and she rose and waited on him.*

<u>Mark 1:29-31:</u> *[29] On leaving the synagogue he entered the house of Simon and Andrew with James and John. [30] Simon's mother-in-law lay sick with a fever. They immediately told him about her. [31] He approached, grasped her hand, and helped her up. Then the fever left her, and she waited on them.*

<u>Luke 4:38-39:</u> *[38] After he left the synagogue, he entered the house of Simon. Simon's mother-in-law was afflicted with a severe fever, and they interceded with him about her. [39] He stood over her, rebuked the fever, and it left her. She got up immediately and waited on them.*

Although the far majority of healings performed by our Lord were to total strangers, there were occasional healings offered for friends. In this particular case, not much is said about circumstances; but the mother-in-law of Simon Peter was "afflicted with a severe fever." Jesus performed the healing, and she responded immediately.

In comparison to the previous healings described above, there is no specific indication of a request for healing;

although the Apostles did bring it to Jesus' attention. Regardless of request or not, our Lord responded to her need out of love.

Lord, I know that it is out of love for us that You grant all the blessings that we receive. Let me always keep this in mind and never believe that I have earned these blessings in some way. Amen.

The Sick Healed at Evening

Matthew 8:16-17: *[16] When it was evening, they brought him many who were possessed by demons, and he drove out the spirits by a word and cured all the sick, [17] to fulfill what had been said by Isaiah the prophet: "He took away our infirmities and bore our diseases."*

Mark 1:32-34: *[32] When it was evening, after sunset, they brought to him all who were ill or possessed by demons. [33] The whole town was gathered at the door. [34] He cured many who were sick with various diseases, and he drove out many demons, not permitting them to speak because they knew him.*

Luke 4:40-41: *[40] At sunset, all who had people sick with various diseases brought them to him. He laid his hands on each of them and cured them. [41] And demons also came out from many, shouting, "You are the Son of God." But he rebuked them and did not allow them to speak because they knew that he was the Messiah.*

This is not surprising at all. Whenever there is a celebrity in the area, people come out by the hundreds to see him or her. This is especially true if something is being given away free. This is not cynical, it is realistic. I have

167

seen it over and over. I have to admit that I have taken some share of the giveaways.

In this case, the celebrity was Jesus. He was in the area all day; and, into the evening, people continued to come to Him. They sought not only His words of love and consolation, but they also wanted the free gifts. He was offering healings and exorcisms. Our Lord's capacity to love was unlimited. Yet, there were times when His human body could only take so much.

When He expelled the demons from their hosts, He had to silence them. The fact that they recognized Him as the Son of God had to be silenced for now. He would reveal His divinity at the proper time.

The thing I learn from this and other similar passages is that Jesus always was concerned about others. His love and compassion were unlimited. He helped. He never sought recompense or praise. He was here to do His Father's will.

Lord, there are many times when I help others unselfishly. But there are times also when I fail to do what I believe You called me to do. Give me the strength to follow through with what I believe You want me to do. Amen.

On Following Jesus, The Would-be Followers

Matthew 8:18-22: *[18] When Jesus saw a crowd around him, he gave orders to cross to the other side. [19] A scribe approached and said to him, "Teacher, I will follow you wherever you go." [20] Jesus answered him, "Foxes have dens and birds of the sky have nests, but the Son of Man has nowhere to rest his head." [21] Another of [his] disciples said to him, "Lord, let me* *go first and bury my father."* ²² *But Jesus answered him, "Follow me, and let the dead bury their dead."*

<u>Luke 9:57-62:</u> *⁵⁷ As they were proceeding on their journey someone said to him, "I will follow you wherever you go." ⁵⁸ Jesus answered him, "Foxes have dens and birds of the sky have nests, but the Son of Man has nowhere to rest his head." ⁵⁹ And to another he said, "Follow me." But he replied, "[Lord,] let me go first and bury my father." ⁶⁰ But he answered him, "Let the dead bury their dead. But you, go and proclaim the kingdom of God." ⁶¹ And another said, "I will follow you, Lord, but first let me say farewell to my family at home." ⁶² [To him] Jesus said, "No one who sets a hand to the plow and looks to what was left behind is fit for the kingdom of God."*

There is not much to be said here. Our Lord makes it very clear that He wants followers who truly want to be there. One of the clear lessons I learned from reading almost everything written by Venerable Fulton J. Sheen over the years is that God wants us – ALL of us – not just part of the time but all of the time – not just 10% or 50% or 75%, but 100% of us. He does not want us to be constantly thinking about our old life. He wants us here and now. He is present for us, and we must be present for Him. He will not be satisfied with less.

Lord, I have failed in this regularly. I am so wrapped up in this earthly life of mine, that I fail to give You the full attention that You not only deserve but have a right to. Help me to push aside the rest and focus on You. Amen.

Calming of the Storm at Sea

<u>Matthew 8:23-27:</u> [23] *He got into a boat and his disciples followed him.* [24] *Suddenly a violent storm came up on the sea, so that the boat was being swamped by waves; but he was asleep.* [25] *They came and woke him, saying, "Lord, save us! We are perishing!"* [26] *He said to them, "Why are you terrified, O you of little faith?" Then he got up, rebuked the winds and the sea, and there was great calm.* [27] *The men were amazed and said, "What sort of man is this, whom even the winds and the sea obey?"*

<u>Mark 4:35-41:</u> [35] *On that day, as evening drew on, he said to them, "Let us cross to the other side."* [36] *Leaving the crowd, they took him with them in the boat just as he was. And other boats were with him.* [37] *A violent squall came up and waves were breaking over the boat, so that it was already filling up.* [38] *Jesus was in the stern, asleep on a cushion. They woke him and said to him, "Teacher, do you not care that we are perishing?"* [39] *He woke up, rebuked the wind, and said to the sea, "Quiet! Be still!" The wind ceased and there was great calm.* [40] *Then he asked them, "Why are you terrified? Do you not yet have faith?"* [41] *They were filled with great awe and said to one another, "Who then is this whom even wind and sea obey?"*

<u>Luke 8:22-25:</u> [22] *One day he got into a boat with his disciples and said to them, "Let us cross to the other side of the lake." So they set sail,* [23] *and while they were sailing he fell asleep. A squall blew over the lake, and they were taking in water and were in danger.* [24] *They came and woke him saying, "Master, master, we are perishing!" He awakened, rebuked the wind and the waves, and they subsided and there was a calm.* [25] *Then he asked them, "Where is your faith?" But they were filled with*

awe and amazed and said to one another, "Who then is this, who commands even the winds and the sea, and they obey him?"

As with a number of the stories in Christ's life, this one has shown up in the Gospels of Matthew, Mark, and Luke. Although all three are not necessarily consistent on when this took place, they are consistent in the details of what took place.

It was the evening and Jesus and His disciples sought refuge in their boats to get away from the crowds. Wherever He went, the crowds were there, seeking Him out to receive His special blessings, His gifts, His healings, His miracles. As always, these encounters were exhausting for our Lord; and it is not surprising to find Him asleep in the boat while the others, experienced fishermen, took care of business.

Storms at sea can be life or death experiences; so, I am not at all surprised that the disciples were frightened. What surprises me is our Lord's reaction, "Why are you terrified? Do you not yet have faith?" If it was anyone from the crowds that had come to Him all day, He would have accepted their fear as natural. But, I suppose, after the disciples had been with Him for so long, He expected more faith than fear.

This passage is not so much about fear and His ordering the wind to be still, it is about the faith of His disciples. They had witnessed His control and authority over the human body. They had witnessed His control and authority over demons. They had seen Him bring a dead man back to life. Yet they feared that the winds and the seas would overcome Jesus and them with Him. Where was their faith?

Then, as usual, He astounded them with His authority over the wind and the sea. He did not ask the disciples to do what was necessary and to be calm while they waited out the

171

storm. If He had not been with them, that is exactly what they would have done. Instead, He simply told the sea and the wind to be calm and they responded immediately. It was the disciples' faith that had to grow, not their skills as boatmen.

Out of love for His disciples, He showed them that they can depend on Him in their need.

Lord, later in the Gospels, You will tell Your disciples how their faith is smaller than a mustard seed. I wish I could say with confidence that my faith is greater than theirs. I guess I have not been tested enough. Guide me in growing my faith. Amen.

The Gadarene Demoniacs

Matthew 8:28-34: *[28] When he came to the other side, to the territory of the Gadarenes, two demoniacs who were coming from the tombs met him. They were so savage that no one could travel by that road. [29] They cried out, "What have you to do with us, Son of God? Have you come here to torment us before the appointed time?" [30] Some distance away a herd of many swine was feeding. [31] The demons pleaded with him, "If you drive us out, send us into the herd of swine." [32] And he said to them, "Go then!" They came out and entered the swine, and the whole herd rushed down the steep bank into the sea where they drowned. [33] The swine herds ran away; and when they came to the town, they reported everything, including what had happened to the demoniacs. [34] Thereupon the whole town came out to meet Jesus; and when they saw him, they begged him to leave their district.*

Mark 5:1-20: *[1] They came to the other side of the sea, to the territory of the Gerasenes. [2] When he got out of the boat, at* once a man from the tombs who had an unclean spirit met him. ³ The man had been dwelling among the tombs, and no one could restrain him any longer, even with a chain. ⁴ In fact, he had frequently been bound with shackles and chains, but the chains had been pulled apart by him and the shackles smashed, and no one was strong enough to subdue him. ⁵ Night and day among the tombs and on the hillsides, he was always crying out and bruising himself with stones. ⁶ Catching sight of Jesus from a distance, he ran up and prostrated himself before him, ⁷ crying out in a loud voice, "What have you to do with me, Jesus, Son of the Most High God? I adjure you by God, do not torment me!" ⁸ (He had been saying to him, "Unclean spirit, come out of the man!") ⁹ He asked him, "What is your name?" He replied, "Legion is my name. There are many of us." ¹⁰ And he pleaded earnestly with him not to drive them away from that territory. ¹¹ Now a large herd of swine was feeding there on the hillside. ¹² And they pleaded with him, "Send us into the swine. Let us enter them." ¹³ And he let them, and the unclean spirits came out and entered the swine. The herd of about two thousand rushed down a steep bank into the sea, where they were drowned. ¹⁴ The swine herds ran away and reported the incident in the town and throughout the countryside. And people came out to see what had happened. ¹⁵ As they approached Jesus, they caught sight of the man who had been possessed by Legion, sitting there clothed and in his right mind. And they were seized with fear. ¹⁶ Those who witnessed the incident explained to them what had happened to the possessed man and to the swine. ¹⁷ Then they began to beg him to leave their district. ¹⁸ As he was getting into the boat, the man who had been possessed pleaded to remain with him. ¹⁹ But he would not permit him but told him instead, "Go home to your family and announce to them all that the Lord in his pity has done for you." ²⁰ Then the man went off and began to proclaim in the Decapolis what Jesus had done for him; and all were amazed.

Luke 8:26-39: [26] Then they sailed to the territory of the Gerasenes, which is opposite Galilee. [27] When he came ashore a man from the town who was possessed by demons met him. For a long time, he had not worn clothes; he did not live in a house but lived among the tombs. [28] When he saw Jesus, he cried out and fell down before him; in a loud voice he shouted, "What have you to do with me, Jesus, son of the Most High God? I beg you, do not torment me!" [29] For he had ordered the unclean spirit to come out of the man. (It had taken hold of him many times, and he used to be bound with chains and shackles as a restraint, but he would break his bonds and be driven by the demon into deserted places.) [30] Then Jesus asked him, "What is your name?" He replied, "Legion," because many demons had entered him. [31] And they pleaded with him not to order them to depart to the abyss. [32] A herd of many swine was feeding there on the hillside, and they pleaded with him to allow them to enter those swine; and he let them. [33] The demons came out of the man and entered the swine, and the herd rushed down the steep bank into the lake and was drowned. [34] When the swineherds saw what had happened, they ran away and reported the incident in the town and throughout the countryside. [35] People came out to see what had happened and, when they approached Jesus, they discovered the man from whom the demons had come out sitting at his feet. He was clothed and in his right mind, and they were seized with fear. [36] Those who witnessed it told them how the possessed man had been saved. [37] The entire population of the region of the Gerasenes asked Jesus to leave them because they were seized with great fear. So he got into a boat and returned. [38] The man from whom the demons had come out begged to remain with him, but he sent him away,

174

saying, [39] "Return home and recount what God has done for you." The man went off and proclaimed throughout the whole town what Jesus had done for him.

    The three passages are essentially the same except for a couple of variations in Matthew. Matthew indicates two demoniacs; and the area was Gadarenes, not Garasenes. Other than that, the stories are the same.

    I believe it is important to note that the demoniac recognized Jesus as the son of the Most High. The demons could see who He is, yet we humans did not recognize Him. This is probably because the demons exist in the spiritual world where they could recognize His divinity.

    I have always been troubled by Jesus sending the demons into the herd of swine. The swine herd represented the livelihood of the people of the town. Why would Jesus destroy their livelihood? At first, I thought that it had something to do with the swine being forbidden food for the Jews. In doing so, Jesus certainly got the attention of the people of the town. We will not always understand God's reasons for what He does.

Lord, I may not always understand Your reasons for doing what You do, but it is important that I accept what You decide. Make my acceptance be a natural part of my relationship with You. Amen.

The Daughter of Jairus and
The Woman with the Hemorrhage

<u>Matthew 9:18-26:</u> *[18] While he was saying these things to them, an official came forward, knelt down before him, and said, "My daughter has just died. But come, lay your hand on*

her, and she will live." [19] Jesus rose and followed him, and so did his disciples. [20] A woman suffering hemorrhages for twelve years came up behind him and touched the tassel on his cloak. [21] She said to herself, "If only I can touch his cloak, I shall be cured." [22] Jesus turned around and saw her, and said, "Courage, daughter! Your faith has saved you." And from that hour the woman was cured. [23] When Jesus arrived at the official's house and saw the flute players and the crowd who were making a commotion, [24] he said, "Go away! The girl is not dead but sleeping." And they ridiculed him. [25] When the crowd was put out, he came and took her by the hand, and the little girl arose. [26] And news of this spread throughout all that land.

Mark 5-21-43: [21] When Jesus had crossed again [in the boat] to the other side, a large crowd gathered around him, and he stayed close to the sea. [22] One of the synagogue officials, named Jairus, came forward. Seeing him he fell at his feet [23] and pleaded earnestly with him, saying, "My daughter is at the point of death. Please, come lay your hands on her that she may get well and live." [24] He went off with him, and a large crowd followed him and pressed upon him. [25] There was a woman afflicted with hemorrhages for twelve years. [26] She had suffered greatly at the hands of many doctors and had spent all that she had. Yet she was not helped but only grew worse. [27] She had heard about Jesus and came up behind him in the crowd and touched his cloak. [28] She said, "If I but touch his clothes, I shall be cured." [29] Immediately her flow of blood dried up. She felt in her body that she was healed of her affliction. [30] Jesus, aware at once that power had gone out from him, turned around in the crowd and asked, "Who has touched my clothes?" [31] But his disciples said to him, "You see how the crowd is pressing upon you, and yet you ask, 'Who touched me?'" [32] And he looked around to see who had done it. [33] The *woman, realizing what had happened to her, approached in fear and trembling. She fell down before Jesus and told him the whole truth. ³⁴ He said to her, "Daughter, your faith has saved you. Go in peace and be cured of your affliction." ³⁵ While he was still speaking, people from the synagogue official's house arrived and said, "Your daughter has died; why trouble the teacher any longer?" ³⁶ Disregarding the message that was reported, Jesus said to the synagogue official, "Do not be afraid; just have faith." ³⁷ He did not allow anyone to accompany him inside except Peter, James, and John, the brother of James. ³⁸ When they arrived at the house of the synagogue official, he caught sight of a commotion, people weeping and wailing loudly. ³⁹ So he went in and said to them, "Why this commotion and weeping? The child is not dead but asleep." ⁴⁰ And they ridiculed him. Then he put them all out. He took along the child's father and mother and those who were with him and entered the room where the child was. ⁴¹He took the child by the hand and said to her, "Talitha koum," which means, "Little girl, I say to you, arise!" ⁴² The girl, a child of twelve, arose immediately and walked around. [At that] they were utterly astounded. ⁴³ He gave strict orders that no one should know this and said that she should be given something to eat.*

Luke 8:40-56: *⁴⁰ When Jesus returned, the crowd welcomed him, for they were all waiting for him. ⁴¹ And a man named Jairus, an official of the synagogue, came forward. He fell at the feet of Jesus and begged him to come to his house, ⁴² because he had an only daughter, about twelve years old, and she was dying. As he went, the crowds almost crushed him. ⁴³ And a woman afflicted with hemorrhages for twelve years, who [had spent her whole livelihood on doctors and] was unable to be cured by anyone, ⁴⁴ came up behind him and touched the tassel on his cloak. Immediately her bleeding*

177

stopped. [45] Jesus then asked, "Who touched me?" While all were denying it, Peter said, "Master, the crowds are pushing and pressing in upon you." [46] But Jesus said, "Someone has touched me; for I know that power has gone out from me." [47] When the woman realized that she had not escaped notice, she came forward trembling. Falling down before him, she explained in the presence of all the people why she had touched him and how she had been healed immediately. [48] He said to her, "Daughter, your faith has saved you; go in peace." [49] While he was still speaking, someone from the synagogue official's house arrived and said, "Your daughter is dead; do not trouble the teacher any longer." [50] On hearing this, Jesus answered him, "Do not be afraid; just have faith and she will be saved." [51] When he arrived at the house he allowed no one to enter with him except Peter and John and James, and the child's father and mother. [52] All were weeping and mourning for her, when he said, "Do not weep any longer, for she is not dead, but sleeping." [53] And they ridiculed him, because they knew that she was dead. [54] But he took her by the hand and called to her, "Child, arise!" [55] Her breath returned, and she immediately arose. He then directed that she should be given something to eat. [56] Her parents were astounded, and he instructed them to tell no one what had happened.

As can be clearly seen in all three versions of this story, we have two separate tales of strong faith: Jairus, the synagogue official, and the unnamed woman suffering with hemorrhages for many years.

Starting out with Jairus, he approached Jesus with the belief that Jesus could restore her health. In Matthew, his daughter is already dead, while in Mark and Luke, his daughter is dying. The key here was that Jairus had heard all the stories of healings (he may even had witnessed some), and he believed Jesus had the power to do the same for his daughter. Jairus' faith was rewarded when Jesus arrived at his home, in spite of the reports that his daughter was already dead and that he should bother Jesus no longer. It would be easy to say that Jesus had compassion for the synagogue official and his family and performed the healing out of that compassion. And this may have come into play here. However, I believe that Jesus was rewarding Jairus' faith.

The same holds true for the unnamed woman. It was her faith that she would be cured. But, if she could not get His attention, maybe by simply touching Jesus' clothing. And that is what happened. She was healed. She felt it. The miracle occurred even before she revealed herself to Jesus. Jesus confirmed her belief.

Over the years, I have read many stories about healings that took place under various circumstances. Although not always the case, the faith of the person receiving the healing or the faith of the person requesting the healing was strong. God does work miracles simply out of His love for us. There is no doubt of that even if we don't ask for it out of faith.

Lord, I believe that my faith is strong; but, then again, I have never really been tested. I hope and pray that, when and if the time comes, my faith will prove to be strong. Amen.

Two Blind Men Healed

Matthew 9:27-31: *²⁷ And as Jesus passed on from there, two blind men followed [him], crying out, "Son of David, have pity on us!" ²⁸ When he entered the house, the blind men approached him and Jesus said to them, "Do you believe that I can do this?" "Yes, Lord," they said to him. ²⁹ Then he touched their eyes and said, "Let it be done for you according to your faith." ³⁰ And their eyes were opened. Jesus warned*

179

them sternly, "See that no one knows about this." ³¹ But they went out and spread word of him through all that land.

__Matthew 20:29-34:__ ²⁹ As they left Jericho, a great crowd followed him. ³⁰ Two blind men were sitting by the roadside, and when they heard that Jesus was passing by, they cried out, "[Lord,] Son of David, have pity on us!" ³¹ The crowd warned them to be silent, but they called out all the more, "Lord, Son of David, have pity on us!" ³² Jesus stopped and called them and said, "What do you want me to do for you?" ³³ They answered him, "Lord, let our eyes be opened." ³⁴ Moved with pity, Jesus touched their eyes. Immediately they received their sight and followed him.

These two stories, both from Matthew, seem to be referring to the same episode. The significance of this story is similar to the previous stories of Jairus and the unnamed woman. It is their faith that Jesus believed, and He granted their request.

It is also worth mentioning the same thing that is common among all the healing stories. They spread the word even though Jesus asked them not to. Who could blame them? When something good happens that causes joy, we tend to want everyone to be joyful with us.

Lord, help my faith to grow and my willingness to be grateful for the blessings I have received. Amen.

The Mute Demoniac Healed

__Matthew 9:32-34:__ ³² As they were going out, a demoniac who could not speak was brought to him, ³³ and when the demon was driven out the mute person spoke. The crowds were amazed and said, "Nothing like this has ever been seen in

180

Israel." [34] *But the Pharisees said, "He drives out demons by the prince of demons."*

<u>Matthew 12:22-24:</u> [22] *Then they brought to him a demoniac who was blind and mute. He cured the mute person so that he could speak and see.* [23] *All the crowd was astounded, and said, "Could this perhaps be the Son of David?"* [24] *But when the Pharisees heard this, they said, "This man drives out demons only by the power of Beelzebul, the prince of demons."*

<u>Mark 3:22:</u> *The scribes who had come from Jerusalem said, "He is possessed by Beelzebul," and "By the prince of demons he drives out demons."*

<u>Luke 11:14-15:</u> [14] *He was driving out a demon [that was] mute, and when the demon had gone out, the mute person spoke and the crowds were amazed.* [15] *Some of them said, "By the power of Beelzebul, the prince of demons, he drives out demons."*

There are two common themes here. One is that the healings continue, and the crowds are amazed. The second is that the Pharisees accuse Jesus of healing through the power of the prince of demons, Beelzebul.

As Jesus travels through the countryside, He fills the people with both blessings and amazements. They have not seen anyone with this type of power or authority before. All they have heard were stories of amazing things that were performed by the prophets of ages past. The fact that God had sent someone among them to provide all the tremendous blessings they are witnessing must have been overwhelming. The excitement must have filled their evening story telling for weeks to follow. God had truly blessed His people. And, as the stories go, He blessed the pagans and gentiles as well.

Then, naturally, the Pharisees had to continue their search for some wrongdoing to accuse Jesus. In this case, they could not accept the fact that Jesus was performing His miracles through either the power of God or His own power. He had to be proven false. Yet, at least in this instance, Jesus did not respond. There had been times when Jesus spoke, not necessarily justifying His own actions but showing the fault in their accusations. Not so here. However, we have to admit that not all of the stories in the Bible are filled with detail.

Lord, I want to always be amazed by Your words and actions. Fill my heart with the newness of all You say and do. May it never be "old hat." Amen.

The Harvest is Great

Matthew 9:35-38: *[35] Jesus went around to all the towns and villages, teaching in their synagogues, proclaiming the gospel of the kingdom, and curing every disease and illness. [36] At the sight of the crowds, his heart was moved with pity for them because they were troubled and abandoned, like sheep without a shepherd. [37] Then he said to his disciples, "The harvest is abundant, but the laborers are few; [38] so ask the master of the harvest to send out laborers for his harvest."*

Mark 6:6: *He went around to the villages in the vicinity teaching.*

Mark 6:34: *When he disembarked and saw the vast crowd, his heart was moved with pity for them, for they were like sheep without a shepherd; and he began to teach them many things.*

Luke 8:1: *Afterward he journeyed from one town and village to another, preaching and proclaiming the good news of the kingdom of God. Accompanying him were the Twelve.*

Luke 10:2: *He said to them, "The harvest is abundant, but the laborers are few; so ask the master of the harvest to send out laborers for his harvest.*

The message is clear. *The harvest is abundant, but the laborers are few; so, ask the master of the harvest to send out laborers for his harvest.* There is only so much that an individual can do. There are so many people in this world who need to hear the word of God. Obviously, not everyone has been chosen to be a preacher of the Word. We must pray for God to send more laborers into the field.

We should never assume that we are NOT one of the laborers. We should be ready to spread the word at the proper opportunity. Later in the Gospels, Jesus will tell His disciples that they should not prepare what to say. The Holy Spirit will provide them with the words to say when the appropriate time comes. We, as individuals, may be called on once in our lifetime to say the right thing to the right person. The call is God's. We must be willing to say "yes" to the opportunity.

Lord, not all of us have been called to be preachers of Your words. I know You have given me a gift for writing. Help me to understand the words You want me to write and to use this gift as You would desire. Amen.

Commissioning the Twelve

Matthew 10:1-16: *[1] Then he summoned his twelve disciples and gave them authority over unclean spirits to drive* *them out and to cure every disease and every illness. ² The names of the twelve Apostles are these: first, Simon called Peter, and his brother Andrew; James, the son of Zebedee, and his brother John; ³ Philip and Bartholomew, Thomas and Matthew the tax collector; James, the son of Alphaeus, and Thaddeus; ⁴ Simon the Cananean, and Judas Iscariot who betrayed him.*

⁵ Jesus sent out these twelve after instructing them thus, "Do not go into pagan territory or enter a Samaritan town. ⁶ Go rather to the lost sheep of the house of Israel. ⁷ As you go, make this proclamation: 'The kingdom of heaven is at hand.' ⁸ Cure the sick, raise the dead, cleanse lepers, drive out demons. Without cost you have received; without cost you are to give. ⁹ Do not take gold or silver or copper for your belts; ¹⁰ no sack for the journey, or a second tunic, or sandals, or walking stick. The laborer deserves his keep. ¹¹ Whatever town or village you enter, look for a worthy person in it, and stay there until you leave. ¹² As you enter a house, wish it peace. ¹³ If the house is worthy, let your peace come upon it; if not, let your peace return to you. ¹⁴ Whoever will not receive you or listen to your words—go outside that house or town and shake the dust from your feet. ¹⁵ Amen, I say to you, it will be more tolerable for the land of Sodom and Gomorrah on the day of judgment than for that town.

¹⁶ "Behold, I am sending you like sheep in the midst of wolves; so be shrewd as serpents and simple as doves.

Mark 6:7-11: *⁷ He summoned the Twelve and began to send them out two by two and gave them authority over unclean spirits. ⁸ He instructed them to take nothing for the journey but a walking stick—no food, no sack, no money in their belts. ⁹ They were, however, to wear sandals but not a second tunic. ¹⁰ He said to them, "Wherever you enter a house, stay there until you leave from there. ¹¹ Whatever place does not* *welcome you or listen to you, leave there and shake the dust off your feet in testimony against them. "*

<u>Mark 3:13-19:</u> *[13] He went up the mountain and summoned those whom he wanted, and they came to him. [14] He appointed twelve [whom he also named Apostles] that they might be with him and he might send them forth to preach [15] and to have authority to drive out demons: [16] [he appointed the twelve:] Simon, whom he named Peter; [17] James, son of Zebedee, and John the brother of James, whom he named Boanerges, that is, sons of thunder; [18] Andrew, Philip, Bartholomew, Matthew, Thomas, James the son of Alphaeus; Thaddeus, Simon the Cananean, [19] and Judas Iscariot who betrayed him.*

<u>LUKE 6:12-16:</u> *[12] In those days he departed to the mountain to pray, and he spent the night in prayer to God. [13] When day came, he called his disciples to himself, and from them he chose Twelve, whom he also named Apostles: [14] Simon, whom he named Peter, and his brother Andrew, James, John, Philip, Bartholomew, [15] Matthew, Thomas, James the son of Alphaeus, Simon who was called a Zealot, [16] and Judas the son of James, and Judas Iscariot, who became a traitor.*

<u>Luke 9:1-6:</u> *[1] He summoned the Twelve and gave them power and authority over all demons and to cure diseases, [2] and he sent them to proclaim the kingdom of God and to heal [the sick]. [3] He said to them, "Take nothing for the journey, neither walking stick, nor sack, nor food, nor money, and let no one take a second tunic. [4] Whatever house you enter, stay there and leave from there. [5] And as for those who do not welcome you, when you leave that town, shake the dust from your feet in testimony against them." [6] Then they set out and went from village to village proclaiming the good news and curing diseases everywhere.*

185

Luke 10:3: *Go on your way; behold, I am sending you like lambs among wolves.*

No one will ever know the Mind of God. This is not a criticism of the choices made for Apostleship. There is no explanation in the Gospels for why someone was chosen to be an Apostle. We know, at least I believe, that God molds us into whom He wants us to be. God qualifies the chosen.

Here are the chosen – the ones that Jesus will depend on to help mold the other disciples. All three gospel accounts are in agreement as far as the choices are concerned – with the exception of the also-known-as names. The writers of the synoptic gospels were reporters. John was not, and there is a lot missing from John's gospel that appears in the others. But, then again, John's gospel presents more insight into Jesus' humanity and divinity.

We may each have our thoughts about why certain men were chosen. I have a personal belief about Matthew. Matthew was a tax collector and his life as a tax collector had him keeping records constantly of who paid and who owed taxes. His records had to be accurate. I believe his drive to record meant that he kept records of what happened during his time with Jesus, things Jesus did, and words Jesus spoke. I believe his records were accurate. Whether or not he was directly commissioned by Jesus to keep these records is not known. But I believe God uses the gifts He gives us to do His work.

In these passages, Jesus not only commissions His Apostles, but He gifts them with the power to cure and the power to cast out demons. This is not simply incidental to their selection. Jesus has chosen these twelve to fulfill a special purpose: namely, to lead His flock after He returns to His Father. Jesus knows they will need these gifts to carry on their mission; however, they will have to learn how to use them. The Apostles will make their share of mistakes while they are learning.

Mark and Luke also remind us that Jesus was a man with a regular prayer life.

Lord, since the first time that I was moved into a leadership role at the age of 15, I have been in leadership roles throughout my life. I know I have made my share of mistakes, but I also realize that You were there guiding me and molding me into who I should be. Knowing that I am still not all You want me to be, I ask that you keep on molding this lump of clay till it reaches Your expectation. Amen.

The Coming Fate and Persecution of the Disciples

<u>Matthew 10:17-25:</u> *[17] But beware of people, for they will hand you over to courts and scourge you in their synagogues, [18] and you will be led before governors and kings for my sake as a witness before them and the pagans. [19] When they hand you over, do not worry about how you are to speak or what you are to say. You will be given at that moment what you are to say. [20] For it will not be you who speak but the Spirit of your Father speaking through you. [21] Brother will hand over brother to death, and the father his child; children will rise up against parents and have them put to death. [22] You will be hated by all because of my name, but whoever endures to the end will be saved. [23] When they persecute you in one town, flee to another. Amen, I say to you, you will not finish the towns of Israel before the Son of Man comes. [24] No disciple is above his teacher, no slave above his master. [25] It is enough for the disciple that he becomes like his teacher, for the slave that he*

becomes like his master. If they have called the master of the house Beelzebul, how much more those of his household!

<u>Matthew 24:9-14:</u> *⁹ Then they will hand you over to persecution, and they will kill you. You will be hated by all nations because of my name. ¹⁰ And then many will be led into sin; they will betray and hate one another. ¹¹ Many false prophets will arise and deceive many; ¹² and because of the increase of evildoing, the love of many will grow cold. ¹³ But the one who perseveres to the end will be saved. ¹⁴ And this gospel of the kingdom will be preached throughout the world as a witness to all nations, and then the end will come.*

<u>Mark 13:9-13:</u> *⁹ "Watch out for yourselves. They will hand you over to the courts. You will be beaten in synagogues. You will be arraigned before governors and kings because of me, as a witness before them. ¹⁰ But the gospel must first be preached to all nations. ¹¹ When they lead you away and hand you over, do not worry beforehand about what you are to say. But say whatever will be given to you at that hour. For it will not be you who are speaking but the holy Spirit. ¹² Brother will hand over brother to death, and the father his child; children will rise up against parents and have them put to death. ¹³ You will be hated by all because of my name. But the one who perseveres to the end will be saved.*

<u>Luke 6:40:</u> *No disciple is superior to the teacher; but when fully trained, every disciple will be like his teacher.*

<u>Luke 12:11-12:</u> *¹¹ When they take you before synagogues and before rulers and authorities, do not worry about how or what your defense will be or about what you are to say. ¹² For the holy Spirit will teach you at that moment what you should say."*

Luke 21:12-19: *[12] "Before all this happens, however, they will seize and persecute you, they will hand you over to the synagogues and to prisons, and they will have you led before kings and governors because of my name. [13] It will lead to your giving testimony. [14] Remember, you are not to prepare your defense beforehand, [15] for I myself shall give you wisdom in speaking that all your adversaries will be powerless to resist or refute. [16] You will even be handed over by parents, brothers, relatives, and friends, and they will put some of you to death. [17] You will be hated by all because of my name, [18] but not a hair on your head will be destroyed. [19] By your perseverance you will secure your lives.*

John 13:16: *Amen, amen, I say to you, no slave is greater than his master nor any messenger greater than the one who sent him.*

This had to have been hard for the Apostles to hear. On the one hand, Jesus is selecting them to be the leaders over all His disciples, with special powers similar to those of Jesus Himself. They must have been on an emotional high and anxious to learn and put all of this into practice. Now the ceiling caves in.

Here is where Jesus gives them the big "but…" They will have all of these powers and responsibilities; they will spread the good news of Jesus; BUT they will be tracked down, persecuted, and killed because they are the followers of Jesus. What?!! Wait a minute, this cannot be true. Jesus is the Messiah, the Son of the Living God, is He not? Is this what we have been waiting thousands of years for?

Jesus eases their pain by telling them the holy Spirit will be with them, guiding them, helping them to formulate the responses they will make to those who will persecute them.

189

Not all will die, but many. This is how mankind treats the prophets, the followers of the one true God.

So bottom line, the new leaders of Jesus' followers, will be gifted with speech and special powers; and then they will be persecuted, and some will die for what they believe. Well, at least they know what to expect. We could never accuse Jesus of withholding some of the important stuff.

But the one who perseveres to the end will be saved. I am not sure that this ending statement was much consolation after what was unloaded upon the new Apostles. It is a single statement offering hope; but did it actually sink in after all the rest was said?

There is no doubt in my mind that Jesus was being transparent and not hiding the truth of what was to come. Knowing their master was being honest with them, I am sure they were still hoping it would not be as bad as He said it would be.

Lord, I have been in leadership roles almost all of my life and I have to admit that I have really never faced persecution (or even expected it). I cannot say I know how the Apostles felt after this. But, Lord, I do ask that, if I ever face anything close to what the Apostles dealt with, You, Your Father, and the Holy Spirit will be with me and help me to deal with it as you said You would. Amen.

Exhortation to Fearless Confession

Matthew 10:26-33: *[26] "Therefore do not be afraid of them. Nothing is concealed that will not be revealed, nor secret that will not be known. [27] What I say to you in the darkness, speak in the light; what you hear whispered, proclaim on the housetops. [28] And do not be afraid of those who kill the body but cannot kill the soul; rather, be afraid of the one who can*

190

destroy both soul and body in Gehenna. ²⁹ Are not two sparrows sold for a small coin? Yet not one of them falls to the ground without your Father's knowledge. ³⁰ Even all the hairs of your head are counted. ³¹ So do not be afraid; you are worth more than many sparrows. ³² Everyone who acknowledges me before others I will acknowledge before my heavenly Father. ³³ But whoever denies me before others, I will deny before my heavenly Father.

<u>Luke 12:2-9:</u> *² "There is nothing concealed that will not be revealed, nor secret that will not be known. ³ Therefore whatever you have said in the darkness will be heard in the light, and what you have whispered behind closed doors will be proclaimed on the housetops. ⁴ I tell you, my friends, do not be afraid of those who kill the body but after that can do no more. ⁵ I shall show you whom to fear. Be afraid of the one who after killing has the power to cast into Gehenna; yes, I tell you, be afraid of that one. ⁶ Are not five sparrows sold for two small coins? Yet not one of them has escaped the notice of God. ⁷ Even the hairs of your head have all been counted. Do not be afraid. You are worth more than many sparrows. ⁸ I tell you, everyone who acknowledges me before others the Son of Man will acknowledge before the angels of God. ⁹ But whoever denies me before others will be denied before the angels of God.*

This is a time of highs and lows. First, our Lord chooses the twelve to be leaders among His disciples. He gives them the powers to cast out demons and to heal. Then He tells them that they will have to suffer persecution and die because of this. Now Jesus is soothing the fright He just gave them.

He talks to them about how important they are to the future. He tells them, "Do not be afraid." It is a greeting He

191

use often with His disciples. "Peace be with you." Jesus wants His followers to be at peace, to accept what is to come. He will be with them. This reminds me of the "measure with which you measure will be measured back to you." *Everyone who acknowledges me before others I will acknowledge before my heavenly Father. But whoever denies me before others, I will deny before my heavenly Father.*

Lord, fear of the unknown can easily grab hold of anyone. Fear based on knowledge that ill tidings are coming your way can cause deeper stress. Help me to be always confident that you are with me, and I will be able to endure all that is to come. Amen.

Divisions Within Households

Matthew 10:34-36: *[34] "Do not think that I have come to bring peace upon the earth. I have come to bring not peace but the sword. [35] For I have come to set a man 'against his father, a daughter against her mother, and a daughter-in-law against her mother-in-law; [36] and one's enemies will be those of his household.'*

Luke 12:51-53: *[51] Do you think that I have come to establish peace on the earth? No, I tell you, but rather division. [52] From now on a household of five will be divided, three against two and two against three; [53] a father will be divided against his son and a son against his father, a mother against her daughter and a daughter against her mother, a mother-in-law against her daughter-in-law and a daughter-in-law against her mother-in-law."*

"Let's face reality," Jesus said, "what I have been saying is causing controversy and will continue to do so – even to the point of splitting up families." Following the Will of God is not going to be easy. It is not impossible, but not easy. Jesus is showing the way. It boils down to us making choices, lots of choices, all day, every day. We will always be faced with the choice to do what God wants of us or to do what the world is calling us to do. Father against son, mother against daughter...

Are the teachings of Jesus making things easier for us or harder? His teachings are not really any different than what the Israelites have been taught all their lives. Jesus did not come the change any of that. He came to fulfill it. Jesus came to show us how to live the Will of God. It is more than just a philosophy. It is a way of life.

Lord, the hardest decision to make is deciding if this is Your will for me. Once I have discerned this, give me the strength I need to follow through and do what you wish. I can face the controversy as long as I believe this is what You want. Amen.

Conditions of Discipleship

Matthew 10:37-39: [37] *"Whoever loves father or mother more than me is not worthy of me, and whoever loves son or daughter more than me is not worthy of me;* [38] *and whoever does not take up his cross and follow after me is not worthy of me.* [39] *Whoever finds his life will lose it, and whoever loses his life for my sake will find it.*

Luke 14:25-27: [25] *Great crowds were traveling with him, and he turned and addressed them,* [26] *"If any one comes to me without hating his father and mother, wife and children,*

193

brothers and sisters, and even his own life, he cannot be my disciple. [27] *Whoever does not carry his own cross and come after me cannot be my disciple.*

Luke 17:33: *Whoever seeks to preserve his life will lose it, but whoever loses it will save it.*

John 12:25: *Whoever loves his life loses it, and whoever hates his life in this world will preserve it for eternal life.*

Whoa! This is tough to hear (or read). But the truth is that God wants 100% of us. God does not want you spending the far majority of your time chasing after the things the world has to offer and tokenizing your time with Him. Jesus is explicit. If you spend your time in search of the world, you may or may not gain it; but you will lose your chance for eternal life.

In his book "Just Like Jesus," Max Lucado wrote: "God rewards those who seek *Him.* Not those who seek doctrine or religions or systems or creeds. Many settle for the lesser passions, but the reward goes to those who settle for nothing less than Jesus Himself. And what is the reward? What awaits those who seek Jesus? Nothing short of the heart of Jesus.

Lord, help me to realize at all times that it is You who I should seek, not the things of this world that are constantly before me. Help me to avoid being sidetracked and lose my way. Amen.

Rewards of Discipleship

Matthew 10:40-42: [40] *"Whoever receives you receives me, and whoever receives me receives the one who sent me.* [41] *Whoever*

194

receives a prophet because he is a prophet will receive a prophet's reward, and whoever receives a righteous man because he is righteous will receive a righteous man's reward. [42] *And whoever gives only a cup of cold water to one of these little ones to drink because he is a disciple—amen, I say to you, he will surely not lose his reward.* "

<u>Mark 9:41</u>: *Anyone who gives you a cup of water to drink because you belong to Christ, amen, I say to you, will surely not lose his reward.*

<u>Luke 10:16</u>: *Whoever listens to you listens to me. Whoever rejects you rejects me. And whoever rejects me rejects the one who sent me.*

<u>John 13:20</u>: *Amen, amen, I say to you, whoever receives the one I send receives me, and whoever receives me receives the one who sent me.*

Jesus assures us that in following Him, we follow the one who sent Him. It is like the chain of command. However, in this case, it is a closer relationship. In following Jesus, we are following God the Father, Jesus' Father, our Father.

Bottom line though, Jesus tells us here that we will be rewarded for following Him and His teachings. What that reward is going to be comprised of and when it will be received are not stated, but the reward will be appropriate. So, following Him does have its benefits. Those benefits may be manifested in this life or the next.

Why was it so important for Jesus to tell us that we will be rewarded? The reason is that we, mere human beings, do not do anything unless we gain some benefit from it. No matter what we do, we have to gain something to our benefit;

or we simply do not do it. The benefit may be a tangible reward: something we have desired, something that will make our lives easier: money, trips, goods, etc. It may be something intangible: credit for something required of us, a good feeling, avoidance of something unpleasant, etc. There is always a benefit. Once again, Jesus does not say what; but we will be rewarded for following Him.

Lord, in the long run, I desire to be with You in Your heavenly kingdom. But my motive for now, in doing this study, is to understand better what You are teaching; so, I may live this life in a way that will please You. Amen.

John the Baptist's Question

<u>Matthew 11:1-6:</u> *¹ When Jesus finished giving these commands to his twelve disciples, he went away from that place to teach and to preach in their towns. ² When John heard in prison of the works of the Messiah, he sent his disciples to him ³ with this question, "Are you the one who is to come, or should we look for another?" ⁴ Jesus said to them in reply, "Go and tell John what you hear and see: ⁵ the blind regain their sight, the lame walk, lepers are cleansed, the deaf hear, the dead are raised, and the poor have the good news proclaimed to them. ⁶ And blessed is the one who takes no offense at me."*

<u>Luke 7:18-23:</u> *¹⁸ The disciples of John told him about all these things. John summoned two of his disciples ¹⁹ and sent them to the Lord to ask, "Are you the one who is to come, or should we look for another?" ²⁰ When the men came to him, they said, "John the Baptist has sent us to you to ask, 'Are you the one who is to come, or should we look for another?'" ²¹ At that time he cured many of their diseases, sufferings, and evil spirits; he also granted sight to many who were blind. ²² And he said to*

them in reply, "Go and tell John what you have seen and heard: the blind regain their sight, the lame walk, lepers are cleansed, the deaf hear, the dead are raised, the poor have the good news proclaimed to them. [23] And blessed is the one who takes no offense at me."

John the Baptist had told his followers that he was not the Messiah. However, he did give them hope by pointing them to Jesus of Nazareth. The question he gave them was simple enough and he expected Jesus to give them an appropriate answer. However, Jesus' answer was not a direct response.

All of the miracles that He was performing were significant and could only come from God or through the power of God. But was this what the disciples of John were expecting? Has John's preparation changed their expectation of one who would be their ruler and free them from the Roman domination? What Jesus was doing had nothing to do with freeing the Israelites from Rome. My guess is that, at a minimum, Jesus wanted John's disciples to stick around and learn more.

What lesson do I learn from this encounter? I believe that Jesus expects us to observe, learn, and reason out what the answers are and not expect God to present the answers word for word. God gave us the gift of reason and expects us to use it. Obviously, we will not be able to solve everything through our own gift; but we will come up with a lot of answers. We must always remember that God wants us to both use the gifts He has given us and also remember that we are dependent on Him.

Lord, all of the miracles showed You have the power and authority to confront and control nature. But miracles are only a small part of Your message to mankind. Help me to continue to seek deeply to understand Your message for us. Amen.

Jesus' Witness Concerning John

Matthew 11:7-19: [7] *As they were going off, Jesus began to speak to the crowds about John, "What did you go out to the desert to see? A reed swayed by the wind?* [8] *Then what did you go out to see? Someone dressed in fine clothing? Those who wear fine clothing are in royal palaces.* [9] *Then why did you go out? To see a prophet? Yes, I tell you, and more than a prophet.* [10] *This is the one about whom it is written: 'Behold, I am sending my messenger ahead of you; he will prepare your way before you.'* [11] *Amen, I say to you, among those born of women there has been none greater than John the Baptist; yet the least in the kingdom of heaven is greater than he.* [12] *From the days of John the Baptist until now, the kingdom of heaven suffers violence, and the violent are taking it by force.* [13] *All the prophets and the law prophesied up to the time of John.* [14] *And if you are willing to accept it, he is Elijah, the one who is to come.* [15] *Whoever has ears ought to hear.* [16] *"To what shall I compare this generation? It is like children who sit in marketplaces and call to one another,* [17] *'We played the flute for you, but you did not dance, we sang a dirge but you did not mourn.'* [18] *For John came neither eating nor drinking, and they said, 'He is possessed by a demon.'* [19] *The Son of Man came eating and drinking and they said, 'Look, he is a glutton and a drunkard, a friend of tax collectors and sinners.' But wisdom is vindicated by her works."*

Luke 7:24-35: [24] *When the messengers of John had left, Jesus began to speak to the crowds about John. "What did you go out to the desert to see—a reed swayed by the wind?* [25] *Then what did you go out to see? Someone dressed in fine garments?*

198

Those who dress luxuriously and live sumptuously are found in royal palaces. [26] Then what did you go out to see? A prophet? Yes, I tell you, and more than a prophet. [27] This is the one about whom scripture says: 'Behold, I am sending my messenger ahead of you, he will prepare your way before you.' [28] I tell you, among those born of women, no one is greater than John; yet the least in the kingdom of God is greater than he." [29] (All the people who listened, including the tax collectors, and who were baptized with the baptism of John, acknowledged the righteousness of God; [30] but the Pharisees and scholars of the law, who were not baptized by him, rejected the plan of God for themselves.) [31] "Then to what shall I compare the people of this generation? What are they like? [32] They are like children who sit in the marketplace and call to one another, 'We played the flute for you, but you did not dance. We sang a dirge, but you did not weep.' [33] For John the Baptist came neither eating food nor drinking wine, and you said, 'He is possessed by a demon.' [34] The Son of Man came eating and drinking and you said, 'Look, he is a glutton and a drunkard, a friend of tax collectors and sinners.' [35] But wisdom is vindicated by all her children."

Luke 16:16: *"The law and the prophets lasted until John; but from then on the kingdom of God is proclaimed, and everyone who enters does so with violence."*

There is both a question and an explanation in this passage. The question is important as well as the explanation. "Why did you come in search of John the Baptist?" People go in search of others for various reasons, and I am sure that the crowds who came for John had various motivations as well. However, Jesus nails the reality. They came for John because they were hoping he was the long-awaited Messiah. And even after John said that he was not the Messiah, they were hoping he was a prophet. The words John spoke sounded like they were coming from Yaweh Himself.

So, Jesus assured them that John the Baptist was not only a prophet but the greatest of them all. John is the one that scriptures foretold that he would be the precursor of the Messiah. He has the spirit of Elijah. This revelation not only confirmed John's status but also His own, because John had pointed Jesus out as the one foretold to come.

As always, Jesus was open and honest in His statements. The statements were not always easy to understand; but in the long run, the truth became clear.

Lord, I know I must pay close attention to what You say. As I noted, not all Your statements, as I read them in the Bible, are absolutely clear; and some require meditation and discernment. Help me to understand all You say to me. Amen.

Woes Pronounced on Galilean Cities

Matthew 11:20-24: *[20] Then he began to reproach the towns where most of his mighty deeds had been done, since they had not repented. [21] "Woe to you, Chorazin! Woe to you, Bethsaida! For if the mighty deeds done in your midst had been done in Tyre and Sidon, they would long ago have repented in sackcloth and ashes. [22] But I tell you, it will be more tolerable for Tyre and Sidon on the day of judgment than for you. [23] And as for you, Capernaum: 'Will you be exalted to heaven? You will go down to the netherworld.' For if the mighty deeds done in your midst had been done in Sodom, it would have remained until this day. [24] But I tell you, it will be more tolerable for the land of Sodom on the day of judgment than for you."*

Luke 10:12-15: *[12] I tell you, it will be more tolerable for Sodom on that day than for that town. [13] "Woe to you, Chorazin! Woe to you, Bethsaida! For if the mighty deeds done in your midst had been done in Tyre and Sidon, they would long ago have repented, sitting in sackcloth and ashes. [14] But it will be more tolerable for Tyre and Sidon at the judgment than for you. [15] And as for you, Capernaum, 'Will you be exalted to heaven? You will go down to the netherworld.'*

It is inevitable. Let us be realistic. Not everyone who heard the words of our Lord or witnessed the miracles were convinced that Jesus was the Messiah. No matter how much people heard of Jesus, not everyone felt drawn to seek Him out. From the sounds of Jesus' melancholy, the majority of those living in the towns and cities He identified paid little attention to Him. Even Capernaum, the city where He often resided with His disciples, was the object of His woes.

Unfortunately, no matter how much we would want it otherwise, there will be lost souls. Not everyone will accept God's message. Not everyone will follow the Will of God. There will be a portion of humanity that will be lost.

Lord, help me to stay on track, to not only listen to Your will and follow it, but to search it out. My life belongs to You. Help me to keep it that way. Amen.

Jesus' Thanksgiving to the Father

Matthew 11:25-27: *[25] At that time Jesus said in reply, "I give praise to you, Father, Lord of heaven and earth, for although you have hidden these things from the wise and the learned you have revealed them to the childlike. [26] Yes, Father, such has been your gracious will. [27] All things have been handed*

201

over to me by my Father. No one knows the Son except the Father, and no one knows the Father except the Son and anyone to whom the Son wishes to reveal him.

Luke 10:21-22: *[21] At that very moment he rejoiced [in] the holy Spirit and said, "I give you praise, Father, Lord of heaven and earth, for although you have hidden these things from the wise and the learned you have revealed them to the childlike. Yes, Father, such has been your gracious will. [22] All things have been handed over to me by my Father. No one knows who the Son is except the Father, and who the Father is except the Son and anyone to whom the Son wishes to reveal him."*

Here is an example of what Jesus is expecting from each of us. No matter what the circumstances, we must be grateful to God for what He has given us. In His sadness about the loss of the souls in the various cities, Jesus is grateful to His Father for the souls who will be saved. From a personal standpoint, we are all the result of the experiences of lives – the good, the bad, and the ugly. We are who we are because of what we have lived through and learned about life and about God. Nothing can change that. And everyone is unique in our experiences. We must show our gratitude to our Father in heaven just as His only begotten Son does.

Lord, remind me to take the time each day to recollect and thank You for all of my life's experiences. Gratitude must be an important part of my life, especially in growing closer to You. Amen.

"Come unto Me"

Matthew 11:28-30: *[28] "Come to me, all you who labor and are burdened, and I will give you rest. [29] Take my yoke upon you*

202

and learn from me, for I am meek and humble of heart; and you will find rest for yourselves. [30] For my yoke is easy, and my burden light."

I believe that many people have misinterpreted this statement. Many people believe that Jesus is saying, if we give our burdens to Him, the burdens will go away. That is not only an unreasonable expectation, but also a false expectation. When people unload themselves to our Lord, the load does not disappear; our Lord shares the load – not bears the load.

Jesus says clearly, "Take My yoke upon you." A yoke is used to put two animals (oxen or horses is what the Israelites can relate to) together to share a heavy load and manage it together. That is what our Lord is saying here. Do not just expect to abandon your problems, expect Jesus to help you with your load.

I know, Lord, that when I come to You with my problems, You will help me through them. I learned this lesson long ago. Help me to never forget it. Amen.

Plucking Grain on the Sabbath

Matthew 12:1-8: *[1] At that time Jesus was going through a field of grain on the sabbath. His disciples were hungry and began to pick the heads of grain and eat them. [2] When the Pharisees saw this, they said to him, "See, your disciples are doing what is unlawful to do on the sabbath." [3] He said to them, "Have you not read what David did when he and his companions were hungry, [4] how he went into the house of God and ate the bread of offering, which neither he nor his companions but only the priests could lawfully eat? [5] Or have you not read in the law that on the sabbath the priests serving in the temple violate the* *sabbath and are innocent? ⁶ I say to you, something greater than the temple is here. ⁷ If you knew what this meant, 'I desire mercy, not sacrifice,' you would not have condemned these innocent men. ⁸ For the Son of Man is Lord of the sabbath."*

<u>Mark 2:23-28:</u> *²³ As he was passing through a field of grain on the sabbath, his disciples began to make a path while picking the heads of grain. ²⁴ At this the Pharisees said to him, "Look, why are they doing what is unlawful on the sabbath?" ²⁵ He said to them, "Have you never read what David did when he was in need and he and his companions were hungry? ²⁶ How he went into the house of God when Abiathar was high priest and ate the bread of offering that only the priests could lawfully eat and shared it with his companions?" ²⁷ Then he said to them, "The sabbath was made for man, not man for the sabbath. ²⁸ That is why the Son of Man is lord even of the sabbath."*

<u>Luke 6:1-5:</u> *¹ While he was going through a field of grain on a sabbath, his disciples were picking the heads of grain, rubbing them in their hands, and eating them. ² Some Pharisees said, "Why are you doing what is unlawful on the sabbath?" ³ Jesus said to them in reply, "Have you not read what David did when he and those [who were] with him were hungry? ⁴ [How] he went into the house of God, took the bread of offering, which only the priests could lawfully eat, ate of it, and shared it with his companions." ⁵ Then he said to them, "The Son of Man is lord of the sabbath."*

The Pharisees are at it again. Constantly looking for something that our Lord could be charged with as a violation of the Law. In this case, on the sabbath the disciples are pulling grains from their stalks and eating them. It could just as easily have been fruit from vines or olives from trees.

The fact is that it was being done on the Sabbath; therefore, it was a violation of working on the Holy Day. Jesus will be accused of this a number of times in the future.

Jesus' response to them was simply to explain that there are circumstances that provide overriding justification for certain actions. In this case he uses a historical event related to King David that can be found in the scriptures. There are three key statements here: "...something greater than the temple is here," "The sabbath was made for man, not man for the sabbath," and "The son of Man is Lord of the sabbath."

The Law, the rules, all have a place. They are intended to keep people in line with God's will. They are intended to help an individual to live his or her life in a way that is pleasing to God. They are intended to help an individual to live his or her life in a way that allows them to live with others with dignity and peace. But, as everyone is well aware, there are circumstances that do not conform to the rigidity of those rules. The circumstances under which the disciples are being accused are an example of exceptions. The rules were made to help men be better; men were not made to follow the rules.

Lord, I often get lost in the details and forget to look at the big picture. It is in these circumstances that I often make the wrong choices. Help me to step back and keep the big picture in mind, to make choices that will please You, or, at least, to make my decisions in a way that will please you. Amen.

The Man with the Withered Hand

<u>Matthew 12:9-14:</u> *⁹Moving on from there, he went into their synagogue. ¹⁰And behold, there was a man there who had a*

withered hand. They questioned him, "Is it lawful to cure on the sabbath?" so that they might accuse him. [11] He said to them, "Which one of you who has a sheep that falls into a pit on the sabbath will not take hold of it and lift it out? [12] How much more valuable a person is than a sheep. So, it is lawful to do good on the sabbath." [13] Then he said to the man, "Stretch out your hand." He stretched it out, and it was restored as sound as the other. [14] But the Pharisees went out and took counsel against him to put him to death.

Mark 3:1-6: [1] Again he entered the synagogue. There was a man there who had a withered hand. [2] They watched him closely to see if he would cure him on the sabbath so that they might accuse him. [3] He said to the man with the withered hand, "Come up here before us." [4] Then he said to them, "Is it lawful to do good on the sabbath rather than to do evil, to save life rather than to destroy it?" But they remained silent. [5] Looking around at them with anger and grieved at their hardness of heart, he said to the man, "Stretch out your hand." He stretched it out and his hand was restored. [6] The Pharisees went out and immediately took counsel with the Herodians against him to put him to death.

Luke 6:6-11: [6] On another sabbath he went into the synagogue and taught, and there was a man there whose right hand was withered. [7] The scribes and the Pharisees watched him closely to see if he would cure on the sabbath so that they might discover a reason to accuse him. [8] But he realized their intentions and said to the man with the withered hand, "Come up and stand before us." And he rose and stood there. [9] Then Jesus said to them, "I ask you, is it lawful to do good on the sabbath rather than to do evil, to save life rather than to destroy it?" [10] Looking around at them all, he then said to him, "Stretch out your hand." He did so and his hand was *restored. ¹¹ But they became enraged and discussed together what they might do to Jesus.*

Here, the three stories are essentially the same except that Matthew portrays the Pharisees asking the question about curing on the sabbath. Mark and Luke portray Jesus asking the question. Other than that, the stories are the same.

I believe that what should be taken from this story is that Jesus was not intimidated by the constant watch by the Pharisees and others, hoping that Jesus would violate the Law. It is the spirit behind the Law that Jesus is promoting. Jesus is plainly saying that it is within the spirit of the Law that one can do good on the sabbath. Remember from the previous segment: the sabbath was made for man, not man for the sabbath.

Jesus also showed once again that He has power over nature. He can heal or cure any and all maladies. And the crowds keep coming. His following keeps growing. And His enemies keep wringing their hands, watching, and planning.

Lord, there are times when I smile at the scenes where You outwit those opposed to You. But I realize that I should be sad rather than happy because they are lost souls. I pray for the souls that are lost so they can see Your light and follow You. Amen.

Jesus Heals Multitudes by the Sea

Matthew 12:15-21: ¹⁵ *When Jesus realized this, he withdrew from that place. Many [people] followed him, and he cured them all, ¹⁶ but he warned them not to make him known. ¹⁷ This was to fulfill what had been spoken through Isaiah the prophet: ¹⁸ "Behold, my servant whom I have chosen, my*

207

beloved in whom I delight; I shall place my spirit upon him, and he will proclaim justice to the Gentiles. [19] He will not contend or cry out, nor will anyone hear his voice in the streets. [20] A bruised reed he will not break, a smoldering wick he will not quench, until he brings justice to victory. [21] And in his name the Gentiles will hope."

Mark 3:7-12: [7] Jesus withdrew toward the sea with his disciples. A large number of people [followed] from Galilee and from Judea. [8] Hearing what he was doing, a large number of people came to him also from Jerusalem, from Idumea, from beyond the Jordan, and from the neighborhood of Tyre and Sidon. [9] He told his disciples to have a boat ready for him because of the crowd, so that they would not crush him. [10] He had cured many and, as a result, those who had diseases were pressing upon him to touch him. [11] And whenever unclean spirits saw him, they would fall down before him and shout, "You are the Son of God." [12] He warned them sternly not to make him known.

Luke 6:17-19: [17] And he came down with them and stood on a stretch of level ground. A great crowd of his disciples and a large number of the people from all Judea and Jerusalem and the coastal region of Tyre and Sidon [18] came to hear him and to be healed of their diseases; and even those who were tormented by unclean spirits were cured. [19] Everyone in the crowd sought to touch him because power came forth from him and healed them all.

People came from all over: Galilee, the Decapolis, Jerusalem, Judea, beyond the Jordan, Idumea, Tyre, and Sidon. They wanted to be healed of their diseases. Even those possessed by unclean spirits were cured. *Everyone in the crowd sought to touch Him because power came forth from Him and healed them all.*

Our Lord's compassion is immeasurable. As indicated earlier, Jesus was available. He allowed people to come to Him and He allowed the power within Him to go out to them. It had nothing to do with whether or not they were Jewish, whether or not they were worthy. His love outweighed all human restraints.

They kept coming and word about Him spread throughout the land, even though *He warned them not to make Him known.*

Lord, love cannot be quantified. It cannot be measured. For it to be true, it must be without restraint. It must be without condition. Help me to love as You do. Amen.

The Woman with the Ointment

<u>Matthew 26:6-13:</u> *⁶ Now when Jesus was in Bethany in the house of Simon the leper, ⁷ a woman came up to him with an alabaster jar of costly perfumed oil and poured it on his head while he was reclining at table. ⁸ When the disciples saw this, they were indignant and said, "Why this waste? ⁹ It could have been sold for much, and the money given to the poor." ¹⁰ Since Jesus knew this, he said to them, "Why do you make trouble for the woman? She has done a good thing for me. ¹¹ The poor you will always have with you; but you will not always have me. ¹² In pouring this perfumed oil upon my body, she did it to prepare me for burial. ¹³ Amen, I say to you, wherever this gospel is proclaimed in the whole world, what she has done will be spoken of, in memory of her."*

<u>Mark 14:3-9:</u> *³ When he was in Bethany reclining at table in the house of Simon the leper, a woman came with an alabaster*

209

jar of perfumed oil, costly genuine spikenard. She broke the alabaster jar and poured it on his head. ⁴ There were some who were indignant. "Why has there been this waste of perfumed oil? ⁵ It could have been sold for more than three hundred days' wages and the money given to the poor." They were infuriated with her. ⁶ Jesus said, "Let her alone. Why do you make trouble for her? She has done a good thing for me. ⁷ The poor you will always have with you, and whenever you wish you can do good to them, but you will not always have me. ⁸ She has done what she could. She has anticipated anointing my body for burial. ⁹ Amen, I say to you, wherever the gospel is proclaimed to the whole world, what she has done will be told in memory of her."

Luke 7:36-50: *³⁶ A Pharisee invited him to dine with him, and he entered the Pharisee's house and reclined at table. ³⁷ Now there was a sinful woman in the city who learned that he was at table in the house of the Pharisee. Bringing an alabaster flask of ointment, ³⁸ she stood behind him at his feet weeping and began to bathe his feet with her tears. Then she wiped them with her hair, kissed them, and anointed them with the ointment. ³⁹ When the Pharisee who had invited him saw this, he said to himself, "If this man were a prophet, he would know who and what sort of woman this is who is touching him, that she is a sinner." ⁴⁰ Jesus said to him in reply, "Simon, I have something to say to you." "Tell me, teacher," he said. ⁴¹ "Two people were in debt to a certain creditor; one owed five hundred days' wages and the other owed fifty. ⁴² Since they were unable to repay the debt, he forgave it for both. Which of them will love him more?" ⁴³ Simon said in reply, "The one, I suppose, whose larger debt was forgiven." He said to him, "You have judged rightly." ⁴⁴ Then he turned to the woman and said to Simon, "Do you see this woman? When I entered your house, you did not give me water for my feet, but she has* *bathed them with her tears and wiped them with her hair. ⁴⁵ You did not give me a kiss, but she has not ceased kissing my feet since the time I entered. ⁴⁶ You did not anoint my head with oil, but she anointed my feet with ointment. ⁴⁷ So I tell you, her many sins have been forgiven; hence, she has shown great love. But the one to whom little is forgiven, loves little." ⁴⁸ He said to her, "Your sins are forgiven." ⁴⁹ The others at table said to themselves, "Who is this who even forgives sins?" ⁵⁰ But he said to the woman, "Your faith has saved you; go in peace."*

<u>John 12:1-8:</u> *¹ Six days before Passover Jesus came to Bethany, where Lazarus was, whom Jesus had raised from the dead. ² They gave a dinner for him there, and Martha served, while Lazarus was one of those reclining at table with him. ³ Mary took a liter of costly perfumed oil made from genuine aromatic nard and anointed the feet of Jesus and dried them with her hair; the house was filled with the fragrance of the oil. ⁴ Then Judas the Iscariot, one [of] his disciples, and the one who would betray him, said, ⁵ "Why was this oil not sold for three hundred days' wages and given to the poor?" ⁶ He said this not because he cared about the poor but because he was a thief and held the money bag and used to steal the contributions. ⁷ So Jesus said, "Leave her alone. Let her keep this for the day of my burial. ⁸ You always have the poor with you, but you do not always have me."*

Between the four accounts, there are many similarities; but there are also differences. Once again, my purpose is not to analyze the various passages of the Gospels but to learn what I can about Jesus Himself. I will leave the rest to competent theologians.

My purpose in this study is also not to identify who that woman was. Only John identifies her as Mary, the sister of

Lazarus. The others identify her simply as a sinful woman. Nor is it important how much of a sinner she really was. What is important is she realized that she was sinful; and she sought some way to make amends to the one who was, in her mind, graced by God. I do not believe she expected to have her sins forgiven. Obviously, the others in the room did not. Only God could forgive sins.

The actual cleansing of Jesus' feet with her tears is only an example of an omitted courtesy by the host. Generally, the host would have a servant cleanse the feet of an honored guest. If the host was indeed Simon the Leper, a Pharisee, then the omitted courtesy would have been expected. I am sure that Jesus was expecting little from the Pharisee.

An important thing to remember here is that Jesus presented something to all present that they did not expect. He forgave her sins. Out of His love for her and His mercy, He gave her something she really needed – a cleansing for a cleansing.

Another lesson has special meaning for me as a member of the Society of St. Vincent de Paul. Our ministry calls for us to help those in need in the best way we can. Jesus reminds us that the poor will always be with us. It is not our job as servants of the poor or simply as human beings to eliminate poverty. That is an impossible task for us. The poor will always be with us. It is our role as Christians, as humans, as servants of the poor to give aid wherever and whenever we can to make life easier for those in need.

Lord, as Psalm 139 states, You probed me and You know me. You know what I need before I do. Out of Your love and mercy, forgive me, a sinner. Amen.

Jesus' Return Home

Luke 8:1-3: *[1] Afterward he journeyed from one town and village to another, preaching and proclaiming the good news of the kingdom of God. Accompanying him were the Twelve [2] and some women who had been cured of evil spirits and infirmities, Mary, called Magdalene, from whom seven demons had gone out, [3] Joanna, the wife of Herod's steward Chuza, Susanna, and many others who provided for them out of their resources.*

Mark 3:20-21: *[20] He came home. Again, [the] crowd gathered, making it impossible for them even to eat. [21] When his relatives heard of this, they set out to seize him, for they said, "He is out of his mind."*

Although these two passages are not directly related, they do point out two important points. Jesus did not travel alone. He, in fact, has a pretty large entourage. He was accompanied by His chosen Apostles and by a number of women who chose to follow and serve Him and the others. This means that there was plenty of time to discuss His mission with His Apostles. This also means that the women were there to serve as needed.

However, when He finally arrived home, and a crowd started to gather again, things became difficult for Jesus and those with Him. But the difficulty did not come from the crowds, it came from His relatives. His relatives did not understand Him or His mission and thought He was out of His mind to allow the crowds to come. Not only to come, but to spend His time teaching and healing.

Jesus continued to do the will of His Father in spite of what others may have thought.

Lord, help me to never believe that I understand all You do and/or the reasons You do them. The mystery of You keeps me wanting to know more. Amen.

On Collusion with Satan

<u>Matthew 12:22-30:</u> *[22] Then they brought to him a demoniac who was blind and mute. He cured the mute person so that he could speak and see. [23] All the crowd was astounded, and said, "Could this perhaps be the Son of David?" [24] But when the Pharisees heard this, they said, "This man drives out demons only by the power of Beelzebul, the prince of demons." [25] But he knew what they were thinking and said to them, "Every kingdom divided against itself will be laid waste, and no town or house divided against itself will stand. [26] And if Satan drives out Satan, he is divided against himself; how, then, will his kingdom stand? [27] And if I drive out demons by Beelzebul, by whom do your own people drive them out? Therefore, they will be your judges. [28] But if it is by the Spirit of God that I drive out demons, then the kingdom of God has come upon you. [29] How can anyone enter a strong man's house and steal his property, unless he first ties up the strong man? Then he can plunder his house. [30] Whoever is not with me is against me, and whoever does not gather with me scatters.*

<u>Mark 3:22-27:</u> *[22] The scribes who had come from Jerusalem said, "He is possessed by Beelzebul," and "By the prince of demons he drives out demons." [23] Summoning them, he began to speak to them in parables, "How can Satan drive out Satan? [24] If a kingdom is divided against itself, that kingdom cannot stand. [25] And if a house is divided against itself, that house will not be able to stand. [26] And if Satan has risen up against himself and is divided, he cannot stand; that is the end of him. [27] But no one can enter a strong man's house to*

214

plunder his property unless he first ties up the strong man.
Then he can plunder his house.

Luke 11:14-15, 17-23: *[14] He was driving out a demon [that was] mute, and when the demon had gone out, the mute person spoke; and the crowds were amazed. [15] Some of them said, "By the power of Beelzebul, the prince of demons, he drives out demons." [17] But he knew their thoughts and said to them, "Every kingdom divided against itself will be laid waste and house will fall against house. [18] And if Satan is divided against himself, how will his kingdom stand? For you say that it is by Beelzebul that I drive out demons. [19] If I, then, drive out demons by Beelzebul, by whom do your own people drive them out? Therefore, they will be your judges. [20] But if it is by the finger of God that [I] drive out demons, then the kingdom of God has come upon you. [21] When a strong man fully armed guards his palace, his possessions are safe. [22] But when one stronger than he attacks and overcomes him, he takes away the armor on which he relied and distributes the spoils. [23] Whoever is not with me is against me, and whoever does not gather with me scatters.*

Once again, we find our Lord both driving out demons and healing. But, in this case, the significant activity is the conflict with the Pharisees. Always looking for things to accuse our Lord, they now accuse Him of acting as a tool of Satan. Jesus can easily deflect their accusation. But the fact is that He does it in a way that upsets the Pharisees more. Their accusation has no merit. This is an important lesson about Jesus and how He is an example to be followed.

Jesus always had the right thing to say for the situation; and He promised us that, if we live as His Father wants us to, then the Holy Spirit will provide us with the words we need when we need them. It is a matter of faith and trust in God.

The last statement is especially important to remember. *"Whoever is not with me is against me, and whoever does not gather with me scatters."* This statement should be remembered later when Jesus talks about being lukewarm. God wants us completely. He does not want us to be "iffy" about our devotion to Him. If we are only "iffy," then we are as good as against Him.

Lord, help me to grow my faith and trust in You; so that I may gather rather than scatter. Amen.

The Sin Against the Holy Spirit

<u>Matthew 12:31-37:</u> *³¹ Therefore, I say to you, every sin and blasphemy will be forgiven people, but blasphemy against the Spirit will not be forgiven. ³² And whoever speaks a word against the Son of Man will be forgiven; but whoever speaks against the holy Spirit will not be forgiven, either in this age or in the age to come. ³³ "Either declare the tree good and its fruit is good or declare the tree rotten and its fruit is rotten, for a tree is known by its fruit. ³⁴ You brood of vipers, how can you say good things when you are evil? For from the fullness of the heart the mouth speaks. ³⁵ A good person brings forth good out of a store of goodness, but an evil person brings forth evil out of a store of evil. ³⁶ I tell you, on the day of judgment people will render an account for every careless word they speak. ³⁷ By your words you will be acquitted, and by your words you will be condemned."*

<u>Matthew 7:16-20:</u> *¹⁶ By their fruits you will know them. Do people pick grapes from thornbushes, or figs from thistles? ¹⁷ Just so, every good tree bears good fruit, and a*

216

rotten tree bears bad fruit. *[18] A good tree cannot bear bad fruit, nor can a rotten tree bear good fruit.* *[19] Every tree that does not bear good fruit will be cut down and thrown into the fire.* *[20] So by their fruits you will know them.*

Mark 3:28-30: *[28] Amen, I say to you, all sins and all blasphemies that people utter will be forgiven them.* *[29] But whoever blasphemes against the holy Spirit will never have forgiveness but is guilty of an everlasting sin." [30] For they had said, "He has an unclean spirit."*

Luke 12:10: *"Everyone who speaks a word against the Son of Man will be forgiven, but the one who blasphemes against the holy Spirit will not be forgiven."*

Luke 6:43-45: *[43] "A good tree does not bear rotten fruit, nor does a rotten tree bear good fruit.* *[44] For every tree is known by its own fruit. For people do not pick figs from thornbushes, nor do they gather grapes from brambles.* *[45] A good person out of the store of goodness in his heart produces good, but an evil person out of a store of evil produces evil; for from the fullness of the heart the mouth speaks."*

Jesus was definitely upset by what the Pharisees said in the previous passage: *"By the power of Beelzebul, the prince of demons, he drives out demons."* In reading the footnotes of this passage in the Bible, I read that a blasphemy against the Holy Spirit is attributing to Satan what is the work of the Spirit of God. This statement from the Pharisees clearly meets the definition. So, the Pharisees committed an unforgiveable sin.

It was not very often that Jesus got upset. I wish I could say the same about myself. So, it is clear that I still have work to do to control my emotions.

The following words about good fruit coming from good people and bad fruit coming from bad people must be accepted along with the belief that this is not a permanent condition. Bad people can change and can start to produce good fruit. Just as the opposite is true. After all, if that was not true, then why did God come to live with us and show us how to live?

Lord, I still have work to do to be able to control my emotions as well as to carefully select the words I want to say. Help me to stay on the proper path. Amen.

Against Seeking Signs, the Sign of Jonah

Matthew 12:38-42: *[38] Then some of the scribes and Pharisees said to him, "Teacher, we wish to see a sign from you." [39] He said to them in reply, "An evil and unfaithful generation seeks a sign, but no sign will be given it except the sign of Jonah the prophet. [40] Just as Jonah was in the belly of the whale three days and three nights, so will the Son of Man be in the heart of the earth three days and three nights. [41] At the judgment, the men of Nineveh will arise with this generation and condemn it, because they repented at the preaching of Jonah; and there is something greater than Jonah here. [42] At the judgment the queen of the south will arise with this generation and condemn it, because she came from the ends of the earth to hear the wisdom of Solomon; and there is something greater than Solomon here.*

Matthew 16:1-4: *[1] The Pharisees and Sadducees came and, to test him, asked him to show them a sign from heaven. [2] He said to them in reply, "[In the evening you say, 'Tomorrow will be fair, for the sky is red'; [3] and, in the morning, 'Today will be stormy, for the sky is red and threatening.' You know how to*

218

judge the appearance of the sky, but you cannot judge the signs of the times.] ⁴ An evil and unfaithful generation seeks a sign, but no sign will be given it except the sign of Jonah." Then he left them and went away.

Mark 8:11-12: *¹¹ The Pharisees came forward and began to argue with him, seeking from him a sign from heaven to test him. ¹² He sighed from the depth of his spirit and said, "Why does this generation seek a sign? Amen, I say to you, no sign will be given to this generation."*

Luke 11:16: *Others, to test him, asked him for a sign from heaven.*

Luke 11:29-32: *²⁹ While still more people gathered in the crowd, he said to them, "This generation is an evil generation; it seeks a sign, but no sign will be given it, except the sign of Jonah. ³⁰ Just as Jonah became a sign to the Ninevites, so will the Son of Man be to this generation. ³¹ At the judgment the queen of the south will rise with the men of this generation; and she will condemn them, because she came from the ends of the earth to hear the wisdom of Solomon, and there is something greater than Solomon here. ³² At the judgment the men of Nineveh will arise with this generation and condemn it, because at the preaching of Jonah they repented, and there is something greater than Jonah here.*

No sign will be given. That is the first lesson from this passage. Jesus does not perform miracles to prove His abilities or His power. He is not presenting a show. The miracles have already been performed. The signs have already been given. It is up to us to recognize the signs and act upon them.

The second lesson is that of Nineveh. The people of Nineveh heard the words of Jonah, recognized the truth of their sinfulness, and repented. And God was merciful. God is both just and merciful. For all who are truly repentant, God will grant mercy. And we cannot fool God.

Lord, You probe me and know what is in my heart. I cannot ask for more than Your love. Amen.

The Return of the Unclean Spirit

<u>Matthew 12:43-45</u>: [43] *"When an unclean spirit goes out of a person it roams through arid regions searching for rest but finds none. [44] Then it says, 'I will return to my home from which I came.' But upon returning, it finds it empty, swept clean, and put in order. [45] Then it goes and brings back with itself seven other spirits more evil than itself, and they move in and dwell there; and the last condition of that person is worse than the first. Thus, it will be with this evil generation."*

<u>Luke 11:24-26</u>: [24] *"When an unclean spirit goes out of someone, it roams through arid regions searching for rest but, finding none, it says, 'I shall return to my home from which I came.' [25] But upon returning, it finds it swept clean and put in order. [26] Then it goes and brings back seven other spirits more wicked than itself who move in and dwell there, and the last condition of that person is worse than the first."*

"This evil generation" has shown over and over again that it prefers the things of this world and will continue to fall for the traps of the evil one, Satan. So even though someone may have been freed of the demons within, they may quickly invite the demons back into their home. They may, in fact, be worse off than they were to begin with. This

220

is a warning from Jesus. The healings He performs, the demons He drives out, all His miracles, are not guarantees of future safety and health. Everything He has done is for the moment. It is up to us to do what is necessary to keep ourselves clean.

Lord, it is only by following the path You set out that I can truly achieve happiness. Help me to stay on that path and not backslide to the ways that lead away from You. Amen.

Jesus' True Kindred Relatives

<u>Matthew 12:46-50:</u> *[46] While he was still speaking to the crowds, his mother and his brothers appeared outside, wishing to speak with him. [47] [Someone told him, "Your mother and your brothers are standing outside, asking to speak with you."] [48] But he said in reply to the one who told him, "Who is my mother? Who are my brothers?" [49] And stretching out his hand toward his disciples, he said, "Here are my mother and my brothers. [50] For whoever does the will of my heavenly Father is my brother, and sister, and mother."*

<u>Mark 3:31-35:</u> *[31] His mother and his brothers arrived. Standing outside they sent word to him and called him. [32] A crowd seated around him told him, "Your mother and your brothers [and your sisters] are outside asking for you." [33] But he said to them in reply, "Who are my mother and [my] brothers?" [34] And looking around at those seated in the circle he said, "Here are my mother and my brothers. [35] [For] whoever does the Will of God is my brother and sister and mother."*

<u>Luke 8:19-21:</u> *[19] Then his mother and his brothers came to him but were unable to join him because of the crowd. [20] He*

was told, "Your mother and your brothers are standing outside, and they wish to see you." ^{21} He said to them in reply, "My mother and my brothers are those who hear the word of God and act on it."

<u>John 15:14:</u> *You are my friends if you do what I command you.*

I believe the first thing I have to acknowledge or recognize is that Jesus is not rejecting His mother and brothers. When I was young, this was the immediate impression I got when reading or hearing this passage. It was simply an opportunity for Jesus to explain that all who believed in Him and followed Him were truly part of His family. And that is the essential message here.

Jesus' mission on earth was to follow the will of His Father in heaven. Those, who believed in Jesus and followed His will, are the adopted children of His Father and, therefore, members of His family. Everyone can be in His family. All it takes is faith and following the Will of God.

Lord, help me to recommit myself every day to building my faith and to do what I understand to be Your will for me. Amen.

The Parable of the Sower

<u>Matthew 13:1-17:</u> *^{1} On that day, Jesus went out of the house and sat down by the sea. ^{2} Such large crowds gathered around him that he got into a boat and sat down, and the whole crowd stood along the shore. ^{3} And he spoke to them at length in parables, saying: "A sower went out to sow. ^{4} And as he sowed, some seed fell on the path, and birds came and ate it up. ^{5} Some fell on rocky ground, where it had little soil. It sprang up at*

222

once because the soil was not deep, ⁶ and when the sun rose it was scorched, and it withered for lack of roots. ⁷ Some seed fell among thorns, and the thorns grew up and choked it. ⁸ But some seed fell on rich soil, and produced fruit, a hundred or sixty or thirtyfold. ⁹ Whoever has ears ought to hear." ¹⁰ The disciples approached him and said, "Why do you speak to them in parables?" ¹¹ He said to them in reply, "Because knowledge of the mysteries of the kingdom of heaven has been granted to you, but to them it has not been granted. ¹² To anyone who has, more will be given, and he will grow rich; from anyone who has not, even what he has will be taken away. ¹³ This is why I speak to them in parables, because 'they look but do not see and hear but do not listen or understand.' ¹⁴ Isaiah's prophecy is fulfilled in them, which says: 'You shall indeed hear but not understand, you shall indeed look but never see. ¹⁵ Gross is the heart of this people, they will hardly hear with their ears, they have closed their eyes, lest they see with their eyes and hear with their ears and understand with their heart and be converted, and I heal them.' ¹⁶ "But blessed are your eyes, because they see, and your ears, because they hear. ¹⁷ Amen, I say to you, many prophets and righteous people longed to see what you see but did not see it, and to hear what you hear but did not hear it."

Mark 4:1-12: *¹On another occasion he began to teach by the sea. A very large crowd gathered around him so that he got into a boat on the sea and sat down. And the whole crowd was beside the sea on land. ² And he taught them at length in parables, and in the course of his instruction he said to them, ³"Hear this! A sower went out to sow. ⁴ And as he sowed, some seed fell on the path, and the birds came and ate it up. ⁵ Other seed fell on rocky ground where it had little soil. It sprang up at once because the soil was not deep. ⁶ And when the sun rose, it was scorched, and it withered for lack of*

223

roots. [7] *Some seed fell among thorns, and the thorns grew up and choked it and it produced no grain.* [8] *And some seed fell on rich soil and produced fruit. It came up and grew and yielded thirty, sixty, and a hundredfold."* [9] *He added, "Whoever has ears to hear ought to hear."* [10] *And when he was alone, those present along with the Twelve questioned him about the parables.* [11] *He answered them, "The mystery of the kingdom of God has been granted to you. But to those outside everything comes in parables,* [12] *so that 'they may look and see but not perceive, and hear and listen but not understand, in order that they may not be converted and be forgiven.'"*

Mark 4:25: *"To the one who has, more will be given; from the one who has not, even what he has will be taken away."*

Luke 8:4-10: [4] *When a large crowd gathered, with people from one town after another journeying to him, he spoke in a parable.* [5] *"A sower went out to sow his seed. And as he sowed, some seed fell on the path and was trampled, and the birds of the sky ate it up.* [6] *Some seed fell on rocky ground, and when it grew, it withered for lack of moisture.* [7] *Some seed fell among thorns, and the thorns grew with it and choked it.* [8] *And some seed fell on good soil, and when it grew, it produced fruit a hundredfold." After saying this, he called out, "Whoever has ears to hear ought to hear."* [9] *Then his disciples asked him what the meaning of this parable might be.* [10] *He answered, "Knowledge of the mysteries of the kingdom of God has been granted to you; but to the rest, they are made known through parables so that 'they may look but not see and hear but not understand.'"*

Luke 8:18: *"Take care, then, how you hear. To anyone who has, more will be given, and from the one who has not, even what he seems to have will be taken away."*

224

Luke 10:23-24: *[23] Turning to the disciples in private he said, "Blessed are the eyes that see what you see. [24] For I say to you, many prophets and kings desired to see what you see, but did not see it, and to hear what you hear, but did not hear it."*

The parable of the sower is one of the most popular that Jesus presented to the crowds. However, the parable can be misinterpreted. The actual meaning will be shared in the next passage. What is important here is that Jesus tells His Apostles that not everyone will understand His parables. The parables are really intended for His Apostles to understand and to explain the meaning to others.

What is surprising to me is that the Apostles are much like the crowds. Actually, it should not be surprising. Jesus made every effort to select ordinary men to take the lead. They do not understand either and need to have the parable explained to them. The Apostles are Jesus' chosen leaders. They are the ones who need to understand.

It is important here to remember that the parables that Jesus presented to the crowds were stories based on ordinary things of the time and place. The people and circumstances in the parables are things the people can relate to. Although they can relate to the people and circumstances, they still need to have the parables explained to them. That is not much different from stories told today by our spiritual leaders.

Lord, help me to not lose interest when I hear something that may be a little difficult to understand at first. Grant me the grace to seek the answers and meanings. Amen.

Interpretation of the Parable of the Sower

<u>Matthew 13:18-23:</u> [18] *"Hear then the parable of the sower.* [19] *The seed sown on the path is the one who hears the word of the kingdom without understanding it, and the evil one comes and steals away what was sown in his heart.* [20] *The seed sown on rocky ground is the one who hears the word and receives it at once with joy.* [21] *But he has no root and lasts only for a time. When some tribulation or persecution comes because of the word, he immediately falls away.* [22] *The seed sown among thorns is the one who hears the word, but then worldly anxiety and the lure of riches choke the word; and it bears no fruit.* [23] *But the seed sown on rich soil is the one who hears the word and understands it, who indeed bears fruit and yields a hundred or sixty or thirtyfold."*

<u>Mark 4:13-20:</u> [13] *Jesus said to them, "Do you not understand this parable? Then how will you understand any of the parables?* [14] *The sower sows the word.* [15] *These are the ones on the path where the word is sown. As soon as they hear, Satan comes at once and takes away the word sown in them.* [16] *And these are the ones sown on rocky ground who, when they hear the word, receive it at once with joy.* [17] *But they have no root; they last only for a time. Then when tribulation or persecution comes because of the word, they quickly fall away.* [18] *Those sown among thorns are another sort. They are the people who hear the word,* [19] *but worldly anxiety, the lure of riches, and the craving for other things intrude and choke the word, and it bears no fruit.* [20] *But those sown on rich soil are the ones who hear the word and accept it and bear fruit thirty and sixty and a hundredfold."*

<u>Luke 8:11-15:</u> [11] *"This is the meaning of the parable. The seed is the word of God.* [12] *Those on the path are the ones who have*

226

heard, but the devil comes and takes away the word from their hearts that they may not believe and be saved. [13] Those on rocky ground are the ones who, when they hear, receive the word with joy, but they have no root; they believe only for a time and fall away in time of trial. [14] As for the seed that fell among thorns, they are the ones who have heard, but as they go along, they are choked by the anxieties and riches and pleasures of life, and they fail to produce mature fruit. [15] But as for the seed that fell on rich soil, they are the ones who, when they have heard the word, embrace it with a generous and good heart, and bear fruit through perseverance.

I want to particularly point out the statement in Mark: *"Jesus said to them, "Do you not understand this parable? Then how will you understand any of the parables?"* The impression that I get in reading this is that Jesus was a bit frustrated with His Apostles. Jesus was expecting that they would have begun to grasp the meaning of His stories by that time. However, I have to keep reminding myself that the Apostles were ordinary men, like those in the crowds – not born leaders, not among the Pharisees, not well educated on the scriptures.

Next I want to recognize that this explanation is being given to the Apostles only. The way the passages have been presented indicates that after the initial telling of the parable to the crowd, Jesus comments were presented to the Apostles only – and any other disciples in hearing distance. There is nothing that explicitly says Jesus explained the parable to the crowd.

Also, Jesus speaks of Satan. He has spoken of the devil, Beelzebub, the evil one, and demons. It surprises me how many people who call themselves Christians and say they believe Christ is God; and yet, they refuse to acknowledge the existence of Satan. Jesus Himself speaks of Him. They

227

refer to Satan as a fairy tale character. Why would God, who is the God of truth, speak of Satan if he does not exist?

I will not go into an explanation of the meaning of the parable except that I believe Jesus ranked 11 of His 12 Apostles as seeds falling on fertile soil. I believe the reader knows who the one is that fell among the thorns.

Lord, help me to understand and be faithful to Your teachings. I know there are times when I backslide and act as if I was born among thorns, but I honestly believe You placed me in fertile soil. Help me to stay there. Amen.

He Who Has Ears …

Mark 4:21-25: *[21] He said to them, "Is a lamp brought in to be placed under a bushel basket or under a bed, and not to be placed on a lampstand? [22] For there is nothing hidden except to be made visible; nothing is secret except to come to light. [23] Anyone who has ears to hear ought to hear." [24] He also told them, "Take care what you hear. The measure with which you measure will be measured out to you, and still more will be given to you. [25] To the one who has, more will be given; from the one who has not, even what he has will be taken away."*

Luke 8:16-18: *[16] "No one who lights a lamp conceals it with a vessel or sets it under a bed; rather, he places it on a lampstand so that those who enter may see the light. [17] For there is nothing hidden that will not become visible, and nothing secret that will not be known and come to light. [18] Take care, then, how you hear. To anyone who has, more will be given, and from the one who has not, even what he seems to have will be taken away."*

Matthew 5:15: *Nor do they light a lamp and then put it under a bushel basket; it is set on a lampstand, where it gives light to all in the house.*

Matthew 7:2: *For as you judge, so will you be judged, and the measure with which you measure will be measured out to you.*

Matthew 10:26: *"Therefore do not be afraid of them. Nothing is concealed that will not be revealed, nor secret that will not be known.*

Matthew 13:12: *To anyone who has, more will be given, and he will grow rich; from anyone who has not, even what he has will be taken away.*

The passages in Mark and Luke are depicted as following upon the previous passages. The passages from Matthew reflect places in his gospel that reflect the same sentiments.

What I learn here is that all we learn about our Lord and God we should seek to understand and then share what we learn with others. As in the previous passages, I believe Jesus is still addressing His Apostles. He is instructing them that what He explains to them should be understood and then explained to all. *"Take care, then, how you hear. To anyone who has, more will be given, and from the one who has not, even what he seems to have will be taken away."* Jesus is telling us that unless we strive to understand, we will lose what we have. The more we strive to understand, and the more we share what we know, the more will be revealed to us.

Lord, I will strive to understand all you are teaching us. Help me to never give up on the search. Amen.

Parable of the Seed Growing Secretly

Mark 4:26-29: *²⁶ He said, "This is how it is with the kingdom of God; it is as if a man were to scatter seed on the land ²⁷ and would sleep and rise night and day and the seed would sprout and grow, he knows not how. ²⁸ Of its own accord the land yields fruit, first the blade, then the ear, then the full grain in the ear. ²⁹ And when the grain is ripe, he wields the sickle at once, for the harvest has come."*

We must realize that we will never know how everything exists and works. We can observe God's creation. We can study God's creation. We can analyze God's creation. And some things we will understand. But the secrets of God's creation are known only to Him and to those few of us to whom He chooses to unveil some of them. It is up to us to accept what is, to observe and to question, but always to accept.

Lord, acceptance is difficult, especially when the current condition is contrary to what we believe is right. Help me to always work to improve what we have, but to accept rather than cry out and rebel. Amen.

Parable of the Tares (Weeds)

Matthew 13:24-30: *²⁴ He proposed another parable to them. "The kingdom of heaven may be likened to a man who sowed good seed in his field. ²⁵ While everyone was asleep his enemy came and sowed weeds all through the wheat, and then went off. ²⁶ When the crop grew and bore fruit, the weeds appeared as well. ²⁷ The slaves of the householder came to him and said, 'Master, did you not sow good seed in your field?*

Where have the weeds come from?' [28] *He answered, 'An enemy has done this.' His slaves said to him, 'Do you want us to go and pull them up?'* [29] *He replied, 'No, if you pull up the weeds you might uproot the wheat along with them.* [30] *Let them grow together until harvest; then at harvest time I will say to the harvesters, "First collect the weeds and tie them in bundles for burning; but gather the wheat into my barn. "*

The weeds and wheat growing together are what we see on a daily basis in our normal lives. We are living out this parable. We are the wheat. The enemy is Satan. And the weeds are the people who are following the way of the world. It is on judgment day that the weeds will be separated from the wheat and burned. Although Jesus speaks in terms that people are familiar with, they do not always understand. As Jesus said earlier, "Anyone who has ears to hear ought to hear."

Lord, help me to both hear and understand the words You speak to us. Amen.

Parables of the Mustard Seed and Leaven

<u>Matthew 13:31-33:</u> [31] *He proposed another parable to them. "The kingdom of heaven is like a mustard seed that a person took and sowed in a field.* [32] *It is the smallest of all the seeds, yet when full-grown it is the largest of plants. It becomes a large bush, and the 'birds of the sky come and dwell in its branches.'"* [33] *He spoke to them another parable. "The kingdom of heaven is like yeast that a woman took and mixed with three measures of wheat flour until the whole batch was leavened."*

Mark 4:30-32: *[30] He said, "To what shall we compare the kingdom of God, or what parable can we use for it? [31] It is like a mustard seed that, when it is sown in the ground, is the smallest of all the seeds on the earth. [32] But once it is sown, it springs up and becomes the largest of plants and puts forth large branches, so that the birds of the sky can dwell in its shade."*

Luke 13:18-19: *[18] Then he said, "What is the kingdom of God like? To what can I compare it? [19] It is like a mustard seed that a person took and planted in the garden. When it was fully grown, it became a large bush and 'the birds of the sky dwelt in its branches.'" [20] Again he said, "To what shall I compare the kingdom of God? [21] It is like yeast that a woman took and mixed [in] with three measures of wheat flour until the whole batch of dough was leavened."*

The smallest of all the seeds is what He calls it. Our Lord is the seed that was planted 2,000 years ago and now His body consists of over a billion people. Going back even further and using Abraham as the seed and now the body is over two billion people who profess belief in the one true God. The Kingdom of God is like this. This is a message of hope from our Lord – the hope for the manifestation of the Kingdom of God, the Church. Hope for something better must fill our hearts or we will have nothing to live for.

However, the kingdom does not grow on its own; something must be injected to help it grow. So, what is our leaven? Is it the message of hope? Is it love? Is it faith? It is all of the above. Faith, hope, and love will fill us with the drive to learn more and to do more, to be part of our Lord's body – His Kingdom.

232

Lord, You are my faith. You are my hope. You are my love.
Fill me. Quench my thirst. Give me something to live for
and to grow for. Amen.

Jesus' Use of Parables

Matthew 13:34-35: *[34] All these things Jesus spoke to the crowds in parables. He spoke to them only in parables, [35] to fulfill what had been said through the prophet: "I will open my mouth in parables, I will announce what has lain hidden from the foundation [of the world]." [36] Then, dismissing the crowds, he went into the house. His disciples approached him and said, "Explain to us the parable of the weeds in the field." [37] He said in reply, "He who sows good seed is the Son of Man, [38] the field is the world, the good seed the children of the kingdom. The weeds are the children of the evil one, [39] and the enemy who sows them is the devil. The harvest is the end of the age, and the harvesters are angels. [40] Just as weeds are collected and burned [up] with fire, so will it be at the end of the age. [41] The Son of Man will send his angels, and they will collect out of his kingdom all who cause others to sin and all evildoers. [42] They will throw them into the fiery furnace, where there will be wailing and grinding of teeth. [43] Then the righteous will shine like the sun in the kingdom of their Father. Whoever has ears ought to hear.*

Mark 4:33-34: *[33] With many such parables he spoke the word to them as they were able to understand it. [34] Without parables he did not speak to them, but to his own disciples he explained everything in private.*

All these things Jesus spoke to the crowds in parables.
But to His disciples he explained everything in private. How
I envy the disciples who accompanied Jesus. Several years

233

ago, I attended a three-day retreat. The retreat master was captivating in his talks. At this time, however, I cannot recall what he spoke about; but that does not matter here. Every evening, we would gather with the retreat master in the common room of the retreat house. We would simply talk about anything and everything: the topics of the talks that day or the day before, or just anything that came to our minds. It was wonderful. It was casual. It was comfortable. And it was informative. I can picture Jesus and His disciples sitting in someone's home or around a camp fire doing the same thing. Jesus explained His teachings to His disciples. Here, he would go into details He could not or would not with the crowds. Here He would prepare His disciples for their mission. There is so much that can be learned in private conversation that is not simply a Q&A session after a talk.

Lord, open up my mind and my heart to what it is that You would have me learn. I look forward to the discussions in private that we will have in Your kingdom. Amen.

Parables: Hidden Treasure, Pearl, Net, Treasures New and Old

<u>Matthew 13:44-52:</u> *⁴⁴"The kingdom of heaven is like a treasure buried in a field, which a person finds and hides again, and out of joy goes and sells all that he has and buys that field. ⁴⁵ Again, the kingdom of heaven is like a merchant searching for fine pearls. ⁴⁶ When he finds a pearl of great price, he goes and sells all that he has and buys it. ⁴⁷ Again, the kingdom of heaven is like a net thrown into the sea, which collects fish of every kind. ⁴⁸ When it is full they haul it ashore and sit down to put what is good into buckets. What is bad they throw away. ⁴⁹ Thus it will be at the end of the age. The angels*

234

will go out and separate the wicked from the righteous ^{50} *and throw them into the fiery furnace, where there will be wailing and grinding of teeth.* ^{51} *"Do you understand all these things?"* *They answered, "Yes."* ^{52} *And he replied, "Then every scribe who has been instructed in the kingdom of heaven is like the head of a household who brings from his storeroom both the new and the old."*

Whether we are conscious of it or not, whether we want to admit it or not, we are always in search of that special treasure. We may not recognize it until we find it. We may work hard for it or happen upon it. However, when we come across it and recognize it, we will do whatever is necessary to keep it. It does not matter how much we already have. A treasure is a treasure is a treasure; and we must have it.

It is important for us to recognize the treasures we come across in the way of wisdom as well. We obviously do not know everything. So, to be completely honest, we are more likely to come across treasures of knowledge and understanding rather than of material value. We need to be able to store those up and call upon them as we need them. The teachings of Jesus, His wisdom, is one of those treasures.

Lord, open my mind and my heart to find what You are leading me to. The treasure I seek should always be You. Help me to stay on track. Amen.

Healing at the Pool at Bethesda

<u>John 5:1-47:</u> ^{1} *After this, there was a feast of the Jews, and Jesus went up to Jerusalem.* ^{2} *Now there is in Jerusalem at the Sheep [Gate] a pool called in Hebrew Bethesda, with five porticoes.* ^{3} *In these lay a large number of ill, blind, lame, and*

235

crippled. [⁴ *]* ⁵ *One man was there who had been ill for thirty-eight years.* ⁶ *When Jesus saw him lying there and knew that he had been ill for a long time, he said to him, "Do you want to be well?"* ⁷ *The sick man answered him, "Sir, I have no one to put me into the pool when the water is stirred up; while I am on my way, someone else gets down there before me."* ⁸ *Jesus said to him, "Rise, take up your mat, and walk."* ⁹ *Immediately the man became well, took up his mat, and walked. Now that day was a sabbath.* ¹⁰ *So the Jews said to the man who was cured, "It is the sabbath, and it is not lawful for you to carry your mat."* ¹¹ *He answered them, "The man who made me well told me, 'Take up your mat and walk.'"* ¹² *They asked him, "Who is the man who told you, 'Take it up and walk'?"* ¹³ *The man who was healed did not know who it was, for Jesus had slipped away, since there was a crowd there.* ¹⁴ *After this Jesus found him in the temple area and said to him, "Look, you are well; do not sin any more so that nothing worse may happen to you."* ¹⁵ *The man went and told the Jews that Jesus was the one who had made him well.* ¹⁶ *Therefore, the Jews began to persecute Jesus because he did this on a sabbath.* ¹⁷ *But Jesus answered them, "My Father is at work until now, so I am at work."* ¹⁸ *For this reason the Jews tried all the more to kill him, because he not only broke the sabbath, but he also called God his own father, making himself equal to God.* ¹⁹ *Jesus answered and said to them, "Amen, amen, I say to you, a son cannot do anything on his own, but only what he sees his father doing; for what he does, his son will do also.* ²⁰ *For the Father loves his Son and shows him everything that he himself does, and he will show him greater works than these, so that you may be amazed.* ²¹ *For just as the Father raises the dead and gives life, so also does the Son give life to whomever he wishes.* ²² *Nor does the Father judge anyone, but he has given all judgment to his Son,* ²³ *so that all may honor the Son just as they honor the Father. Whoever does not honor the Son does* *not honor the Father who sent him. ²⁴ Amen, amen, I say to you, whoever hears my word and believes in the one who sent me has eternal life and will not come to condemnation but has passed from death to life. ²⁵ Amen, amen, I say to you, the hour is coming and is now here when the dead will hear the voice of the Son of God, and those who hear will live. ²⁶ For just as the Father has life in himself, so also he gave to his Son the possession of life in himself. ²⁷ And he gave him power to exercise judgment, because he is the Son of Man. ²⁸ Do not be amazed at this, because the hour is coming in which all who are in the tombs will hear his voice ²⁹ and will come out, those who have done good deeds to the resurrection of life, but those who have done wicked deeds to the resurrection of condemnation. ³⁰ "I cannot do anything on my own; I judge as I hear, and my judgment is just, because I do not seek my own will but the will of the one who sent me. ³¹ "If I testify on my own behalf, my testimony cannot be verified. ³² But there is another who testifies on my behalf, and I know that the testimony he gives on my behalf is true. ³³ You sent emissaries to John, and he testified to the truth. ³⁴ I do not accept testimony from a human being, but I say this so that you may be saved. ³⁵ He was a burning and shining lamp, and for a while you were content to rejoice in his light. ³⁶ But I have testimony greater than John's. The works that the Father gave me to accomplish, these works that I perform testify on my behalf that the Father has sent me. ³⁷ Moreover, the Father who sent me has testified on my behalf. But you have never heard his voice nor seen his form, ³⁸ and you do not have his word remaining in you, because you do not believe in the one whom he has sent. ³⁹ You search the scriptures, because you think you have eternal life through them; even they testify on my behalf. ⁴⁰ But you do not want to come to me to have life. ⁴¹ "I do not accept human praise; ⁴² moreover, I know that you do not have the love of God in you. ⁴³ I came in the name of my*

Father, but you do not accept me; yet if another comes in his own name, you will accept him. [44] How can you believe, when you accept praise from one another and do not seek the praise that comes from the only God? [45] Do not think that I will accuse you before the Father: the one who will accuse you is Moses, in whom you have placed your hope. [46] For if you had believed Moses, you would have believed me, because he wrote about me. [47] But if you do not believe his writings, how will you believe my words?"

There is a lot to learn from this story. So much so that I will take it in segments.

In this particular case, Jesus went to the man who was ill and offered to heal him rather than the man seeking a healing from Jesus. This is not the first time. Jesus has shown His compassion on other occasions. And even though the sabbath only occurs once in seven days, this healing was on the sabbath. It is not necessary to go into the ramifications of this. This has happened in the past and we know how the scribes and Pharisees react to this. However, there is one little statement here that is not common.

Jesus said, *"Look, you are well; do not sin anymore, so that nothing worse may happen to you."* For years, when I was young, I thought that if the man sinned again, his illness that he had for thirty-eight years would come back. All Jesus is saying is that, if he does not follow the straight and narrow path, some worse mishap may come upon him. Not "will" but "may." It was a warning, a precaution, not a threat. When God heals someone, the healing is real; not just a relief of symptoms that will return later.

Jesus said to the Jews who were persecuting Him, *"My Father is at work until now, so I am at work."* The day of the week does not matter; God, Jesus' Father, works always, not just on certain days of the week or times of the day. So,

238

Jesus follows what His Father does. Sons learn from their fathers. They generally model their lives after what they see in their fathers.

He went on, *"For just as the Father raises the dead and gives life, so also does the Son give life to whomever he wishes."* As the Son of God, Jesus can do what He chooses: healing whoever He wants, giving life to whoever He chooses. And He can pass this power on to whoever he chooses. Up to this point, Jesus has not said so much about His relationship with His Father to the Jews. He may have in His talks with His disciples apart from the crowds, but not directly to the Jews. This is a special passage in the Gospels.

"I cannot do anything on my own; I judge as I hear, and my judgment is just, because I do not seek my own will but the will of the one who sent me." He said it before and He says it again, He is here to do the will of His Father. Here is where Jesus testifies to the authenticity and mission of John the Baptist, His precursor. But an even greater than John foretold of Jesus' coming, Moses himself.

In this passage, we have a healing; but that is only a lead in to a justification of Jesus' power and authority. He is the Son of God. He is here to do the Will of His Father in heaven. He has the power to heal, to command nature, to exorcize demons, and to give life. Jesus is God.

Lord, You have the power to heal, to command nature, to exorcize demons, and to give life. You are here to fulfill the Will of Your Father. All of this You have shown. Why is it so hard for us to accept? Help me to KNOW this and show this in all I say and do. Amen.

239

Herod and John the Baptist

Matthew 14:1-12: *[1] At that time Herod the tetrarch heard of the reputation of Jesus [2] and said to his servants, "This man is John the Baptist. He has been raised from the dead; that is why mighty powers are at work in him." [3] Now Herod had arrested John, bound [him], and put him in prison on account of Herodias, the wife of his brother Philip, [4] for John had said to him, "It is not lawful for you to have her." [5] Although he wanted to kill him, he feared the people, for they regarded him as a prophet. [6] But at a birthday celebration for Herod, the daughter of Herodias performed a dance before the guests and delighted Herod [7] so much that he swore to give her whatever she might ask for. [8] Prompted by her mother, she said, "Give me here on a platter the head of John the Baptist." [9] The king was distressed, but because of his oaths and the guests who were present, he ordered that it be given, [10] and he had John beheaded in the prison. [11] His head was brought in on a platter and given to the girl, who took it to her mother. [12] His disciples came and took away the corpse and buried him; and they went and told Jesus.*

Mark 6:14-29: *[14] King Herod heard about it, for his fame had become widespread, and people were saying, "John the Baptist has been raised from the dead; that is why mighty powers are at work in him." [15] Others were saying, "He is Elijah"; still others, "He is a prophet like any of the prophets." [16] But when Herod learned of it, he said, "It is John whom I beheaded. He has been raised up." [17] Herod was the one who had John arrested and bound in prison on account of Herodias, the wife of his brother Philip, whom he had married. [18] John had said to Herod, "It is not lawful for you to have your brother's wife." [19] Herodias harbored a grudge against him and wanted to kill him but was unable to do so. [20] Herod feared John,* *knowing him to be a righteous and holy man, and kept him in custody. When he heard him speak, he was very much perplexed; yet he liked to listen to him.* [21] *She had an opportunity one day when Herod, on his birthday, gave a banquet for his courtiers, his military officers, and the leading men of Galilee.* [22] *Herodias's own daughter came in and performed a dance that delighted Herod and his guests. The king said to the girl, "Ask of me whatever you wish, and I will grant it to you."* [23] *He even swore [many things] to her, "I will grant you whatever you ask of me, even to half of my kingdom."* [24] *She went out and said to her mother, "What shall I ask for?" She replied, "The head of John the Baptist."* [25] *The girl hurried back to the king's presence and made her request, "I want you to give me at once on a platter the head of John the Baptist."* [26] *The king was deeply distressed, but because of his oaths and the guests he did not wish to break his word to her.* [27] *So he promptly dispatched an executioner with orders to bring back his head. He went off and beheaded him in the prison.* [28] *He brought in the head on a platter and gave it to the girl. The girl in turn gave it to her mother.* [29] *When his disciples heard about it, they came and took his body and laid it in a tomb.*

Luke 9:7-9: [7] *Herod the tetrarch heard about all that was happening, and he was greatly perplexed because some were saying, "John has been raised from the dead"; [8] others were saying, "Elijah has appeared"; still others, "One of the ancient prophets has arisen."* [9] *But Herod said, "John I beheaded. Who then is this about whom I hear such things?" And he kept trying to see him.*

Luke 3:19-20: [19] *Now Herod the tetrarch, who had been censured by him because of Herodias, his brother's wife, and* *because of all the evil deeds Herod had committed, [20] added still another to these by [also] putting John in prison.*

This story of Herod and John the Baptist does not give me much insight into Jesus, His teachings, and His works. However, it does give some insight into both Herod and John the Baptist.

Herod shows up later in the gospels in relation to Jesus' trial during the time of His passion and death. Herod is depicted as a man suffering from mental torment, and this story explains some of what was behind that torment. The fact that Herod is unstable in confirmed during the passion trial.

John the Baptist was outspoken in His righteousness. It is what ultimately caused the loss of His life. The specific circumstances that led up to his death make for an interesting story. A question does come up related to John and these circumstances. Actually, it is a question of martyrdom and possibilities. If John had not accused Herod, would his ministry have continued? Would he have been able to bring more souls to repentance and to God? Obviously, we will never know the answer to that. However, what we do know is that John said he must decrease, and Jesus must increase. The focus had to move to Jesus. John's ministry had to change to something other than an itinerant preacher. It seems that John was following the Will of God in his encounters with Herod.

Lord, as I learn more and more about You and doing the Will of Your Father, I realize that I should not be trying to second guess His will. I should not be trying to analyze woulda, coulda, shoulda moments. I need to accept what is and focus on what is Your will for me. Amen.

The Feeding of the Five Thousand

<u>Matthew 14:13-21:</u> *[13] When Jesus heard of it, he withdrew in a boat to a deserted place by himself. The crowds heard of this and followed him on foot from their towns. [14] When he disembarked and saw the vast crowd, his heart was moved with pity for them, and he cured their sick. [15] When it was evening, the disciples approached him and said, "This is a deserted place and it is already late; dismiss the crowds so that they can go to the villages and buy food for themselves." [16] [Jesus] said to them, "There is no need for them to go away; give them some food yourselves." [17] But they said to him, "Five loaves and two fish are all we have here." [18] Then he said, "Bring them here to me," [19] and he ordered the crowds to sit down on the grass. Taking the five loaves and the two fish, and looking up to heaven, he said the blessing, broke the loaves, and gave them to the disciples, who in turn gave them to the crowds. [20] They all ate and were satisfied, and they picked up the fragments left over—twelve wicker baskets full. [21] Those who ate were about five thousand men, not counting women and children.*

<u>Mark 6:30-44:</u> *[30] The Apostles gathered together with Jesus and reported all they had done and taught. [31] He said to them, "Come away by yourselves to a deserted place and rest a while." People were coming and going in great numbers, and they had no opportunity even to eat. [32] So they went off in the boat by themselves to a deserted place. [33] People saw them leaving and many came to know about it. They hastened there on foot from all the towns and arrived at the place before them. [34] When he disembarked and saw the vast crowd, his heart was moved with pity for them, for they were like sheep without a shepherd; and he began to teach them many things. [35] By now it was already late, and his disciples approached him and said, "This is a deserted place, and it is*

already very late. ³⁶ Dismiss them so that they can go to the surrounding farms and villages and buy themselves something to eat." ³⁷ He said to them in reply, "Give them some food yourselves." But they said to him, "Are we to buy two hundred days' wages worth of food and give it to them to eat?" ³⁸ He asked them, "How many loaves do you have? Go and see." And when they had found out they said, "Five loaves and two fish." ³⁹ So he gave orders to have them sit down in groups on the green grass. ⁴⁰The people took their places in rows by hundreds and by fifties. ⁴¹ Then, taking the five loaves and the two fish and looking up to heaven, he said the blessing, broke the loaves, and gave them to [his] disciples to set before the people; he also divided the two fish among them all. ⁴² They all ate and were satisfied. ⁴³ And they picked up twelve wicker baskets full of fragments and what was left of the fish. ⁴⁴ Those who ate [of the loaves] were five thousand men.

Luke 9:10-17: *¹⁰ When the Apostles returned, they explained to him what they had done. He took them and withdrew in private to a town called Bethsaida. ¹¹ The crowds, meanwhile, learned of this and followed him. He received them and spoke to them about the kingdom of God, and he healed those who needed to be cured. ¹² As the day was drawing to a close, the Twelve approached him and said, "Dismiss the crowd so that they can go to the surrounding villages and farms and find lodging and provisions; for we are in a deserted place here." ¹³ He said to them, "Give them some food yourselves." They replied, "Five loaves and two fish are all we have, unless we ourselves go and buy food for all these people." ¹⁴ Now the men there numbered about five thousand. Then he said to his disciples, "Have them sit down in groups of [about] fifty." ¹⁵ They did so and made them all sit down. ¹⁶ Then taking the five loaves and the two fish, and looking up to heaven, he said the blessing over them, broke them, and gave them to the disciples to set before the crowd.* [17] *They all ate and were satisfied. And when the leftover fragments were picked up, they filled twelve wicker baskets.*

John 6:1-15: [1] *After this, Jesus went across the Sea of Galilee [of Tiberias].* [2] *A large crowd followed him, because they saw the signs he was performing on the sick.* [3] *Jesus went up on the mountain, and there he sat down with his disciples.* [4] *The Jewish feast of Passover was near.* [5] *When Jesus raised his eyes and saw that a large crowd was coming to him, he said to Philip, "Where can we buy enough food for them to eat?"* [6] *He said this to test him, because he himself knew what he was going to do.* [7] *Philip answered him, "Two hundred days' wages worth of food would not be enough for each of them to have a little [bit]."* [8] *One of his disciples, Andrew, the brother of Simon Peter, said to him,* [9] *"There is a boy here who has five barley loaves and two fish; but what good are these for so many?"* [10] *Jesus said, "Have the people recline." Now there was a great deal of grass in that place. So, the men reclined, about five thousand in number.* [11] *Then Jesus took the loaves, gave thanks, and distributed them to those who were reclining, and also as much of the fish as they wanted.* [12] *When they had had their fill, he said to his disciples, "Gather the fragments left over, so that nothing will be wasted."* [13] *So they collected them, and filled twelve wicker baskets with fragments from the five barley loaves that had been more than they could eat.* [14] *When the people saw the sign he had done, they said, "This is truly the Prophet, the one who is to come into the world."* [15] *Since Jesus knew that they were going to come and carry him off to make him king, he withdrew again to the mountain alone.*

I want to acknowledge something I heard in the homily at Mass this morning. The Gospel was the Feeding of the

Five Thousand. Our Pastor commented on the phrase "His heart was moved with pity." This acknowledgement of compassion in our Lord is not a typical Jewish expression. This translation is more modern. The typical Jewish expression would be related to the gut, not the heart, such as gut-wrenching. So, gut-wrenching would be the expression used by Jews to reflect compassion. Just a bit of trivia to store up. Jesus' compassion for people is brought out many times in the Gospel, so this instance is not unexpected.

After the people were seated in groups, Jesus said a blessing over the meal. The Gospels do not say if this was a spontaneous prayer or if it was a typical blessing prayer. It obviously was not the typical Catholic meal blessing: "bless us, O Lord, and these Thy gifts ..." I googled "Jewish meal blessing prayer" and was provided two possibilities. The first: "Blessed is the Oneness that makes us holy. Blessed is the Creator of the fruit of the vine." The second: "Blessed are You, Lord our God, Ruler of the universe, Who brings forth bread from the earth." It does not matter what form the blessing took. The Gospels do not indicate whether or not He explicitly called the bread and fish to multiply. I guess that is why there is so much dialogue around the idea of the "miracle" of the loaves and fishes. What is important to get out of this story is that, because of the compassion of our Lord on the crowd of more than 5,000, everyone was fed to their satisfaction and there was a great amount of food left over.

Then, *"Jesus knew that they were going to come and carry Him off to make him king, He withdrew again to the mountain alone."* Here, as in other instances in the Gospels, Jesus avoids the crowds who want to make Him king. After exerting Himself to help the crowds, Jesus once again goes off to be by Himself (probably to pray and recuperate).

246

Lord, when I am weary after a hard day, I want to rest. I seldom ever go off to pray. Help me to use that time to give You praise and thanksgiving as only You deserve before I lay down to rest. Amen.

Walking on the Water

<u>Matthew 14:22-33:</u> *[22] Then he made the disciples get into the boat and precede him to the other side, while he dismissed the crowds. [23] After doing so, he went up on the mountain by himself to pray. When it was evening, he was there alone. [24] Meanwhile the boat, already a few miles offshore, was being tossed about by the waves, for the wind was against it. [25] During the fourth watch of the night, he came toward them, walking on the sea. [26] When the disciples saw him walking on the sea, they were terrified. "It is a ghost," they said, and they cried out in fear. [27] At once [Jesus] spoke to them, "Take courage, it is I; do not be afraid." [28] Peter said to him in reply, "Lord, if it is you, command me to come to you on the water." [29] He said, "Come." Peter got out of the boat and began to walk on the water toward Jesus. [30] But when he saw how [strong] the wind was, he became frightened; and, beginning to sink, he cried out, "Lord, save me!" [31] Immediately Jesus stretched out his hand and caught him, and said to him, "O you of little faith, why did you doubt?" [32] After they got into the boat, the wind died down. [33] Those, who were in the boat, did him homage, saying, "Truly, you are the Son of God."*

<u>Mark 6:45-52:</u> *[45] Then he made his disciples get into the boat and precede him to the other side toward Bethsaida, while he dismissed the crowd. [46] And when he had taken leave of them, he went off to the mountain to pray. [47] When it was evening, the boat was far out on the sea, and he was alone on*

shore. ⁴⁸ Then he saw that they were tossed about while rowing, for the wind was against them. About the fourth watch of the night, he came toward them walking on the sea. He meant to pass by them. ⁴⁹ But when they saw him walking on the sea, they thought it was a ghost and cried out. ⁵⁰ They had all seen him and were terrified. But at once he spoke with them, "Take courage, it is I, do not be afraid!" ⁵¹ He got into the boat with them and the wind died down. They were [completely] astounded. ⁵² They had not understood the incident of the loaves. On the contrary, their hearts were hardened.

John 6:16-21: *¹⁶ When it was evening, his disciples went down to the sea, ¹⁷ embarked in a boat, and went across the sea to Capernaum. It had already grown dark, and Jesus had not yet come to them. ¹⁸ The sea was stirred up because a strong wind was blowing. ¹⁹ When they had rowed about three or four miles, they saw Jesus walking on the sea and coming near the boat; and they began to be afraid. ²⁰ But he said to them, "It is I. Do not be afraid." ²¹ They wanted to take him into the boat, but the boat immediately arrived at the shore to which they were heading.*

He went off by Himself in order to pray. This is another instance of Jesus' taking time to be alone and to commune with His Father.

One of the things that has bothered me about this story is that, throughout the Gospels, Jesus never performed a miracle to help Himself. So, why was He walking on water to get to His Apostles? The only answer I came up with is that it was to test their faith. And that He did! As seemingly appropriate, Simon Peter was the chosen one. Realistically, Jesus could have sustained Peter's ability to walk on the water; but if He did, then it would not have been Peter's faith that allowed Him to do it. It was the test of faith that was the central point of this passage.

Lord, I am always fearful You will test my faith, and I will fail. I should not be. An example is right here. Even though Peter's faith was not strong enough to sustain his walk, Jesus forgave his weakness and gave him more chances to prove himself. I believe that, in Your love for me, You would give me another chance as well. Amen.

Healings at Gennesaret

Matthew 14:34-36: *[34] After making the crossing, they came to land at Gennesaret. [35] When the men of that place recognized him, they sent word to all the surrounding country. People brought to him all those who were sick [36] and begged him that they might touch only the tassel on his cloak, and as many as touched it were healed.*

Mark 6:53-56: *[53] After making the crossing, they came to land at Gennesaret and tied up there. [54] As they were leaving the boat, people immediately recognized him. [55] They scurried about the surrounding country and began to bring in the sick on mats to wherever they heard he was. [56] Whatever villages or towns or countryside he entered, they laid the sick in the marketplaces and begged him that they might touch only the tassel on his cloak; and as many as touched it were healed.*

John 6:22-25: *[22] The next day, the crowd that remained across the sea saw that there had been only one boat there, and that Jesus had not gone along with his disciples in the boat, but only his disciples had left. [23] Other boats came from Tiberias near the place where they had eaten the bread when the Lord gave thanks. [24] When the crowd saw that neither Jesus nor his* *disciples were there, they themselves got into boats and came to Capernaum looking for Jesus. ²⁵ And when they found him across the sea they said to him, "Rabbi, when did you get here?"*

The crowds continued to pursue Him. Their faith was strong, even if only in His healing power. And their faith was rewarded. Jesus traveled from village-to-village teaching and healing.

Lord, you spoke of faith the size of a mustard seed. For some among those taught and healed, I hope their faith grew. I hope my faith is growing as I study Your life and teachings. Amen.

The Bread of Life

<u>John 6:26-59</u>: *²⁶ Jesus answered them and said, "Amen, amen, I say to you, you are looking for me not because you saw signs but because you ate the loaves and were filled. ²⁷ Do not work for food that perishes but for the food that endures for eternal life, which the Son of Man will give you. For on him the Father, God, has set his seal." ²⁸ So they said to him, "What can we do to accomplish the works of God?" ²⁹ Jesus answered and said to them, "This is the work of God, that you believe in the one he sent." ³⁰ So they said to him, "What sign can you do, that we may see and believe in you? What can you do? ³¹ Our ancestors ate manna in the desert, as it is written: 'He gave them bread from heaven to eat.'" ³² So Jesus said to them, "Amen, amen, I say to you, it was not Moses who gave the bread from heaven; my Father gives you the true bread from heaven. ³³ For the bread of God is that which comes down from heaven and gives life to the world." ³⁴ So they said to him, "Sir,*

give us this bread always." *35* Jesus said to them, "I am the bread of life; whoever comes to me will never hunger, and whoever believes in me will never thirst. *36* But I told you that although you have seen [me], you do not believe. *37* Everything that the Father gives me will come to me, and I will not reject anyone who comes to me, *38* because I came down from heaven not to do my own will but the will of the one who sent me. *39* And this is the will of the one who sent me, that I should not lose anything of what he gave me, but that I should raise it [on] the last day. *40* For this is the will of my Father, that everyone who sees the Son and believes in him may have eternal life, and I shall raise him [on] the last day." *41* The Jews murmured about him because he said, "I am the bread that came down from heaven," *42* and they said, "Is this not Jesus, the son of Joseph? Do we not know his father and mother? Then how can he say, 'I have come down from heaven'?" *43* Jesus answered and said to them, "Stop murmuring among yourselves. *44* No one can come to me unless the Father who sent me draw him, and I will raise him on the last day. *45* It is written in the prophets: 'They shall all be taught by God.' Everyone who listens to my Father and learns from him comes to me. *46* Not that anyone has seen the Father except the one who is from God; he has seen the Father. *47* Amen, amen, I say to you, whoever believes has eternal life. *48* I am the bread of life. *49* Your ancestors ate the manna in the desert, but they died; *50* this is the bread that comes down from heaven so that one may eat it and not die. *51* I am the living bread that came down from heaven; whoever eats this bread will live forever; and the bread that I will give is my flesh for the life of the world." *52* The Jews quarreled among themselves, saying, "How can this man give us [his] flesh to eat?" *53* Jesus said to them, "Amen, amen, I say to you, unless you eat the flesh of the Son of Man and drink his blood, you do not have life within you. *54* Whoever eats my flesh and *drinks my blood has eternal life, and I will raise him on the last day. [55] For my flesh is true food, and my blood is true drink. [56] Whoever eats my flesh and drinks my blood remains in me and I in him. [57] Just as the living Father sent me and I have life because of the Father, so also the one who feeds on me will have life because of me. [58] This is the bread that came down from heaven. Unlike your ancestors who ate and still died, whoever eats this bread will live forever." [59] These things he said while teaching in the synagogue in Capernaum.*

One lesson I learn here is that Jesus was always honest with the people He encountered. It was not only scribes and Pharisees that He challenged, but He also challenged the common folk. Here, Jesus confronts them for why they follow Him. Accepting and acknowledging the truth is ever important. He has been performing miracles throughout the region. Many were witnessed by the very people who have come to Him; yet they ask Him for a sign. A sign will not be given. Jesus does not perform for an audience.

Here is where Jesus introduces the Bread of Life. *"I am the bread of life; whoever comes to me will never hunger, and whoever believes in me will never thirst."* Here it starts to become confusing for the crowd. They are looking for an easy answer. They are looking for the benefit to them. *"Stop murmuring among yourselves. No one can come to me unless the Father who sent me draw him, and I will raise him on the last day."* More confusion, because they are looking for an answer for today, not for the last day. They are too grounded in the world. As we will see, some will begin to leave. *"I am the living bread that came down from heaven; whoever eats this bread will live forever; and the bread that I will give is my flesh for the life of the world. ... Whoever eats my flesh and drinks my blood has eternal life, and I will raise him on the last day."* Again, Jesus speaks about raising on the last day.

People have to grasp hold of the concept. What Jesus is presenting to us in the Eucharist, His living example, and all of His teachings is the way to live this life and prepare ourselves for our heavenly journey. The Israelites have been taught that the Messiah would be their earthly leader. Now they have to decide what is more important.

For today's Israelite, this choice is the same. This is not, however, the same choice we Christians have. Christians have to decide how far we are going to commit ourselves to what Jesus has taught through words and example. We have already accepted Him as our Messiah, not the one expected by the Jewish people. Jesus, our God, wants a full commitment from us. God is willing to forgive us our mistakes as we go, but we must be firm in the path we are taking. He wants our paths to lead to Him.

Lord, You are truly present in the Blessed Sacrament: body, blood, soul and divinity. It is Your true presence. Help me to always seek You out so I may have life eternal. Amen.

What Defiles a Person - Traditional and Real

<u>Matthew 15:1-20:</u> *[1] Then Pharisees and scribes came to Jesus from Jerusalem and said, [2] "Why do your disciples break the tradition of the elders? They do not wash [their] hands when they eat a meal." [3] He said to them in reply, "And why do you break the commandment of God for the sake of your tradition? [4] For God said, 'Honor your father and your mother,' and 'Whoever curses father or mother shall die.' [5] But you say, 'Whoever says to father or mother, "Any*

support you might have had from me is dedicated to God," [6] need not honor his father.' You have nullified the word of God for the sake of your tradition. [7] Hypocrites, well did Isaiah prophesy about you when he said: [8] 'This people honors me with their lips, but their hearts are far from me; [9] in vain do they worship me, teaching as doctrines human precepts.'"
[10] He summoned the crowd and said to them, "Hear and understand. [11] It is not what enters one's mouth that defiles that person; but what comes out of the mouth is what defiles one." [12] Then his disciples approached and said to him, "Do you know that the Pharisees took offense when they heard what you said?" [13] He said in reply, "Every plant that my heavenly Father has not planted will be uprooted. [14] Let them alone; they are blind guides (of the blind). If a blind person leads a blind person, both will fall into a pit." [15] Then Peter said to him in reply, "Explain [this] parable to us." [16] He said to them, "Are even you still without understanding? [17] Do you not realize that everything that enters the mouth passes into the stomach and is expelled into the latrine? [18] But the things that come out of the mouth come from the heart, and they defile. [19] For from the heart come evil thoughts, murder, adultery, unchastity, theft, false witness, blasphemy. [20] These are what defile a person, but to eat with unwashed hands does not defile."

Mark 7:1-23: *[1] Now when the Pharisees with some scribes who had come from Jerusalem gathered around him, [2] they observed that some of his disciples ate their meals with unclean, that is, unwashed, hands. [3] (For the Pharisees and, in fact, all Jews, do not eat without carefully washing their hands, keeping the tradition of the elders. [4] And on coming from the marketplace they do not eat without purifying themselves. And there are many other things that they have traditionally observed, the purification of cups and jugs and*

254

kettles [and beds].) ⁵ So the Pharisees and scribes questioned him, "Why do your disciples not follow the tradition of the elders but instead eat a meal with unclean hands?" ⁶ He responded, "Well did Isaiah prophesy about you hypocrites, as it is written: 'This people honors me with their lips, but their hearts are far from me; ⁷ In vain do they worship me, teaching as doctrines human precepts.' ⁸ You disregard God's commandment but cling to human tradition." ⁹ He went on to say, "How well you have set aside the commandment of God in order to uphold your tradition! ¹⁰ For Moses said, 'Honor your father and your mother,' and 'Whoever curses father or mother shall die.' ¹¹ Yet you say, 'If a person says to father or mother, "Any support you might have had from me is qorban"' (meaning, dedicated to God), ¹² you allow him to do nothing more for his father or mother. ¹³ You nullify the word of God in favor of your tradition that you have handed on. And you do many such things." ¹⁴ He summoned the crowd again and said to them, "Hear me, all of you, and understand. ¹⁵ Nothing that enters one from outside can defile that person; but the things that come out from within are what defile." [¹⁶] ¹⁷ When he got home away from the crowd his disciples questioned him about the parable. ¹⁸ He said to them, "Are even you likewise without understanding? Do you not realize that everything that goes into a person from outside cannot defile, ¹⁹ since it enters not the heart but the stomach and passes out into the latrine?" (Thus, he declared all foods clean.) ²⁰ "But what comes out of a person, that is what defiles. ²¹ From within people, from their hearts, come evil thoughts, unchastity, theft, murder, ²² adultery, greed, malice, deceit, licentiousness, envy, blasphemy, arrogance, folly. ²³ All these evils come from within, and they defile."

__Luke 11:37-41:__ *³⁷ After he had spoken, a Pharisee invited him to dine at his home. He entered and reclined at table to* *eat.* [38] *The Pharisee was amazed to see that he did not observe the prescribed washing before the meal.* [39] *The Lord said to him, "Oh you Pharisees! Although you cleanse the outside of the cup and the dish, inside you are filled with plunder and evil.* [40] *You fools! Did not the maker of the outside also make the inside?* [41] *But as to what is within, give alms, and behold, everything will be clean for you.*

<u>Luke 6:39:</u> *And he told them a parable, "Can a blind person guide a blind person? Will not both fall into a pit?*

  "Hypocrites, well did Isaiah prophesy about you when he said: 'This people honors me with their lips, but their hearts are far from me; in vain do they worship me, teaching as doctrines human precepts.'" Once again, we see the conflict between Jesus and the Pharisees. This is about the strict rules that the Pharisees of past ages formulated for the people. The social doctrines of society have no place in the doctrines of the faith. When Jesus speaks with the Pharisees, it seems that He is always somewhere between frustration and anger, yet He is always in control. This passage is very important for us because Jesus wants us to understand the reality of what we are told to do. We have to make the right decision and not follow hollow or false precepts.

  And there are times when He reaches frustration with His disciples as well. *"Do you not realize that everything that enters the mouth passes into the stomach and is expelled into the latrine? But the things that come out of the mouth come from the heart, and they defile. For from the heart come evil thoughts, murder, adultery, unchastity, theft, false witness, blasphemy. These are what defile a person, but to eat with unwashed hands does not defile."* His teaching here is very clear. *"Thus, He declared all foods clean."*

The conflicts will continue with the scribes, Pharisees, and Sanhedrin throughout the rest of Jesus life on earth. This is important for us to remember. The rules do not change simply because someone points out that they are wrong or unfair. The Jewish people will continue to follow the earthly precepts set down by their leaders centuries ago. It takes a choice to change our thinking, even when it is from wrong to right. That is part of what Jesus brought to us. That choice takes time to evolve enough to change a culture.

Lord, grant me the wisdom to know when I am being told the truth. Sometimes it is really difficult to know when someone is using their authority for personal gain. It is difficult to serve You in truth when I do not recognize it. Amen.

The Canaanite Woman

<u>Matthew 15:21-28:</u> *[21] Then Jesus went from that place and withdrew to the region of Tyre and Sidon. [22] And behold, a Canaanite woman of that district came and called out, "Have pity on me, Lord, Son of David! My daughter is tormented by a demon." [23] But he did not say a word in answer to her. His disciples came and asked him, "Send her away, for she keeps calling out after us." [24] He said in reply, "I was sent only to the lost sheep of the house of Israel." [25] But the woman came and did him homage, saying, "Lord, help me." [26] He said in reply, "It is not right to take the food of the children and throw it to the dogs." [27] She said, "Please, Lord, for even the dogs eat the scraps that fall from the table of their masters." [28] Then Jesus said to her in reply, "O woman, great is your faith! Let it be done for you as you wish." And her daughter was healed from that hour.*

Mark 7:24-30: *[24] From that place he went off to the district of Tyre. He entered a house and wanted no one to know about it, but he could not escape notice. [25] Soon a woman whose daughter had an unclean spirit heard about him. She came and fell at his feet. [26] The woman was a Greek, a Syrophoenician by birth, and she begged him to drive the demon out of her daughter. [27] He said to her, "Let the children be fed first. For it is not right to take the food of the children and throw it to the dogs." [28] She replied and said to him, "Lord, even the dogs under the table eat the children's scraps." [29] Then he said to her, "For saying this, you may go. The demon has gone out of your daughter." [30] When the woman went home, she found the child lying in bed and the demon gone.*

Here is another case where Jesus provides loving assistance to someone who shows strong faith. It does not relate whether or not she believed Jesus to be the Son of God; however, she certainly believed He had the power to heal. In this case also, like the Centurian, she believed He could do so at a distance. Her daughter's presence was not required for the healing. This incident emphasizes the importance of faith. She also accepted His word that her daughter was healed and went home.

Another important aspect of this encounter is that Jesus heard her and went out of His way to engage her in dialogue. The disciples were ready to push her aside as they probably usually as part of their crowd management; however, Jesus cares and He showed it to this non-Jew.

Lord, this Canaanite woman came to you seeking help for her daughter. You recognized the truth of her faith. Help me to discern the truth when it is presented to me. Amen.

Healing of a Deaf Mute and
Many Others

Matthew 15:29-31: [29] *Moving on from there Jesus walked by the Sea of Galilee, went up on the mountain, and sat down there.* [30] *Great crowds came to him, having with them the lame, the blind, the deformed, the mute, and many others. They placed them at his feet, and he cured them.* [31] *The crowds were amazed when they saw the mute speaking, the deformed made whole, the lame walking, and the blind able to see, and they glorified the God of Israel.*

Mark 7:31-37: [31] *Again he left the district of Tyre and went by way of Sidon to the Sea of Galilee, into the district of the Decapolis.* [32] *And people brought to him a deaf man who had a speech impediment and begged him to lay his hand on him.* [33] *He took him off by himself away from the crowd. He put his finger into the man's ears and, spitting, touched his tongue;* [34] *then he looked up to heaven and groaned, and said to him, "Ephphatha!" (that is, "Be opened!")* [35] *And [immediately] the man's ears were opened, his speech impediment was removed, and he spoke plainly.* [36] *He ordered them not to tell anyone. But the more he ordered them not to, the more they proclaimed it.* [37] *They were exceedingly astonished; and they said, "He has done all things well. He makes the deaf hear and [the] mute speak."*

Wherever Jesus went, the crowds gathered. Healings took place. Jesus taught. This is the story over and over again. And, as much as He cautioned people not to spread the word, they did. His popularity increased. All of this leads us here to the second feeding of the masses. That story is next.

At this point, however, I must look at what I learn from these few verses. Is it simply a repetition of what we have read before? The fact is that more people are beginning to believe. They are listening to what He is teaching. They want to hear what He has to say; and the amazing part is that, as He said Himself, He was here to fulfill the law, not to change it. He is a living example of what everyone should do in living their daily lives.

Lord, open my mind and my heart so that I can discern Your will for me, so that I can understand what it is You want me to learn. Amen.

Feeding of the Four Thousand

Matthew 15:32-39: *³² Jesus summoned his disciples and said, "My heart is moved with pity for the crowd, for they have been with me now for three days and have nothing to eat. I do not want to send them away hungry, for fear they may collapse on the way." ³³ The disciples said to him, "Where could we ever get enough bread in this deserted place to satisfy such a crowd?" ³⁴ Jesus said to them, "How many loaves do you have?" "Seven," they replied, "and a few fish." ³⁵ He ordered the crowd to sit down on the ground. ³⁶ Then he took the seven loaves and the fish, gave thanks, broke the loaves, and gave them to the disciples, who in turn gave them to the crowds. ³⁷ They all ate and were satisfied. They picked up the fragments left over—seven baskets full. ³⁸ Those who ate were four thousand men, not counting women and children. ³⁹ And when he had dismissed the crowds, he got into the boat and came to the district of Magadan.*

Mark 8:1-10: *¹ In those days when there again was a great crowd without anything to eat, he summoned the disciples and* said, [2] *"My heart is moved with pity for the crowd, because they have been with me now for three days and have nothing to eat. [3] If I send them away hungry to their homes, they will collapse on the way, and some of them have come a great distance." [4] His disciples answered him, "Where can anyone get enough bread to satisfy them here in this deserted place?" [5] Still he asked them, "How many loaves do you have?" "Seven," they replied. [6] He ordered the crowd to sit down on the ground. Then, taking the seven loaves he gave thanks, broke them, and gave them to his disciples to distribute, and they distributed them to the crowd. [7] They also had a few fish. He said the blessing over them and ordered them distributed also. [8] They ate and were satisfied. They picked up the fragments left over—seven baskets. [9] There were about four thousand people. He dismissed them [10] and got into the boat with his disciples and came to the region of Dalmanutha.*

Similar to the feeding of the five thousand related earlier in the Gospels, this reflects the compassion of our Lord on the crowds that have come to see Him, hear Him, and be cured by Him. Based on the area in which this took place, the crowd may have contained a significant number of Gentiles. The messages that Jesus gave to the crowd, I am sure, were the same given to the many crowds He taught in the past. The healings were similar as well. Although some people may have had some food with them, after three days there probably was not much to share with others. Our Lord was ever thoughtful of the people who came to Him.

Lord, You fed thousands out of compassion for their needs. Help me to love those I encounter with a love similar to Yours, keeping them foremost in my mind and heart. Amen.

The Pharisees Seek a Sign

Matthew 16:1-4: *[1] The Pharisees and Sadducees came and, to test him, asked him to show them a sign from heaven. [2] He said to them in reply, "[In the evening you say, 'Tomorrow will be fair, for the sky is red'; [3] and, in the morning, 'Today will be stormy, for the sky is red and threatening.' You know how to judge the appearance of the sky, but you cannot judge the signs of the times.] [4] An evil and unfaithful generation seeks a sign, but no sign will be given it except the sign of Jonah." Then he left them and went away.*

Matthew 12:38-39: *[38] Then some of the scribes and Pharisees said to him, "Teacher, we wish to see a sign from you." [39] He said to them in reply, "An evil and unfaithful generation seeks a sign, but no sign will be given it except the sign of Jonah the prophet.*

Mark 8:11-13: *[11] The Pharisees came forward and began to argue with him, seeking from him a sign from heaven to test him. [12] He sighed from the depth of his spirit and said, "Why does this generation seek a sign? Amen, I say to you, no sign will be given to this generation." [13] Then he left them, got into the boat again, and went off to the other shore.*

Luke 11:16: *Others, to test him, asked him for a sign from heaven.*

Luke 11:29: *While still more people gathered in the crowd, he said to them, "This generation is an evil generation; it seeks a sign, but no sign will be given it, except the sign of Jonah.*

Luke 12:54-56: *[54] He also said to the crowds, "When you see [a] cloud rising in the west you say immediately that it is going* *to rain—and so it does; * *⁵⁵ and when you notice that the wind is* *blowing from the south you say that it is going to be hot—and* *so it is. * *⁵⁶ You hypocrites! You know how to interpret the* *appearance of the earth and the sky; why do you not know how* *to interpret the present time?*

Again, as noted earlier, Jesus does not perform before those who want to be shown signs. He has been performing miracles and teaching throughout Israel and still they ask for a sign. No sign will be given except the sign of Jonah. Jonah went to Nineveh and proclaimed the end was near and the people needed to repent their sins. The people believed and repented. And the Lord blessed them. The other sign of Jonah was yet to come; Jesus' death and resurrection is like the death of Jonah within the whale and Jonah's being brought back to life.

At first, it amazed me as to how patient our Lord is with the scribes and Pharisees. Then I realized that patience and repetition is necessary when someone is teaching. I have been training adults for about 40 years and I find myself repeating over and over again. For the most part, the people I am speaking to have not heard my message in the past; so even though it is repetition to me, it is not to them. Even those who have heard me before need a reminder every once in a while. Our Lord is a patient teacher.

Lord, sometimes I am as weak as the Pharisees, seeking *signs to show I am on the right path. Help me to grow my* *faith so I can read the signs that already exist. Amen.*

The Leaven (Yeast) of the Pharisees

<u>Matthew 16:5-12:</u> *⁵ In coming to the other side of the sea, the* *disciples had forgotten to bring bread. * *⁶ Jesus said to them,*

263

"Look out, and beware of the leaven of the Pharisees and Sadducees." [7] *They concluded among themselves, saying, "It is because we have brought no bread."* [8] *When Jesus became aware of this he said, "You of little faith, why do you conclude among yourselves that it is because you have no bread?* [9] *Do you not yet understand, and do you not remember the five loaves for the five thousand, and how many wicker baskets you took up?* [10] *Or the seven loaves for the four thousand, and how many baskets you took up?* [11] *How do you not comprehend that I was not speaking to you about bread? Beware of the leaven of the Pharisees and Sadducees."* [12] *Then they understood that he was not telling them to beware of the leaven of bread, but of the teaching of the Pharisees and Sadducees.*

<u>Mark 8:14-21:</u> [14] *They had forgotten to bring bread, and they had only one loaf with them in the boat.* [15] *He enjoined them, "Watch out, guard against the leaven of the Pharisees and the leaven of Herod."* [16] *They concluded among themselves that it was because they had no bread.* [17] *When he became aware of this he said to them, "Why do you conclude that it is because you have no bread? Do you not yet understand or comprehend? Are your hearts hardened?* [18] *Do you have eyes and not see, ears and not hear? And do you not remember,* [19] *when I broke the five loaves for the five thousand, how many wicker baskets full of fragments you picked up?"* *They answered him, "Twelve."* [20] *"When I broke the seven loaves for the four thousand, how many full baskets of fragments did you pick up?"* *They answered [him], "Seven."* [21] *He said to them, "Do you still not understand?"*

<u>Luke 12:1:</u> [1] *Meanwhile, so many people were crowding together that they were trampling one another underfoot. He began to speak, first to his disciples, "Beware of the leaven— that is, the hypocrisy—of the Pharisees.*

264

It is surprising how thick headed the Apostles could be at times. Our Lord must once again explain what He means by His statement. His patience is shown again. His explanation was required but sufficient. *"Then they understood that he was not telling them to beware of the leaven of bread, but of the teaching of the Pharisees and Sadducees."*

Lord, I know that there are times when I am as thick headed as Your Apostles. Be patient with me as You were with them. Amen.

A Blind Man is Healed at Bethsaida

<u>Mark 8:22-26:</u> *[22] When they arrived at Bethsaida, they brought to him a blind man and begged him to touch him. [23] He took the blind man by the hand and led him outside the village. Putting spittle on his eyes he laid his hands on him and asked, "Do you see anything?" [24] Looking up he replied, "I see people looking like trees and walking." [25] Then he laid hands on his eyes a second time and he saw clearly; his sight was restored, and he could see everything distinctly. [26] Then he sent him home and said, "Do not even go into the village."*

Although Jesus treated those who came to Him uniquely based on their circumstances, it seems strange that He would take this blind man outside of the village in order to heal Him. It may have had something to do with the fact that the blind man was not from that village. I have learned that I will not always understand everything our Lord says and does.

The method of this healing is different as well. Using spittle and having to do so a second time is different from what we have encountered in the past. Jesus had shown over and over again that He did not need anything material to help Him perform His miracles. All he had to do was to will it to happen. It may have had something to do with the strength of the blind man's faith.

After the healing, Jesus sent the blind man home and cautioned him not to go into the village. This is not unusual. It could be that He found a lack of faith in Bethsaida.

Lord, in my search to understand You and the way You lived, keep me on track and help me to analyze each incident and discern what I must do to imitate You. Amen.

Part 7

The Way to the Cross

Many Disciples Take Offense at Jesus

John 6:60-66: *[60] Then many of his disciples who were listening said, "This saying is hard; who can accept it?" [61] Since Jesus knew that his disciples were murmuring about this, he said to them, "Does this shock you? [62] What if you were to see the Son of Man ascending to where he was before? [63] It is the spirit that gives life, while the flesh is of no avail. The words I have spoken to you are spirit and life. [64] But there are some of you who do not believe." Jesus knew from the beginning the ones who would not believe and the one who would betray him. [65] And he said, "For this reason I have told you that no one can come to me unless it is granted him by my Father." [66] As a result of this, many [of] his disciples returned to their former way of life and no longer accompanied him.*

From this point on, we will be focusing on Jesus' journey to His passion, death, and resurrection. Before doing so, we must back up briefly a few chapters to the discussion of the Bread of Life. It is following that discussion that this passage from John proceeds.

After Jesus spoke of the Bread of Life, His body and blood, many of His disciples simply could not believe what they heard Him say. *"This saying is hard; who can accept it?"* Many of His disciples simply left and went back to their former normal lives.

We have to accept the fact that faith is a gift – a gift from God. God has to select us and grant us this gift if we ever hope to grow close to Him and spend eternal life with Him. God has chosen us – not the other way around. He has gifted us with the faith to follow His only begotten Son. And if we can continue to accept and feed this faith, we will have life with Him throughout eternity.

Lord, help me to be ever persistent in whatever it takes to grow my faith. If I start to have doubts, help me to stay the course. Help me to truly appreciate this gift You have given me. Amen.

Peter's Confession at Caesarea Philippi

Matthew 16:13-20: [13] **When Jesus went into the region of Caesarea Philippi he asked his disciples, "Who do people say that the Son of Man is?"** [14] **They replied, "Some say John the Baptist, others Elijah, still others Jeremiah or one of the prophets."** [15] **He said to them, "But who do you say that I am?"** [16] **Simon Peter said in reply, "You are the Messiah, the Son of the living God."** [17] **Jesus said to him in reply, "Blessed are you, Simon son of Jonah. For flesh and blood has not revealed this to you, but my heavenly Father.** [18] **And so I say to you, you are Peter, and upon this rock I will build my church, and the gates of the netherworld shall not prevail against it.** [19] **I will give you the keys to the kingdom of heaven. Whatever you bind on earth shall be bound in heaven; and whatever you loose on earth shall be loosed in heaven."** [20] **Then he strictly ordered his disciples to tell no one that he was the Messiah.**

Mark 8:27-30: [27] **Now Jesus and his disciples set out for the villages of Caesarea Philippi. Along the way he asked his disciples, "Who do people say that I am?"** [28] **They said in reply, "John the Baptist, others Elijah, still others one of the prophets."** [29] **And he asked them, "But who do you say that I am?" Peter said to him in reply, "You are the Messiah."** [30] **Then he warned them not to tell anyone about him.**

Luke 9:18-21: *[18] Once when Jesus was praying in solitude, and the disciples were with him, he asked them, "Who do the crowds say that I am?" [19] They said in reply, "John the Baptist; others, Elijah; still others, 'One of the ancient prophets has arisen.'" [20] Then he said to them, "But who do you say that I am?" Peter said in reply, "The Messiah of God." [21] He rebuked them and directed them not to tell this to anyone.*

John 6:67-71: *[67] Jesus then said to the Twelve, "Do you also want to leave?" [68] Simon Peter answered him, "Master, to whom shall we go? You have the words of eternal life. [69] We have come to believe and are convinced that you are the Holy One of God." [70] Jesus answered them, "Did I not choose you twelve? Yet is not one of you a devil?" [71] He was referring to Judas, son of Simon the Iscariot; it was he who would betray him, one of the Twelve.*

Peter's response to Jesus' question is truly important at this point. *"You are the Messiah, the Son of the living God."* Jesus wants His Apostles to believe, but He is not ready for everyone to know it. So, He cautions them not to spread this word. All four of the Gospels record Peter's acknowledgement; however, only Matthew records Jesus' formal commissioning of Peter to lead the Church.

Upon Peter, the rock, the Church will grow; and nothing will destroy it. Peter is given the keys to the kingdom of heaven. Whatever Peter binds on earth will be bound in heaven. Whatever he unbinds on earth will be unbound in heaven. How well did Peter understand all of this? I am sure he spent some private time with Jesus, questioning what it all meant.

I truly believe that Jesus spent a lot of time with His Apostles explaining many of His statements. His Apostles were simple men. That does not mean they were ignorant, but they were not highly educated. They needed simple explanations to move forward. Being commissioned to build a Church and lead it into the future must have been mind-boggling to Peter and the others.

Being involved in adult education for years, I know that not everyone hears and understands what I say in the same way. I have to choose my words carefully, and still there are times when I have to go back and explain.

Lord, help me to understand that not everyone always understands what they read and hear. Clarity is important. Explanations are usually required. Help me to carefully plan what I am called on to teach. Amen.

Jesus Foretells His Passion

Matthew 16:21-23: *[21] From that time on, Jesus began to show his disciples that he must go to Jerusalem and suffer greatly from the elders, the chief priests, and the scribes, and be killed and on the third day be raised. [22] Then Peter took him aside and began to rebuke him, "God forbid, Lord! No such thing shall ever happen to you." [23] He turned and said to Peter, "Get behind me, Satan! You are an obstacle to me. You are thinking not as God does, but as human beings do."*

Mark 8:31-33: *[31] He began to teach them that the Son of Man must suffer greatly and be rejected by the elders, the chief priests, and the scribes, and be killed, and rise after three days. [32] He spoke this openly. Then Peter took him aside and began to rebuke him. [33] At this he turned around and, looking at his disciples, rebuked Peter and said, "Get behind me, Satan. You are thinking not as God does, but as human beings do."*

Luke 9:22: *He said, "The Son of Man must suffer greatly and be rejected by the elders, the chief priests, and the scribes, and be killed and on the third day be raised."*

The Apostles, as well as His other disciples, had to be told. Jesus already told them that He was doing the will of His Father. They had to know that He was there to suffer and die for mankind. Of course, these passages do not go into why this is necessary or what this will accomplish overall. Did Jesus explain that as well at this time? We will never know. Jesus let them know part of the game plan, but we do not know to what depth.

I feel sorry for Peter. He has a tendency to speak before he has time to think it through. He obviously did not react to the full plan – only the little they were told. He was reacting as he or any human would to news such as that – especially about someone he cared deeply for. He rejected the idea. This is not a good plan. Why must this happen?

I also believe that they overlooked the part that He would rise on the third day. The shock of His passion and death was what they focused on.

But Jesus would not have it as Peter proclaimed. Jesus will do the will of His Father in heaven. Jesus read Peter's protest as a temptation sent by the devil to sway Him away from doing His Father's will. In reading these passages from the bible, we have to try to place ourselves in the mindset of both sides of the conversation.

Lord, help me to understand all aspects of what is presented in these passages. Much has to be discerned. But help me to keep in mind that Jesus always does the right thing. Amen.

"If any man would come after Me"

__Matthew 16:24-28:__ *[24] Then Jesus said to his disciples, "Whoever wishes to come after me must deny himself, take up his cross, and follow me. [25] For whoever wishes to save his life will lose it, but whoever loses his life for my sake will find it. [26] What profit would there be for one to gain the whole world and forfeit his life? Or what can one give in exchange for his life? [27] For the Son of Man will come with his angels in his Father's glory, and then he will repay everyone according to his conduct. [28] Amen, I say to you, there are some standing here who will not taste death until they see the Son of Man coming in his kingdom."*

__Mark 8:34-9:1:__ *[34] He summoned the crowd with his disciples and said to them, "Whoever wishes to come after me must deny himself, take up his cross, and follow me. [35] For whoever wishes to save his life will lose it, but whoever loses his life for my sake and that of the gospel will save it. [36] What profit is there for one to gain the whole world and forfeit his life? [37] What could one give in exchange for his life? [38] Whoever is ashamed of me and of my words in this faithless and sinful generation, the Son of Man will be ashamed of when he comes in his Father's glory with the holy angels." [9:1] He also said to them, "Amen, I say to you, there are some standing here who will not taste death until they see that the kingdom of God has come in power."*

__Luke 9:23-27:__ *[23] Then he said to all, "If anyone wishes to come after me, he must deny himself and take up his cross daily and follow me. [24] For whoever wishes to save his life will lose it, but whoever loses his life for my sake will save it. [25] What profit is there for one to gain the whole world yet lose or forfeit himself? [26] Whoever is ashamed of me and of my words, the*

Son of Man will be ashamed of when he comes in his glory and in the glory of the Father and of the holy angels. ²⁷ Truly I say to you, there are some standing here who will not taste death until they see the kingdom of God."

John 12:25: *Whoever loves his life loses it, and whoever hates his life in this world will preserve it for eternal life.*

We all have choices to make. Jesus is telling us that we must decide if we are going to follow the world or follow Him. We cannot have both. Yes, we must live in this world and make the best of it; but we must not let the world control us. We must place our trust in God and live as He wants us to. It is all a matter of choice.

It falls back to an earlier statement in the Gospels. The measure with which you measure will be measured back to you. Here the simple meaning is that, if you choose the world, that is what you will get. Period. Eternal life comes from choosing and following God – not the world.

In the statement: *there are some standing here who will not taste death until they see the kingdom of God*, the kingdom of God refers to the time when Christ's reign begins, after the resurrection. Jesus is not predicting that some will live until judgment day.

Lord, once again, You speak to us of choices to be made. I need Your regular guidance in making my choices. Keep my mind and heart open to what You have to tell me. Amen.

The Transfiguration

Matthew 17:1-9: *¹ After six days Jesus took Peter, James, and John his brother, and led them up a high mountain by themselves. ² And he was transfigured before them; his face* shone like the sun and his clothes became white as light. *³ And behold, Moses and Elijah appeared to them, conversing with him. ⁴ Then Peter said to Jesus in reply, "Lord, it is good that we are here. If you wish, I will make three tents here, one for you, one for Moses, and one for Elijah." ⁵ While he was still speaking, behold, a bright cloud cast a shadow over them, then from the cloud came a voice that said, "This is my beloved Son, with whom I am well pleased; listen to him." ⁶ When the disciples heard this, they fell prostrate and were very much afraid. ⁷ But Jesus came and touched them, saying, "Rise, and do not be afraid." ⁸ And when the disciples raised their eyes, they saw no one else but Jesus alone. ⁹ As they were coming down from the mountain, Jesus charged them, "Do not tell the vision to anyone until the Son of Man has been raised from the dead."*

Mark 9:2-10: *² After six days Jesus took Peter, James, and John and led them up a high mountain apart by themselves. And he was transfigured before them, ³ and his clothes became dazzling white, such as no fuller on earth could bleach them. ⁴ Then Elijah appeared to them along with Moses, and they were conversing with Jesus. ⁵ Then Peter said to Jesus in reply, "Rabbi, it is good that we are here! Let us make three tents: one for you, one for Moses, and one for Elijah." ⁶ He hardly knew what to say, they were so terrified. ⁷ Then a cloud came, casting a shadow over them; then from the cloud came a voice, "This is my beloved Son. Listen to him." ⁸ Suddenly, looking around, they no longer saw anyone but Jesus alone with them. ⁹ As they were coming down from the mountain, he charged them not to relate what they had seen to anyone, except when the Son of Man had risen from the dead. ¹⁰ So they kept the matter to themselves, questioning what rising from the dead meant.*

Luke 9:28-36: *²⁸About eight days after he said this, he took Peter, John, and James and went up the mountain to pray. ²⁹While he was praying his face changed in appearance and his clothing became dazzling white. ³⁰And behold, two men were conversing with him, Moses and Elijah, ³¹who appeared in glory and spoke of his exodus that he was going to accomplish in Jerusalem. ³²Peter and his companions had been overcome by sleep, but becoming fully awake, they saw his glory and the two men standing with him. ³³As they were about to part from him, Peter said to Jesus, "Master, it is good that we are here; let us make three tents, one for you, one for Moses, and one for Elijah." But he did not know what he was saying. ³⁴While he was still speaking, a cloud came and cast a shadow over them, and they became frightened when they entered the cloud. ³⁵Then from the cloud came a voice that said, "This is my chosen Son; listen to him." ³⁶After the voice had spoken, Jesus was found alone. They fell silent and did not at that time tell anyone what they had seen.*

The Gospels do not tell us much about why our Lord chose this trio to be the leaders of the Apostles. Two things are definite. Peter was the one who always took charge, spoke openly what he felt (right or wrong in his thinking), and acted. John was the more spiritual of the three. We do not get much of an impression of James. It is my belief that, in this trio, James and John were able to temper down Peter. So, the three would be a good leadership combination. Of course, this is my own opinion. None of us, on our own, could lead any type of movement without the advice of others who are trusted.

There were no images allowed within the Israelite community, so identifying Moses and Elijah had to be revealed to the three by Jesus or by the Holy Spirit who had to be present as well. Our triune God was present since God the Father acknowledged His Son for the second time, the first being at Jesus' baptism by John.

There is a time and place set aside by God for revealing special messages or events. Obviously, our Lord did not want the other Apostles to know at this time about the Transfiguration. However, it was especially important for Peter, James, and John to have Jesus' divinity revealed to them.

Lord, my natural human curiosity drives me to know everything about everything. However, I resign myself to the belief that You will reveal to me what I need to know when I need to know it. Amen.

The Coming of Elijah

Matthew 17:10-13: *[10] Then the disciples asked him, "Why do the scribes say that Elijah must come first?" [11] He said in reply, "Elijah will indeed come and restore all things; [12] but I tell you that Elijah has already come, and they did not recognize him but did to him whatever they pleased. So also, will the Son of Man suffer at their hands." [13] Then the disciples understood that he was speaking to them of John the Baptist.*

Mark 9:11-13: *[11] Then they asked him, "Why do the scribes say that Elijah must come first?" [12] He told them, "Elijah will indeed come first and restore all things, yet how is it written regarding the Son of Man that he must suffer greatly and be treated with contempt? [13] But I tell you that Elijah has come, and they did to him whatever they pleased, as it is written of him."*

Here we have a re-affirmation that Elijah has already come. The spirit of Elijah returned in John the Baptist. This

277

is important because it is part of the prophecy of the coming of the Messiah.

Here also is another opportunity that our Lord took to forecast His coming passion and death. Jesus would be treated in the way John the Baptist was treated: abusively.

Lord, help me to always keep in mind what You suffered for love of me. Amen.

Healing a Boy Possessed

<u>Matthew 17:14-21:</u> *[14] When they came to the crowd a man approached, knelt down before him, [15] and said, "Lord, have pity on my son, for he is a lunatic and suffers severely; often he falls into fire, and often into water. [16] I brought him to your disciples, but they could not cure him." [17] Jesus said in reply, "O faithless and perverse generation, how long will I be with you? How long will I endure you? Bring him here to me." [18] Jesus rebuked him, and the demon came out of him, and from that hour the boy was cured. [19] Then the disciples approached Jesus in private and said, "Why could we not drive it out?" [20] He said to them, "Because of your little faith. Amen, I say to you, if you have faith the size of a mustard seed, you will say to this mountain, 'Move from here to there,' and it will move. Nothing will be impossible for you." [[21] "But this kind does not come out except by prayer and fasting"]*

<u>Mark 9:14-29:</u> *[14] When they came to the disciples, they saw a large crowd around them and scribes arguing with them. [15] Immediately on seeing him, the whole crowd was utterly amazed. They ran up to him and greeted him. [16] He asked them, "What are you arguing about with them?" [17] Someone from the crowd answered him, "Teacher, I have brought to you my son possessed by a mute*

278

spirit. ¹⁸ *Wherever it seizes him, it throws him down; he foams at the mouth, grinds his teeth, and becomes rigid. I asked your disciples to drive it out, but they were unable to do so."* ¹⁹ *He said to them in reply, "O faithless generation, how long will I be with you? How long will I endure you? Bring him to me."* ²⁰ *They brought the boy to him. And when he saw him, the spirit immediately threw the boy into convulsions. As he fell to the ground, he began to roll around and foam at the mouth.* ²¹ *Then he questioned his father, "How long has this been happening to him?" He replied, "Since childhood.* ²² *It has often thrown him into fire and into water to kill him. But if you can do anything, have compassion on us and help us."* ²³ *Jesus said to him, "'If you can!' Everything is possible to one who has faith."* ²⁴ *Then the boy's father cried out, "I do believe, help my unbelief!"* ²⁵ *Jesus, on seeing a crowd rapidly gathering, rebuked the unclean spirit and said to it, "Mute and deaf spirit, I command you: come out of him and never enter him again!"* ²⁶ *Shouting and throwing the boy into convulsions, it came out. He became like a corpse, which caused many to say, "He is dead!"* ²⁷ *But Jesus took him by the hand, raised him, and he stood up.* ²⁸ *When he entered the house, his disciples asked him in private, "Why could we not drive it out?"* ²⁹ *He said to them, "This kind can only come out through prayer."*

Luke 9:37-43: ³⁷ *On the next day, when they came down from the mountain, a large crowd met him.* ³⁸ *There was a man in the crowd who cried out, "Teacher, I beg you, look at my son; he is my only child.* ³⁹ *For a spirit seizes him and he suddenly screams, and it convulses him until he foams at the mouth; it releases him only with difficulty, wearing him out.* ⁴⁰ *I begged your disciples to cast it out, but they could not."* ⁴¹ *Jesus said in reply, "O faithless and perverse generation, how long will I be with you and endure you? Bring your son here."* ⁴² *As he was*

279

coming forward, the demon threw him to the ground in a convulsion; but Jesus rebuked the unclean spirit, healed the boy, and returned him to his father. *⁴³ And all were astonished by the majesty of God.*

<u>Luke 17:6:</u> *The Lord replied, "If you have faith the size of a mustard seed, you would say to [this] mulberry tree, 'Be uprooted and planted in the sea,' and it would obey you.*

"*Everything is possible to one who has faith.*" "*I do believe, help my unbelief!*" These are two really important statements. Jesus emphasizes that faith is absolutely necessary for miracles to take place. This has been shown over and over again. The faith must be strong in the person to be healed or in the person making the request.

The second statement affirms that we all are lacking in faith. The father of the boy realizes his faith is not very strong, and so he asks Jesus to strengthen his faith. We must all strive to grow in faith. The Apostles, who tried to do the healing, realized their faith alone was not strong enough to perform the miracle. "*This kind can only come out through prayer.*" Some healings also require prayer. Remember: it is God who heals, not the person saying the words.

Lord, never let me be filled with the belief that good is performed by me. It is performed by You through me. I am Your instrument. Amen.

The Passion Foretold Again

<u>Matthew 17:22-23:</u> *²² As they were gathering in Galilee, Jesus said to them, "The Son of Man is to be handed over to men, ²³ and they will kill him, and he will be raised on the third day." And they were overwhelmed with grief.*

Mark 9:30-32: *30 They left from there and began a journey through Galilee, but he did not wish anyone to know about it. 31 He was teaching his disciples and telling them, "The Son of Man is to be handed over to men and they will kill him, and three days after his death he will rise." 32 But they did not understand the saying, and they were afraid to question him.*

Luke 9:43-45: *43 While they were all amazed at his every deed, he said to his disciples, 44 "Pay attention to what I am telling you. The Son of Man is to be handed over to men." 45 But they did not understand this saying; its meaning was hidden from them so that they should not understand it, and they were afraid to ask him about this saying.*

And they were afraid to ask him about this saying. Jesus had foretold this before. They did not want to hear it then. They do not want to hear it now. They have grown to love their teacher, the Son of Man. They did not want to hear that He would be turned over to those who hate Him, that He would be killed, and that He would rise again (whatever that meant). This was a hard saying to hear. Why would they want to hear more? They will hear more later.

Lord, open my mind and heart to all You want to tell me, even if it is something I do not want to hear. Help me to understand how important Your words are. Amen.

Payment of the Temple Tax

Matthew 17:24-27: *24 When they came to Capernaum, the collectors of the temple tax approached Peter and said, "Doesn't your teacher pay the temple tax?" 25 "Yes," he said. When he came into the house, before he had time to*

281

speak, Jesus asked him, "What is your opinion, Simon? From whom do the kings of the earth take tolls or census tax? From their subjects or from foreigners?" ²⁶ When he said, "From foreigners," Jesus said to him, "Then the subjects are exempt. ²⁷ But that we may not offend them, go to the sea, drop in a hook, and take the first fish that comes up. Open its mouth and you will find a coin worth twice the temple tax. Give that to them for me and for you."

This was a strange lesson for Simon Peter. In one moment, Jesus is effectively telling Peter that they really do not owe the temple tax. Then in the next moment, He is telling Peter to pay the tax. He is not only saying to pay it, but He is also providing the money to pay it by a miracle. So, what is Jesus' message to Peter? Is it that sometimes we are forced to do things we are not really obligated to do? Is it that God will provide for our needs? Well, it is not that God will perform a miracle so that we will be able to pay our taxes every year. The lesson for Peter and the other disciples is that there are times when we will be required to do things we are not really obligated to do, and we will do them to avoid offending others or causing conflict.

Lord, there will be times when I am simply obliged to do what I believe I should not have to do. Help me to know when those times are. Help me also to reconcile my action with my mind and heart. Amen.

True Greatness

Matthew 18:1-5: *¹ At that time the disciples approached Jesus and said, "Who is the greatest in the kingdom of heaven?" ² He called a child over, placed it in their midst, ³ and said, "Amen, I say to you, unless you turn and become like children, you*

282

will not enter the kingdom of heaven. *4 Whoever humbles himself like this child is the greatest in the kingdom of heaven.* *5 And whoever receives one child such as this in my name receives me.*

<u>Mark 9:33-37:</u> *33 They came to Capernaum and, once inside the house, he began to ask them, "What were you arguing about on the way?" 34 But they remained silent. They had been discussing among themselves on the way who was the greatest. 35 Then he sat down, called the Twelve, and said to them, "If anyone wishes to be first, he shall be the last of all and the servant of all." 36 Taking a child he placed it in their midst, and putting his arms around it he said to them, 37 "Whoever receives one child such as this in my name, receives me; and whoever receives me, receives not me but the One who sent me."*

<u>Luke 9:46-48:</u> *46 An argument arose among the disciples about which of them was the greatest. 47 Jesus realized the intention of their hearts and took a child and placed it by his side 48 and said to them, "Whoever receives this child in my name receives me, and whoever receives me receives the one who sent me. For the one who is least among all of you is the one who is the greatest."*

<u>John 13:20:</u> *"Amen, amen, I say to you, whoever receives the one I send receives me, and whoever receives me receives the one who sent me."*

"For the one who is least among all of you is the one who is the greatest." That statement from Jesus seems to me to answer the question posed to Jesus; but each passage is slightly different as remembered by the Apostles. Here, I see the emphasis on both humility and compassion. We are

283

to humble ourselves before God and man. We are also to love each other with the love that Jesus taught us. Those are the two traits that are outstanding in children. That is why Jesus is pointing to the child. We must learn to be like children. For all the time of mankind's existence, we have taught our children to be like (grow into) adults. Now Jesus is telling us the opposite. There is so much for us to learn.

"Amen, amen, I say to you, whoever receives the one I send receives me, and whoever receives me receives the one who sent me." This is the second message I get from these passages. As long as we accept what Jesus is teaching us, then we are also accepting the will of His Father in Heaven. For Jesus came to fulfill the will of His Father.

Lord, Your lessons are very simple and basic. Why is it so difficult for us to grasp and follow. Open my mind and my heart to You. Amen.

The Strange Exorcist

Mark 9:38-41: [38] *John said to him, "Teacher, we saw someone driving out demons in your name, and we tried to prevent him because he does not follow us."* [39] *Jesus replied, "Do not prevent him. There is no one who performs a mighty deed in my name who can at the same time speak ill of me.* [40] *For whoever is not against us is for us.* [41] *Anyone who gives you a cup of water to drink because you belong to Christ, amen, I say to you, will surely not lose his reward."*

Luke 9:49-50: [49] *Then John said in reply, "Master, we saw someone casting out demons in your name and we tried to prevent him because he does not follow in our company."* [50] *Jesus said to him, "Do not prevent him, for whoever is not against you is for you."*

Matthew 10:42: *"And whoever gives only a cup of cold water to one of these little ones to drink because he is a disciple—amen, I say to you, he will surely not lose his reward."*

"There is no one who performs a mighty deed in my name who can at the same time speak ill of me. For whoever is not against us is for us." This is the key message coming from our Lord. The exorcism was a circumstance. Regardless of "religious" affiliation, if the person doing the mighty deed is Christian and does the deed in Jesus' name, then we should accept it as something good. You cannot do good deeds in the name of Jesus and be against Him at the same time.

Lord, help me to judge actions and words and not people. This is so hard because we tend to judge people by their words and actions. This is not what You want. Help me to accept the good in everyone. Amen.

Warnings Concerning Temptations

Matthew 18:6-9: *⁶ "Whoever causes one of these little ones who believe in me to sin, it would be better for him to have a great millstone hung around his neck and to be drowned in the depths of the sea. ⁷ Woe to the world because of things that cause sin! Such things must come, but woe to the one through whom they come! ⁸ If your hand or foot causes you to sin, cut it off and throw it away. It is better for you to enter into life maimed or crippled than with two hands or two feet to be thrown into eternal fire. ⁹ And if your eye causes you to sin, tear it out and throw it away. It is better for you to enter into life with one eye than with two eyes to be thrown into fiery Gehenna."*

285

Matthew 5:13: *"You are the salt of the earth. But if salt loses its taste, with what can it be seasoned? It is no longer good for anything but to be thrown out and trampled underfoot."*

Mark 9:42-50: [42] *"Whoever causes one of these little ones who believe [in me] to sin, it would be better for him if a great millstone were put around his neck and he were thrown into the sea.* [43] *If your hand causes you to sin, cut it off. It is better for you to enter into life maimed than with two hands to go into Gehenna, into the unquenchable fire. [[44]]* [45] *And if your foot causes you to sin, cut it off. It is better for you to enter into life crippled than with two feet to be thrown into Gehenna. [[46]]* [47] *And if your eye causes you to sin, pluck it out. Better for you to enter into the kingdom of God with one eye than with two eyes to be thrown into Gehenna,* [48] *where 'their worm does not die, and the fire is not quenched.'* [49] *"Everyone will be salted with fire.* [50] *Salt is good, but if salt becomes insipid, with what will you restore its flavor? Keep salt in yourselves and you will have peace with one another."*

Luke 17:1-2: [1] *He said to his disciples, "Things that cause sin will inevitably occur, but woe to the person through whom they occur.* [2] *It would be better for him if a millstone were put around his neck and he be thrown into the sea than for him to cause one of these little ones to sin."*

Luke 14-34-35: [34] *"Salt is good, but if salt itself loses its taste, with what can its flavor be restored?* [35] *It is fit neither for the soil nor for the manure pile; it is thrown out. Whoever has ears to hear ought to hear."*

There are two lessons in this passage.

"Things that cause sin will inevitably occur, but woe to the person through whom they occur. It would be better for him if a millstone were put around his neck and he be thrown into the sea than for him to cause one of these little ones to sin." Luke pretty well sums things up nicely. We are all tempted in many different ways. But we still have the choice to give in to the temptation or to push it aside. The choice is ours. But the punishment is severe for the ones who cause others to sin.

"Salt is good, but if salt becomes insipid, with what will you restore its flavor?" Here, the Evangelists are referring to our passion, our fervor, our zeal. This is what keeps our faith strong and keeps us growing. If we lose that zeal, there is no simple solution to bringing it back. We must strive to keep our passion alive.

Lord, the loss of my fervor for my faith can make me readily susceptible to temptations. Help me to always strive to grow in my faith and seek to please You in all I do. Amen.

Parable of the Lost Sheep

Matthew 18:10-14: *[10] "See that you do not despise one of these little ones, for I say to you that their angels in heaven always look upon the face of my heavenly Father. [11] [12] What is your opinion? If a man has a hundred sheep and one of them goes astray, will he not leave the ninety-nine in the hills and go in search of the stray? [13] And if he finds it, amen, I say to you, he rejoices more over it than over the ninety-nine that did not stray. [14] In just the same way, it is not the will of your heavenly Father that one of these little ones be lost.*

Luke 15:3-7: *[3] So to them he addressed this parable. [4] "What man among you having a hundred sheep and losing one of* *them would not leave the ninety-nine in the desert and go after the lost one until he finds it? [5] And when he does find it, he sets it on his shoulders with great joy [6] and, upon his arrival home, he calls together his friends and neighbors and says to them, 'Rejoice with me because I have found my lost sheep.' [7] I tell you, in just the same way there will be more joy in heaven over one sinner who repents than over ninety-nine righteous people who have no need of repentance.*

"*See that you do not despise one of these little ones, for I say to you that their angels in heaven always look upon the face of my heavenly Father.*" In Matthew's passage, our Lord assures us that we have Guardian Angels. This is not a fairy tale for children. I firmly believe in Guardian Angels; and I firmly believe that each of us has more than one, one to guide us through life and additional angels to help us through our challenges, our difficulties. God wants us to come home to Him, so He will give us all the help we need.

Have you ever misplaced or lost something that has special importance to you? You search and search, looking everywhere you have been, anxiously going through everything you have recently touched, opened, or closed. Everything else is on hold until you find the missing item. I have prayed to St. Anthony of Padua for help in finding lost items. The lost sheep has that kind of value to the shepherd. And our souls have that kind of value to God. He will do all within His power to draw you back to Him, except to deny our free will and force us to come back. We are the lost sheep. It is also up to us to try to find our way back. Our Guardian Angels are ever present to help us.

Lord, never let me lose sight of the fact that I am important to You. Let me never forget that I need to keep my focus on

You. Help me to understand and follow the guidance
provided by my Guardian Angels. Amen.

On Reproving One's Brother

<u>Matthew 18:15-18:</u> [15] *"If your brother sins [against you], go*
and tell him his fault between you and him alone. If he listens
to you, you have won over your brother. [16] *If he does not listen,*
take one or two others along with you, so that 'every fact may
be established on the testimony of two or three witnesses.' [17] *If*
he refuses to listen to them, tell the church. If he refuses to
listen even to the church, then treat him as you would a Gentile
or a tax collector. [18] *Amen, I say to you, whatever you bind on*
earth shall be bound in heaven, and whatever you loose on
earth shall be loosed in heaven.

<u>Luke 17:3:</u> *Be on your guard! If your brother sins, rebuke*
him; and if he repents, forgive him.

<u>John 20:23:</u> *Whose sins you forgive are forgiven them, and*
whose sins you retain are retained.

In spite of the formal procedure defined in Matthew's
text, the basic message is: *if your brother sins, rebuke him;*
and if he repents, forgive him. It is all about love. If you
love your brother, then you want him to know that what he
has done is wrong and should cease doing and correct his
ways. The rebuke is not to be vindictive but corrective. If
he agrees, then you have won him over. If he refuses, then
he should be treated as an outsider.

This does not sound like the "Christian" way to treat our
brothers. It would seem like we should continue to love him
and try to get him to correct his ways. However, Jesus
makes a very good point in that those opposed to the right

way to do things may eventually have an adverse influence on you and cause you to ultimately go along with the wrong way. That is why the unrepentant should be treated as outsiders.

Lord, it is not always easy to love our brothers and sisters. It is even harder to try to correct them when they do something that is wrong. Help me to respond to their sinfulness in the way You would have me do so. Amen.

Where Two or Three are Gathered

Matthew 18:19-20: *[19] Again, [amen,] I say to you, if two of you agree on earth about anything for which they are to pray, it shall be granted to them by my heavenly Father. [20] For where two or three are gathered together in my name, there am I in the midst of them.*

If two of you agree on earth about anything for which they are to pray, it shall be granted to them by my heavenly Father. Except … Yes, there is an exception. There always is. If what is requested is deemed by our heavenly Father to be inappropriate or inopportune at this time, then the answer can be "no."

I am a firm believer in the power of prayer, and I have received the benefits of many prayers over the years. However, I realize not everything I have prayed for or asked others to pray for would meet God's criteria for granting the requests. God loves us and knows what is best for us, in spite of what we ask for.

Lord, grant me the willingness to accept our heavenly Father's decision about what we pray for even if the answer for now is "no." Amen.

On Reconciliation

Matthew 18:21-22: *[21] Then Peter approaching asked him, "Lord, if my brother sins against me, how often must I forgive him? As many as seven times?" [22] Jesus answered, "I say to you, not seven times but seventy-seven times.*

Luke 17:4: *And if he wrongs you seven times in one day and returns to you seven times saying, 'I am sorry,' you should forgive him.*

The fact is that we should be willing to forgive our brother whether it is seven times, seven times seven times, seventy-seven times, on to infinity. Jesus is not saying to forgive on certain conditions, He is saying we should forgive. Period. If we truly love someone, then we should be willing to forgive whenever and as often as necessary. God is the prime example of this because He is willing to forgive us over and over again.

Lord, I am not aware of anyone I have not forgiven, but sometimes my memory is faulty. Help me to follow Your example. Help me to love everyone I encounter in the way You would do so. Amen.

The Unforgiving Servant

Matthew 18:23-35: *[23] That is why the kingdom of heaven may be likened to a king who decided to settle accounts with his servants. [24] When he began the accounting, a debtor was brought before him who owed him a huge amount. [25] Since he had no way of paying it back, his master ordered him to be sold,* *along with his wife, his children, and all his property, in payment of the debt. ²⁶ At that, the servant fell down, did him homage, and said, 'Be patient with me, and I will pay you back in full.' ²⁷ Moved with compassion the master of that servant let him go and forgave him the loan. ²⁸ When that servant had left, he found one of his fellow servants who owed him a much smaller amount. He seized him and started to choke him, demanding, 'Pay back what you owe.' ²⁹ Falling to his knees, his fellow servant begged him, 'Be patient with me, and I will pay you back.' ³⁰ But he refused. Instead, he had him put in prison until he paid back the debt. ³¹ Now when his fellow servants saw what had happened, they were deeply disturbed and went to their master and reported the whole affair. ³² His master summoned him and said to him, 'You wicked servant! I forgave you your entire debt because you begged me to. ³³ Should you not have had pity on your fellow servant, as I had pity on you?' ³⁴ Then in anger his master handed him over to the torturers until he should pay back the whole debt. ³⁵ So will my heavenly Father do to you, unless each of you forgives his brother from his heart."*

The measure with which you measure will be measured back to you. The unforgiving servant did not learn from the compassion his master felt and displayed toward him. Instead of forgiving his fellow servant, the unforgiving servant punished him to the highest degree he could. That was the measure. The master then treated the unforgiving servant in the same manner. This is an often-repeated lesson throughout the gospels. It is likely that the unforgiving servant was upset about losing his job, forgetting the fact that he received mercy from his master. He was taking his anger out on his fellow servant. He did not want to go down alone. He had already been forgiven but chose to hate rather than grant mercy.

Lord, I often make mistakes in judgment; but help me to never let those mistakes cause harm to others. Help me to keep love, forgiveness, and mercy at the forefront of any actions I take. Amen.

Part 8

The Last Journey

to Jerusalem

(according to Luke)

Jesus is rejected by the Samaritans

Luke 9:51-56: *[51]When the days for his being taken up were fulfilled, he resolutely determined to journey to Jerusalem, [52]and he sent messengers ahead of him. On the way they entered a Samaritan village to prepare for his reception there, [53]but they would not welcome him because the destination of his journey was Jerusalem. [54]When the disciples James and John saw this they asked, "Lord, do you want us to call down fire from heaven to consume them?" [55]Jesus turned and rebuked them, [56]and they journeyed to another village.*

Matthew 19:1-2: *[1]When Jesus finished these words, he left Galilee and went to the district of Judea across the Jordan. [2]Great crowds followed him, and he cured them there.*

Mark 10:1: *He set out from there and went into the district of Judea [and] across the Jordan. Again, crowds gathered around him; and, as was his custom, he again taught them.*

Jesus' work in Galilee was completed for now. Jesus and His disciples moved into Judea and started His last journey to Jerusalem.

Not everyone welcomed Jesus in their midst. In this case, the people in the Samaritan town would not welcome Him; but it was not because of His teachings and miracles. It was because they were going to Jerusalem to be among the Israelites. We cannot always assume that people reject Jesus because He is God or because of His teachings and miracles. Personal agendas often come into play. In this case, it is the hatred Samaritans and Israelites have for each other.

The sons of thunder are then rebuked by our Lord. At least this time, it was not Peter.

Lord, one of the sad things about being human is that we have personal priorities that sometimes cause us to bypass opportunities You send our way. Help me to keep You as my highest priority. Amen.

Commissioning the Seventy

<u>Luke 10:1-12:</u> *¹After this the Lord appointed seventy[-two] others whom he sent ahead of him in pairs to every town and place he intended to visit. ²He said to them, "The harvest is abundant, but the laborers are few; so, ask the master of the harvest to send out laborers for his harvest. ³Go on your way; behold, I am sending you like lambs among wolves. ⁴Carry no money bag, no sack, no sandals; and greet no one along the way. ⁵Into whatever house you enter, first say, 'Peace to this household.' ⁶If a peaceful person lives there, your peace will rest on him; but if not, it will return to you. ⁷Stay in the same house and eat and drink what is offered to you, for the laborer deserves his payment. Do not move about from one house to another. ⁸Whatever town you enter and they welcome you, eat what is set before you, ⁹cure the sick in it and say to them, 'The kingdom of God is at hand for you.' ¹⁰Whatever town you enter and they do not receive you, go out into the streets and say, ¹¹'The dust of your town that clings to our feet, even that we shake off against you.' Yet know this: the kingdom of God is at hand. ¹²I tell you it will be more tolerable for Sodom on that day than for that town.*

<u>Matthew 9:37-38:</u> *³⁷Then he said to his disciples, "The harvest is abundant, but the laborers are few; ³⁸so ask the master of the harvest to send out laborers for his harvest."*

I first want to address the decision Jesus made to send out His disciples "in pairs." This is especially important to me because, as a member of the St. Vincent de Paul Society, we focus our service to those in need on visiting them in their homes. We insist, in imitation of Jesus, that our members do these visits in pairs. There are many good reasons for this having to do with safety, discretion, multiple opinions, and reliance of one member on the other.

"The harvest is abundant, but the laborers are few." This has not changed over the past two thousand years. There are so many people in this world who would welcome the word of God, but we have so few people to bring it to them. The 72 disciples that Jesus is sending out to spread the word are the first real Christian missionaries. Their mission term may have been short and not for a long distance, but their purpose was to evangelize.

I wonder how many of the 72 were like Peter, James, and John, ready to act, often before thinking. They were explicitly given the authority to preach and heal. Both of these gifts would not have been easy for these chosen followers to use. To preach and spread the word is difficult, even for the gifted. As a writer and speaker, I know. But the gift of healing, especially in the eyes of those who watched Jesus and found it hard to believe, would be really hard to perform until results were seen. The more we use the gifts we are given, the more confidence we have in our ability to use them.

Lord, each of us has been given gifts or talents to be used on behalf of others. Help me to remember that. Your gifts are to be used on behalf of others – not selfishly. Amen.

Return of the Seventy-Two

Luke 10:17-20: *[17] The seventy[-two] returned rejoicing, and said, "Lord, even the demons are subject to us because of your name." [18] Jesus said, "I have observed Satan fall like lightning from the sky. [19] Behold, I have given you the power 'to tread upon serpents' and scorpions and upon the full force of the enemy and nothing will harm you. [20] Nevertheless, do not rejoice because the spirits are subject to you, but rejoice because your names are written in heaven."*

From this passage, I surmise that the journeys of the seventy-two were successful. They were happy. Nothing is said about how long they were gone. I believe it would be safe to assume they were gone a few days, maybe as long as a week. Nothing is said about where they went except it was in the general vicinity, within reasonable walking distance. Nothing is said about what Jesus did or where He went while they were gone. The point is they were sent on a mission by Jesus, and they were happy when they returned.

Again, as I mentioned earlier, Jesus refers to Satan. Satan is not a myth, Lucifer does exist, and hell is real.

"Rejoice because your names are written in heaven." This is not about power or authority. This is about growing close to God, doing His will, and spending eternity with Him.

Lord, it is so easy to get caught up in the moment. Help me to keep things in perspective, to know what my true goal is. Amen.

The Blessedness of the Disciples

Luke 10:21-24: *²¹ At that very moment he rejoiced [in] the holy Spirit and said, "I give you praise, Father, Lord of heaven and earth, for although you have hidden these things from the wise and the learned you have revealed them to the childlike. Yes, Father, such has been your gracious will. ²² All things have been handed over to me by my Father. No one knows who the Son is except the Father, and who the Father is except the Son and anyone to whom the Son wishes to reveal him." ²³ Turning to the disciples in private he said, "Blessed are the eyes that see what you see. ²⁴ For I say to you, many prophets and kings desired to see what you see, but did not see it, and to hear what you hear, but did not hear it."*

Here is an incident of Jesus rejoicing. I do not want this to sound like it was a very isolated incident. Jesus lived among us humans for 33 years. Although 99% of all depictions of Jesus show Him with a serious or stern face, there had to be lots of times when Jesus was happy, smiling, and rejoicing. I have a picture at home of the smiling Jesus, and that is the picture of Him that I like best. Why would any men, women, or children follow Jesus if He did not smile and laugh and enjoy life?

Here He is rejoicing in the blessings His disciples received on their missionary journeys. We know from other Gospel passages that Jesus often prayed to, talked with His Father. He prayed on behalf of the people who came to hear His words. He prayed for those He healed. He prayed for those who hated Him. Here He is sharing in the rejoicing of His disciples.

Lord, life is filled with all kinds of experiences. Never let me forget that You want us to enjoy the life we have. It is not

*always easy, but there are plenty of times for rejoicing.
Amen.*

The Lawyer's Question

<u>Matthew 22:34-40</u>: *[34] When the Pharisees heard that he had silenced the Sadducees, they gathered together, [35] and one of them [a scholar of the law] tested him by asking, [36] "Teacher, which commandment in the law is the greatest?" [37] He said to him, "You shall love the Lord, your God, with all your heart, with all your soul, and with all your mind. [38] This is the greatest and the first commandment. [39] The second is like it: You shall love your neighbor as yourself. [40] The whole law and the prophets depend on these two commandments."*

<u>Mark 12:28-34</u>: *[28] One of the scribes, when he came forward and heard them disputing and saw how well he had answered them, asked him, "Which is the first of all the commandments?" [29] Jesus replied, "The first is this: 'Hear, O Israel! The Lord our God is Lord alone! [30] You shall love the Lord your God with all your heart, with all your soul, with all your mind, and with all your strength.' [31] The second is this: 'You shall love your neighbor as yourself.' There is no other commandment greater than these." [32] The scribe said to him, "Well said, teacher. You are right in saying, 'He is One and there is no other than he.' [33] And 'to love him with all your heart, with all your understanding, with all your strength, and to love your neighbor as yourself' is worth more than all burnt offerings and sacrifices." [34] And when Jesus saw that [he] answered with understanding, he said to him, "You are not far from the kingdom of God." And no one dared to ask him any more questions.*

Luke 10:25-28: *²⁵ There was a scholar of the law who stood up to test him and said, "Teacher, what must I do to inherit eternal life?" ²⁶ Jesus said to him, "What is written in the law? How do you read it?" ²⁷ He said in reply, "You shall love the Lord, your God, with all your heart, with all your being, with all your strength, and with all your mind, and your neighbor as yourself." ²⁸ He replied to him, "You have answered correctly; do this and you will live."*

Whether this was a Pharisee, a scribe, or a scholar of the law does not really matter. However, I find it interesting that in Mattew and Mark, the two commandments are stated by Jesus. In Luke, the lawyer is the one who pronounces the two, and Jesus confirms his statement. I have always referred to the two great commandments as having been given to us by Jesus. In Luke's version, although confirmed by Jesus, the words actually come from someone else.

In all three accounts, the question was a challenge to Jesus. They were essentially trying to catch Him as teaching something contrary to the law. However, Jesus countered and gave them what they needed, not what they wanted.

Lord, You always give us what we need in spite of what we ask for. Help me to follow Your commandments of love. Amen.

The Parable of the Good Samaritan

Luke 10:29-37: *²⁹ But because he wished to justify himself, he said to Jesus, "And who is my neighbor?" ³⁰ Jesus replied, "A man fell victim to robbers as he went down from Jerusalem to Jericho. They stripped and beat him and went off leaving him half-dead. ³¹ A priest happened to be going down that road, but when he saw him, he passed by on the opposite side. ³² Likewise*

301

a Levite came to the place, and when he saw him, he passed by on the opposite side. [33] But a Samaritan traveler who came upon him was moved with compassion at the sight. [34] He approached the victim, poured oil and wine over his wounds and bandaged them. Then he lifted him up on his own animal, took him to an inn and cared for him. [35] The next day he took out two silver coins and gave them to the innkeeper with the instruction, 'Take care of him. If you spend more than what I have given you, I shall repay you on my way back.' [36] Which of these three, in your opinion, was neighbor to the robbers' victim?" [37] He answered, "The one who treated him with mercy." Jesus said to him, "Go and do likewise."

This passage in Luke is a continuation of the prior conversation. The scholar of the law was bested by Jesus and is now trying to justify himself; once again trying to catch Jesus. Jesus turns things around and gets the lawyer to pronounce the answer. And again, Jesus confirms the lawyer's answer.

The answers to both of the above questions are important teachings of Jesus; however, their importance is drawn from two angles. First, Jesus is confirming that the one questioning Him has a good understanding of the law. Second, it confirms the fact that Jesus came to fulfill the law, not to change it.

Lord, in every case in which Your enemies tested You, You bested them by answering with patience and love. You provided them with what they needed rather than what they wanted. Help me to use patience and love to make my way through challenges that come before me. Amen.

Mary and Martha

Luke 10:38-42: *³⁸ As they continued their journey, he entered a village where a woman whose name was Martha welcomed him. ³⁹ She had a sister named Mary [who] sat beside the Lord at his feet listening to him speak. ⁴⁰ Martha, burdened with much serving, came to him and said, "Lord, do you not care that my sister has left me by myself to do the serving? Tell her to help me." ⁴¹ The Lord said to her in reply, "Martha, Martha, you are anxious and worried about many things. ⁴² There is need of only one thing. Mary has chosen the better part, and it will not be taken from her."*

This may have been the first time that Jesus encountered Mary and Martha. Lazarus, their brother, is mentioned later as a close friend of Jesus. After Jesus and his disciples entered the Village where Martha and Mary lived, she welcomed them into her home.

Martha was being a good hostess and heavily involved in serving Jesus and, at least, some of His disciples. I believe it is best to assume there was a lot of work involved in this. Martha was probably justified in wanting her sister to help with the tasks. However, Jesus sets the priority, indicating that Mary's desire to hear Him was more important at this time. Being someone who likes to follow the normal order of things, I can sympathize with Martha. She was trying to be a proper hostess to her guests. And, having the desire that I have of learning more about Jesus, I can also understand Mary's choice. But Jesus did set the priority.

Lord, we humans have our own ways of determining the order of things. We set our priorities as best we can. Help us to recognize and reset our priorities when it comes to matters of You and our faith. Amen.

Inopportune Friend at Midnight

Luke 11:5-8: *⁵ And he said to them, "Suppose one of you has a friend to whom he goes at midnight and says, 'Friend, lend me three loaves of bread, ⁶ for a friend of mine has arrived at my house from a journey and I have nothing to offer him,' ⁷ and he says in reply from within, 'Do not bother me; the door has already been locked and my children and I are already in bed. I cannot get up to give you anything.' ⁸ I tell you, if he does not get up to give him the loaves because of their friendship, he will get up to give him whatever he needs because of his persistence.*

Our motivations for helping someone in need vary with the circumstances surrounding the request. Friendship should be the driving force, or so it would seem. In the many interpretations of the law, helping someone in need is promoted as a valid fulfillment of the law. Persistence of the requestor is not viewed as a loving response to a friend or even fulfillment of the law. Granted, we should never place our families or ourselves in danger, but these circumstances do not reflect any possible danger. If our Lord places someone in need in our path, we should strongly consider helping our Lord in the person of the one in need.

Lord, when someone in need makes themselves known to me, it is so easy to ignore them (especially the homeless) and go about my business. Help me to see Your face in those I encounter and treat them as I would You. Amen.

Discourses Against Pharisees and Lawyers

<u>Luke 11:37-54:</u> *[37] After he had spoken, a Pharisee invited him to dine at his home. He entered and reclined at table to eat. [38] The Pharisee was amazed to see that he did not observe the prescribed washing before the meal. [39] The Lord said to him, "Oh you Pharisees! Although you cleanse the outside of the cup and the dish, inside you are filled with plunder and evil. [40] You fools! Did not the maker of the outside also make the inside? [41] But as to what is within, give alms, and behold, everything will be clean for you. [42] Woe to you Pharisees! You pay tithes of mint and of rue and of every garden herb, but you pay no attention to judgment and to love for God. These you should have done, without overlooking the others. [43] Woe to you Pharisees! You love the seat of honor in synagogues and greetings in marketplaces. [44] Woe to you! You are like unseen graves over which people unknowingly walk." [45] Then one of the scholars of the law said to him in reply, "Teacher, by saying this you are insulting us too." [46] And he said, "Woe also to you scholars of the law! You impose on people burdens hard to carry, but you yourselves do not lift one finger to touch them. [47] Woe to you! You build the memorials of the prophets whom your ancestors killed. [48] Consequently, you bear witness and give consent to the deeds of your ancestors, for they killed them and you do the building. [49] Therefore, the wisdom of God said, 'I will send to them prophets and Apostles; some of them they will kill and persecute' [50] in order that this generation might be charged with the blood of all the prophets shed since the foundation of the world, [51] from the blood of Abel to the blood of Zechariah who died between the altar and the temple building. Yes, I tell you, this generation will be charged with their blood! [52] Woe to you, scholars of the law! You have taken away the key of knowledge. You yourselves did not enter and you stopped those trying to enter." [53] When he left, the scribes*

and Pharisees began to act with hostility toward him and to interrogate him about many things, ⁵⁴ for they were plotting to catch him at something he might say.

Jesus' message was certainly heard. He was talking to the men who formulated and interpreted the laws and to the men who taught and enforced the laws. Jesus accused them. They placed heavy burdens on the ordinary people, burdens which they themselves cannot follow. Everything Jesus said was the truth and they knew it. The fact is that this has been going on for centuries. That is why they plotted against Him. It was a matter of maintaining their power and control over the Israelite nation. However, they learned the hard way that they could not trap our Lord. They were never able to get Him to fall for one of their little tricks.

One additional lesson I learned in this passage as well as the prior gospel passages is that Jesus did not go out seeking to pick a fight with Pharisees and scholars of the law. The fight always came to Him. He did not shy away from these encounters but used them to teach. Jesus seldom argues a point but rather provides another point of view that teaches a new behavior.

Lord, I have influence over a lot of people. Let me never abuse that influence to gain power and control over those who listen to me. Help me to serve them well as You have taught us. Amen.

Warning Against Greed for Wealth and the Parable of the Rich Fool

<u>Luke 12:13-21:</u> *¹³ Someone in the crowd said to him, "Teacher, tell my brother to share the inheritance with*

306

me." *[14]* *He replied to him, "Friend, who appointed me as your judge and arbitrator?" [15] Then he said to the crowd, "Take care to guard against all greed, for though one may be rich, one's life does not consist of possessions." [16] Then he told them a parable. "There was a rich man whose land produced a bountiful harvest. [17] He asked himself, 'What shall I do, for I do not have space to store my harvest?' [18] And he said, 'This is what I shall do: I shall tear down my barns and build larger ones. There I shall store all my grain and other goods [19] and I shall say to myself, "Now as for you, you have so many good things stored up for many years, rest, eat, drink, be merry!"' [20] But God said to him, 'You fool, this night your life will be demanded of you; and the things you have prepared, to whom will they belong?' [21] Thus will it be for the one who stores up treasure for himself but is not rich in what matters to God."*

There is a difference between greed and having wealth. It is primarily in the attitude toward what you have. Greed wants more and more. Greed is never satisfied. Having wealth is not greed if the wealth is used for the good of others. I will not try to go into how much is enough or what is the point where having wealth becomes greedy. Our Lord's point is essentially that you cannot take it with you. What is the purpose of the gathering if it is going to be lost anyway?

"...one's life does not consist of possessions." Our lives consist of our relationships with others and how we use what we have. Our lives should be bringing us closer to God rather than building walls between us. The more we are focused on our treasures, the less we are able to keep God in our lives.

Lord, I know that You never intended for me to be wealthy. It is not that I get swept up in greed. In my case, I do not know how to keep it or use it properly. Help me to keep You as my focus and my treasure. Amen.

Watchfulness and Faithfulness

Luke 12:35-48: *[35] "Gird your loins and light your lamps [36] and be like servants who await their master's return from a wedding, ready to open immediately when he comes and knocks. [37] Blessed are those servants whom the master finds vigilant on his arrival. Amen, I say to you, he will gird himself, have them recline at table, and proceed to wait on them. [38] And should he come in the second or third watch and find them prepared in this way, blessed are those servants. [39] Be sure of this: if the master of the house had known the hour when the thief was coming, he would not have let his house be broken into. [40] You also must be prepared, for at an hour you do not expect, the Son of Man will come." [41] Then Peter said, "Lord, is this parable meant for us or for everyone?" [42] And the Lord replied, "Who, then, is the faithful and prudent steward whom the master will put in charge of his servants to distribute [the] food allowance at the proper time? [43] Blessed is that servant whom his master on arrival finds doing so. [44] Truly, I say to you, he will put him in charge of all his property. [45] But if that servant says to himself, 'My master is delayed in coming,' and begins to beat the menservants and the maidservants, to eat and drink and get drunk, [46] then that servant's master will come on an unexpected day and at an unknown hour and will punish him severely and assign him a place with the unfaithful. [47] That servant who knew his master's will but did not make preparations nor act in accord with his will shall be beaten severely; [48] and the servant who was ignorant of his master's will but acted in a way deserving of a severe beating* *shall be beaten only lightly. Much will be required of the person entrusted with much, and still more will be demanded of the person entrusted with more.*

Matthew 24:42-51: *⁴² Therefore, stay awake! For you do not know on which day your Lord will come. ⁴³ Be sure of this: if the master of the house had known the hour of night when the thief was coming, he would have stayed awake and not let his house be broken into. ⁴⁴ So too, you also must be prepared, for at an hour you do not expect, the Son of Man will come. ⁴⁵ "Who, then, is the faithful and prudent servant, whom the master has put in charge of his household to distribute to them their food at the proper time? ⁴⁶ Blessed is that servant whom his master on his arrival finds doing so. ⁴⁷ Amen, I say to you, he will put him in charge of all his property. ⁴⁸ But if that wicked servant says to himself, 'My master is long delayed,' ⁴⁹ and begins to beat his fellow servants, and eat and drink with drunkards, ⁵⁰ the servant's master will come on an unexpected day and at an unknown hour ⁵¹ and will punish him severely and assign him a place with the hypocrites, where there will be wailing and grinding of teeth.*

"... you also must be prepared, for at an hour you do not expect, the Son of Man will come." This is what our Lord wants us to understand. The parable is just an explanation. The reality is that we will never know when our Lord is going to call us to account for what we have been doing. So, our Lord's advice is to do things according to God's will; and, when God calls on us, all will be well. This is a very simple formula, yet it is so hard for people to follow.

Also, our Lord warns us of the punishments that are due to disobedience. It is very common among us humans to avoid actions because of potential punishment. Potential punishment has always been a deterrent of improper behavior, as long as the punishment is sufficient to force the decision. We must not fear punishment as much as offending God by our disobedience. If we simply avoid actions because of potential punishment, then we are no better than Pavlov's dog.

Lord, we know not the day nor the hour; but we do know that we should live according to Your will for us. We have enough clues from Your teachings and from the laws of nature to know what is right and what is wrong. Help us to always choose what is right. Amen.

Repentance or Destruction

<u>Luke 13:1-9:</u> *[1] At that time some people who were present there told him about the Galileans whose blood Pilate had mingled with the blood of their sacrifices. [2] He said to them in reply, "Do you think that because these Galileans suffered in this way, they were greater sinners than all other Galileans? [3] By no means! But I tell you, if you do not repent, you will all perish as they did! [4] Or those eighteen people who were killed when the tower at Siloam fell on them—do you think they were more guilty than everyone else who lived in Jerusalem? [5] By no means! But I tell you, if you do not repent, you will all perish as they did!" [6] And he told them this parable: "There once was a person who had a fig tree planted in his orchard, and when he came in search of fruit on it but found none, [7] he said to the gardener, 'For three years now I have come in search of fruit on this fig tree but have found none. [So] cut it down. Why should it exhaust the soil?' [8] He said to him in reply, 'Sir, leave it for this year also, and I shall cultivate the ground around it and fertilize it; [9] it may bear fruit in the future. If not, you can cut it down.'*

310

We are all sinners. Period. Exclamation mark! It does not matter whose sins are greater. We are all subject to judgment and punishment. Jesus is calling for all to repent of their sins. This was also the message of John the Baptist. However, there is a difference, Jesus is going to give us the method by which our sins can be forgiven (the sacrament of reconciliation).

The parable tells us that as long as we are still alive, we have an opportunity to repent and grow. However, we need to take action to follow the Will of God. It will not just happen. God looks at each of us based on who we are today, not what we have done in the past. We *may bear fruit in the future.*

Lord, although You remind us that we are sinful creatures, You offer us chance after chance to grow and become better. Grant me the courage to admit my sins and seek reconciliation so that I may bear fruit in the future. Amen.

The Healing of the Crippled Woman on the Sabbath

Luke 13:10-17: *[10] He was teaching in a synagogue on the sabbath. [11] And a woman was there who for eighteen years had been crippled by a spirit; she was bent over, completely incapable of standing erect. [12] When Jesus saw her, he called to her and said, "Woman, you are set free of your infirmity." [13] He laid his hands on her, and she at once stood up straight and glorified God. [14] But the leader of the synagogue, indignant that Jesus had cured on the sabbath, said to the crowd in reply, "There are six days when work should be done. Come on those days to be cured, not on the*

311

sabbath day." [15] *The Lord said to him in reply, "Hypocrites! Does not each one of you on the sabbath untie his ox or his ass from the manger and lead it out for watering?* [16] *This daughter of Abraham, whom Satan has bound for eighteen years now, ought she not to have been set free on the sabbath day from this bondage?"* [17] *When he said this, all his adversaries were humiliated; and the whole crowd rejoiced at all the splendid deeds done by him.*

It seems that we have another instance when Jesus heals someone who did not ask to be healed. At least, there is no indication one way or the other. However, it again shows our Lord's compassion for those who are burdened. He knows that she has suffered for eighteen years and wishes to free her. Unfortunately, it happens to be the Sabbath.

Jesus knew it was the Sabbath. The "leader of the synagogue" was outspoken in his criticism. However, the words he used were targeted to the crowd, not to Jesus. But it is once again the Jewish leadership that challenges healing on the Sabbath. This is not work. It is compassion. Jesus points out that people will do what is necessary to be done regardless of the day of the week. That does not mean they are dishonoring God on that day. The crowd understood His message and rejoiced.

Lord, when it comes to acts of compassion, help me to be sure that it is the right thing to do, regardless of what day it is. Amen.

Exclusion from the Kingdom,
The Narrow Gate

<u>Luke 13:22-30:</u> *[22] He passed through towns and villages, teaching as he went and making his way to Jerusalem. [23] Someone asked him, "Lord, will only a few people be saved?" He answered them, [24] "Strive to enter through the narrow door, for many, I tell you, will attempt to enter but will not be strong enough. [25] After the master of the house has arisen and locked the door, then will you stand outside knocking and saying, 'Lord, open the door for us.' He will say to you in reply, 'I do not know where you are from.' [26] And you will say, 'We ate and drank in your company and you taught in our streets.' [27] Then he will say to you, 'I do not know where [you] are from. Depart from me, all you evildoers!' [28] And there will be wailing and grinding of teeth when you see Abraham, Isaac, and Jacob and all the prophets in the kingdom of God and you yourselves cast out. [29] And people will come from the east and the west and from the north and the south and will recline at table in the kingdom of God. [30] For behold, some are last who will be first, and some are first who will be last."*

<u>Matthew 7:13-14:</u> *[13] "Enter through the narrow gate; for the gate is wide and the road broad that leads to destruction, and those who enter through it are many. [14] How narrow the gate and constricted the road that leads to life. And those who find it are few.*

<u>Matthew 7:22-23:</u> *[22] Many will say to me on that day, 'Lord, Lord, did we not prophesy in your name? Did we not drive out demons in your name? Did we not do mighty deeds in your*

name?' [23] *Then I will declare to them solemnly, 'I never knew you. Depart from me, you evildoers.'*

Matthew 8:11-12: [11] *I say to you, many will come from the east and the west, and will recline with Abraham, Isaac, and Jacob at the banquet in the kingdom of heaven,* [12] *but the children of the kingdom will be driven out into the outer darkness, where there will be wailing and grinding of teeth."*

Matthew 19:30: *But many who are first will be last, and the last will be first.*

Mark 10:31: *But many that are first will be last, and [the] last will be first.*

The law is the path through the narrow gate. It is the Will of God. Unless we do the will of His Father in heaven, we will not enter the kingdom. The Israelites were given the law. They were raised by the law. They were expected to live by the law. Yet so many lived by the standards of the world, answering the call of the world to its treasures instead. Then the pagans heard the word of God, Jesus, the way, and became intrigued with it. They began to follow the will of the Father. The first to be called drifted away, but the last to be called moved in ahead of them, finding their way through the narrow gate.

Jesus' warning in this parable should have frightened the "followers of the law" but it did not. It only angered the Jewish leaders because it accused them of hypocrisy. They promoted one way of living and lived another. However, Jesus' warning was not only for them, but for all sinners. Following the law, living the will of the Father, as Jesus showed us the way, will lead us through the narrow gate.

Lord, You are the compass of my life. Open my mind and my heart to follow your lead. Show me the way and help me to see, so I may find my way through the narrow gate. Amen.

A Warning Against Herod

Luke 13:31-33: [31] *At that time some Pharisees came to him and said, "Go away, leave this area because Herod wants to kill you." [32] He replied, "Go and tell that fox, 'Behold, I cast out demons and I perform healings today and tomorrow, and on the third day I accomplish my purpose. [33] Yet I must continue on my way today, tomorrow, and the following day, for it is impossible that a prophet should die outside of Jerusalem.'*

Let us be realistic. The Pharisees are not trying to save Jesus. They simply are trying to scare Him into leaving the area. They know that, if He gives in to the warning, they will have a tactic to use against Him. Jesus knows what the Pharisees are up to and will not give in.

"Yet I must continue on my way today, tomorrow, and the following day, for it is impossible that a prophet should die outside of Jerusalem." Here, Jesus is telling His disciples that He will suffer and die in Jerusalem. Little hints along the way that His followers are slow to grasp.

Lord, I am not very different from Your other disciples. I suppose that, if I were there with them at that time, Your words would fly over my head as well. It is only after the fact that I know the truth. Help me to not judge them harshly. Amen.

The Lament over Jerusalem

<u>Luke 13:34-35:</u> *[34] "Jerusalem, Jerusalem, you who kill the prophets and stone those sent to you, how many times I yearned to gather your children together as a hen gathers her brood under her wings, but you were unwilling! [35] Behold, your house will be abandoned. [But] I tell you, you will not see me until [the time comes when] you say, 'Blessed is he who comes in the name of the Lord.'"*

<u>Matthew 23:37-39:</u> *[37] "Jerusalem, Jerusalem, you who kill the prophets and stone those sent to you, how many times I yearned to gather your children together, as a hen gathers her young under her wings, but you were unwilling! [38] Behold, your house will be abandoned, desolate. [39] I tell you, you will not see me again until you say, 'Blessed is he who comes in the name of the Lord.'"*

Jesus is not talking to the city, Jerusalem, or the people of the city. He is speaking to the Israelite nation. Jesus is lamenting all of the rejection God has experienced from them. Over and over, God has come to their aid. Over and over, they have rejected God and those He sent in His name. It has reached a point now that Jesus tells them and all sinners that they will not see God until they acknowledge Him.

Lord, I pray that all people will be given the grace to accept You as their savior and Lord. I also pledge to do whatever You want of me to help make this happen. Amen.

316

Healing of the Man with Dropsy

<u>Luke 14:1-6:</u> *¹ On a sabbath he went to dine at the home of one of the leading Pharisees, and the people there were observing him carefully. ² In front of him there was a man suffering from dropsy. ³ Jesus spoke to the scholars of the law and Pharisees in reply, asking, "Is it lawful to cure on the sabbath or not?" ⁴ But they kept silent; so, he took the man and, after he had healed him, dismissed him. ⁵ Then he said to them, "Who among you, if your son or ox falls into a cistern, would not immediately pull him out on the sabbath day?" ⁶ But they were unable to answer his question.*

It is the Sabbath once again. Jesus is in the home of a Pharisee – not just any Pharisee, one of the leaders. There were scholars of the law among the guests. Jesus performed His miracle, another healing *on the Sabbath*. This time there was no response from the Pharisee or any of his other guests. Our Lord made His point, but did He win the Pharisee over to His side?

Lord, life is full of its challenges, and I have lived through many. But I have never had to face an enemy over and over as You had. Give me Your strength to endure all I encounter. Amen.

The Teaching about Humility

<u>Luke 14:7-14:</u> *⁷ He told a parable to those who had been invited, noticing how they were choosing the places of honor at the table. ⁸ "When you are invited by someone to a wedding banquet, do not recline at table in the place of honor. A more distinguished guest than you may have been invited by*

him, [9] and the host who invited both of you may approach you and say, 'Give your place to this man,' and then you would proceed with embarrassment to take the lowest place. [10] Rather, when you are invited, go and take the lowest place; so that when the host comes to you, he may say, 'My friend, move up to a higher position.' Then you will enjoy the esteem of your companions at the table. [11] For everyone who exalts himself will be humbled, but the one who humbles himself will be exalted." [12] Then he said to the host who invited him, "When you hold a lunch or a dinner, do not invite your friends or your brothers or your relatives or your wealthy neighbors, in case they may invite you back and you have repayment. [13] Rather, when you hold a banquet, invite the poor, the crippled, the lame, the blind; [14] blessed indeed will you be because of their inability to repay you. For you will be repaid at the resurrection of the righteous."

Jesus is appealing to human emotions based on logic. This will work for most people. It probably will not work for those who are vain and filled with pride. However, even those who are vain will see the advantage of being asked to move from a lowly place to a higher place. They would probably expect it.

Although I see Jesus' advice about banquets as a good thing to do, the celebrations, such as weddings, are usually intended for family and friends to celebrate the special occasion. I believe that God wants us to be joyful and celebrate appropriate events. I agree that there are times when such gatherings are used only to impress others and build the self-esteem of the hosts. This is contrary to what I believe God wants us to do. But to invite the poor and downtrodden to special events is always a good idea.

318

Lord, help me to recognize the times when it is most appropriate to humble myself before others. The more often I do so, the more likely the virtue will be part of my being. Amen.

The Parable of the Great Feast

<u>Luke 14:15-24:</u> [15] *One of his fellow guests on hearing this said to him, "Blessed is the one who will dine in the kingdom of God."* [16] *He replied to him, "A man gave a great dinner to which he invited many.* [17] *When the time for the dinner came, he dispatched his servant to say to those invited, 'Come, everything is now ready.'* [18] *But one by one, they all began to excuse themselves. The first said to him, 'I have purchased a field and must go to examine it; I ask you, consider me excused.'* [19] *And another said, 'I have purchased five yoke of oxen and am on my way to evaluate them; I ask you, consider me excused.'* [20] *And another said, 'I have just married a woman, and therefore I cannot come.'* [21] *The servant went and reported this to his master. Then the master of the house in a rage commanded his servant, 'Go out quickly into the streets and alleys of the town and bring in here the poor and the crippled, the blind and the lame.'* [22] *The servant reported, 'Sir, your orders have been carried out and still there is room.'* [23] *The master then ordered the servant, 'Go out to the highways and hedgerows and make people come in that my home may be filled.* [24] *For, I tell you, none of those men who were invited will taste my dinner.'"*

<u>Matthew 22:1-14:</u> [1] *Jesus again in reply spoke to them in parables, saying,* [2] *"The kingdom of heaven may be likened to a king who gave a wedding feast for his son.* [3] *He dispatched his servants to summon the invited guests to the feast, but they refused to come.* [4] *A second time he sent other servants, saying,*

319

'Tell those invited: "Behold, I have prepared my banquet, my calves and fattened cattle are killed, and everything is ready; come to the feast."' ⁵ Some ignored the invitation and went away, one to his farm, another to his business. ⁶ The rest laid hold of his servants, mistreated them, and killed them. ⁷ The king was enraged and sent his troops, destroyed those murderers, and burned their city. ⁸ Then he said to his servants, 'The feast is ready, but those who were invited were not worthy to come. ⁹ Go out, therefore, into the main roads and invite to the feast whomever you find.' ¹⁰ The servants went out into the streets and gathered all they found, bad and good alike, and the hall was filled with guests. ¹¹ But when the king came in to meet the guests, he saw a man there not dressed in a wedding garment. ¹² He said to him, 'My friend, how is it that you came in here without a wedding garment?' But he was reduced to silence. ¹³ Then the king said to his attendants, 'Bind his hands and feet, and cast him into the darkness outside, where there will be wailing and grinding of teeth.' ¹⁴ Many are invited, but few are chosen."

There are a couple of messages here. The first is that those who were given the grace of faith are the ones who are invited, whether they were original invitees or secondarily called. However, not all of them valued that gift; and they eventually lost it. They simply lost the desire to partake in the great feast. In the end, they missed the feast.

The second message is that those who do not value the gift will make no effort to develop it. Those who do not value the gift will spend no time or resources to grow it. In the end, they will miss the feast also.

The ones who value the gift of faith will follow the precepts of the faith and spend time and resources to grow it. They will be welcomed to the feast and enjoy it.

Lord, I pray that I never lose my fervor for my faith. I pray that I always strive to learn more and comply with Your will for me. May my will correspond to Your will in all things. Amen.

Parables of the Lost Sheep
and the Lost Coin

<u>Luke 15:1-10:</u> *[1] The tax collectors and sinners were all drawing near to listen to him, [2] but the Pharisees and scribes began to complain, saying, "This man welcomes sinners and eats with them." [3] So to them he addressed this parable. [4] "What man among you having a hundred sheep and losing one of them would not leave the ninety-nine in the desert and go after the lost one until he finds it? [5] And when he does find it, he sets it on his shoulders with great joy [6] and, upon his arrival home, he calls together his friends and neighbors and says to them, 'Rejoice with me because I have found my lost sheep.' [7] I tell you, in just the same way there will be more joy in heaven over one sinner who repents than over ninety-nine righteous people who have no need of repentance. [8] "Or what woman having ten coins and losing one would not light a lamp and sweep the house, searching carefully until she finds it? [9] And when she does find it, she calls together her friends and neighbors and says to them, 'Rejoice with me because I have found the coin that I lost.' [10] In just the same way, I tell you, there will be rejoicing among the angels of God over one sinner who repents."*

<u>Matthew 18:12-14:</u> *[12] What is your opinion? If a man has a hundred sheep and one of them goes astray, will he not leave the ninety-nine in the hills and go in search of the stray? [13] And if he finds it, amen, I say to you, he rejoices more over it than*

*over the ninety-nine that did not stray. *¹⁴* In just the same way, it is not the will of your heavenly Father that one of these little ones be lost.*

"... there will be more joy in heaven over one sinner who repents than over ninety-nine righteous people who have no need of repentance." Here we have the message that Jesus wants His audience to remember. Jesus was sent by His Father to gather in the lost sheep of the house of Israel. That is why He was regularly in the presence of sinners. But let us face the fact, the Pharisees, scribes, and scholars of the law did not consider themselves as sinners. They were the elite, the righteous, who did not need His guidance. Jesus wants them to know that God will make every effort to find sinners and bring them back to the fold.

The parable of the lost coin is essentially the same as that of the lost sheep. God's enduring love for us strives to bring us home.

Lord, I am a sinner. I pray You will continue to call me in whatever way it takes to return to the fold. Amen.

Parable of the Prodigal Son

<u>Luke 15:11-32:</u> *¹¹ Then he said, "A man had two sons, ¹² and the younger son said to his father, 'Father, give me the share of your estate that should come to me.' So, the father divided the property between them. ¹³ After a few days, the younger son collected all his belongings and set off to a distant country where he squandered his inheritance on a life of dissipation. ¹⁴ When he had freely spent everything, a severe famine struck that country, and he found himself in dire need. ¹⁵ So he hired himself out to one of the local citizens who sent him to his farm to tend the swine. ¹⁶ And he longed to eat*

his fill of the pods on which the swine fed, but nobody gave him any. [17] Coming to his senses he thought, 'How many of my father's hired workers have more than enough food to eat, but here am I, dying from hunger. [18] I shall get up and go to my father and I shall say to him, "Father, I have sinned against heaven and against you. [19] I no longer deserve to be called your son; treat me as you would treat one of your hired workers."' [20] So he got up and went back to his father. While he was still a long way off, his father caught sight of him and was filled with compassion. He ran to his son, embraced him and kissed him. [21] His son said to him, 'Father, I have sinned against heaven and against you; I no longer deserve to be called your son.' [22] But his father ordered his servants, 'Quickly bring the finest robe and put it on him; put a ring on his finger and sandals on his feet. [23] Take the fattened calf and slaughter it. Then let us celebrate with a feast, [24] because this son of mine was dead, and has come to life again; he was lost, and has been found.' Then the celebration began. [25] Now the older son had been out in the field and, on his way back, as he neared the house, he heard the sound of music and dancing. [26] He called one of the servants and asked what this might mean. [27] The servant said to him, 'Your brother has returned, and your father has slaughtered the fattened calf because he has him back safe and sound.' [28] He became angry, and when he refused to enter the house, his father came out and pleaded with him. [29] He said to his father in reply, 'Look, all these years I served you and not once did I disobey your orders; yet you never gave me even a young goat to feast on with my friends. [30] But when your son returns who swallowed up your property with prostitutes, for him you slaughter the fattened calf.' [31] He said to him, 'My son, you are here with me always; everything I have is yours. [32] But now we must celebrate and rejoice, because your brother was dead and has come to life again; he was lost and has been found.'"

This story has been told in many different contexts ever since our Lord first told the story. The first message is the same as the parables of the lost sheep and the coin. God is always in search of the lost one to welcome him home. But in this parable, there is more to learn.

The prodigal son has a lot to learn about life and about himself. In this story, he suffers, learns, and realizes he has made bad choices and wants to return to where he knows he will be loved and cared for. Not all sinners come to that realization. He humbles himself before his loving and forgiving father, who welcomes him home and wants to celebrate his return. Again, this is similar to the prior parables.

The difference here in this story is the reaction of the older brother to the younger brother's return. It sounds like jealousy but is more like simple anger. The anger is toward both his brother for taking and blowing his inheritance and his father for simply welcoming his younger brother home. Should the younger son not make some attempt at reconciliation? Should the father not punish the younger son for his seriously poor choices? The father was acting out of love and the joy of his son's return.

Nothing is said in the parable about the older son changing his mind and welcoming his younger brother. So, we will never know, but we can hope that the older son will eventually welcome his young brother out of forgiveness and love for him. Yes, forgiveness is correct. The younger son did sin against his brother as well as his father. He left the family causing hardship, both materially and emotionally, against all who remained. Love once again is the answer if the older brother can find it in himself to express it.

Lord, fill my mind and my heart with Your love always, so that the first thing I draw on in my reactions to what I encounter is always love. Amen.

Parable of the Unjust Steward

<u>Luke 16:1-13:</u> *[1] Then he also said to his disciples, "A rich man had a steward who was reported to him for squandering his property. [2] He summoned him and said, 'What is this I hear about you? Prepare a full account of your stewardship, because you can no longer be my steward.' [3] The steward said to himself, 'What shall I do, now that my master is taking the position of steward away from me? I am not strong enough to dig and I am ashamed to beg. [4] I know what I shall do so that, when I am removed from the stewardship, they may welcome me into their homes.' [5] He called in his master's debtors one by one. To the first, he said, 'How much do you owe my master?' [6] He replied, 'One hundred measures of olive oil.' He said to him, 'Here is your promissory note. Sit down and quickly write one for fifty.' [7] Then to another he said, 'And you, how much do you owe?' He replied, 'One hundred kors of wheat.' He said to him, 'Here is your promissory note; write one for eighty.' [8] And the master commended that dishonest steward for acting prudently. "For the children of this world are more prudent in dealing with their own generation than are the children of light. [9] I tell you, make friends for yourselves with dishonest wealth, so that when it fails, you will be welcomed into eternal dwellings. [10] The person who is trustworthy in very small matters is also trustworthy in great ones; and the person who is dishonest in very small matters is also dishonest in great ones. [11] If, therefore, you are not trustworthy with dishonest wealth, who will trust you with true wealth? [12] If you are not trustworthy with what belongs to another, who will give you what is yours? [13] No servant can*

serve two masters. He will either hate one and love the other or be devoted to one and despise the other. You cannot serve God and mammon."

There are two lessons in this passage, and both can be found in the last few verses. The story of the unjust steward shows that he was not only shrewd but a thief as well. In adjusting the debt to his employer, he was trying to ensure a place to go to when he lost his job. But in doing what he did, the people he helped would be sorry indeed if they hired someone they knew would steal from his employer. But this is not one of the lessons.

The person who is trustworthy in very small matters is also trustworthy in great ones; and the person who is dishonest in very small matters is also dishonest in great ones. My father once told me something that turned out to be a valuable lesson. He said that my name is on everything I do. I will be known if I am trustworthy by what I do. If I am, I will be given more trust. That is essentially the lesson here. If I am not trustworthy, I will be treated appropriately. We see that all the time in our daily lives. We experience it as well. Trust is such an important factor in our day-to-day living.

No servant can serve two masters. He will either hate one and love the other or be devoted to one and despise the other. Many of us try to do just the opposite. That is because we are put in the position to try to serve more than one master. We cannot live by what God wants us to do and by what the world calls us to do at the same time. You cannot give 100% of yourself to both, because both want 100% of you. Not being able to give your whole self will keep you in constant conflict until you decide who your master truly is.

Lord, I want to be trustworthy to You in all I do. I can only do that by being trustworthy with everyone I know and meet, a real challenge that only You can help me attain. Amen.

Concerning the Law and Divorce

Luke 16:17-18: *[17] It is easier for heaven and earth to pass away than for the smallest part of a letter of the law to become invalid. [18] "Everyone who divorces his wife and marries another commits adultery, and the one who marries a woman divorced from her husband commits adultery.*

The law is the law, and it will be until the end of time. When God gave us the law to live by, He intended that it would apply to us for all time, not until something better comes along. Nothing better is going to come along. It is the rule of love, and nothing surpasses it. So, we need to treat it as the only guide for our lives.

Jesus is expounding on a proper understanding of the meaning of adultery. But I believe this is incomplete. Jesus is telling us that both of these instances are examples of adultery. However, in practice, the women are usually the ones who are blamed and punished, rather than the men. Jesus may have gone into more detail when reviewing this with His disciples, but it is not shown here. The law is meant to apply to everyone, not just men and not just women.

Lord, grant me a clear understanding of the law. It is meant for all and not just some. When You created me, You made me a follower of rules. Help me to understand. Amen.

The Rich Man and Lazarus

<u>Luke 16:19-31:</u> *[19] "There was a rich man who dressed in purple garments and fine linen and dined sumptuously each day. [20] And lying at his door was a poor man named Lazarus, covered with sores, [21] who would gladly have eaten his fill of the scraps that fell from the rich man's table. Dogs even used to come and lick his sores. [22] When the poor man died, he was carried away by angels to the bosom of Abraham. The rich man also died and was buried, [23] and from the netherworld, where he was in torment, he raised his eyes and saw Abraham far off and Lazarus at his side. [24] And he cried out, 'Father Abraham, have pity on me. Send Lazarus to dip the tip of his finger in water and cool my tongue, for I am suffering torment in these flames.' [25] Abraham replied, 'My child, remember that you received what was good during your lifetime while Lazarus likewise received what was bad; but now he is comforted here, whereas you are tormented. [26] Moreover, between us and you a great chasm is established to prevent anyone from crossing who might wish to go from our side to yours or from your side to ours.' [27] He said, 'Then I beg you, father, send him to my father's house, [28] for I have five brothers, so that he may warn them, lest they too come to this place of torment.' [29] But Abraham replied, 'They have Moses and the prophets. Let them listen to them.' [30] He said, 'Oh no, father Abraham, but if someone from the dead goes to them, they will repent.' [31] Then Abraham said, 'If they will not listen to Moses and the prophets, neither will they be persuaded if someone should rise from the dead.'"*

As an aside, this story from Luke's Gospel about the rich man and Lazarus has special meaning for me. A number of years ago, I was doing a recruitment for the Society of St. Vincent de Paul. Part of the recruitment process was to give a short pulpit announcement after Communion at each Mass in the parish. I was ready when I arrived at the parish that Sunday morning. However, the pastor had different plans. Instead of giving me two minutes after Communion, he told me I was to give the homily and fold my recruitment plea into the homily. I was really surprised since I am not a priest or a deacon. But he was serious. I had 15 minutes to mentally put together a homily and my recruitment speech. I have to admit that the parishioners were happy because the homily was short, only about 10 minutes. The pastor was satisfied, and he had me do the homilies for the next two Masses. I recruited 15 people that day. Happily, I have never had to give a homily at Mass again.

There are two important lessons in this passage. The first has to do with the relationship between a rich man and Lazarus. They were in each other's presence every day, yet Lazarus was invisible to the rich man. He totally ignored the fact that Lazarus was there. I am sure Mother Teresa encountered much like this during her ministry in India. We encounter it today with the homeless population. People try to ignore them until they cannot. They are real and their needs are real, so we should not simply look or walk the other way.

The second lesson has to do with the last sentence in the passage: *If they will not listen to Moses and the prophets, neither will they be persuaded if someone should rise from the dead.* Jesus forewarned us that, even though He foretold His passion, death, and resurrection, all people would not believe and repent of their sins. His disciples would have a lot of work ahead of them. It is only with God's grace that people will believe; but even with His grace, they still must choose to believe and follow God's will.

Lord, there are people in need around us always. We encounter them almost daily. Some are homeless, some suffer from illness, some from addiction; there are many reasons. Help us to not simply ignore them. Help us to do what is necessary to show them Your love for them. Amen.

We are Unprofitable Servants

Luke 17:7-10: [7] **"Who among you would say to your servant who has just come in from plowing or tending sheep in the field, 'Come here immediately and take your place at table'?** [8] **Would he not rather say to him, 'Prepare something for me to eat. Put on your apron and wait on me while I eat and drink. You may eat and drink when I am finished'?** [9] **Is he grateful to that servant because he did what was commanded?** [10] **So should it be with you. When you have done all you have been commanded, say, 'We are unprofitable servants; we have done what we were obliged to do.'"**

Our sense of pride would most likely object to what is presented here. And that is the point. We are called to be humble. We are called to humble ourselves before God.

Lord, do not let my pride interfere with what I am doing to serve You and others. Amen.

The Cleansing of the Ten Lepers

Luke 17:11-19: [11] **As he continued his journey to Jerusalem, he traveled through Samaria and Galilee.** [12] **As he was entering a village, ten lepers met [him]. They stood at a distance from him** [13] **and raised their voice, saying, "Jesus, Master! Have pity on us!"** [14] **And when he saw them, he said,**

330

"Go show yourselves to the priests." As they were going, they were cleansed. [15] *And one of them, realizing he had been healed, returned, glorifying God in a loud voice;* [16] *and he fell at the feet of Jesus and thanked him. He was a Samaritan.* [17] *Jesus said in reply, "Ten were cleansed, were they not? Where are the other nine?* [18] *Has none but this foreigner returned to give thanks to God?"* [19] *Then he said to him, "Stand up and go; your faith has saved you."*

The importance of this passage is not so much the healing of the lepers but the return of the Samaritan to give thanks. Once again, Jesus marvels at the faith and virtue of the Samaritan. The Samaritan is the "foreigner." You would expect thanks to come from the Israelites, but not from the foreigner. Here Jesus recognizes the gratitude and the faith of the Samaritan. Sometimes it is the one you least expect to respond who actually does. I can also understand Jesus' sadness that only one returned to give thanks. We are all called to be grateful for all of the blessings, known and unknown, that Jesus pours on us.

Lord, I know that I have biases in my thinking and expectations. It comes with being human. Help me to keep an open mind and not let those biases control my thoughts and actions. Amen.

The Coming of the Kingdom of God

Luke 17:20-21: [20] *Asked by the Pharisees when the kingdom of God would come, he said in reply, "The coming of the kingdom of God cannot be observed,* [21] *and no one will announce, 'Look, here it is,' or 'There it is.' For behold, the kingdom of God is among you."*

331

There is a close connection between this passage from Luke and the next. But I want to focus here. The Pharisees are asking a question about when the Messiah will come. It is the Messiah who will bring the kingdom of God. Jesus' answer is that they will not be able to see it coming in advance. It is, as a matter of fact, now, the beginning of the kingdom since Jesus is the Messiah.

Lord, You are the long-awaited Messiah and the only ones who foresaw it were three wise men from the east. Grant me the graces I need to be ready for, not foresee, Your second coming. Amen.

The Day of the Son of Man

<u>Luke 17:22-37:</u> *[22] Then he said to his disciples, "The days will come when you will long to see one of the days of the Son of Man, but you will not see it. [23] There will be those who will say to you, 'Look, there he is,' [or] 'Look, here he is.' Do not go off, do not run in pursuit. [24] For just as lightning flashes and lights up the sky from one side to the other, so will the Son of Man be [in his day]. [25] But first he must suffer greatly and be rejected by this generation. [26] As it was in the days of Noah, so it will be in the days of the Son of Man; [27] they were eating and drinking, marrying and giving in marriage up to the day that Noah entered the ark, and the flood came and destroyed them all. [28] Similarly, as it was in the days of Lot: they were eating, drinking, buying, selling, planting, building; [29] on the day when Lot left Sodom, fire and brimstone rained from the sky to destroy them all. [30] So it will be on the day the Son of Man is revealed. [31] On that day, a person who is on the housetop and whose belongings are in the house must not go down to get them, and likewise a person in the field must not return to what was left behind. [32] Remember the wife of Lot. [33] Whoever seeks*

to preserve his life will lose it, but whoever loses it will save it. [34] I tell you, on that night there will be two people in one bed; one will be taken, the other left. [35] And there will be two women grinding meal together; one will be taken, the other left." [36]] [37] They said to him in reply, "Where, Lord?" He said to them, "Where the body is, there also the vultures will gather."

The day of the Son of Man cannot be predicted. Over the last two thousand years, there have been attempts to predict or proclaim the day of the Son of Man. However, Jesus told us that we will not be able to predict it. When He comes, everyone will know at that instant.

Jesus, with this statement, is giving us a warning that we should be prepared for His coming. We will not know when in advance, but we will know when He arrives. When He comes, it will be too late to start preparing ourselves. The things of this world will have no meaning. It is only us and God, and our state of being at that time. Remember, God is concerned with who we are today. How we got to this state of being is a result of our choices.

Lord, it is my choices, my decisions, that will determine my state of being when You come. Help me to make those choices in a way that would please You. Amen.

Parable of the Persistent Widow

<u>Luke 18:1-8:</u> *[1] Then he told them a parable about the necessity for them to pray always without becoming weary. He said, [2] "There was a judge in a certain town who neither feared God nor respected any human being. [3] And a widow in that town used to come to him and say, 'Render a just decision for me against my adversary.' [4] For a long time the judge was*

333

unwilling, but eventually he thought, 'While it is true that I neither fear God nor respect any human being, [5] because this widow keeps bothering me I shall deliver a just decision for her lest she finally come and strike me.'" [6] The Lord said, "Pay attention to what the dishonest judge says. [7] Will not God then secure the rights of his chosen ones who call out to him day and night? Will he be slow to answer them? [8] I tell you, he will see to it that justice is done for them speedily. But when the Son of Man comes, will he find faith on earth?"

Luke summarized the parable in verse 1: *Then he told them a parable about the necessity for them to pray always without becoming weary.* We have to be persistent in the things we pray for, at least the things that are really important to us. Jesus' point is that God will answer our prayers out of love for us, not because we are nagging Him. However, He is not saying that God will always give us what we want.

The last statement in verse 8 almost seems cynical, but it is a realistic question. At Jesus' second coming, how many people of faith will He find? This depends on our persistence in following the precepts of our faith. There is a fine line between being persistent and being stubborn. Being stubborn is a fault. Being persistent can be a virtue. Do not let "being stubborn" be the thing that is remembered about you.

Lord, grant me the wisdom to know when I should be persistent in my prayers and to know when what I am praying for is not important. Amen.

334

The Pharisee and the Tax Collector

Luke 18:9-14: *[9] He then addressed this parable to those who were convinced of their own righteousness and despised everyone else. [10] "Two people went up to the temple area to pray; one was a Pharisee and the other was a tax collector. [11] The Pharisee took up his position and spoke this prayer to himself, 'O God, I thank you that I am not like the rest of humanity—greedy, dishonest, adulterous—or even like this tax collector. [12] I fast twice a week, and I pay tithes on my whole income.' [13] But the tax collector stood off at a distance and would not even raise his eyes to heaven but beat his breast and prayed, 'O God, be merciful to me a sinner.' [14] I tell you, the latter went home justified, not the former; for everyone who exalts himself will be humbled, and the one who humbles himself will be exalted."*

It is really difficult for a person to convict himself of being a sinner and really mean it. Pride convinces us that we are good, in spite of some minor faults. This is especially true when that person is in a position of power and/or influence. To be realistic, it takes a lot of soul searching to get one to truly admit to being a sinner. I believe our Lord chose the two characters in this parable, not because they were specific people He knew (although He may very well have had two specific people in mind), but because people were expected to respect Pharisees, scribes, and scholars of the law as good people, worthy of imitation. People looked on tax collectors as the scum of the earth. So, for our Lord to praise the tax collector for humbling himself before God was contrary to the thinking of most people.

I look at myself as an example. I have spent most of my life in roles of power and influence, not the kind to affect significant portions of the world, but small segments.

Through my work and my writings, I have a lot of influence on people; and I have earned the respect of many. My pride can easily build me up as a righteous person. I could easily become like the Pharisee in this parable. In fact, there are times when I patted myself on the back for being a good person. However, there have also been plenty of times when the Holy Spirit has convicted me of my excessive pride; and I recognize my faults and humble myself before God.

I read something this morning that applies to this. It is from *Devotion to the Sacred Heart of Jesus* by Fr. John Croiset, S.J.: "We love fame, applause, and praise for all we do. We see some who labor much for God but are always saying how much they do. They are always uncomfortable, hurried, fatigued, and oppressed; one would say they are inviting everyone to have compassion on them, in their labors. The truth is, that vanity has a great part in so much labor. We think ourselves very important and necessary; we wish to appear so. Pride comes in, even in the very actions that belong to humility. We love to distinguish ourselves in the practice of certain virtues, and even in the exercise of good works. But all this alacrity is not for God alone, it is also to secure our own distinction. Finally, that excessive sadness and discouragement which we feel after a relapse into our former failings is not the effect of tenderness of conscience, as some imagine. It is the effect of a secret pride, which makes us think ourselves more holy than we really are."

Our Lord wants us to recognize the faults in our lives. Every one of us is a sinner. Some are greater sinners than others. There goes pride again! We all need to admit our failings and humble ourselves before our Lord and Creator.

O God, be merciful to me a sinner.

Part 9

Jesus at the

Feast of the Tabernacles

(according to John)

The Journey to Jerusalem in Secret

John 7:1-13: *¹ After this, Jesus moved about within Galilee; but he did not wish to travel in Judea, because the Jews were trying to kill him. ² But the Jewish feast of Tabernacles was near. ³ So his brothers said to him, "Leave here and go to Judea, so that your disciples also may see the works you are doing. ⁴ No one works in secret if he wants to be known publicly. If you do these things, manifest yourself to the world." ⁵ For his brothers did not believe in him. ⁶ So Jesus said to them, "My time is not yet here, but the time is always right for you. ⁷ The world cannot hate you, but it hates me, because I testify to it that its works are evil. ⁸ You go up to the feast. I am not going up to this feast, because my time has not yet been fulfilled." ⁹ After he had said this, he stayed on in Galilee. ¹⁰ But when his brothers had gone up to the feast, he himself also went up, not openly but [as it were] in secret. ¹¹ The Jews were looking for him at the feast and saying, "Where is he?" ¹² And there was considerable murmuring about him in the crowds. Some said, "He is a good man," [while] others said, "No; on the contrary, he misleads the crowd." ¹³ Still, no one spoke openly about him because they were afraid of the Jews.*

To go or not to go, that is the question. There is no question in Jesus' mind. It is not out of fear that Jesus is sending His disciples and staying behind. It is not yet His time. There are so many opposed to Him and looking to attack Him that there could be danger to His disciples just because of His presence. Later, we will see that His disciples fear for Him to go to Jerusalem because of the danger to Jesus. Jesus will follow the will of His Father in all cases.

But when his brothers had gone up to the feast, He Himself also went up, not openly but [as it were] in secret. The will of His Father evidently was for Jesus to go to the feast but separate from His disciples.

Lord, Your mission essentially was to follow the will of Your Father. And You did so in all cases, in spite of the bidding You received from those around You. Help me to be as faithful to Your call as You are to that of Your Father. Amen.

Teaching in the Temple

<u>John 7:14-39:</u> *[14] When the feast was already half over, Jesus went up into the temple area and began to teach. [15] The Jews were amazed and said, "How does he know scripture without having studied?" [16] Jesus answered them and said, "My teaching is not my own but is from the one who sent me. [17] Whoever chooses to do his will shall know whether my teaching is from God or whether I speak on my own. [18] Whoever speaks on his own seeks his own glory, but whoever seeks the glory of the one who sent him is truthful, and there is no wrong in him. [19] Did not Moses give you the law? Yet none of you keeps the law. Why are you trying to kill me?" [20] The crowd answered, "You are possessed! Who is trying to kill you?" [21] Jesus answered and said to them, "I performed one work and all of you are amazed [22] because of it. Moses gave you circumcision—not that it came from Moses but rather from the patriarchs—and you circumcise a man on the sabbath. [23] If a man can receive circumcision on a sabbath so that the law of Moses may not be broken, are you angry with me because I made a*

whole person well on a sabbath? ²⁴ Stop judging by appearances but judge justly." ²⁵ So some of the inhabitants of Jerusalem said, "Is he not the one they are trying to kill? ²⁶ And look, he is speaking openly, and they say nothing to him. Could the authorities have realized that he is the Messiah? ²⁷ But we know where he is from. When the Messiah comes, no one will know where he is from." ²⁸ So Jesus cried out in the temple area as he was teaching and said, "You know me and also know where I am from. Yet I did not come on my own, but the one who sent me, whom you do not know, is true. ²⁹ I know him, because I am from him, and he sent me." ³⁰ So they tried to arrest him, but no one laid a hand upon him, because his hour had not yet come. ³¹ But many of the crowd began to believe in him, and said, "When the Messiah comes, will he perform more signs than this man has done?" ³² The Pharisees heard the crowd murmuring about him to this effect, and the chief priests and the Pharisees sent guards to arrest him. ³³ So Jesus said, "I will be with you only a little while longer, and then I will go to the one who sent me. ³⁴ You will look for me but not find [me], and where I am you cannot come." ³⁵ So the Jews said to one another, "Where is he going that we will not find him? Surely, he is not going to the dispersion among the Greeks to teach the Greeks, is he? ³⁶ What is the meaning of his saying, 'You will look for me and not find [me], and where I am you cannot come'?" ³⁷ On the last and greatest day of the feast, Jesus stood up and exclaimed, "Let anyone who thirsts come to me and drink. ³⁸ Whoever believes in me, as scripture says: 'Rivers of living water will flow from within him.'"

⁹ He said this in reference to the Spirit that those who came to believe in him were to receive. There was, of course, no Spirit yet, because Jesus had not yet been glorified.

Whoever speaks on his own seeks his own glory, but whoever seeks the glory of the one who sent him is truthful, and there is no wrong in him. If I am to do the Will of God, then I must follow it completely. If I vary it at all, it becomes my will, not His. As Jesus says, if we start inserting our own ideas, then it is not the truth as God revealed His will to us.

He is speaking openly, and they say nothing to him. This exchange is helping people to realize that Jesus could be the long-awaited Messiah. He speaks the simple truth. What He says makes sense. The Pharisees, scribes, and scholars of the law are all out to have Him killed, but they are afraid to take Him. If I am to imitate the life of Jesus, then I must not fear; I must have courage to follow the will of Him who sent me. *So, they tried to arrest him, but no one laid a hand upon him, because his hour had not yet come.*

Lord, You always know what to say and how to respond in the circumstances presented to You. Grant me the confidence to know that the Holy Spirit will provide me with the guidance and words I need as I need them. Grant me the trust and strength I need at all times. Amen.

Division Among the People
Regarding Jesus

<u>John 7:40-52:</u> *[40] Some in the crowd who heard these words said, "This is truly the Prophet." [41] Others said, "This is the Messiah." But others said, "The Messiah will not come from Galilee, will he? [42] Does not scripture say that the Messiah will be of David's family and come from Bethlehem, the village where David lived?" [43] So a division occurred in the crowd because of him. [44] Some of them even wanted to arrest him, but no one laid hands on him. [45] So the guards went to the chief priests and Pharisees, who asked them, "Why did you not bring him?" [46] The guards answered, "Never before has anyone spoken like this one." [47] So the Pharisees answered them, "Have you also been deceived? [48] Have any of the authorities or the Pharisees believed in him? [49] But this crowd, which does not know the law, is accursed." [50] Nicodemus, one of their members who had come to him earlier, said to them, [51] "Does our law condemn a person before it first hears him and finds out what he is doing?" [52] They answered and said to him, "You are not from Galilee also, are you? Look and see that no prophet arises from Galilee."*

The split of opinions about Jesus would have been expected. That's simply what happens when you have a controversial subject. However, in the gospels, there is no reference to the source that the Pharisees would have used to determine if Jesus fit the prophecies of the Messiah. All we hear is that Jesus in not the promised one. The only lesson I receive here about Jesus' way of life is, once again, His patience in dealing with the Pharisees. There seems to be just as much of a split of opinions on what is being said by the Pharisees.

342

Lord, although I realize that there is more to come in the way of controversy spewed out by the Pharisees, grant me the patience I need to continue with this study and not become cynical. Amen.

The Woman Caught in Adultery

John 7:53-8:11: *[53] Then each went to his own house, [1] while Jesus went to the Mount of Olives. [2] But early in the morning he arrived again in the temple area, and all the people started coming to him, and he sat down and taught them. [3] Then the scribes and the Pharisees brought a woman who had been caught in adultery and made her stand in the middle. [4] They said to him, "Teacher, this woman was caught in the very act of committing adultery. [5] Now in the law, Moses commanded us to stone such women. So, what do you say?" [6] They said this to test him, so that they could have some charge to bring against him. Jesus bent down and began to write on the ground with his finger. [7] But when they continued asking him, he straightened up and said to them, "Let the one among you who is without sin be the first to throw a stone at her." [8] Again he bent down and wrote on the ground. [9] And in response, they went away one by one, beginning with the elders. So he was left alone with the woman before him. [10] Then Jesus straightened up and said to her, "Woman, where are they? Has no one condemned you?" [11] She replied, "No one, sir." Then Jesus said, "Neither do I condemn you. Go, [and] from now on do not sin anymore."*

Jesus took every opportunity He could to go off by Himself and spend time in communion with His Father. That is something I must learn to do as well. The nice thing about being retired is that I can devote some time every day to prayer. I do so in the morning, evening, and at bedtime. Each morning is when I devote most of my time to it. However, the devotion of my time is probably not nearly as high in quality as the few minutes Jesus may have spent with His Father. Somehow, I feel that, in spite of the amount of time, I feel my prayer life is lacking. I hope to develop it into something more meaningful.

Jesus came into the temple area alone, without His disciples and started teaching the people who gathered. Once again, the Pharisees challenged Him with the woman caught in adultery. They wanted to see if He would contradict the law as Moses gave it to them. However, Jesus had said He was not here to change the law but to fulfill it. He proved it by making a simple answer: *Let the one among you who is without sin be the first to throw a stone at her.* The crowd responded as He had expected. No one was sinless, so no one cast the first stone, not even the Pharisees. Jesus did not condemn her and simply advised her to sin no more. There is nothing stated or implied that she had faith, her sins were forgiven or that she even asked for forgiveness. Our Lord was merciful to her, a sinner.

Lord, help me, guide me to go and sin no more. Amen.

"I am the Light of the World"

John 8:12-20: *[12] Jesus spoke to them again, saying, "I am the light of the world. Whoever follows me will not walk in darkness, but will have the light of life." [13] So the Pharisees said to him, "You testify on your own behalf, so your testimony cannot be verified." [14] Jesus answered and said to them, "Even if I do testify on my own behalf, my testimony can be verified, because I know where I came from and where I am going. But you do not know where I come from or where I am*

344

going. ^{15} *You judge by appearances, but I do not judge anyone.* ^{16} *And even if I should judge, my judgment is valid, because I am not alone, but it is I and the Father who sent me.* ^{17} *Even in your law it is written that the testimony of two men can be verified.* ^{18} *I testify on my behalf and so does the Father who sent me."* ^{19} *So they said to him, "Where is your father?" Jesus answered, "You know neither me nor my Father. If you knew me, you would know my Father also."* ^{20} *He spoke these words while teaching in the treasury in the temple area. But no one arrested him, because his hour had not yet come.*

Almost everything that Jesus taught corresponds to the law – the law as presented by God, not the law as interpreted and enhanced by the Pharisees and scholars of the law. To follow the law is to walk in the light. Jesus, in fulfilling the law, is the light. Those who follow Him *will not walk in darkness.*

Lord, I need to continue to ask the question: what would Jesus do? In following where You lead me, my path is clear. Light my way. Amen.

Discussion with the Jews

John 8:21-29: ^{21} *He said to them again, "I am going away and you will look for me, but you will die in your sin. Where I am going you cannot come."* ^{22} *So the Jews said, "He is not going to kill himself, is he, because he said, 'Where I am going you cannot come'?"* ^{23} *He said to them, "You belong to what is below, I belong to what is above. You belong to this world, but I do not belong to this world.* ^{24} *That is why I told you that you will die in your sins. For if you do not believe that I AM, you will die in your sins."* ^{25} *So they said to him, "Who are*

345

you?" Jesus said to them, "What I told you from the beginning. ²⁶ I have much to say about you in condemnation. But the one who sent me is true, and what I heard from him I tell the world." ²⁷ They did not realize that he was speaking to them of the Father. ²⁸ So Jesus said [to them], "When you lift up the Son of Man, then you will realize that I AM, and that I do nothing on my own, but I say only what the Father taught me. ²⁹ The one who sent me is with me. He has not left me alone, because I always do what is pleasing to him."

Jesus' statements in this passage provide a clear message, although it probably was confusing to some of those who heard Him. If we do not believe that Jesus is God, then we cannot go with Him to His heavenly kingdom. That is the one thing that all Christians should have in common – the belief that Jesus is God, one of three persons in the Blessed Trinity. If they do not believe this, then they should not be calling themselves Christians. Even with that said, many who call themselves Christians are more dedicated to the world than to their faith. *"For if you do not believe that I AM, you will die in your sins."*

Lord, grant me Your graces so that my faith will be strong and never lose my belief that You, Your Father, and Your Holy Spirit are the Blessed Trinity, the one true God. Amen.

The Truth will Make You Free

John 8:30-36: *³⁰ Because he spoke this way, many came to believe in him. ³¹ Jesus then said to those Jews who believed in him, "If you remain in my word, you will truly be my disciples, ³² and you will know the truth, and the truth will set you free." ³³ They answered him, "We are descendants of Abraham and have never been enslaved to anyone. How can*

you say, 'You will become free'?" [34] *Jesus answered them,*
"Amen, amen, I say to you, everyone who commits sin is a slave
of sin. [35] *A slave does not remain in a household forever, but a*
son always remains. [36] *So if a son frees you, then you will truly*
be free.

This is the topic of one of the chapters in my book "One-Liners to Guide Our Lives." Here are some of the considerations I wrote.

"This particular passage from the Gospel of John can be confusing. It would seem that sometimes knowing the truth can restrict you in what you might want to do. It would seem that sometimes knowing the truth would cause you to be embarrassed and have to withdraw something you said – undo a mistake. ...

If you believe honestly that something is true, then that knowledge removes from you the decision to say or do something contrary. Obviously, people have free will and they can choose to do or say anything they want. However, when you do or say something that is contrary to what you say you believe, then you are forced to try to justify that in some way – even to yourself. You are professing one belief and then contradicting yourself. That causes conflict within yourself."

Following our faith frees us from that conflict. We are free. However, following our faith does require courage and fortitude in addition to knowledge and understanding.

Lord, grant me the wisdom to understand the values of my faith, but especially grant me the strength to stand behind those values. Amen.

Children of the Devil

John 8:37-47: *[37] I know that you are descendants of Abraham. But you are trying to kill me, because my word has no room among you. [38] I tell you what I have seen in the Father's presence; then do what you have heard from the Father." [39] They answered and said to him, "Our father is Abraham." Jesus said to them, "If you were Abraham's children, you would be doing the works of Abraham. [40] But now you are trying to kill me, a man who has told you the truth that I heard from God; Abraham did not do this. [41] You are doing the works of your father!" [So,] they said to him, "We are not illegitimate. We have one Father, God." [42] Jesus said to them, "If God were your Father, you would love me, for I came from God and am here; I did not come on my own, but he sent me. [43] Why do you not understand what I am saying? Because you cannot bear to hear my word. [44] You belong to your father the devil, and you willingly carry out your father's desires. He was a murderer from the beginning and does not stand in truth, because there is no truth in him. When he tells a lie, he speaks in character, because he is a liar and the father of lies. [45] But because I speak the truth, you do not believe me. [46] Can any of you charge me with sin? If I am telling the truth, why do you not believe me? [47] Whoever belongs to God hears the words of God; for this reason, you do not listen, because you do not belong to God."*

This is part of a long dialogue between our Lord and the Jews. When I refer to the Jews, I believe this includes Pharisees, scribes, and scholars of the law, because those three groups seem to be everywhere that Jesus spoke. Primarily the argument is coming from the Pharisees. Jesus is right. If they do not follow Jesus' teachings which come from God the Father, then they must be following the devil.

The more Jesus speaks to the people, the more followers He gets. Unfortunately, it does not seem like He is getting through to the Pharisees, scribes, and scholars of the law.

Lord, help me to always recognize what is coming from our Father in heaven. It is You, our Father, and the Holy Spirit that I wish to follow. Amen.

Before Abraham was, I Am.

<u>John 8:48-59:</u> *[48] The Jews answered and said to him, "Are we not right in saying that you are a Samaritan and are possessed?" [49] Jesus answered, "I am not possessed; I honor my Father, but you dishonor me. [50] I do not seek my own glory; there is one who seeks it and he is the one who judges. [51] Amen, amen, I say to you, whoever keeps my word will never see death." [52] [So] the Jews said to him, "Now we are sure that you are possessed. Abraham died, as did the prophets, yet you say, 'Whoever keeps my word will never taste death.' [53] Are you greater than our father Abraham, who died? Or the prophets, who died? Who do you make yourself out to be?" [54] Jesus answered, "If I glorify myself, my glory is worth nothing; but it is my Father who glorifies me, of whom you say, 'He is our God.' [55] You do not know him, but I know him. And if I should say that I do not know him, I would be like you a liar. But I do know him, and I keep his word. [56] Abraham, your father rejoiced to see my day; he saw it and was glad. [57] So the Jews said to him, "You are not yet fifty years old, and you have seen Abraham?" [58] Jesus said to them, "Amen, amen, I say to you, before Abraham came to be, I AM." [59] So they picked up stones to throw at him; but Jesus hid and went out of the temple area.*

And the dialogue continues to no avail. Finally, our Lord states the absolute truth: "I AM." This statement was used by God as He spoke to Moses. To the Jews, it is blasphemy to say you are God; and so, they were ready to stone Him. There was no trial. There was no attempt to determine the truth of what Jeus said. Saying the words was an automatic death sentence. This is the same reaction we will see from Caiphas in demanding our Lord's execution.

Lord, it is sad to see that throughout history, the mob can be insighted by a bare few to act upon circumstances where the truth has not been revealed. Help me, guide me to never follow the mob; and to look to You for the truth. Amen.

Jesus Heals the Man Born Blind

John 9:1-41: *[1] As he passed by he saw a man blind from birth. [2] His disciples asked him, "Rabbi, who sinned, this man or his parents, that he was born blind?" [3] Jesus answered, "Neither he nor his parents sinned; it is so that the works of God might be made visible through him. [4] We have to do the works of the one who sent me while it is day. Night is coming when no one can work. [5] While I am in the world, I am the light of the world." [6] When he had said this, he spat on the ground and made clay with the saliva, and smeared the clay on his eyes, [7] and said to him, "Go wash in the Pool of Siloam" (which means Sent). So, he went and washed and came back able to see. [8] His neighbors and those who had seen him earlier as a beggar said, "Isn't this the one who used to sit and beg?" [9] Some said, "It is," but others said, "No, he just looks like him." He said, "I am." [10] So they said to him, "[So] how were your eyes opened?" [11] He replied, "The man called Jesus made clay and anointed my eyes and told me, 'Go to Siloam and wash.' So I went there and washed and was able to see." [12] And they said to him, "Where is he?" He said, "I don't know." [13] They brought the one who was once blind to the*

350

Pharisees. ¹⁴ Now Jesus had made clay and opened his eyes on a sabbath. ¹⁵ So then the Pharisees also asked him how he was able to see. He said to them, "He put clay on my eyes, and I washed, and now I can see." ¹⁶ So some of the Pharisees said, "This man is not from God, because he does not keep the sabbath." [But] others said, "How can a sinful man do such signs?" And there was a division among them. ¹⁷ So they said to the blind man again, "What do you have to say about him, since he opened your eyes?" He said, "He is a prophet." ¹⁸ Now the Jews did not believe that he had been blind and gained his sight until they summoned the parents of the one who had gained his sight. ¹⁹ They asked them, "Is this your son, who you say was born blind? How does he now see?" ²⁰ His parents answered and said, "We know that this is our son and that he was born blind. ²¹ We do not know how he sees now, nor do we know who opened his eyes. Ask him, he is of age; he can speak for himself." ²² His parents said this because they were afraid of the Jews, for the Jews had already agreed that if anyone acknowledged him as the Messiah, he would be expelled from the synagogue. ²³ For this reason his parents said, "He is of age; question him." ²⁴ So a second time they called the man who had been blind and said to him, "Give God the praise! We know that this man is a sinner." ²⁵ He replied, "If he is a sinner, I do not know. One thing I do know is that I was blind and now I see." ²⁶ So they said to him, "What did he do to you? How did he open your eyes?" ²⁷ He answered them, "I told you already and you did not listen. Why do you want to hear it again? Do you want to become his disciples, too?" ²⁸ They ridiculed him and said, "You are that man's disciple; we are disciples of Moses! ²⁹ We know that God spoke to Moses, but we do not know where this one is from." ³⁰ The man answered and said to them, "This is what is so amazing, that you do not know where he is from, yet he opened my eyes. ³¹ We know that God does not listen to sinners, but if one is devout and does his will, he listens to him. [32] It is unheard of that anyone ever opened the eyes of a person born blind. [33] If this man were not from God, he would not be able to do anything." [34] They answered and said to him, "You were born totally in sin, and are you trying to teach us?" Then they threw him out. [35] When Jesus heard that they had thrown him out, he found him and said, "Do you believe in the Son of Man?" [36] He answered and said, "Who is he, sir, that I may believe in him?" [37] Jesus said to him, "You have seen him and the one speaking with you is he." [38] He said, "I do believe, Lord," and he worshiped him. [39] Then Jesus said, "I came into this world for judgment, so that those who do not see might see, and those who do see might become blind." [40] Some of the Pharisees who were with him heard this and said to him, "Surely we are not also blind, are we?" [41] Jesus said to them, "If you were blind, you would have no sin; but now you are saying, 'We see,' so your sin remains.

This is another case of a cure for someone who did not explicitly ask to be cured. Even the question of "who sinned" may not have brought attention to the blind man. It may simply be as Jesus said; it is an opportunity to show His Father's love and mercy. The cure was a blessing to show God's benevolence.

Another thought is that God does not punish anyone for someone else's sin. That is a lesson I learned a long time ago.

Once again, Jesus cured on the Sabbath. The blind man was brought to the Pharisees who added another charge to their already long list of things that Jesus had done in violation of the law. The Pharisees would not accept the man being healed, so they contacted the parents of the blind man. The parents confirmed that he was their son and that he was born blind. The parents may have had some fear of what the Pharisees could blame on them, but they were not intimidated and put the charge back where it belonged. Question their son, he is of age.

Then comes the wisdom of a simple man born blind: *"This is what is so amazing, that you do not know where he is from, yet he opened my eyes. We know that God does not listen to sinners, but if one is devout and does his will, he listens to him. It is unheard of that anyone ever opened the eyes of a person born blind. If this man were not from God, he would not be able to do anything."* Like his parents, the man born blind was not intimidated by the Pharisees and simply told the truth as he understood it. We should never be intimidated by the devil and his cohorts. The Pharisees were blind – to their own sins.

Lord, there are times when people who have authority can wield it in such a way to intimidate others into following what they want them to believe. Help us to always seek and follow the truth. Amen.

I am the Good Shepherd

John 10:1-18: *[1] "Amen, amen, I say to you, whoever does not enter a sheepfold through the gate but climbs over elsewhere is a thief and a robber. [2] But whoever enters through the gate is the shepherd of the sheep. [3] The gatekeeper opens it for him, and the sheep hear his voice, as he calls his own sheep by name and leads them out. [4] When he has driven out all his own, he walks ahead of them, and the sheep follow him, because they recognize his voice. [5] But they will not follow a stranger; they will run away from him, because they do not recognize the voice of strangers." [6] Although Jesus used this figure of speech, they did not realize what he was trying to tell them.*

353

[7]So Jesus said again, "Amen, amen, I say to you, I am the gate for the sheep. [8]All who came [before me] are thieves and robbers, but the sheep did not listen to them. [9]I am the gate. Whoever enters through me will be saved and will come in and go out and find pasture. [10]A thief comes only to steal and slaughter and destroy; I came so that they might have life and have it more abundantly. [11]I am the good shepherd. A good shepherd lays down his life for the sheep. [12]A hired man, who is not a shepherd and whose sheep are not his own, sees a wolf coming and leaves the sheep and runs away, and the wolf catches and scatters them. [13]This is because he works for pay and has no concern for the sheep. [14]I am the good shepherd, and I know mine and mine know me, [15]just as the Father knows me and I know the Father; and I will lay down my life for the sheep. [16]I have other sheep that do not belong to this fold. These also I must lead, and they will hear my voice, and there will be one flock, one shepherd. [17]This is why the Father loves me, because I lay down my life in order to take it up again. [18]No one takes it from me, but I lay it down on my own. I have power to lay it down, and power to take it up again. This command I have received from my Father."

Although Jesus used this figure of speech, they did not realize what he was trying to tell them. This seems to be true in a lot of the dialogues that Jesus had with the Jews, ordinary folk as well as leadership. His disciples had difficulty as well with many of the things He said because they were of a different mindset and their experiences in life would not allow them to relate well with what His teachings were. Jesus had to retell what He said in a different way or explain in detail what He meant. In reading Jesus' life and teachings, it is up to us to reach an understanding of the lessons He wants us to learn. Sometimes this can only be done over time and after much investigation.

I have other sheep that do not belong to this fold. Jesus is here referring to the Gentiles and pagans who will follow Him. They are all also part of His flock. They recognize Him as their shepherd, as all Christians do.

Finally, He tells them that He is willing to and will lay down His life for His sheep because His Father wills it. This is what any shepherd should be willing to do for his sheep.

Lord, open up my mind and my heart to what it is that You would have me understand. If You will not directly give me the understanding, then grant me the wisdom to find the right path to the answer. Amen.

Division Among the Jews Again

<u>John 10:19-21:</u> *¹⁹ Again there was a division among the Jews because of these words. ²⁰ Many of them said, "He is possessed and out of his mind; why listen to him?" ²¹ Others said, "These are not the words of one possessed; surely a demon cannot open the eyes of the blind, can he?"*

This was not unexpected. No matter what premise is presented to a group of people, there will be a variety of opinions from those listening. I am sure our Lord knew this would be the case.

Lord, help me, guide me; so that I may always understand what You are saying and follow the path You are leading. Amen.

Part 10

The Ministry

in Judea

Jesus Blesses the Children

Matthew 19:13-15: [13] *Then children were brought to him that he might lay his hands on them and pray. The disciples rebuked them,* [14] *but Jesus said, "Let the children come to me, and do not prevent them; for the kingdom of heaven belongs to such as these."* [15] *After he placed his hands on them, he went away.*

Mark 10:13-16: [13] *And people were bringing children to him that he might touch them, but the disciples rebuked them.* [14] *When Jesus saw this, he became indignant and said to them, "Let the children come to me; do not prevent them, for the kingdom of God belongs to such as these.* [15] *Amen, I say to you, whoever does not accept the kingdom of God like a child will not enter it."* [16] *Then he embraced them and blessed them, placing his hands on them.*

Luke 18:15-17: [15] *People were bringing even infants to him that he might touch them, and when the disciples saw this, they rebuked them.* [16] *Jesus, however, called the children to himself and said, "Let the children come to me and do not prevent them; for the kingdom of God belongs to such as these.* [17] *Amen, I say to you, whoever does not accept the kingdom of God like a child will not enter it."*

There are a couple of lessons to be learned here. The first relates to the rebuke of the disciples. It only makes sense that the disciples were being protective of our Lord in trying to keep children from being brought to Him. Jesus had been spending the far majority of His time with adults in healing and teaching. I think "rebuke" is too harsh a word for this situation.

Then, Jesus referred to the innocence of the children as well as their ultimate love and dependence on their parents and others to care for and protect them. That is the type of relationship that we should have with our Father in heaven.

Lord, I bow my head before You in hopes You will bless me as You did the children who were brought to You. Amen.

The Rich Young Man

Matthew 19:16-22: *[16] Now someone approached him and said, "Teacher, what good must I do to gain eternal life?" [17] He answered him, "Why do you ask me about the good? There is only One who is good. If you wish to enter into life, keep the commandments." [18] He asked him, "Which ones?" And Jesus replied, "'You shall not kill; you shall not commit adultery; you shall not steal; you shall not bear false witness; [19] honor your father and your mother'; and 'you shall love your neighbor as yourself.'" [20] The young man said to him, "All of these I have observed. What do I still lack?" [21] Jesus said to him, "If you wish to be perfect, go, sell what you have and give to [the] poor, and you will have treasure in heaven. Then come, follow me." [22] When the young man heard this statement, he went away sad, for he had many possessions.*

Mark 10:17-22: *[17] As he was setting out on a journey, a man ran up, knelt down before him, and asked him, "Good teacher, what must I do to inherit eternal life?" [18] Jesus answered him, "Why do you call me good? No one is good but God alone. [19] You know the commandments: 'You shall not kill; you shall not commit adultery; you shall not steal; you shall not bear false witness; you shall not defraud; honor your father and your mother.'" [20] He replied and said to him, "Teacher, all of these I have observed from my* *youth." [21] Jesus, looking at him, loved him and said to him, "You are lacking in one thing. Go, sell what you have, and give to [the] poor and you will have treasure in heaven; then come, follow me." [22] At that statement his face fell, and he went away sad, for he had many possessions.*

Luke 18:18-23: *[18] An official asked him this question, "Good teacher, what must I do to inherit eternal life?" [19] Jesus answered him, "Why do you call me good? No one is good but God alone. [20] You know the commandments, 'You shall not commit adultery; you shall not kill; you shall not steal; you shall not bear false witness; honor your father and your mother.'" [21] And he replied, "All of these I have observed from my youth." [22] When Jesus heard this he said to him, "There is still one thing left for you: sell all that you have and distribute it to the poor, and you will have a treasure in heaven. Then come, follow me." [23] But when he heard this, he became quite sad, for he was very rich.*

Here are three renditions of the same story. And to top it off, that was the Gospel passage from this morning's Mass. Jesus told him, "You know the commandments." So, it boils down to what the real question from the man was: am I doing enough, have I done enough, or is there more to do in order to gain eternal life? And the real answer from Jesus is not sell and distribute, but that there will always be more to do? It is the will of our Father in heaven that we live by His commandments and do His will throughout our lives, not just at certain times or for a period of time. Showing our love for God and all those we encounter is an ongoing venture that we will hopefully be happy to experience.

Lord, grant me the wisdom to know that my love for You and all Your creation is an ongoing mission that I must fulfill; and grant me the graces I need to persevere in that mission. Amen.

On Riches and the Rewards of Discipleship

<u>Matthew 19:23-30:</u> *[23] Then Jesus said to his disciples, "Amen, I say to you, it will be hard for one who is rich to enter the kingdom of heaven. [24] Again I say to you, it is easier for a camel to pass through the eye of a needle than for one who is rich to enter the kingdom of God." [25] When the disciples heard this, they were greatly astonished and said, "Who then can be saved?" [26] Jesus looked at them and said, "For human beings this is impossible, but for God all things are possible." [27] Then Peter said to him in reply, "We have given up everything and followed you. What will there be for us?" [28] Jesus said to them, "Amen, I say to you that you who have followed me, in the new age, when the Son of Man is seated on his throne of glory, will yourselves sit on twelve thrones, judging the twelve tribes of Israel. [29] And everyone who has given up houses or brothers or sisters or father or mother or children or lands for the sake of my name will receive a hundred times more, and will inherit eternal life. [30] But many who are first will be last, and the last will be first.*

<u>Mark 10:23-31:</u> *[23] Jesus looked around and said to his disciples, "How hard it is for those who have wealth to enter the kingdom of God!" [24] The disciples were amazed at his words. So, Jesus again said to them in reply, "Children, how hard it is to enter the kingdom of God! [25] It is easier for a camel to pass through [the] eye of [a] needle than for one who is rich*

to enter the kingdom of God." *26 They were exceedingly astonished and said among themselves, "Then who can be saved?" *27 Jesus looked at them and said, "For human beings it is impossible, but not for God. All things are possible for God." *28 Peter began to say to him, "We have given up everything and followed you." *29 Jesus said, "Amen, I say to you, there is no one who has given up house or brothers or sisters or mother or father or children or lands for my sake and for the sake of the gospel *30 who will not receive a hundred times more now in this present age: houses and brothers and sisters and mothers and children and lands, with persecutions, and eternal life in the age to come. *31 But many that are first will be last, and [the] last will be first."*

Luke 18:24-30: *24 Jesus looked at him [now sad] and said, "How hard it is for those who have wealth to enter the kingdom of God! *25 For it is easier for a camel to pass through the eye of a needle than for a rich person to enter the kingdom of God." *26 Those who heard this said, "Then who can be saved?" *27 And he said, "What is impossible for human beings is possible for God." *28 Then Peter said, "We have given up our possessions and followed you." *29 He said to them, "Amen, I say to you, there is no one who has given up house or wife or brothers or parents or children for the sake of the kingdom of God *30 who will not receive [back] an overabundant return in this present age and eternal life in the age to come."*

Luke 22:28-30: *28 It is you who have stood by me in my trials; *29 and I confer a kingdom on you, just as my Father has conferred one on me, *30 that you may eat and drink at my table in my kingdom; and you will sit on thrones judging the twelve tribes of Israel.*

These passages are a continuation of the previous passages. The wealthy will find it difficult to enter the kingdom of heaven because they will be dedicated too much to acquiring and keeping the treasures of this world. However, this does not apply to all who are wealthy. It is only through God that some will be saved. All things are possible with God.

The disciples who have given up all to follow Jesus are concerned, what is in it for them? Jesus then satisfies them with the promise of rewards both here on earth and in heaven. However, those rewards do not contain earthly treasures. They are the intangibles that come with love, friendship and service to each other. And these rewards will continue on through all eternity.

Lord, I already know that the wealth of this world is not and will not be part of my life. Help me always to strive to follow Your will and look forward to the rewards to come. Amen.

The Laborers in the Vineyard

Matthew 20:1-16: *[1] "The kingdom of heaven is like a landowner who went out at dawn to hire laborers for his vineyard. [2] After agreeing with them for the usual daily wage, he sent them into his vineyard. [3] Going out about nine o'clock, he saw others standing idle in the marketplace, [4] and he said to them, 'You too go into my vineyard, and I will give you what is just.' [5] So they went off. [And] he went out again around noon, and around three o'clock, and did likewise. [6] Going out about five o'clock, he found others standing around, and said to them, 'Why do you stand here idle all day?' [7] They answered, 'Because no one has hired us.' He said to them, 'You too go into my vineyard.' [8] When it was evening the owner of the vineyard said to his foreman, 'Summon the laborers and give*

362

them their pay, beginning with the last and ending with the first.' ⁹ When those who had started about five o'clock came, each received the usual daily wage. ¹⁰ So when the first came, they thought that they would receive more, but each of them also got the usual wage. ¹¹ And on receiving it they grumbled against the landowner, ¹² saying, 'These last ones worked only one hour, and you have made them equal to us, who bore the day's burden and the heat.' ¹³ He said to one of them in reply, 'My friend, I am not cheating you. Did you not agree with me for the usual daily wage? ¹⁴ Take what is yours and go. What if I wish to give this last one the same as you? ¹⁵ [Or] am I not free to do as I wish with my own money? Are you envious because I am generous?' ¹⁶ Thus, the last will be first, and the first will be last."

I wrote about this earlier; not this particular parable, but this topic. God is interested in who we are now, today. God always exists in the present. The past cannot be changed, and the future is unknown. What is true is who we are today. When our final judgment comes, it will be based on who we are today. What we have done and experienced in the past helped make us who we are today. The reward is the same for all those who follow God and His will. So, even the evilest person who ever lived, who experiences a conversion, may be invited to enter the kingdom of heaven. With God, all things are possible. Let us pray that we will be there to rejoice with him.

Lord, all that I believe about heaven, separate from what You have told us, is speculation. What I believe is that You are all love, You are all just, and You are all merciful. Guide me through the right path; and in the end, be merciful to me a sinner. Amen.

Jesus at the Feast of Dedication

<u>John 10:22-39:</u> *[22] The feast of the Dedication was then taking place in Jerusalem. It was winter. [23] And Jesus walked about in the temple area on the Portico of Solomon. [24] So the Jews gathered around him and said to him, "How long are you going to keep us in suspense? If you are the Messiah, tell us plainly." [25] Jesus answered them, "I told you and you do not believe. The works I do in my Father's name testify to me. [26] But you do not believe, because you are not among my sheep. [27] My sheep hear my voice; I know them, and they follow me. [28] I give them eternal life, and they shall never perish. No one can take them out of my hand. [29] My Father, who has given them to me, is greater than all, and no one can take them out of the Father's hand. [30] The Father and I are one." [31] The Jews again picked up rocks to stone him. [32] Jesus answered them, "I have shown you many good works from my Father. For which of these are you trying to stone me?" [33] The Jews answered him, "We are not stoning you for a good work but for blasphemy. You, a man, are making yourself God." [34] Jesus answered them, "Is it not written in your law, 'I said, "You are gods"'? [35] If it calls them gods to whom the word of God came, and scripture cannot be set aside, [36] can you say that the one whom the Father has consecrated and sent into the world blasphemes because I said, 'I am the Son of God'? [37] If I do not perform my Father's works, do not believe me; [38] but if I perform them, even if you do not believe me, believe the works, so that you may realize [and understand] that the Father is in me and I am in the Father." [39] [Then] they tried again to arrest him; but he escaped from their power. [40] He went back across the Jordan to the place where John first baptized, and there he remained. [41] Many came to him and said, "John performed no sign, but everything John said about this man was true." [42] And many there began to believe in him.*

Once again, we see the dialogue with the Jews. This time it seems a little more heated. The Jews are asking questions but not listening to the answers. They want only one answer from our Lord: the admission that He is the Son of God. And Jesus gives it to them. Once again, they charge Him with blasphemy and try to stone Him. Jesus escapes again to a place where people value His works and words.

Jesus has been open and honest in all His healings and teachings. Those who are prompted by the devil will not value truth. They only value the purpose of their mission. No matter what Jesus would have said, they would have continued the pursuit. No amount of reasoning will open a closed mind.

Lord, I ask that You open my mind to Your words and guidance and close my mind to the promptings of the devil, so that I may always recognize You alone as my shepherd. Amen.

The Raising of Lazarus

<u>John 11:1-44:</u> *¹ Now a man was ill, Lazarus from Bethany, the village of Mary and her sister Martha. ² Mary was the one who had anointed the Lord with perfumed oil and dried his feet with her hair; it was her brother Lazarus who was ill. ³ So the sisters sent word to him, saying, "Master, the one you love is ill." ⁴ When Jesus heard this he said, "This illness is not to end in death, but is for the glory of God, that the Son of God may be glorified through it." ⁵ Now Jesus loved Martha and her sister and Lazarus. ⁶ So when he heard that he was ill, he remained for two days in the place where he was. ⁷ Then after this he said to his disciples, "Let us go back to Judea." ⁸ The disciples said to him, "Rabbi, the Jews were just trying to stone*

you, and you want to go back there?" ⁹ *Jesus answered, "Are there not twelve hours in a day? If one walks during the day, he does not stumble, because he sees the light of this world.* ¹⁰ *But if one walks at night, he stumbles, because the light is not in him."* ¹¹ *He said this, and then told them, "Our friend Lazarus is asleep, but I am going to awaken him."* ¹² *So the disciples said to him, "Master, if he is asleep, he will be saved."* ¹³ *But Jesus was talking about his death, while they thought that he meant ordinary sleep.* ¹⁴ *So then Jesus said to them clearly, "Lazarus has died.* ¹⁵ *And I am glad for you that I was not there, that you may believe. Let us go to him."* ¹⁶ *So Thomas, called Didymus, said to his fellow disciples, "Let us also go to die with him."* ¹⁷ *When Jesus arrived, he found that Lazarus had already been in the tomb for four days.* ¹⁸ *Now Bethany was near Jerusalem, only about two miles away.* ¹⁹ *And many of the Jews had come to Martha and Mary to comfort them about their brother.* ²⁰ *When Martha heard that Jesus was coming, she went to meet him; but Mary sat at home.* ²¹ *Martha said to Jesus, "Lord, if you had been here, my brother would not have died.* ²² *[But] even now I know that whatever you ask of God, God will give you."* ²³ *Jesus said to her, "Your brother will rise."* ²⁴ *Martha said to him, "I know he will rise, in the resurrection on the last day."* ²⁵ *Jesus told her, "I am the resurrection and the life; whoever believes in me, even if he dies, will live,* ²⁶ *and everyone who lives and believes in me will never die. Do you believe this?"* ²⁷ *She said to him, "Yes, Lord. I have come to believe that you are the Messiah, the Son of God, the one who is coming into the world."* ²⁸ *When she had said this, she went and called her sister Mary secretly, saying, "The teacher is here and is asking for you."* ²⁹ *As soon as she heard this, she rose quickly and went to him.* ³⁰ *For Jesus had not yet come into the village but was still where Martha had met him.* ³¹ *So when the Jews who were with her in the house comforting her saw Mary get up quickly and go out, they followed her, presuming that she was going to the tomb to weep there. ³² When Mary came to where Jesus was and saw him, she fell at his feet and said to him, "Lord, if you had been here, my brother would not have died." ³³ When Jesus saw her weeping and the Jews who had come with her weeping, he became perturbed and deeply troubled, ³⁴ and said, "Where have you laid him?" They said to him, "Sir, come and see." ³⁵ And Jesus wept. ³⁶ So the Jews said, "See how he loved him." ³⁷ But some of them said, "Could not the one who opened the eyes of the blind man have done something so that this man would not have died?" ³⁸ So Jesus, perturbed again, came to the tomb. It was a cave, and a stone lay across it. ³⁹ Jesus said, "Take away the stone." Martha, the dead man's sister, said to him, "Lord, by now there will be a stench; he has been dead for four days." ⁴⁰ Jesus said to her, "Did I not tell you that if you believe you will see the glory of God?" ⁴¹ So they took away the stone. And Jesus raised his eyes and said, "Father, I thank you for hearing me. ⁴² I know that you always hear me; but because of the crowd here I have said this, that they may believe that you sent me." ⁴³ And when he had said this, he cried out in a loud voice, "Lazarus, come out!" ⁴⁴ The dead man came out, tied hand and foot with burial bands, and his face was wrapped in a cloth. So, Jesus said to them, "Untie him and let him go."*

There are multiple lessons to be learned in this passage. The first is that our Lord did love Martha, Mary, and Lazarus. However, what was more important was for Jesus to follow the will of His Father and bring glory to His name: *This illness is not to end in death, but is for the glory of God, that the Son of God may be glorified through it.* So, Jesus waited and let nature take its course. Jesus' love for others can still be manifested in following the will of His Father even when that is not apparent to us.

"Our friend Lazarus is asleep, but I am going to awaken him." Jesus did not fear for His life for His hour had not yet come. He was on His way to raise His friend and bring glory to God. Then, Thomas who later became known as Doubting Thomas, who feared vengeance of the Jews as much as the other disciples, encouraged the other disciples to accompany Jesus who would likely go to His death in Judea. Love of our Lord can inspire us to have the courage necessary to face our fears.

"Lord, if you had been here, my brother would not have died. [But] even now I know that whatever you ask of God, God will give you." Martha's love of Jesus was also manifested in her faith. Then our Lord moves her one step further: *"Yes, Lord. I have come to believe that you are the Messiah, the Son of God, the one who is coming into the world."* Jesus is no longer just a friend and loved one; but He is the Messiah, the Son of God.

Martha called for her sister Mary to come; and when she did so without hesitation, the glory of God was about to become manifest. Love for Jesus, sorrow for her brother, and hope all drew Mary to her Lord.

The crowd, as always, had a mixture of believers, hopefuls, and cynics. Jesus simply called out, *"Lazarus, come out!"* Lazarus responded to Jesus' call. The glory of God was manifested in the raising of Lazarus. The love of Jesus for His friend was manifested. All is possible with God.

Lord, the story of the raising of Lazarus shows that anything is possible through Your love for us. Give me the strength to persevere in my faith, that I may always go to You even when things seem impossible. Amen.

The Chief Priests and Pharisees
Take Counsel Against Jesus

<u>John 11:45-53:</u> *[45] Now many of the Jews who had come to Mary and seen what he had done began to believe in him. [46] But some of them went to the Pharisees and told them what Jesus had done. [47] So the chief priests and the Pharisees convened the Sanhedrin and said, "What are we going to do? This man is performing many signs. [48] If we leave him alone, all will believe in him, and the Romans will come and take away both our land and our nation." [49] But one of them, Caiaphas, who was high priest that year, said to them, "You know nothing, [50] nor do you consider that it is better for you that one man should die instead of the people, so that the whole nation may not perish." [51] He did not say this on his own, but since he was high priest for that year, he prophesied that Jesus was going to die for the nation, [52] and not only for the nation, but also to gather into one the dispersed children of God. [53] So from that day on they planned to kill him.*

…it is better for you that one man should die instead of the people, so that the whole nation may not perish. Caiaphas, the high priest, knew what needed to be done to unify the leaders of the Jews. It did not matter to them if Jesus was the true Messiah. They had to rid themselves of Him, for the sake of the nation. *So, from that day on they planned to kill him.*

Lord, evildoers normally can find the words to unify and instigate the crowd. Help me to never fall into the web they weave. Amen.

369

The Third Prediction of the Passion

<u>John 11:54-57:</u> *54 So Jesus no longer walked about in public among the Jews, but he left for the region near the desert, to a town called Ephraim, and there he remained with his disciples. 55 Now the Passover of the Jews was near, and many went up from the country to Jerusalem before Passover to purify themselves. 56 They looked for Jesus and said to one another as they were in the temple area, "What do you think? That he will not come to the feast?" 57 For the chief priests and the Pharisees had given orders that if anyone knew where he was, he should inform them, so that they might arrest him.*

<u>Matthew 20:17-19:</u> *17 As Jesus was going up to Jerusalem, he took the twelve [disciples] aside by themselves, and said to them on the way, 18 "Behold, we are going up to Jerusalem, and the Son of Man will be handed over to the chief priests and the scribes, and they will condemn him to death, 19 and hand him over to the Gentiles to be mocked and scourged and crucified, and he will be raised on the third day."*

<u>Mark 10:32-34:</u> *32 They were on the way, going up to Jerusalem, and Jesus went ahead of them. They were amazed, and those who followed were afraid. Taking the Twelve aside again, he began to tell them what was going to happen to him. 33 "Behold, we are going up to Jerusalem, and the Son of Man will be handed over to the chief priests and the scribes, and they will condemn him to death and hand him over to the Gentiles 34 who will mock him, spit upon him, scourge him, and put him to death, but after three days he will rise."*

<u>Luke 18:31-34:</u> *31 Then he took the Twelve aside and said to them, "Behold, we are going up to Jerusalem and everything written by the prophets about the Son of Man will be*

fulfilled. [32] He will be handed over to the Gentiles and he will be mocked and insulted and spat upon; [33] and after they have scourged him, they will kill him, but on the third day he will rise." [34] But they understood nothing of this; the word remained hidden from them, and they failed to comprehend what he said.

Jesus was making His final journey to Jerusalem with His Apostles. While on this journey, Jesus made His third prediction of His upcoming passion, death, and resurrection. *But they understood nothing of this; the word remained hidden from them, and they failed to comprehend what he said.* This was the third time He predicted His upcoming sufferings. I am not sure if they did not understand or if they simply wanted it to go away. They were learning from our Lord. They were happy to be in His presence, and they wanted it to continue. Why does it have to end? Why does it especially have to end with suffering and death?

Our Lord has always spoken the truth to them. They recognize that He is the Son of God. They acknowledge His love for them. However, they do not want to lose Him. Jesus is now speaking of things they do not want to hear.

Lord, You have spoken to me many times in many different ways. Help me to understand what You want me to know and be ever willing to do Your bidding. Amen.

Request for the Sons of Zebedee

<u>Matthew 20:20-28:</u> *[20] Then the mother of the sons of Zebedee approached him with her sons and did him homage, wishing to ask him for something. [21] He said to her, "What do you wish?" She answered him, "Command that these two sons of mine sit, one at your right and the other at your left, in your*

371

kingdom." ²² Jesus said in reply, "You do not know what you are asking. Can you drink the cup that I am going to drink?" They said to him, "We can." ²³ He replied, "My cup you will indeed drink, but to sit at my right and at my left [, this] is not mine to give but is for those for whom it has been prepared by my Father." ²⁴ When the ten heard this, they became indignant at the two brothers. ²⁵ But Jesus summoned them and said, "You know that the rulers of the Gentiles lord it over them, and the great ones make their authority over them felt. ²⁶ But it shall not be so among you. Rather, whoever wishes to be great among you shall be your servant; ²⁷ whoever wishes to be first among you shall be your slave. ²⁸ Just so, the Son of Man did not come to be served but to serve and to give his life as a ransom for many."

<u>Mark 10:35-45:</u> ³⁵ Then James and John, the sons of Zebedee, came to him and said to him, "Teacher, we want you to do for us whatever we ask of you." ³⁶ He replied, "What do you wish [me] to do for you?" ³⁷ They answered him, "Grant that in your glory we may sit one at your right and the other at your left." ³⁸ Jesus said to them, "You do not know what you are asking. Can you drink the cup that I drink or be baptized with the baptism with which I am baptized?" ³⁹ They said to him, "We can." Jesus said to them, "The cup that I drink, you will drink, and with the baptism with which I am baptized, you will be baptized; ⁴⁰ but to sit at my right or at my left is not mine to give but is for those for whom it has been prepared." ⁴¹ When the ten heard this, they became indignant at James and John. ⁴² Jesus summoned them and said to them, "You know that those who are recognized as rulers over the Gentiles lord it over them, and their great ones make their authority over them felt. ⁴³ But it shall not be so among you. Rather, whoever wishes to be great among you will be your servant; ⁴⁴ whoever wishes to be first among you will be the slave of all. ⁴⁵ For the

Son of Man did not come to be served but to serve and to give his life as a ransom for many."

Luke 22:24-27: *[24] Then an argument broke out among them about which of them should be regarded as the greatest. [25] He said to them, "The kings of the Gentiles lord it over them and those in authority over them are addressed as 'Benefactors'; [26] but among you it shall not be so. Rather, let the greatest among you be as the youngest, and the leader as the servant. [27] For who is greater: the one seated at table or the one who serves? Is it not the one seated at table? I am among you as the one who serves.*

They did not get it. They spent almost three years with Him, and they still did not get it. It is not about prestige and honor. It is not about who is first. It is not about who is on the right and the left. It is about serving each other, not just serving, but serving out of love. *...but among you it shall not be so. Rather, let the greatest among you be as the youngest, and the leader as the servant.* What we must learn is to be humble before God and each other. This is one key lesson His disciples must learn.

Lord, it is so easy to fall into the trap of what the world wants us to believe: the first are the best, the first shall be served, the first shall be honored. Help me to always understand that being first is an obligation to see that others are served as they should be, even if it means me being the servant. Amen.

The Healing of the Blind Men

Matthew 20:29-34: *[29] As they left Jericho, a great crowd followed him. [30] Two blind men were sitting by the roadside,*

373

and when they heard that Jesus was passing by, they cried out, "[Lord,] Son of David, have pity on us!" [31] *The crowd warned them to be silent, but they called out all the more, "Lord, Son of David, have pity on us!"* [32] *Jesus stopped and called them and said, "What do you want me to do for you?"* [33] *They answered him, "Lord, let our eyes be opened."* [34] *Moved with pity, Jesus touched their eyes. Immediately they received their sight and followed him.*

Mark 10:46-52: [46] *They came to Jericho. And as he was leaving Jericho with his disciples and a sizable crowd, Bartimaeus, a blind man, the son of Timaeus, sat by the roadside begging.* [47] *On hearing that it was Jesus of Nazareth, he began to cry out and say, "Jesus, son of David, have pity on me."* [48] *And many rebuked him, telling him to be silent. But he kept calling out all the more, "Son of David, have pity on me."* [49] *Jesus stopped and said, "Call him." So, they called the blind man, saying to him, "Take courage; get up, he is calling you."* [50] *He threw aside his cloak, sprang up, and came to Jesus.* [51] *Jesus said to him in reply, "What do you want me to do for you?" The blind man replied to him, "Master, I want to see."* [52] *Jesus told him, "Go your way; your faith has saved you." Immediately he received his sight and followed him on the way.*

Luke 18:35-43: [35] *Now as he approached Jericho a blind man was sitting by the roadside begging,* [36] *and hearing a crowd going by, he inquired what was happening.* [37] *They told him, "Jesus of Nazareth is passing by."* [38] *He shouted, "Jesus, Son of David, have pity on me!"* [39] *The people walking in front rebuked him, telling him to be silent, but he kept calling out all the more, "Son of David, have pity on me!"* [40] *Then Jesus stopped and ordered that he be brought to him; and when he came near, Jesus asked him,* [41] *"What do you want me to do for* *you?" He replied, "Lord, please let me see." ⁴² Jesus told him, "Have sight; your faith has saved you." ⁴³ He immediately received his sight and followed him, giving glory to God. When they saw this, all the people gave praise to God.*

Here is another case of Jesus' healing power. In spite of the minor differences in the three passages, they are essentially the same on one important point. The blind man (men) had faith strong enough to believe Jesus could heal them. Jesus saw this and granted the request. Once again, Jesus showed compassion for those who believe.

Lord Jesus, have pity on me. Strengthen my belief. Amen.

Zacchaeus

Luke 19:1-10: *¹ He came to Jericho and intended to pass through the town. ² Now a man there named Zacchaeus, who was a chief tax collector and also a wealthy man, ³ was seeking to see who Jesus was; but he could not see him because of the crowd, for he was short in stature. ⁴ So he ran ahead and climbed a sycamore tree in order to see Jesus, who was about to pass that way. ⁵ When he reached the place, Jesus looked up and said to him, "Zacchaeus, come down quickly, for today I must stay at your house." ⁶ And he came down quickly and received him with joy. ⁷ When they all saw this, they began to grumble, saying, "He has gone to stay at the house of a sinner." ⁸ But Zacchaeus stood there and said to the Lord, "Behold, half of my possessions, Lord, I shall give to the poor, and if I have extorted anything from anyone I shall repay it four times over." ⁹ And Jesus said to him, "Today salvation has come to this house because this man too is a descendant of Abraham. ¹⁰ For the Son of Man has come to seek and to save what was lost."*

Like Matthew, Zacchaeus was a tax collector; however, Zacchaeus is identified as the chief tax collector in Jericho and a wealthy man. I only comment on this because wealthy men were generally accepted as graced by God, yet the people refer to both Matthew and Zacchaeus as sinners.

Once again, Jesus brings grace and forgiveness to sinners. Zacchaeus' life is changed in the presence of Jesus. What I find interesting is that Zacchaeus speaks of reconciliation which is not a topic that is presented often. However, it is important if the request for forgiveness is sincere. If possible, reconciliation for the sin committed should be given.

For the Son of Man has come to seek and to save what was lost. Jesus continues to do the will of His Father in heaven.

Lord, we are all sinners. I know that You bring forgiveness and salvation for all of us. Help me to accept Your forgiveness and strive to follow Your will in all things to come. Amen.

The Parable of the Gold Coins

Luke 19:11-27: *[11] While they were listening to him speak, he proceeded to tell a parable because he was near Jerusalem; and they thought that the kingdom of God would appear there immediately. [12] So he said, "A nobleman went off to a distant country to obtain the kingship for himself and then to return. [13] He called ten of his servants and gave them ten gold coins and told them, 'Engage in trade with these until I return.' [14] His fellow citizens, however, despised him and sent a delegation after him to announce, 'We do not want this man to be our king.' [15] But when he returned after obtaining the*

376

kingship, he had the servants called, to whom he had given the money, to learn what they had gained by trading. [16] *The first came forward and said, 'Sir, your gold coin has earned ten additional ones.'* [17] *He replied, 'Well done, good servant! You have been faithful in this very small matter; take charge of ten cities.'* [18] *Then the second came and reported, 'Your gold coin, sir, has earned five more.'* [19] *And to this servant too he said, 'You, take charge of five cities.'* [20] *Then the other servant came and said, 'Sir, here is your gold coin; I kept it stored away in a handkerchief,* [21] *for I was afraid of you, because you are a demanding person; you take up what you did not lay down and you harvest what you did not plant.'* [22] *He said to him, 'With your own words I shall condemn you, you wicked servant. You knew I was a demanding person, taking up what I did not lay down and harvesting what I did not plant;* [23] *why did you not put my money in a bank? Then on my return I would have collected it with interest.'* [24] *And to those standing by he said, 'Take the gold coin from him and give it to the servant who has ten.'* [25] *But they said to him, 'Sir, he has ten gold coins.'* [26] *'I tell you, to everyone who has, more will be given, but from the one who has not, even what he has will be taken away.* [27] *Now as for those enemies of mine who did not want me as their king, bring them here and slay them before me.'"*

Matthew 25:14-30: [14] *"It will be as when a man who was going on a journey called in his servants and entrusted his possessions to them.* [15] *To one he gave five talents; to another, two; to a third, one—to each according to his ability. Then he went away. Immediately* [16] *the one who received five talents went and traded with them and made another five.* [17] *Likewise, the one who received two made another two.* [18] *But the man who received one went off and dug a hole in the ground and buried his master's money.* [19] *After a long time the master of those servants came back and settled accounts with them.* *²⁰ The one who had received five talents came forward bringing the additional five. He said, 'Master, you gave me five talents. See, I have made five more.' ²¹ His master said to him, 'Well done, my good and faithful servant. Since you were faithful in small matters, I will give you great responsibilities. Come, share your master's joy.' ²² [Then] the one who had received two talents also came forward and said, 'Master, you gave me two talents. See, I have made two more.' ²³ His master said to him, 'Well done, my good and faithful servant. Since you were faithful in small matters, I will give you great responsibilities. Come, share your master's joy.' ²⁴ Then the one who had received the one talent came forward and said, 'Master, I knew you were a demanding person, harvesting where you did not plant and gathering where you did not scatter; ²⁵ so out of fear I went off and buried your talent in the ground. Here it is back.' ²⁶ His master said to him in reply, 'You wicked, lazy servant! So, you knew that I harvest where I did not plant and gather where I did not scatter? ²⁷ Should you not then have put my money in the bank so that I could have got it back with interest on my return? ²⁸ Now then! Take the talent from him and give it to the one with ten. ²⁹ For to everyone who has, more will be given, and he will grow rich; but from the one who has not, even what he has will be taken away. ³⁰ And throw this useless servant into the darkness outside, where there will be wailing and grinding of teeth.'"*

The lesson here is a simple one. God has gifted each of us. And those gifts are different for everyone. However, God does expect a return. He expects each of us to use those gifts to bear fruit. The resulting fruit does not have to equal the value of the gift given, but God does expect us to be fruitful. If we are not fruitful, what we have will be taken from us.

Now as for those enemies of mine who did not want me as their king, bring them here and slay them before me. This last sentence from the passage from Luke is a reminder to us that those who are non-believers or opposed to God and His will shall face eternal punishment.

Lord, You have sent me graces, talents, and gifts for my use. Help me to not be a disappointment to You, and to use them to fulfill Your will. Amen.

Part 11
The Final Ministry
in Jerusalem

The Triumphal Entry into Jerusalem

Matthew 21:1-9: *[1] When they drew near Jerusalem and came to Bethphage on the Mount of Olives, Jesus sent two disciples, [2] saying to them, "Go into the village opposite you, and immediately you will find an ass tethered, and a colt with her. Untie them and bring them here to me. [3] And if anyone should say anything to you, reply, 'The master has need of them.' Then he will send them at once." [4] This happened so that what had been spoken through the prophet might be fulfilled: [5] "Say to daughter Zion, 'Behold, your king comes to you, meek and riding on an ass, and on a colt, the foal of a beast of burden.'" [6] The disciples went and did as Jesus had ordered them. [7] They brought the ass and the colt and laid their cloaks over them, and he sat upon them. [8] The very large crowd spread their cloaks on the road, while others cut branches from the trees and strewed them on the road. [9] The crowds preceding him and those following kept crying out and saying: "Hosanna to the Son of David; blessed is he who comes in the name of the Lord; hosanna in the highest."*

Mark 11:1-10: *[1] When they drew near to Jerusalem, to Bethphage and Bethany at the Mount of Olives, he sent two of his disciples [2] and said to them, "Go into the village opposite you, and immediately on entering it, you will find a colt tethered on which no one has ever sat. Untie it and bring it here. [3] If anyone should say to you, 'Why are you doing this?' reply, 'The Master has need of it and will send it back here at once.'" [4] So they went off and found a colt tethered at a gate outside on the street, and they untied it. [5] Some of the bystanders said to them, "What are you doing, untying the colt?" [6] They answered them just as Jesus had told them to, and they permitted them to do it. [7] So they brought the colt to Jesus and put their cloaks over it. And he sat on it. [8] Many people* *spread their cloaks on the road, and others spread leafy branches that they had cut from the fields. ⁹ Those preceding him as well as those following kept crying out: "Hosanna! Blessed is he who comes in the name of the Lord! ¹⁰ Blessed is the kingdom of our father David that is to come! Hosanna in the highest!"*

Luke 19:28-40: *²⁸ After he had said this, he proceeded on his journey up to Jerusalem. ²⁹ As he drew near to Bethphage and Bethany at the place called the Mount of Olives, he sent two of his disciples. ³⁰ He said, "Go into the village opposite you, and as you enter it you will find a colt tethered on which no one has ever sat. Untie it and bring it here. ³¹ And if anyone should ask you, 'Why are you untying it?' you will answer, 'The Master has need of it.'" ³² So those who had been sent went off and found everything just as he had told them. ³³ And as they were untying the colt, its owners said to them, "Why are you untying this colt?" ³⁴ They answered, "The Master has need of it." ³⁵ So they brought it to Jesus, threw their cloaks over the colt, and helped Jesus to mount. ³⁶ As he rode along, the people were spreading their cloaks on the road; ³⁷ and now as he was approaching the slope of the Mount of Olives, the whole multitude of his disciples began to praise God aloud with joy for all the mighty deeds they had seen. ³⁸ They proclaimed: "Blessed is the king who comes in the name of the Lord. Peace in heaven and glory in the highest." ³⁹ Some of the Pharisees in the crowd said to him, "Teacher, rebuke your disciples." ⁴⁰ He said in reply, "I tell you, if they keep silent, the stones will cry out!"*

John 12:12-19: *¹² On the next day, when the great crowd that had come to the feast heard that Jesus was coming to Jerusalem, ¹³ they took palm branches and went out to meet him and cried out: "Hosanna! Blessed is he who comes in the name of the Lord, [even] the king of Israel." [14] Jesus found an ass and sat upon it, as is written: [15] "Fear no more, O daughter Zion; see, your king comes, seated upon an ass's colt." [16] His disciples did not understand this at first, but when Jesus had been glorified they remembered that these things were written about him and that they had done this for him. [17] So the crowd that was with him when he called Lazarus from the tomb and raised him from death continued to testify. [18] This was [also] why the crowd went to meet him, because they heard that he had done this sign. [19] So the Pharisees said to one another, "You see that you are gaining nothing. Look, the whole world has gone after him."*

Jesus' reputation had spread throughout Galilee and Judea. Obviously, His reputation was a good one, except in the minds of the Pharisees and others in leadership among the Jews. These passages give no extended dialogue other than the Master has need of the colt. The value of a colt was very high, and there had to be a great amount of trust in the mind of its owner for him to release it to the two disciples. Here is an example of God accommodating the need of His Son and moving the heart of the colt's owner to trust he will get his colt back.

This was an important day for our Lord. He knew He was entering upon His final journey into Jerusalem. And His Father in heaven moved the hearts of the people to welcome Him. My hope is that those who welcomed Him were not the same people who condemned Him a few days later. The "people" welcomed Him, and the "people" condemned Him; but that does not mean they were the same "people." Understanding some of the mentality of the mob, it is possible there were some of the same people in both groups. Only God knows what was in the hearts of those in each mob.

Lord, trust in Your words, works, and example is absolutely necessary if I am to grow closer to You. The more I trust You, the more likely it is that I will imitate You. Help me to grow in trust. Amen.

Jesus Weeps Over Jerusalem

Luke 19:41-44: *[41] As he drew near, he saw the city and wept over it, [42] saying, "If this day you only knew what makes for peace—but now it is hidden from your eyes. [43] For the days are coming upon you when your enemies will raise a palisade against you; they will encircle you and hem you in on all sides. [44] They will smash you to the ground and your children within you, and they will not leave one stone upon another within you because you did not recognize the time of your visitation."*

Can God feel sad? I know that Jesus in His humanity could feel sad; but is sadness something that can be felt in His divinity. Is sadness a divine emotion? Logically, I can understand how God could be disappointed. Is that the same as sadness? The Catechism of the Catholic Church does not answer this question directly.

Here, our Lord was clearly sad. The people of Jerusalem, the crown city of Judaism, do not recognize the presence of their God. If our Lord Jesus feels sadness, then His Father in heaven must feel it as well. And the Holy Spirit who proceeds from the Father and the Son must feel it as well. For they are one.

Lord, let me always remember that, in Your humanity, You can feel the same emotions that I feel. Let me never be a disappointment to You. Amen.

384

Cleansing of the Temple

<u>Matthew 21:10-17:</u> *¹⁰ And when he entered Jerusalem the whole city was shaken and asked, "Who is this?" ¹¹ And the crowds replied, "This is Jesus the prophet, from Nazareth in Galilee." ¹² Jesus entered the temple area and drove out all those engaged in selling and buying there. He overturned the tables of the money changers and the seats of those who were selling doves. ¹³ And he said to them, "It is written: 'My house shall be a house of prayer,' but you are making it a den of thieves." ¹⁴ The blind and the lame approached him in the temple area, and he cured them. ¹⁵ When the chief priests and the scribes saw the wondrous things he was doing, and the children crying out in the temple area, "Hosanna to the Son of David," they were indignant ¹⁶ and said to him, "Do you hear what they are saying?" Jesus said to them, "Yes; and have you never read the text, 'Out of the mouths of infants and nurslings you have brought forth praise'?" ¹⁷ And leaving them, he went out of the city to Bethany, and there he spent the night.*

<u>Mark 11:15-17:</u> *¹⁵ They came to Jerusalem, and on entering the temple area he began to drive out those selling and buying there. He overturned the tables of the money changers and the seats of those who were selling doves. ¹⁶ He did not permit anyone to carry anything through the temple area. ¹⁷ Then he taught them saying, "Is it not written: 'My house shall be called a house of prayer for all peoples.' But you have made it a den of thieves."*

<u>Luke 19:45-46:</u> *⁴⁵ Then Jesus entered the temple area and proceeded to drive out those who were selling things, ⁴⁶ saying to them, "It is written, 'My house shall be a house of prayer, but you have made it a den of thieves.'"*

385

This seems to be another case where Jesus is showing an emotion, anger. However, this is not necessarily so. Jesus had been to Jerusalem in the past. He knew what was going on and did not cleanse the temple area on His other visits. This could very simply be something He was compelled to do, the will of His Father in heaven. Doing the will of His Father was His ultimate goal.

Lord, help me to understand and never misjudge Your words or actions. Amen.

Cursing of the Fig Tree

Matthew 21:18-19: *[18] When he was going back to the city in the morning, he was hungry. [19] Seeing a fig tree by the road, he went over to it but found nothing on it except leaves. And he said to it, "May no fruit ever come from you again." And immediately the fig tree withered.*

Mark 11:12-14: *[12] The next day as they were leaving Bethany, he was hungry. [13] Seeing from a distance a fig tree in leaf, he went over to see if he could find anything on it. When he reached it, he found nothing but leaves; it was not the time for figs. [14] And he said to it in reply, "May no one ever eat of your fruit again!" And his disciples heard it.*

This sounds totally out of character for Jesus, except for one possibility. It is a teaching moment. Here is an example of the consequences of the creation not producing the fruit anticipated. This is similar to the parable of the gold coins. Granted, *it was not the time for figs*, but timing is not everything. The disciples will see on their return that way that the tree has withered.

Lord, may I ever be conscious of what I am called to do and never be a disappointment to You. Amen.

The Chief Priests and Scribes Conspire

Mark 11:18-19: *[18] The chief priests and the scribes came to hear of it and were seeking a way to put him to death, yet they feared him because the whole crowd was astonished at his teaching. [19] When evening came, they went out of the city.*

Luke 19:47-48: *[47] And every day he was teaching in the temple area. The chief priests, the scribes, and the leaders of the people, meanwhile, were seeking to put him to death, [48] but they could find no way to accomplish their purpose because all the people were hanging on his words.*

The conspirators continued their task, but they were once again unable to do anything. However, this time it was not something Jesus said. It was simply fear of the crowd. So, they went back to their shadows.

Lord, help me to follow Your way so that I may never conspire to do evil to anyone. Amen.

Lesson from the Withered Tree

Matthew 21:20-22: *[20] When the disciples saw this, they were amazed and said, "How was it that the fig tree withered immediately?" [21] Jesus said to them in reply, "Amen, I say to you, if you have faith and do not waver, not only will you do what has been done to the fig tree, but even if you say to this mountain, 'Be lifted up and thrown into the sea,' it will be*

387

done. [22] Whatever you ask for in prayer with faith, you will receive."

Mark 11:20-26: *[20] Early in the morning, as they were walking along, they saw the fig tree withered to its roots. [21] Peter remembered and said to him, "Rabbi, look! The fig tree that you cursed has withered." [22] Jesus said to them in reply, "Have faith in God. [23] Amen, I say to you, whoever says to this mountain, 'Be lifted up and thrown into the sea,' and does not doubt in his heart but believes that what he says will happen, it shall be done for him. [24] Therefore I tell you, all that you ask for in prayer, [25] When you stand to pray, forgive anyone against whom you have a grievance; so that your heavenly Father may in turn forgive you your transgressions." [[26]]*

So, the withered tree incident was a teaching moment. But our Lord had something else in mind rather than the parable of the gold coins. It is about having faith that what we say in God's name and what we pray for will actually come true. I believe that my faith has not reached the point that Jesus describes here, although I have not tried to move a mountain. There are things that I prayed for; however, I always use an escape clause in case I do not receive what I ask for. I end my petition with "but Thy will be done." I do not know if that is a sign of lack of faith, it might be. Jesus says, "believe that you will receive it, and it shall be yours." I still have to work on this.

Lord, help me to grow in faith so I may believe as You wish me to. Amen.

Jesus' Authority

Matthew 21:23-27: [23] *When he had come into the temple area, the chief priests and the elders of the people approached him as he was teaching and said, "By what authority are you doing these things? And who gave you this authority?"* [24] *Jesus said to them in reply, "I shall ask you one question, and if you answer it for me, then I shall tell you by what authority I do these things.* [25] *Where was John's baptism from? Was it of heavenly or of human origin?" They discussed this among themselves and said, "If we say 'Of heavenly origin,' he will say to us, 'Then why did you not believe him?'* [26] *But if we say, 'Of human origin,' we fear the crowd, for they all regard John as a prophet."* [27] *So they said to Jesus in reply, "We do not know." He himself said to them, "Neither shall I tell you by what authority I do these things.*

Mark 11:27-33: [27] *They returned once more to Jerusalem. As he was walking in the temple area, the chief priests, the scribes, and the elders approached him* [28] *and said to him, "By what authority are you doing these things? Or who gave you this authority to do them?"* [29] *Jesus said to them, "I shall ask you one question. Answer me, and I will tell you by what authority I do these things.* [30] *Was John's baptism of heavenly or of human origin? Answer me."* [31] *They discussed this among themselves and said, "If we say, 'Of heavenly origin,' he will say, '[Then] why did you not believe him?'* [32] *But shall we say, 'Of human origin'?"—they feared the crowd, for they all thought John really was a prophet.* [33] *So they said to Jesus in reply, "We do not know." Then Jesus said to them, "Neither shall I tell you by what authority I do these things."*

Luke 20:1-8: [1] *One day as he was teaching the people in the temple area and proclaiming the good news, the chief priests and scribes, together with the elders, approached him* [2] *and said to him, "Tell us, by what authority are you doing these things? Or who is the one who gave you this authority?"* [3] *He said to them in reply, "I shall ask you a question. Tell me,* [4] *was John's baptism of heavenly or of human origin?"* [5] *They discussed this among themselves, and said, "If we say, 'Of heavenly origin,' he will say, 'Why did you not believe him?'* [6] *But if we say, 'Of human origin,' then all the people will stone us, for they are convinced that John was a prophet."* [7] *So they answered that they did not know from where it came.* [8] *Then Jesus said to them, "Neither shall I tell you by what authority I do these things."*

Two thoughts come to mind with this passage. First, the chief priests and elders show no zeal for what they are doing. They are trying to discredit Jesus, but they are unwilling to take a stand in answering Jesus' question. It reminds me of Jesus' attitude toward those who are 'lukewarm." He will spit them out.

The second thought is that no matter what Jesus says in answer to their question, they will twist it into some way of discrediting Him. Jesus' approach turns things around and ends up putting the chief priests and elders on the defensive and unsure of their next step.

Jesus is able to read the hearts of those who approach Him and always has an appropriate answer for those who challenge Him.

Lord, there are times when I am prepared to discuss matters of faith; however, there are times when the questions come as a surprise, and I am not sure how to answer. Remind me at those times that I should open myself up to the guidance of the Holy Spirit who will provide me with the words I need. Amen.

The Parable of the Two Sons

<u>Matthew 21:28-32:</u> *[28] "What is your opinion? A man had two sons. He came to the first and said, 'Son, go out and work in the vineyard today.' [29] He said in reply, 'I will not,' but afterwards he changed his mind and went. [30] The man came to the other son and gave the same order. He said in reply, 'Yes, sir,' but did not go. [31] Which of the two did his father's will?" They answered, "The first." Jesus said to them, "Amen, I say to you, tax collectors and prostitutes are entering the kingdom of God before you. [32] When John came to you in the way of righteousness, you did not believe him; but tax collectors and prostitutes did. Yet even when you saw that, you did not later change your minds and believe him.*

This is a continuation of Jesus' dialogue with the chief priests and elders. My initial impression on this parable is that both sons disrespected their father. The first said "no" directly to him and the second did say "yes" but did not follow through. Ultimately the first son came around and followed the wish of his father but had already disappointed his father.

However, Jesus' point was that following the will of their father was the important thing. Whether it was done when initially requested or not, doing the father's will was the correct response. This story was used to validate the importance of the efforts John the Baptist made to bring sinners back to God's flock.

Following the Will of God is what is important; but, just as important is the timing. Following God's will now, at the present time, is what God wants. Who you are and what you do today is what is important to God.

Lord, may my response to Your will always be "yes" and my
follow through meet Your expectation. Amen.

Parable of the Wicked Tenant Farmers

<u>**Matthew 21:33-46:**</u> *[33] "Hear another parable. There was a landowner who planted a vineyard, put a hedge around it, dug a wine press in it, and built a tower. Then he leased it to tenants and went on a journey. [34] When vintage time drew near, he sent his servants to the tenants to obtain his produce. [35] But the tenants seized the servants and one they beat, another they killed, and a third they stoned. [36] Again he sent other servants, more numerous than the first ones, but they treated them in the same way. [37] Finally, he sent his son to them, thinking, 'They will respect my son.' [38] But when the tenants saw the son, they said to one another, 'This is the heir. Come, let us kill him and acquire his inheritance.' [39] They seized him, threw him out of the vineyard, and killed him. [40] What will the owner of the vineyard do to those tenants when he comes?" [41] They answered him, "He will put those wretched men to a wretched death and lease his vineyard to other tenants who will give him the produce at the proper times." [42] Jesus said to them, "Did you never read in the scriptures: 'The stone that the builders rejected has become the cornerstone; by the Lord has this been done, and it is wonderful in our eyes'? [43] Therefore, I say to you, the kingdom of God will be taken away from you and given to a people that will produce its fruit. [44] [The one who falls on this stone will be dashed to pieces; and it will crush anyone on whom it falls.]" [45] When the chief priests and the Pharisees heard his parables, they knew that he was speaking about them. [46] And although they were attempting to arrest him, they feared the crowds, for they regarded him as a prophet.*

Mark 12:1-12: [1] *He began to speak to them in parables. "A man planted a vineyard, put a hedge around it, dug a wine press, and built a tower. Then he leased it to tenant farmers and left on a journey.* [2] *At the proper time he sent a servant to the tenants to obtain from them some of the produce of the vineyard.* [3] *But they seized him, beat him, and sent him away empty-handed.* [4] *Again he sent them another servant. And that one they beat over the head and treated shamefully.* [5] *He sent yet another whom they killed. So, too, many others; some they beat, others they killed.* [6] *He had one other to send, a beloved son. He sent him to them last of all, thinking, 'They will respect my son.'* [7] *But those tenants said to one another, 'This is the heir. Come, let us kill him, and the inheritance will be ours.'* [8] *So they seized him and killed him, and threw him out of the vineyard.* [9] *What [then] will the owner of the vineyard do? He will come, put the tenants to death, and give the vineyard to others.* [10] *Have you not read this scripture passage: 'The stone that the builders rejected has become the cornerstone;* [11] *by the Lord has this been done, and it is wonderful in our eyes'?"* [12] *They were seeking to arrest him, but they feared the crowd, for they realized that he had addressed the parable to them. So, they left him and went away.*

Luke 20:9-19: [9] *Then he proceeded to tell the people this parable. "[A] man planted a vineyard, leased it to tenant farmers, and then went on a journey for a long time.* [10] *At harvest time he sent a servant to the tenant farmers to receive some of the produce of the vineyard. But they beat the servant and sent him away empty-handed.* [11] *So he proceeded to send another servant, but him also they beat and insulted and sent away empty-handed.* [12] *Then he proceeded to send a third, but this one too they wounded and threw out.* [13] *The owner of the vineyard said, 'What shall I do? I shall send my beloved son; maybe they will respect him.'* [14] *But when the tenant farmers*

393

saw him they said to one another, 'This is the heir. Let us kill him that the inheritance may become ours.' [15] So they threw him out of the vineyard and killed him. What will the owner of the vineyard do to them? [16] He will come and put those tenant farmers to death and turn over the vineyard to others." When the people heard this, they exclaimed, "Let it not be so!" [17] But he looked at them and asked, "What then does this scripture passage mean: 'The stone which the builders rejected has become the cornerstone'? [18] Everyone who falls on that stone will be dashed to pieces; and it will crush anyone on whom it falls." [19] The scribes and chief priests sought to lay their hands on him at that very hour, but they feared the people, for they knew that he had addressed this parable to them.

This parable has a strong message for the Israelites, but my question is how does this apply to me as an individual and the way I need to live my life? I need to view myself as the Israelite nation. The Jews followed God at times and many times they abandoned Him. They took God's prophets and God's only begotten Son and killed them all. Could the same thing happen in my case? Of course it could, if I allow it. Maybe not literally killing but abandoning the Triune God. There is nothing that would prevent that from happening except the grace of God.

My life must be lived in such a way that I keep the Presence of God ever before me, which means I must continue to study and pray. I must regularly discern His will for me. And I must persevere in doing His will. Is that too much to ask?

Lord, I do not want to be like the tenant farmers in this parable. The only way I can avoid that is with Your saving grace. Grant me what I need to be ever Yours. Amen.

On Paying Tribute to Caeser

<u>Matthew 22:15-22:</u> *[15] Then the Pharisees went off and plotted how they might entrap him in speech. [16] They sent their disciples to him, with the Herodians, saying, "Teacher, we know that you are a truthful man and that you teach the way of God in accordance with the truth. And you are not concerned with anyone's opinion, for you do not regard a person's status. [17] Tell us, then, what is your opinion: Is it lawful to pay the census tax to Caesar or not?" [18] Knowing their malice, Jesus said, "Why are you testing me, you hypocrites? [19] Show me the coin that pays the census tax." Then they handed him the Roman coin. [20] He said to them, "Whose image is this and whose inscription?" [21] They replied, "Caesar's." At that he said to them, "Then repay to Caesar what belongs to Caesar and to God what belongs to God." [22] When they heard this they were amazed and leaving him they went away.*

<u>Mark 12:13-17:</u> *[13] They sent some Pharisees and Herodians to him to ensnare him in his speech. [14] They came and said to him, "Teacher, we know that you are a truthful man and that you are not concerned with anyone's opinion. You do not regard a person's status but teach the way of God in accordance with the truth. Is it lawful to pay the census tax to Caesar or not? Should we pay or should we not pay?" [15] Knowing their hypocrisy he said to them, "Why are you testing me? Bring me a denarius to look at." [16] They brought one to him and he said to them, "Whose image and inscription is this?" They replied to him, "Caesar's." [17] So Jesus said to them, "Repay to Caesar what belongs to Caesar and to God what belongs to God." They were utterly amazed at him.*

Luke 20:20-26: *[20] They watched him closely and sent agents pretending to be righteous who were to trap him in speech, in order to hand him over to the authority and power of the governor. [21] They posed this question to him, "Teacher, we know that what you say and teach is correct, and you show no partiality, but teach the way of God in accordance with the truth. [22] Is it lawful for us to pay tribute to Caesar or not?" [23] Recognizing their craftiness he said to them, [24] "Show me a denarius; whose image and name does it bear?" They replied, "Caesar's." [25] So he said to them, "Then repay to Caesar what belongs to Caesar and to God what belongs to God." [26] They were unable to trap him by something he might say before the people, and so amazed were they at his reply that they fell silent.*

They watched him closely and sent agents pretending to be righteous who were to trap him in speech, in order to hand him over to the authority and power of the governor. But Jesus, *knowing their malice*, did not fall into their trap.

This is the first of the two lessons I gained from this passage. In many incidents throughout the Gospels, Jesus is confronted by the Pharisees, scholars of the law, and elders who want to catch Him or trap Him into doing something against the law. I have experienced this in my life also. Mostly, the incidents have been related to my job in some way. Only a few times have been related to my faith. One time it was by a group of Protestants challenging some of my beliefs as a Catholic. Other times, it was just friends or relatives who also were challenging things I believe. In every case, I was able to answer their challenges appropriately; however, my answers were not enough to convert them. The lesson here is that I must have confidence that the Holy Spirit will provide me with the words I need to say when I need them. I am not afraid to give answers related to my faith. I, however, should never expect a particular result, such as conversion, from what I say.

The other lesson I learn from this passage is that we are expected by God to accept the situation we are in and fulfill the requirements of that situation. In this case, the Jews were under the dominion of the Romans and must follow the rules laid down by the Romans, including paying taxes. We may not be happy about it, and we may work at changing that situation; but, in the meantime, we must follow the rules as they stand. The consequences for not doing so may be more than we can handle.

Lord, so much of my life is dependent on what is presented to me, what standards of life I must follow, whose words I must believe, and the circumstances that I have no control over in my life. I pray You will guide me through this maze of decisions I must make each day. Amen.

Question About the Resurrection

<u>Matthew 22:23-33:</u> *[23] On that day Sadducees approached him, saying that there is no resurrection. They put this question to him, [24] saying, "Teacher, Moses said, 'If a man dies without children, his brother shall marry his wife and raise up descendants for his brother.' [25] Now there were seven brothers among us. The first married and died and, having no descendants, left his wife to his brother. [26] The same happened with the second and the third, through all seven. [27] Finally the woman died. [28] Now at the resurrection, of the seven, whose wife will she be? For they all had been married to her." [29] Jesus said to them in reply, "You are misled because you do not know the scriptures or the power of God. [30] At the resurrection they*

397

neither marry nor are given in marriage but are like the angels in heaven. ³¹ And concerning the resurrection of the dead, have you not read what was said to you by God, ³² 'I am the God of Abraham, the God of Isaac, and the God of Jacob'? He is not the God of the dead but of the living." ³³ When the crowds heard this, they were astonished at his teaching.

<u>**Mark 12:18-27:**</u> *¹⁸ Some Sadducees, who say there is no resurrection, came to him and put this question to him, ¹⁹ saying, "Teacher, Moses wrote for us, 'If someone's brother dies, leaving a wife but no child, his brother must take the wife and raise up descendants for his brother.' ²⁰ Now there were seven brothers. The first married a woman and died, leaving no descendants. ²¹ So the second married her and died, leaving no descendants, and the third likewise. ²² And the seven left no descendants. Last of all the woman also died. ²³ At the resurrection [when they arise] whose wife will she be? For all seven had been married to her." ²⁴ Jesus said to them, "Are you not misled because you do not know the scriptures or the power of God? ²⁵ When they rise from the dead, they neither marry nor are given in marriage, but they are like the angels in heaven. ²⁶ As for the dead being raised, have you not read in the Book of Moses, in the passage about the bush, how God told him, 'I am the God of Abraham, [the] God of Isaac, and [the] God of Jacob'? ²⁷ He is not God of the dead but of the living. You are greatly misled."*

<u>**Luke 20:27-40:**</u> *²⁷ Some Sadducees, those who deny that there is a resurrection, came forward and put this question to him, ²⁸ saying, "Teacher, Moses wrote for us, 'If someone's brother dies leaving a wife but no child, his brother must take the wife and raise up descendants for his brother.' ²⁹ Now there were seven brothers; the first married a woman but died childless. ³⁰ Then the second ³¹ and the third married her, and*

likewise all the seven died childless. ³² Finally the woman also died. ³³ Now at the resurrection whose wife will that woman be? For all seven had been married to her." ³⁴ Jesus said to them, "The children of this age marry and are given in marriage; ³⁵ but those who are deemed worthy to attain to the coming age and to the resurrection of the dead neither marry nor are given in marriage. ³⁶ They can no longer die, for they are like angels; and they are the children of God because they are the ones who will rise. ³⁷ That the dead will rise even Moses made known in the passage about the bush, when he called 'Lord' the God of Abraham, the God of Isaac, and the God of Jacob; ³⁸ and he is not God of the dead, but of the living, for to him all are alive." ³⁹ Some of the scribes said in reply, "Teacher, you have answered well." ⁴⁰ And they no longer dared to ask him anything.

"Teacher, you have answered well." And they no longer dared to ask him anything. But the question I have is: did they change their belief based on what Jesus told them? They did not believe in the afterlife. Has that changed? What Jesus said confirms that there is life after death. He is the God of the living. When our physical bodies expire, we will transition (whatever that means and whatever form that takes) either to eternal life ultimately with God in heaven or eternal damnation in hell. However, in either case it will still be life.

It is clear from this and the prior passage, that even though Jesus had *answered well*, they did not believe Him. That has been true throughout our Christian history. Just because something of our faith is explained, that will not necessarily result in another follower of Jesus. The grace of God must be present, and the choices must be made.

Lord, my life is filled with questions and the devil tries to fill my mind with doubts. Help me to always fall back on Your words of explanation and hope. Amen.

The Question About David's Son

<u>Matthew 22:41-46</u>: *[41] While the Pharisees were gathered together, Jesus questioned them, [42] saying, "What is your opinion about the Messiah? Whose son is he?" They replied, "David's." [43] He said to them, "How, then, does David, inspired by the Spirit, call him 'lord,' saying: [44] 'The Lord said to my lord, "Sit at my right hand until I place your enemies under your feet"'? [45] If David calls him 'lord,' how can he be his son?" [46] No one was able to answer him a word, nor from that day on did anyone dare to ask him any more questions.*

<u>Mark 12:35-37</u>: *[35] As Jesus was teaching in the temple area he said, "How do the scribes claim that the Messiah is the son of David? [36] David himself, inspired by the holy Spirit, said: 'The Lord said to my lord, "Sit at my right hand until I place your enemies under your feet."' [37] David himself calls him 'lord'; so how is he his son?" [The] great crowd heard this with delight.*

<u>Luke 20:41-44</u>: *[41] Then he said to them, "How do they claim that the Messiah is the Son of David? [42] For David himself in the Book of Psalms says: 'The Lord said to my lord, "Sit at my right hand [43] till I make your enemies your footstool."' [44] Now if David calls him 'lord,' how can he be his?"*

There are many things that the Pharisees did not have answers for. There are many things that we do not have answers for. In this particular case, Jesus was able to silence these Pharisees and prevent them from challenging Him further. It is unclear whether the Pharisees believed that the Messiah would be a son of man (a prophet, a king, a representative of God) or the Son of God Himself. So, it is not surprising that they were silenced when questioned about this. But this does ask a question of me and what I believe. I believe Jesus is the divine Son of God who draws His human lineage from King David.

Lord, so much of my life is based on what I believe. Help me to transform that phrase into "what I know." Amen.

Woe to the Scribes and Pharisees

<u>Matthew 23:1-36:</u> *[1] Then Jesus spoke to the crowds and to his disciples, [2]saying, "The scribes and the Pharisees have taken their seat on the chair of Moses. [3] Therefore, do and observe all things whatsoever they tell you, but do not follow their example. For they preach but they do not practice. [4] They tie up heavy burdens [hard to carry] and lay them on people's shoulders, but they will not lift a finger to move them. [5] All their works are performed to be seen. They widen their phylacteries and lengthen their tassels. [6] They love places of honor at banquets, seats of honor in synagogues, [7]greetings in marketplaces, and the salutation 'Rabbi.' [8] As for you, do not be called 'Rabbi.' You have but one teacher, and you are all brothers. [9] Call no one on earth your father; you have but one Father in heaven. [10] Do not be called 'Master'; you have but one master, the Messiah. [11] The greatest among you must be your servant. [12] Whoever exalts himself will be humbled; but whoever humbles himself will be exalted. [13] "Woe to you, scribes and Pharisees, you hypocrites. You lock the kingdom of heaven before human beings. You do not enter yourselves, nor do you allow entrance to those trying to enter. [[14]] [15] "Woe to you, scribes and Pharisees, you hypocrites. You traverse sea*

401

and land to make one convert, and when that happens you make him a child of Gehenna twice as much as yourselves.

[16] *"Woe to you, blind guides, who say, 'If one swears by the temple, it means nothing, but if one swears by the gold of the temple, one is obligated.'* [17] *Blind fools, which is greater, the gold, or the temple that made the gold sacred?* [18] *And you say, 'If one swears by the altar, it means nothing, but if one swears by the gift on the altar, one is obligated.'* [19] *You blind ones, which is greater, the gift, or the altar that makes the gift sacred?* [20] *One who swears by the altar swears by it and all that is upon it;* [21] *one who swears by the temple swears by it and by him who dwells in it;* [22] *one who swears by heaven swears by the throne of God and by him who is seated on it.* [23] *"Woe to you, scribes and Pharisees, you hypocrites. You pay tithes of mint and dill and cummin, and have neglected the weightier things of the law: judgment and mercy and fidelity. [But] these you should have done, without neglecting the others.* [24] *Blind guides, who strain out the gnat and swallow the camel!* [25] *"Woe to you, scribes and Pharisees, you hypocrites. You cleanse the outside of cup and dish, but inside they are full of plunder and self-indulgence.* [26] *Blind Pharisee, cleanse first the inside of the cup, so that the outside also may be clean.* [27] *"Woe to you, scribes and Pharisees, you hypocrites. You are like whitewashed tombs, which appear beautiful on the outside, but inside are full of dead men's bones and every kind of filth.* [28] *Even so, on the outside you appear righteous, but inside you are filled with hypocrisy and evildoing.* [29] *"Woe to you, scribes and Pharisees, you hypocrites. You build the tombs of the prophets and adorn the memorials of the righteous,* [30] *and you say, 'If we had lived in the days of our ancestors, we would not have joined them in shedding the prophets' blood.'* [31] *Thus you bear witness against yourselves that you are the children of those who murdered the prophets;* [32] *now fill up what your ancestors measured out!* [33] *You serpents, you brood of vipers,*

how can you flee from the judgment of Gehenna? [34] *Therefore, behold, I send to you prophets and wise men and scribes; some of them you will kill and crucify, some of them you will scourge in your synagogues and pursue from town to town,* [35] *so that there may come upon you all the righteous blood shed upon earth, from the righteous blood of Abel to the blood of Zechariah, the son of Barachiah, whom you murdered between the sanctuary and the altar.* [36] *Amen, I say to you, all these things will come upon this generation.*

<u>Mark 12:37-40:</u> [37] *[The] great crowd heard this with delight. Denunciation of the Scribes.* [38] *In the course of his teaching he said, "Beware of the scribes, who like to go around in long robes and accept greetings in the marketplaces,* [39] *seats of honor in synagogues, and places of honor at banquets.* [40] *They devour the houses of widows and, as a pretext, recite lengthy prayers. They will receive a very severe condemnation."*

<u>Luke 20:45-47:</u> [45] *Then, within the hearing of all the people, he said to [his] disciples,* [46] *"Be on guard against the scribes, who like to go around in long robes and love greetings in marketplaces, seats of honor in synagogues, and places of honor at banquets.* [47] *They devour the houses of widows and, as a pretext, recite lengthy prayers. They will receive a very severe condemnation."*

It seems to me that Jesus reached a point where something had to be said and this diatribe was the result. As Mark and Luke summarize, the scribes and Pharisees *devour the houses of widows and, as a pretext, recite lengthy prayers. They will receive a very severe condemnation.* Even though not mentioned here, I believe Jesus was referring to the scholars of the law and the Sadducees as

403

well. In general, He was referring to all of the religious leaders of Israel.

Just to keep things clearly in mind, here is a list of the thou-shalt-nots which are based on the sins of these religious leaders:

1. Thou shalt not preach one thing and practice another.
2. Thou shalt not lay heavy burdens on people's shoulders but not lift a finger to help them.
3. Thou shalt not boast of how good a person you are. Thou shalt not seek honors in public gatherings. Thou shalt not seek titles of prestige. Thou shalt not seek greatness but humble yourself.
4. Thou shalt not close the gates of heaven to all who wish to enter.
5. Thou shalt not place higher value on the things of this world rather than on God and all He sends us.
6. Thou shalt not place higher value on the things of this world but ignore judgment, mercy, and fidelity.
7. Thou shalt not cleanse the outside but ignore the evil within.

Jesus' advice to the Israelites as well as to us: *Therefore, do and observe all things whatsoever* these hypocrites *tell you, but do not follow their example.*

Lord, grant me the graces necessary to be able to discern the right action and not follow others simply because they are the official leaders. Amen.

The Widow's Gift of Two Mites

Mark 12:41-44: *[41] He sat down opposite the treasury and observed how the crowd put money into the treasury. Many rich people put in large sums. [42] A poor widow also came and* *put in two small coins worth a few cents.* [43] *Calling his disciples to himself, he said to them, "Amen, I say to you, this poor widow put in more than all the other contributors to the treasury.* [44] *For they have all contributed from their surplus wealth, but she, from her poverty, has contributed all she had, her whole livelihood."*

<u>Luke 21:1-4:</u> [1] *When he looked up he saw some wealthy people putting their offerings into the treasury* [2] *and he noticed a poor widow putting in two small coins.* [3] *He said, "I tell you truly, this poor widow put in more than all the rest;* [4] *for those others have all made offerings from their surplus wealth, but she, from her poverty, has offered her whole livelihood."*

This is a simple but profound message from our Lord. The gift we offer to God must be of value to us or it is meaningless to God. The old expression that "we must give until it hurts" approaches this idea. Giving something to charity that no longer has meaning to us is simply spring cleaning; we are just making room for more stuff. What we are giving has no value. When the value of the gift is higher than "making room for more" or something we "will not miss," then it will have meaning to God.

Lord, let me be always mindful that the gifts I offer to God are for the right reason and have value. Amen.

Part 12

The Discourse on the Mount of Olives

Prediction of the Destruction of the Temple

Matthew 24:1-2: *¹ Jesus left the temple area and was going away, when his disciples approached him to point out the temple buildings. ² He said to them in reply, "You see all these things, do you not? Amen, I say to you, there will not be left here a stone upon another stone that will not be thrown down."*

Mark 13:1-2: *¹ As he was making his way out of the temple area one of his disciples said to him, "Look, teacher, what stones and what buildings!" ² Jesus said to him, "Do you see these great buildings? There will not be one stone left upon another that will not be thrown down."*

Luke 21:5-6: *⁵ While some people were speaking about how the temple was adorned with costly stones and votive offerings, he said, ⁶ "All that you see here—the days will come when there will not be left a stone upon another stone that will not be thrown down."*

Jesus had predicted His passion, death, and resurrection to His disciples, and they were not sure they believed Him. At least, they did not want to believe Him. Now Jesus was predicting the destruction of the temple. God forbid! What should they believe? How much would I have believed if I was among them? First, the man who they believed to be the Messiah was going to die a horrific death, then the temple would be destroyed. What more horror could come from our Lord's mouth?

Lord, to know the future may bring fear to my heart and tears to my eyes. Yet, we all want to know what is going to happen. Give me a glimpse of the future only if it will serve

Your purpose. Otherwise, I am willing to take it one step at a time. Amen.

Signs Before the End

Matthew 24:3-8: *[3] As he was sitting on the Mount of Olives, the disciples approached him privately and said, "Tell us, when will this happen, and what sign will there be of your coming, and of the end of the age?" [4] Jesus said to them in reply, "See that no one deceives you. [5] For many will come in my name, saying, 'I am the Messiah,' and they will deceive many. [6] You will hear of wars and reports of wars; see that you are not alarmed, for these things must happen, but it will not yet be the end. [7] Nation will rise against nation, and kingdom against kingdom; there will be famines and earthquakes from place to place. [8] All these are the beginning of the labor pains."*

Mark 13:3-8: *[3] As he was sitting on the Mount of Olives opposite the temple area, Peter, James, John, and Andrew asked him privately, [4] "Tell us, when will this happen, and what sign will there be when all these things are about to come to an end?" [5] Jesus began to say to them, "See that no one deceives you. [6] Many will come in my name saying, 'I am he,' and they will deceive many. [7] When you hear of wars and reports of wars do not be alarmed; such things must happen, but it will not yet be the end. [8] Nation will rise against nation and kingdom against kingdom. There will be earthquakes from place to place and there will be famines. These are the beginnings of the labor pains."*

Luke 21:7-11: *[7] Then they asked him, "Teacher, when will this happen? And what sign will there be when all these things are about to happen?" [8] He answered, "See that you not be deceived, for many will come in my name, saying, 'I am he,'* *and 'The time has come.' Do not follow them!* ⁹ *When you hear of wars and insurrections, do not be terrified; for such things must happen first, but it will not immediately be the end."* ¹⁰ *Then he said to them, "Nation will rise against nation, and kingdom against kingdom.* ¹¹ *There will be powerful earthquakes, famines, and plagues from place to place; and awesome sights and mighty signs will come from the sky."*

The disciples wanted to know more. Would our Lord give them a precise time or, at least, what conditions to look for. The predictions did not end there. However, Jesus would not give them the precision they were looking for. What Jesus spoke of was leading to the destruction of the temple. Not all of the disciples would be around for that event. All Jesus spoke about has also been happening over the last 2,000 years and He said this is just the beginning: nations warring against nations and the natural disasters brought on by the earth. If this is the beginning, then there will be more to come. The true end definitely was not within the lifetime of the disciples.

Lord, once again I ask You to reveal to me only what I need to know about what is coming. I will leave the rest in Your hands. Amen.

The Desolating Abomination

<u>Matthew 24:15-22:</u> ¹⁵ *"When you see the desolating abomination spoken of through Daniel the prophet standing in the holy place (let the reader understand),* ¹⁶ *then those in Judea must flee to the mountains,* ¹⁷ *a person on the housetop must not go down to get things out of his house,* ¹⁸ *a person in the field must not return to get his cloak.* ¹⁹ *Woe to pregnant women and nursing mothers in those days.* ²⁰ *Pray that your*

flight not be in winter or on the sabbath, ²¹for at that time there will be great tribulation, such as has not been since the beginning of the world until now, nor ever will be. ²² And if those days had not been shortened, no one would be saved; but for the sake of the elect, they will be shortened."

Mark 13:14-20: *¹⁴ "When you see the desolating abomination standing where he should not (let the reader understand), then those in Judea must flee to the mountains, ¹⁵ [and] a person on a housetop must not go down or enter to get anything out of his house, ¹⁶ and a person in a field must not return to get his cloak. ¹⁷ Woe to pregnant women and nursing mothers in those days. ¹⁸ Pray that this does not happen in winter. ¹⁹ For those times will have tribulation such as has not been since the beginning of God's creation until now, nor ever will be. ²⁰ If the Lord had not shortened those days, no one would be saved; but for the sake of the elect whom he chose, he did shorten the days."*

Luke 21:20-24: *²⁰ "When you see Jerusalem surrounded by armies, know that its desolation is at hand. ²¹ Then those in Judea must flee to the mountains. Let those within the city escape from it, and let those in the countryside not enter the city, ²² for these days are the time of punishment when all the scriptures are fulfilled. ²³ Woe to pregnant women and nursing mothers in those days, for a terrible calamity will come upon the earth and a wrathful judgment upon this people. ²⁴ They will fall by the edge of the sword and be taken as captives to all the Gentiles; and Jerusalem will be trampled underfoot by the Gentiles until the times of the Gentiles are fulfilled."*

Of the three passages, my personal preference is Luke's version. The destruction of the temple would be a horrific event for all Jews. The devastating armies would enter the city and destroy the temple. The people would be led away to slavery. We can look back and see that these events did occur. The disciples could only fear in anticipation of what was to come. They could also pray for God's mercy. But did the Israelite nation pray for God's forgiveness and mercy, or change their lives as did the people in Nineveh when Jonah predicted their destruction?!

Lord, only You know what the future holds in store for us. May our daily prayers be in gratitude for all of Your blessings, and an appeal for Your forgiveness and mercy for all of our sins. Amen.

False Christs and False Prophets

Matthew 24:23-28: [23] *If anyone says to you then, 'Look, here is the Messiah!' or, 'There he is!' do not believe it.* [24] *False messiahs and false prophets will arise, and they will perform signs and wonders so great as to deceive, if that were possible, even the elect.* [25] *Behold, I have told it to you beforehand.* [26] *So if they say to you, 'He is in the desert,' do not go out there; if they say, 'He is in the inner rooms,' do not believe it.* [27] *For just as lightning comes from the east and is seen as far as the west, so will the coming of the Son of Man be.* [28] *Wherever the corpse is, there the vultures will gather."*

Mark 13:21-23: [21] *If anyone says to you then, 'Look, here is the Messiah! Look, there he is!' do not believe it.* [22] *False messiahs and false prophets will arise and will perform signs and wonders in order to mislead, if that were possible, the elect.* [23] *Be watchful! I have told it all to you beforehand."*

In Part 8 of this book, I wrote of the *Day of the Son of Man* based on a passage from Luke. Here we have similar

411

predictions. *False messiahs and false prophets will arise. Do not believe it.* So much will happen that will cause fear and astound people, but we are not to believe. Our Lord will return, we are told by an angel, as He left, rising into the heavens.

Lord, let me not fall into the trap of believing in false messiahs and prophets. Let me live my life as You wish until You come again. Amen.

The Coming of the Son of Man

Matthew 24:29-31: *[29]"Immediately after the tribulation of those days, the sun will be darkened, and the moon will not give its light, and the stars will fall from the sky, and the powers of the heavens will be shaken. [30] And then the sign of the Son of Man will appear in heaven, and all the tribes of the earth will mourn, and they will see the Son of Man coming upon the clouds of heaven with power and great glory. [31] And he will send out his angels with a trumpet blast, and they will gather his elect from the four winds, from one end of the heavens to the other."*

Mark 13:24-27: *[24] "But in those days after that tribulation the sun will be darkened, and the moon will not give its light, [25] and the stars will be falling from the sky, and the powers in the heavens will be shaken. [26] And then they will see 'the Son of Man coming in the clouds' with great power and glory, [27] and then he will send out the angels and gather [his] elect from the four winds, from the end of the earth to the end of the sky."*

Luke 21:25-28: *[25] "There will be signs in the sun, the moon, and the stars, and on earth nations will be in dismay, perplexed by the roaring of the sea and the waves. [26] People will die of* *fright in anticipation of what is coming upon the world, for the powers of the heavens will be shaken. * [27] *And then they will see the Son of Man coming in a cloud with power and great glory.* [28] *But when these signs begin to happen, stand erect and raise your heads because your redemption is at hand."*

They will see the Son of Man coming upon the clouds of heaven with power and great glory. According to the Gospels, this was said by our Lord Jesus Himself. So, it is written, so it shall be. All the world will know when He arrives. Until that time, we should not speculate about His coming.

Lord, let me not be enticed by stories of Your return. I will know, as well as everyone else when You arrive. Amen.

Take Heed, Be Watchful!

Matthew 24:32-36: [32] *"Learn a lesson from the fig tree. When its branch becomes tender and sprouts leaves, you know that summer is near.* [33] *In the same way, when you see all these things, know that he is near, at the gates.* [34] *Amen, I say to you, this generation will not pass away until all these things have taken place.* [35] *Heaven and earth will pass away, but my words will not pass away.* [36] *"But of that day and hour no one knows, neither the angels of heaven, nor the Son, but the Father alone.*

Matthew 25:13: *Therefore, stay awake, for you know neither the day nor the hour.*

Mark 13:28-37: [28] *"Learn a lesson from the fig tree. When its branch becomes tender and sprouts leaves, you know that* *summer is near. ²⁹ In the same way, when you see these things happening, know that he is near, at the gates. ³⁰ Amen, I say to you, this generation will not pass away until all these things have taken place. ³¹ Heaven and earth will pass away, but my words will not pass away. ³² "But of that day or hour, no one knows, neither the angels in heaven, nor the Son, but only the Father. ³³ Be watchful! Be alert! You do not know when the time will come. ³⁴ It is like a man traveling abroad. He leaves home and places his servants in charge, each with his work, and orders the gatekeeper to be on the watch. ³⁵ Watch, therefore; you do not know when the lord of the house is coming, whether in the evening, or at midnight, or at cockcrow, or in the morning. ³⁶ May he not come suddenly and find you sleeping. ³⁷ What I say to you, I say to all: 'Watch!'"*

Luke 21:29-36: ²⁹ He taught them a lesson. "Consider the fig tree and all the other trees. ³⁰ When their buds burst open, you see for yourselves and know that summer is now near; ³¹ in the same way, when you see these things happening, know that the kingdom of God is near. ³² Amen, I say to you, this generation will not pass away until all these things have taken place. ³³ Heaven and earth will pass away, but my words will not pass away. ³⁴ "Beware that your hearts do not become drowsy from carousing and drunkenness and the anxieties of daily life, and that day catch you by surprise ³⁵ like a trap. For that day will assault everyone who lives on the face of the earth. ³⁶ Be vigilant at all times and pray that you have the strength to escape the tribulations that are imminent and to stand before the Son of Man."

There are signs that we recognize in our daily lives that lead to events that will occur. Jesus tells of the fig tree and the normal cycle of its life. There are myriad signs that we see throughout our lives; this is no surprise. There are

414

natural events that we can predict. However, we will not be able to predict when His return will occur. He had said on many occasions that He does the will of His Father in heaven. Only His Father knows the day and the time.

However, Jesus advises that we should be watchful. In other words, we should live our lives in such a way that we will be ready for our Lord when He does come.

Lord, lead me, guide me. Help me to be ready when Your hour comes. Amen.

Part 13

Conclusion of the

Account before

the Passion

The Final Judgment

Matthew 25:31-46: [31] *"When the Son of Man comes in his glory, and all the angels with him, he will sit upon his glorious throne,* [32] *and all the nations will be assembled before him. And he will separate them one from another, as a shepherd separates the sheep from the goats.* [33] *He will place the sheep on his right and the goats on his left.* [34] *Then the king will say to those on his right, 'Come, you who are blessed by my Father. Inherit the kingdom prepared for you from the foundation of the world.* [35] *For I was hungry and you gave me food, I was thirsty and you gave me drink, a stranger and you welcomed me,* [36] *naked and you clothed me, ill and you cared for me, in prison and you visited me.'* [37] *Then the righteous will answer him and say, 'Lord, when did we see you hungry and feed you, or thirsty and give you drink?* [38] *When did we see you a stranger and welcome you, or naked and clothe you?* [39] *When did we see you ill or in prison, and visit you?'* [40] *And the king will say to them in reply, 'Amen, I say to you, whatever you did for one of these least brothers of mine, you did for me.'* [41] *Then he will say to those on his left, 'Depart from me, you accursed, into the eternal fire prepared for the devil and his angels.* [42] *For I was hungry and you gave me no food, I was thirsty and you gave me no drink,* [43] *a stranger and you gave me no welcome, naked and you gave me no clothing, ill and in prison, and you did not care for me.'* [44] *Then they will answer and say, 'Lord, when did we see you hungry or thirsty or a stranger or naked or ill or in prison, and not minister to your needs?'* [45] *He will answer them, 'Amen, I say to you, what you did not do for one of these least ones, you did not do for me.'* [46] *And these will go off to eternal punishment, but the righteous to eternal life."*

Here is another passage from the Gospels that has special meaning for me. Once again it is related to my

417

involvement in the Society of St. Vincent de Paul. It is specifically because of the statement: *Amen, I say to you, whatever you did for one of these least brothers of mine, you did for me.* And its counterpart: *Amen, I say to you, what you did not do for one of these least ones, you did not do for me.* One of the things we focus on in our ministry is seeing the face of Christ in those we serve. We believe that, in giving aid to those in need, we are giving aid to our Lord.

Setting aside the specific ministry I am involved in, the only way that we humans can physically show our love for God is to show our love for others. We can talk to God and tell Him how much we love Him, but we cannot do anything for Him or to Him directly. It is in how we treat others that we tell our Lord how we feel about Him.

Keep in mind that we also show God how we feel about Him when we ignore those in need. Remember the counterpart statement above. Obviously, we cannot help everyone, but we do make choices. We choose to do for one and not do for another. We choose to do to one and not do to another. We choose to grant favors. We choose to forgive wrongs done to us. We choose to be merciful or not. The reason behind our choice, our motivation, is what is important.

The final judgment is all about love. We are asked to love those we encounter to the best of our ability. That is what we will be evaluated on by our God. Put on your thinking cap and recall Matthew 7:2: *For as you judge, so will you be judged, and the measure with which you measure will be measured out to you.* That is the message I derive from the final judgment passage. God will treat us as we treat others: loving, caring, forgiving, ignoring, harming, abandoning. In the end, we will face the consequences of our own choices: eternal life or eternal punishment.

Lord, lead me, guide me along the way. Only Your Father knows when the final judgment will take place. Help me to make the right choices and be ready for when You come. Amen.

Greeks Seek Jesus –
Discourse on His Death

<u>Luke 21:37-38:</u> *[37] During the day, Jesus was teaching in the temple area, but at night he would leave and stay at the place called the Mount of Olives. [38] And all the people would get up early each morning to listen to him in the temple area.*

<u>John 12:20-36:</u> *[20] Now there were some Greeks among those who had come up to worship at the feast. [21] They came to Philip, who was from Bethsaida in Galilee, and asked him, "Sir, we would like to see Jesus." [22] Philip went and told Andrew; then Andrew and Philip went and told Jesus. [23] Jesus answered them, "The hour has come for the Son of Man to be glorified. [24] Amen, amen, I say to you, unless a grain of wheat falls to the ground and dies, it remains just a grain of wheat; but if it dies, it produces much fruit. [25] Whoever loves his life loses it, and whoever hates his life in this world will preserve it for eternal life. [26] Whoever serves me must follow me, and where I am, there also will my servant be. The Father will honor whoever serves me. [27] "I am troubled now. Yet what should I say? 'Father, save me from this hour'? But it was for this purpose that I came to this hour. [28] Father, glorify your name." Then a voice came from heaven, "I have glorified it and will glorify it again." [29] The crowd there heard it and said it was thunder; but others said, "An angel has spoken to him." [30] Jesus answered and said, "This voice did not come for*

419

my sake but for yours. ³¹ Now is the time of judgment on this world; now the ruler of this world will be driven out. ³² And when I am lifted up from the earth, I will draw everyone to myself." ³³ He said this indicating the kind of death he would die. ³⁴ So the crowd answered him, "We have heard from the law that the Messiah remains forever. Then how can you say that the Son of Man must be lifted up? Who is this Son of Man?" ³⁵ Jesus said to them, "The light will be among you only a little while. Walk while you have the light, so that darkness may not overcome you. Whoever walks in the dark does not know where he is going. ³⁶ While you have the light, believe in the light, so that you may become children of the light." After he had said this, Jesus left and hid from them.

This is the third time God's voice comes down from heaven and speaks to Jesus and His followers around Him. The first two were when Jesus was being baptized and during the transfiguration. Not everyone who was present heard God's voice. But that is true throughout our history. God speaks to each of us, but we are not always tuned into Him and hear what He is saying to us.

Once again, Jesus speaks about His death, but the Jews do not want to hear it. *We have heard from the law that the Messiah remains forever.* Jesus will ascend into heaven, but He will leave His physical presence here with us in the form of bread and wine, His Body and Blood, His Eucharistic presence.

Lord, I believe You are the Messiah and that You are here with us always in Your Eucharistic presence. Help me to be strong in my faith. Amen.

The Unbelief of the People

John 12:37-43: *[37] Although he had performed so many signs in their presence, they did not believe in him, [38] in order that the word which Isaiah the prophet spoke might be fulfilled: "Lord, who has believed our preaching, to whom has the might of the Lord been revealed? [39] For this reason they could not believe, because again Isaiah said: [40] "He blinded their eyes and hardened their heart, so that they might not see with their eyes and understand with their heart and be converted, and I would heal them." [41] Isaiah said this because he saw his glory and spoke about him. [42] Nevertheless, many, even among the authorities, believed in him, but because of the Pharisees they did not acknowledge it openly in order not to be expelled from the synagogue. [43] For they preferred human praise to the glory of God.*

Face it, we all want to believe there is truth in what we read and hear. The latest authority on everything seems to be the internet. There are so many people who believe that, because it is written and available for all to see, it must be true. However, the facts are clear that we have been lied to orally and in writing repeatedly. People simply are not sure what to believe or who to believe.

It takes a lot for someone to convince some of us that they are worth believing, worth trusting. For others, they want to believe and trust to such a degree that they will follow anyone until they are proven to be false. It is easier to follow the crowd than to oppose it.

In this passage from John, Jesus is speaking about those who oppose Him, those who follow Him, and those who want to openly follow Him but are afraid of the consequences. Life is not easy. It is filled with choices, some lead to good, some lead to bad. Our Lord wants us to trust His word and follow Him, in spite of the potential consequences from those in "authority."

Lord, help me to discern the truth in the matters that are important and grant me the strength to follow You along the right path. Amen.

Judgment by the Word

<u>**John 12:44-50:**</u> *[44] Jesus cried out and said, "Whoever believes in me believes not only in me but also in the one who sent me, [45] and whoever sees me sees the one who sent me. [46] I came into the world as light, so that everyone who believes in me might not remain in darkness. [47] And if anyone hears my words and does not observe them, I do not condemn him, for I did not come to condemn the world but to save the world. [48] Whoever rejects me and does not accept my words has something to judge him: the word that I spoke, it will condemn him on the last day, [49] because I did not speak on my own, but the Father who sent me commanded me what to say and speak. [50] And I know that his commandment is eternal life. So, what I say, I say as the Father told me."*

So, what I say, I say as the Father told me. This whole passage is all about this last statement. Jesus has said repeatedly that He has come to do the will of His Father. In the process of that, He speaks the words His Father would have Him say. What Jesus wants is for us to accept what He says as the words of His Father in heaven; and to realize that, if we reject Him and His words, we are also rejecting His Father. We either believe or we do not.

Lord, I do believe that Your words and actions are those of Your Father, our Father in heaven. Help me through my studies to keep affirming that belief. Amen.

Part 14
The Passion
Narrative

Jesus' Death is Premeditated

<u>Matthew 26:1-5:</u> *¹ When Jesus finished all these words, he said to his disciples, ² "You know that in two days' time it will be Passover, and the Son of Man will be handed over to be crucified." ³ Then the chief priests and the elders of the people assembled in the palace of the high priest, who was called Caiaphas, ⁴ and they consulted together to arrest Jesus by treachery and put him to death. ⁵ But they said, "Not during the festival, that there may not be a riot among the people."*

<u>Mark 14:1-2:</u> *¹ The Passover and the Feast of Unleavened Bread were to take place in two days' time. So the chief priests and the scribes were seeking a way to arrest him by treachery and put him to death. ² They said, "Not during the festival, for fear that there may be a riot among the people."*

<u>Luke 22:1-2:</u> *¹ Now the feast of Unleavened Bread, called the Passover, was drawing near, ² and the chief priests and the scribes were seeking a way to put him to death, for they were afraid of the people.*

Once again, our Lord predicts His coming passion and death. It is being planned by Caiaphas, the chief priests, and scribes. But the arrest had to be in secret. If it was done openly while the feast was being celebrated, there could be a riot because more and more people were following Jesus. It had to be done in such a way that they could justify it and still have little to no resistance from Jesus' followers. The plans to do evil are normally done in the shadows.

Lord, help me to never be involved in evil conspiracy. Amen.

The Betrayal by Judas

<u>Matthes 26:14-16:</u> *[14] Then one of the Twelve, who was called Judas Iscariot, went to the chief priests [15] and said, "What are you willing to give me if I hand him over to you?" They paid him thirty pieces of silver, [16] and from that time on he looked for an opportunity to hand him over.*

<u>Mark 14:10-11:</u> *[10] Then Judas Iscariot, one of the Twelve, went off to the chief priests to hand him over to them. [11] When they heard him, they were pleased and promised to pay him money. Then he looked for an opportunity to hand him over.*

<u>Luke 22:3-6:</u> *[3] Then Satan entered into Judas, the one surnamed Iscariot, who was counted among the Twelve, [4] and he went to the chief priests and temple guards to discuss a plan for handing him over to them. [5] They were pleased and agreed to pay him money. [6] He accepted their offer and sought a favorable opportunity to hand him over to them in the absence of a crowd.*

One of the twelve, one of His closest, had to be the one to betray Him. They were the only ones who were regularly with Him. We were not there. We did not see the signs which led to Judas' betrayal. There are a few things mentioned in the Gospel passages that would lead up to this; but there is not enough to lead investigators to identify Judas in advance as the one who would betray his Master. And, let us face it, as a whole, the Apostles would be the last anyone would suspect.

We are asked to judge actions and circumstances for right or wrong but to never judge people. Discerning the truth about what happened in history helps us to avoid making similar mistakes. However, the judging of individuals must be left in the hands of God.

Lord, it is so easy for us to make judgments about others. We do not know what they are thinking, and we certainly do not know what their motivations are. Help me to be non-judgmental about people around me. Amen.

Preparation for Passover

Matthew 26:17-20: *[17] On the first day of the Feast of Unleavened Bread, the disciples approached Jesus and said, "Where do you want us to prepare for you to eat the Passover?" [18] He said, "Go into the city to a certain man and tell him, 'The teacher says, "My appointed time draws near; in your house I shall celebrate the Passover with my disciples."'" [19] The disciples then did as Jesus had ordered, and prepared the Passover. [20] When it was evening, he reclined at table with the Twelve.*

Mark 14:12-17: *[12] On the first day of the Feast of Unleavened Bread, when they sacrificed the Passover lamb, his disciples said to him, "Where do you want us to go and prepare for you to eat the Passover?" [13] He sent two of his disciples and said to them, "Go into the city and a man will meet you, carrying a jar of water. Follow him. [14] Wherever he enters, say to the master of the house, 'The Teacher says, "Where is my guest room where I may eat the Passover with my disciples?"' [15] Then he will show you a large upper room furnished and ready. Make the preparations for us there." [16] The disciples then went off, entered the city, and found it just as he had told them; and they prepared the Passover. [17] When it was evening, he came with the Twelve.*

Luke 22:7-14: [7] *When the day of the feast of Unleavened Bread arrived, the day for sacrificing the Passover lamb,* [8] *he sent out Peter and John, instructing them, "Go and make preparations for us to eat the Passover."* [9] *They asked him, "Where do you want us to make the preparations?"* [10] *And he answered them, "When you go into the city, a man will meet you carrying a jar of water. Follow him into the house that he enters* [11] *and say to the master of the house, 'The teacher says to you, "Where is the guest room where I may eat the Passover with my disciples?"'* [12] *He will show you a large upper room that is furnished. Make the preparations there."* [13] *Then they went off and found everything exactly as he had told them, and there they prepared the Passover.* [14] *When the hour came, he took his place at table with the Apostles.*

His disciples had been with Him for about three years. They knew that what He said was truth. When He gave those instructions for the preparation of the dinner, they just followed them. They knew how to follow His instructions. Their faith in Jesus was growing each day. Then again, that is the way of faith. You must persevere in your studies in order for your faith to grow. His disciples had the best teacher.

Lord, studying has its high points and its low points. It is difficult to stay focused all the time. Grant me the grace of perseverance so I may never lose track of You and what You mean to my life. Amen.

Washing the Disciples' Feet

John 13:1-20: [1] *Before the feast of Passover, Jesus knew that his hour had come to pass from this world to the Father. He loved his own in the world and he loved them to the end.* [2] *The*

428

devil had already induced Judas, son of Simon the Iscariot, to hand him over. So, during supper, [3] fully aware that the Father had put everything into his power and that he had come from God and was returning to God, [4] he rose from supper and took off his outer garments. He took a towel and tied it around his waist. [5] Then he poured water into a basin and began to wash the disciples' feet and dry them with the towel around his waist. [6] He came to Simon Peter, who said to him, "Master, are you going to wash my feet?" [7] Jesus answered and said to him, "What I am doing, you do not understand now, but you will understand later." [8] Peter said to him, "You will never wash my feet." Jesus answered him, "Unless I wash you, you will have no inheritance with me." [9] Simon Peter said to him, "Master, then not only my feet, but my hands and head as well." [10] Jesus said to him, "Whoever has bathed has no need except to have his feet washed, for he is clean all over; so you are clean, but not all." [11] For he knew who would betray him; for this reason, he said, "Not all of you are clean." [12] So when he had washed their feet [and] put his garments back on and reclined at table again, he said to them, "Do you realize what I have done for you? [13] You call me 'teacher' and 'master,' and rightly so, for indeed I am. [14] If I, therefore, the master and teacher, have washed your feet, you ought to wash one another's feet. [15] I have given you a model to follow, so that as I have done for you, you should also do. [16] Amen, amen, I say to you, no slave is greater than his master nor any messenger greater than the one who sent him. [17] If you understand this, blessed are you if you do it. [18] I am not speaking of all of you. I know those whom I have chosen. But so that the scripture might be fulfilled, 'The one who ate my food has raised his heel against me.' [19] From now on I am telling you before it happens, so that when it happens you may believe that I AM. [20] Amen, amen, I say to you, whoever receives the one I send receives me, and whoever receives me receives the one who sent me."

There are a couple of messages in this passage. Being a leader is not about prestige. Being a leader is about responsibility to those who are followers. The leader has to consider the needs of those who follow because it is about their welfare as well as the cause they are promoting. As leaders, we must ensure that the cause is promoted; however, fulfillment of the cause should not result in the sacrifice of the followers, if at all possible. The leader must ensure that the followers are prepared for the movement ahead, whatever that entails.

The other message is that Jesus is once again assuring us that He is following the lead of the one who sent Him, His Father in heaven. If we accept the message Jesus gives us, then we accept the message of the one who sent Him. If we follow Jesus, then we follow His Father. If we follow Jesus, we follow the Triune God.

Lord, for most of my life, I have served in a leadership or supervisory role. I was fortunate that I had learned a couple of valuable lessons from my father about serving those whom I follow as well as those for whom I am responsible. I know that You are my ultimate guide, and I wish to continue to follow You. Amen.

The Last Supper –
Jesus Foretells His Betrayal

<u>John 13:21-30:</u> *²¹ When he had said this, Jesus was deeply troubled and testified, "Amen, amen, I say to you, one of you will betray me." ²² The disciples looked at one another, at a loss as to whom he meant. ²³ One of his disciples, the one whom Jesus loved, was reclining at Jesus' side. ²⁴ So Simon Peter*

nodded to him to find out whom he meant. *²⁵ He leaned back against Jesus' chest and said to him, "Master, who is it?" ²⁶ Jesus answered, "It is the one to whom I hand the morsel after I have dipped it." So, he dipped the morsel and [took it and] handed it to Judas, son of Simon the Iscariot. ²⁷ After he took the morsel, Satan entered him. So, Jesus said to him, "What you are going to do, do quickly." ²⁸ [Now] none of those reclining at table realized why he said this to him. ²⁹ Some thought that since Judas kept the money bag, Jesus had told him, "Buy what we need for the feast," or to give something to the poor. ³⁰ So he took the morsel and left at once. And it was night.*

Matthew 26:21-29: *²¹ And while they were eating, he said, "Amen, I say to you, one of you will betray me." ²² Deeply distressed at this, they began to say to him one after another, "Surely it is not I, Lord?" ²³ He said in reply, "He who has dipped his hand into the dish with me is the one who will betray me. ²⁴ The Son of Man indeed goes, as it is written of him, but woe to that man by whom the Son of Man is betrayed. It would be better for that man if he had never been born." ²⁵ Then Judas, his betrayer, said in reply, "Surely it is not I, Rabbi?" He answered, "You have said so." ²⁶ While they were eating, Jesus took bread, said the blessing, broke it, and giving it to his disciples said, "Take and eat; this is my body." ²⁷ Then he took a cup, gave thanks, and gave it to them, saying, "Drink from it, all of you, ²⁸ for this is my blood of the covenant, which will be shed on behalf of many for the forgiveness of sins. ²⁹ I tell you, from now on I shall not drink this fruit of the vine until the day when I drink it with you new in the kingdom of my Father."*

Mark 14:18-25: *¹⁸ And as they reclined at table and were eating, Jesus said, "Amen, I say to you, one of you will betray* me, one who is eating with me." *¹⁹* They began to be distressed and to say to him, one by one, "Surely it is not I?" *²⁰* He said to them, "One of the Twelve, the one who dips with me into the dish. *²¹* For the Son of Man indeed goes, as it is written of him, but woe to that man by whom the Son of Man is betrayed. It would be better for that man if he had never been born." *²²* While they were eating, he took bread, said the blessing, broke it, and gave it to them, and said, "Take it; this is my body." *²³* Then he took a cup, gave thanks, and gave it to them, and they all drank from it. *²⁴* He said to them, "This is my blood of the covenant, which will be shed for many. *²⁵* Amen, I say to you, I shall not drink again the fruit of the vine until the day when I drink it new in the kingdom of God."

Luke 22:15-23: *¹⁵* He said to them, "I have eagerly desired to eat this Passover with you before I suffer, *¹⁶* for, I tell you, I shall not eat it [again] until there is fulfillment in the kingdom of God." *¹⁷* Then he took a cup, gave thanks, and said, "Take this and share it among yourselves; *¹⁸* for I tell you [that] from this time on I shall not drink of the fruit of the vine until the kingdom of God comes." *¹⁹* Then he took the bread, said the blessing, broke it, and gave it to them, saying, "This is my body, which will be given for you; do this in memory of me." *²⁰* And likewise the cup after they had eaten, saying, "This cup is the new covenant in my blood, which will be shed for you. *²¹* "And yet behold, the hand of the one who is to betray me is with me on the table; *²²* for the Son of Man indeed goes as it has been determined; but woe to that man by whom he is betrayed." *²³* And they began to debate among themselves who among them would do such a deed.

There are two scenarios here. The portrayals of them vary with the Gospel writer. Whether or not the establishment of the Eucharist occurred before or after Judas left is decided by theologians, not by me. However, I have learned lessons from each scenario.

God knows what is in my heart and what motivates the actions I am considering. There are no secrets I can keep from my Lord. In spite of that fact, He allows me to proceed with the choices I make, even if the choices I make sadden Him. It makes me think of the times in my life as a father when I allowed my children to make choices of their own. I did not always agree with those choices, and some saddened me. But those were decisions they had to make.

This is my body ... this is my blood. This was not something symbolic. If it was, He would have said so. He is with us always, and we must partake in His body and blood in order to have life within us. The first lesson I learn from here is that I must partake in His body and blood, not just acknowledge it. This gift has no meaning for us if we do not accept it. And, it has more meaning for us if we accept it often.

The second lesson is that our Lord is with us always. He comes to us through the Mass and is present to us in tabernacles throughout the world. Jesus is present to us always. Yet we make so little effort to spend time with Him. I am as guilty as anyone else. I have spent time visiting Him in the tabernacle, but not nearly as often as I could have. This is something I must change.

Lord, the choices I make can please You or sadden You; but they are choices You allow me to make. Help me to keep in mind that I want to please You in all I do. And remind me to make meaningful visits to You as often as I can. Amen.

The New Commandment of Love

<u>John 13:31-35:</u> *[31] When he had left, Jesus said, "Now is the Son of Man glorified, and God is glorified in him. [32] [If God is glorified in him,] God will also glorify him in himself, and he will glorify him at once. [33] My children, I will be with you only a little while longer. You will look for me, and as I told the Jews, 'Where I go you cannot come,' so now I say it to you. [34] I give you a new commandment: love one another. As I have loved you, so you also should love one another. [35] This is how all will know that you are my disciples, if you have love for one another."*

I give you a new commandment: love one another. As I have loved you, so you also should love one another. This is different from what we have seen earlier. Jesus' love for us is unconditional. He loves us in spite of who we are, what we say, or what we do. He is willing to forgive every sin we commit if we truly repent. He is willing to be merciful to us, sinners. That is what He is asking of us: do the same.

This is how all will know that you are my disciples, if you have love for one another. I wish I could say that I see this in all Christians I encounter. I wish I could say I see this in all who I care about. It is not. However, it could be. There is still time. But most of all, I hope others see this in me.

Lord, I want to love others as You love me. I want to be an example of Your love for us. Please help me. Amen.

434

Peter's Denial Predicted

<u>Matthew 26:30-35:</u> *[30] Then, after singing a hymn, they went out to the Mount of Olives. [31] Then Jesus said to them, "This night all of you will have your faith in me shaken, for it is written: 'I will strike the shepherd, and the sheep of the flock will be dispersed'; [32] but after I have been raised up, I shall go before you to Galilee." [33] Peter said to him in reply, "Though all may have their faith in you shaken, mine will never be." [34] Jesus said to him, "Amen, I say to you, this very night before the cock crows, you will deny me three times." [35] Peter said to him, "Even though I should have to die with you, I will not deny you." And all the disciples spoke likewise.*

<u>Mark 14:26-31:</u> *[26] Then, after singing a hymn, they went out to the Mount of Olives. [27] Then Jesus said to them, "All of you will have your faith shaken, for it is written: 'I will strike the shepherd, and the sheep will be dispersed.' [28] But after I have been raised up, I shall go before you to Galilee." [29] Peter said to him, "Even though all should have their faith shaken, mine will not be." [30] Then Jesus said to him, "Amen, I say to you, this very night before the cock crows twice you will deny me three times." [31] But he vehemently replied, "Even though I should have to die with you, I will not deny you." And they all spoke similarly.*

<u>Luke 22:31-34:</u> *[31] "Simon, Simon, behold Satan has demanded to sift all of you like wheat, [32] but I have prayed that your own faith may not fail; and once you have turned back, you must strengthen your brothers." [33] He said to him, "Lord, I am prepared to go to prison and to die with you." [34] But he replied, "I tell you, Peter, before the cock crows this day, you will deny three times that you know me."*

John 13:36-38: *[36] Simon Peter said to him, "Master, where are you going?" Jesus answered [him], "Where I am going, you cannot follow me now, though you will follow later." [37] Peter said to him, "Master, why can't I follow you now? I will lay down my life for you." [38] Jesus answered, "Will you lay down your life for me? Amen, amen, I say to you, the cock will not crow before you deny me three times."*

Peter was more outspoken than the others. He believed he was stronger than the others. But our Lord knew better. Jesus knew how Peter would react. However, Peter needed to know that he was as weak as others, that he could be as afraid as others, that he could be *shaken* as others. The same holds true for me. I have often read the Passion descriptions and tried to place myself in Peter's position. I have tried over and over to convince myself that I would not have abandoned my Lord. But, if I am ever in circumstances that are similar to Peter, I can only hope I will do better.

Lord, if ever I am in circumstances where I am being confronted for my belief in You, give me the strength to not abandon You. Amen.

The Two Swords

Luke 22:35-38: *[35] He said to them, "When I sent you forth without a money bag or a sack or sandals, were you in need of anything?" "No, nothing," they replied. [36] He said to them, "But now one who has a money bag should take it, and likewise a sack, and one who does not have a sword should sell his cloak and buy one. [37] For I tell you that this scripture must be fulfilled in me, namely, 'He was counted among the wicked'; and indeed, what is written about me is coming to* *fulfillment.*" *[38] Then they said, "Lord, look, there are two swords here." But he replied, "It is enough!"*

Here is a case in which I believe Jesus wanted to be taken figuratively and not literally. He wanted His disciples to know that they would face much opposition to what He taught and what they believe. Fortunately for me, I believe I have only encountered a few people over the years totally opposed to my Christian beliefs and outspoken about it. I have also encountered a few Christians opposed to my Catholic beliefs. However, I have never faced violence related to my beliefs.

Lord, I know what the world is like and what it could be. I trust in You. Amen.

Let Not Your Hearts Be Troubled

John 14:1-14: *[1] "Do not let your hearts be troubled. You have faith in God; have faith also in me. [2] In my Father's house there are many dwelling places. If there were not, would I have told you that I am going to prepare a place for you? [3] And if I go and prepare a place for you, I will come back again and take you to myself, so that where I am you also may be. [4] Where [I] am going you know the way." [5] Thomas said to him, "Master, we do not know where you are going; how can we know the way?" [6] Jesus said to him, "I am the way and the truth and the life. No one comes to the Father except through me. [7] If you know me, then you will also know my Father. From now on you do know him and have seen him." [8] Philip said to him, "Master, show us the Father, and that will be enough for us." [9] Jesus said to him, "Have I been with you for so long a time, and you still do not know me, Philip? Whoever has seen me has seen the Father. How can*

437

*you say, 'Show us the Father'? *[10]* Do you not believe that I am in the Father and the Father is in me? The words that I speak to you I do not speak on my own. The Father who dwells in me is doing his works. *[11]* Believe me that I am in the Father and the Father is in me, or else, believe because of the works themselves. *[12]* Amen, amen, I say to you, whoever believes in me will do the works that I do, and will do greater ones than these, because I am going to the Father. *[13]* And whatever you ask in my name, I will do, so that the Father may be glorified in the Son. *[14]* If you ask anything of me in my name, I will do it."*

You have faith in God; have faith also in me. Jesus assures us that we should trust in Him. Everything that He has taught has come from His Father. Jesus told us more than once that He came to do His Father's will and He has been doing so in word and deed. It is trust He is asking for.

And whatever you ask in my name, I will do, so that the Father may be glorified in the Son. The love Jesus has for His Father in heaven is shown through obedience to His will. Answering our requests also brings glory to His Father and our Father. This does not mean He will give us everything we ask for. Jesus will give us the same love His Father would. He will answer our requests based on His Father's will.

Lord, I trust in You. I hope all I do will in some way give glory to our heavenly Father. I will accept His will in response to all I ask. Amen.

Promise of the Holy Spirit

<u>John: 14:15-26:</u> *[15]"If you love me, you will keep my commandments. *[16]* And I will ask the Father, and he will give*

438

you another Advocate to be with you always, [17] the Spirit of truth, which the world cannot accept, because it neither sees nor knows it. But you know it, because it remains with you, and will be in you. [18] I will not leave you orphans; I will come to you. [19] In a little while the world will no longer see me, but you will see me, because I live, and you will live. [20] On that day you will realize that I am in my Father and you are in me and I in you. [21] Whoever has my commandments and observes them is the one who loves me. And whoever loves me will be loved by my Father, and I will love him and reveal myself to him." [22] Judas, not the Iscariot, said to him, "Master, [then] what happened that you will reveal yourself to us and not to the world?" [23] Jesus answered and said to him, "Whoever loves me will keep my word, and my Father will love him, and we will come to him and make our dwelling with him. [24] Whoever does not love me does not keep my words; yet the word you hear is not mine but that of the Father who sent me. [25] I have told you this while I am with you. [26] The Advocate, the holy Spirit that the Father will send in my name—he will teach you everything and remind you of all that [I] told you."

I believe this passage boils down to two of Jesus' statements. The first is: *Whoever has my commandments and observes them is the one who loves me. And whoever loves me will be loved by my Father, and I will love him and reveal myself to him.* It is in following God's will that we show our love for Him. It is in following God's will that we will find Jesus, because He will reveal Himself to us.

The second is: *The Advocate, the holy Spirit that the Father will send in my name—he will teach you everything and remind you of all that [I] told you.* After Jesus ascends to His Father, His Father will send the Holy Spirit to be with us always, to teach us what to say, to guide us in what we do. He will remind us of all Jesus taught us. The Holy Spirit will be our guiding light.

Lord, I know Your Holy Spirit is with us always, guiding us. Help me to place my trust in Him and follow His lead in all I do. Amen.

The Gift of Peace

John 14:27-31: *[27] "Peace I leave with you; my peace I give to you. Not as the world gives do I give it to you. Do not let your hearts be troubled or afraid. [28] You heard me tell you, 'I am going away, and I will come back to you.' If you loved me, you would rejoice that I am going to the Father; for the Father is greater than I. [29] And now I have told you this before it happens, so that when it happens you may believe. [30] I will no longer speak much with you, for the ruler of the world is coming. He has no power over me, [31] but the world must know that I love the Father and that I do just as the Father has commanded me. Get up, let us go."*

Once again, Jesus is encouraging His disciples to be at peace, to not be afraid. Yet at the same time He reminds them that the ruler of the world (Satan) is coming. It is hard to imagine what is going through the minds of His disciples at this time. Jesus is talking about going away and asking them to be at peace. He has asked them to love one another as He loved them, to imitate Him; then He reminds them that He does the will of His heavenly Father. What I get from this passage is that Jesus is telling us that, if we do what Jesus does and follow the will of our Father in heaven, then we will be at peace, in spite of what the world throws our way.

Lord, with all that is going on in the world, both in the world at large and also in my little corner of the world, it is hard to remain at peace. Help me to realize that peace can only be achieved and felt when we place our trust in You. Amen.

Jesus the True Vine

<u>John 15:1-8:</u> *[1] "I am the true vine, and my Father is the vine grower. [2] He takes away every branch in me that does not bear fruit, and every one that does he prunes so that it bears more fruit. [3] You are already pruned because of the word that I spoke to you. [4] Remain in me, as I remain in you. Just as a branch cannot bear fruit on its own unless it remains on the vine, so neither can you unless you remain in me. [5] I am the vine, you are the branches. Whoever remains in me and I in him will bear much fruit, because without me you can do nothing. [6] Anyone who does not remain in me will be thrown out like a branch and wither; people will gather them and throw them into a fire and they will be burned. [7] If you remain in me and my words remain in you, ask for whatever you want, and it will be done for you. [8] By this is my Father glorified, that you bear much fruit and become my disciples."*

One of the statements that I have overlooked in the past is truly important: *my Father is the vine grower. He takes away every branch in me that does not bear fruit, and every one that does he prunes so that it bears more fruit.* I do not know if it is naivete, but I have always pictured Jesus as the final judge. Jesus is the one who calls us, we are His chosen ones. We do what we can to follow Him, to bear good fruit. But His Father, our Father in heaven, is the one who judges us. He is the one who determines whether we are producing sufficient fruit to keep on hand. Jesus does the will of His

441

Father, and so must we. By this is His Father glorified, that we bear much fruit and become Jesus' disciples.

Lord, help me to not only understand the will of our Father in heaven, but to follow it as You do. Amen.

Abide in My Love

<u>John 15:9-17:</u> *⁹ "As the Father loves me, so I also love you. Remain in my love. ¹⁰ If you keep my commandments, you will remain in my love, just as I have kept my Father's commandments and remain in his love. ¹¹ I have told you this so that my joy may be in you and your joy may be complete. ¹² This is my commandment: love one another as I love you. ¹³ No one has greater love than this, to lay down one's life for one's friends. ¹⁴ You are my friends if you do what I command you. ¹⁵ I no longer call you slaves, because a slave does not know what his master is doing. I have called you friends, because I have told you everything I have heard from my Father. ¹⁶ It was not you who chose me, but I who chose you and appointed you to go and bear fruit that will remain, so that whatever you ask the Father in my name he may give you. ¹⁷ This I command you: love one another."*

In my mind, everything in this passage boils down to one statement: *I have called you friends, because I have told you everything I have heard from my Father.* Jesus had given us the command to love one another in the past. So, this passage is an important repetition of what He told us before; however, we are no longer simply His disciples, we are His *friends.* Everything that He has revealed to us was from His Father. As he told us before, He does what His Father wills, and He expects us to do the same. As friends of Jesus, we are friends of His Father. And as would be expected, friends treat each other with love.

Lord, help me to ensure that everything I do is a loving response to what I encounter. If I can do this at all times and under all conditions, I believe I will please You. Amen.

The World's Hatred

<u>John 15:18-16:4:</u> *[18] "If the world hates you, realize that it hated me first. [19] If you belonged to the world, the world would love its own; but because you do not belong to the world, and I have chosen you out of the world, the world hates you. [20] Remember the word I spoke to you, 'No slave is greater than his master.' If they persecuted me, they will also persecute you. If they kept my word, they will also keep yours. [21] And they will do all these things to you on account of my name, because they do not know the one who sent me. [22] If I had not come and spoken to them, they would have no sin; but as it is they have no excuse for their sin. [23] Whoever hates me also hates my Father. [24] If I had not done works among them that no one else ever did, they would not have sin; but as it is, they have seen and hated both me and my Father. [25] But in order that the word written in their law might be fulfilled, 'They hated me without cause.' [26] When the Advocate comes whom I will send you from the Father, the Spirit of truth that proceeds from the Father, he will testify to me. [27] And you also testify, because you have been with me from the beginning. [1] I have told you this so that you may not fall away. [2] They will expel you from the synagogues; in fact, the hour is coming when everyone who kills you will think he is offering worship to God. [3] They will do this because they have not known either the Father or me. [4] I have told you this so that when their hour comes you may*

remember that I told you. I did not tell you this from the beginning, because I was with you."

Jesus paints a pretty bleak picture; but it is a realistic one that His Apostles and disciples needed to hear. Jesus had been predicting His passion, death, and resurrection; so, they had to understand that the followers would most likely suffer what the master experiences, maybe not in exactly the same way, but suffer they will. In this date and time, 2,000 years later, Christians are still suffering for their belief. I have to admit that I have been fortunate to live in a country where prejudice against Christians is minimal. I have not had to suffer for my faith. That does not mean I will not in the future. It is pretty obvious that there is a growing trend within our country that is in opposition to our beliefs. It is the acknowledgement and assurance of our Lord that His followers, His disciples, will suffer for belief in Him and His teachings. Our Lord does not set a time limit on this.

Lord, I am aware that there is always the possibility of persecution for my faith. Grant me the strength to persevere and to be a good example to others if I ever have to endure such for You. Amen.

Work of the Advocate

<u>John 16:5-15:</u> *[5] "But now I am going to the one who sent me, and not one of you asks me, 'Where are you going?' [6] But because I told you this, grief has filled your hearts. [7] But I tell you the truth, it is better for you that I go. For if I do not go, the Advocate will not come to you. But if I go, I will send him to you. [8] And when he comes, he will convict the world in regard to sin and righteousness and condemnation: [9] sin, because they do not believe in me; [10] righteousness, because I*

444

am going to the Father and you will no longer see me; [11] condemnation, because the ruler of this world has been condemned. [12] I have much more to tell you, but you cannot bear it now. [13] But when he comes, the Spirit of truth, he will guide you to all truth. He will not speak on his own, but he will speak what he hears and will declare to you the things that are coming. [14] He will glorify me, because he will take from what is mine and declare it to you. [15] Everything that the Father has is mine; for this reason, I told you that he will take from what is mine and declare it to you."

But when he comes, the Spirit of truth, he will guide you to all truth. He will not speak on his own, but he will speak what he hears and will declare to you the things that are coming. God the Father and the Son sent the Holy Spirit, who proceeds from the Father and the Son. The Holy Spirit does not speak on His own. Like Jesus, He speaks what He hears from the Father. The Holy Spirit is our guide to all truth. He will guide us to living our lives as our Father in heaven wants us to live; but we must still say "yes." He will be with us always. This is the work of the Holy Spirit: to guide us to glorifying God through the works we do. Let us hope we are up to the task.

Lord, You sent the Spirit of truth to guide us and bring glory to You and our Father in heaven. Grant me the wisdom to discern the truth in every situation I encounter, so I may bring glory to You in what I do. Amen.

Sorrow Turned to Joy

John 16:16-22: [16] "A little while and you will no longer see me, and again a little while later and you will see me." [17] So some of his disciples said to one another, "What does this mean that

445

he is saying to us, 'A little while and you will not see me, and again a little while and you will see me,' and 'Because I am going to the Father'?" [18] So they said, "What is this 'little while' [of which he speaks]? We do not know what he means." [19] Jesus knew that they wanted to ask him, so he said to them, "Are you discussing with one another what I said, 'A little while and you will not see me, and again a little while and you will see me'? [20] Amen, amen, I say to you, you will weep and mourn, while the world rejoices; you will grieve, but your grief will become joy. [21] When a woman is in labor, she is in anguish because her hour has arrived; but when she has given birth to a child, she no longer remembers the pain because of her joy that a child has been born into the world. [22] So you also are now in anguish. But I will see you again, and your hearts will rejoice, and no one will take your joy away from you."

Much of what Jesus has told His disciples over three years caused them to be confused and to question. But is that not what our Lord wants, for us to question, to meditate, to look for answers? Our Lord will ascend to be with His Father, that is what He told them. And a little while and He will see them again. What is a little while in terms of eternity? It could be a moment. It could be a million years. The fact that after 2,000 years, for all who have come before, it meant through their lifetime. It could mean through our lifetimes. Only the Father knows when Jesus will return. But if we live as the Father wants us to live, we will be with Jesus at the end of our earthly lives.

Lord, let me not worry about the stuff for which I can gain no answer. Help me to focus on what will get me to see You and spend eternity with You. Amen.

Prayer in the Name of Jesus

John 16:23-28: *[23] "On that day you will not question me about anything. Amen, amen, I say to you, whatever you ask the Father in my name he will give you. [24] Until now you have not asked anything in my name; ask and you will receive, so that your joy may be complete. [25] I have told you this in figures of speech. The hour is coming when I will no longer speak to you in figures, but I will tell you clearly about the Father. [26] On that day you will ask in my name, and I do not tell you that I will ask the Father for you. [27] For the Father himself loves you, because you have loved me and have come to believe that I came from God. [28] I came from the Father and have come into the world. Now I am leaving the world and going back to the Father."*

... whatever you ask the Father in my name he will give you. The truth of the matter is that whatever we ask for in the name of Jesus will be given by the Father if it fits into His plans for us or for the one we are praying for. We can never forget about the plans of God. If we ask for something that will deviate from His plans, He may or may not grant it. If He does grant it, He will have some way to bring things in alignment with His plans again.

In all of these recent passages, our Lord has been acquainting His disciples with His Father. He wants His disciples (and us) to love His Father as He loves us, as His Father loves us. There is no secret here. Jesus wants this point to come across clearly. He speaks for His Father. His Father, our Father loves us.

Lord, let me ever be mindful of the love You and our Father in heaven have for me. But let me never forget that what I ask for in Your name will be granted by our Father if it corresponds to His will. Amen.

Prediction of the Disciples' Flight

John 16:29-33: *[29] His disciples said, "Now you are talking plainly, and not in any figure of speech. [30] Now we realize that you know everything and that you do not need to have anyone question you. Because of this we believe that you came from God." [31] Jesus answered them, "Do you believe now? [32] Behold, the hour is coming and has arrived when each of you will be scattered to his own home and you will leave me alone. But I am not alone, because the Father is with me. [33] I have told you this so that you might have peace in me. In the world you will have trouble, but take courage, I have conquered the world."*

I do not know what would happen if I felt a serious threat because of my faith. Would I be one to scatter? I am confident that if I felt a threat to my family, then I definitely would take my family and run. But a threat to me alone, I might be courageous enough to confront it. I have never been in a situation where physical danger was what I faced. So, I honestly do not know how I would react, even though I would like to believe I would be willing to become a martyr.

Jesus' disciples, at least some, I am sure, did not believe that they would run at the sign of danger. Simon Peter, as we will see, did not. This is another prediction of our Lord that the disciples will recall later. We have to remember that running in the face of danger is a natural reaction.

Lord, I do not know how I would react in the face of danger. I only hope that I will listen to You and move as You guide

448

me: stay and face the threat or run and possibly face it another day. Only You know what is in my heart. Amen.

The Intercessory Prayer

<u>John 17:1-26:</u> *[1] When Jesus had said this, he raised his eyes to heaven and said, "Father, the hour has come. Give glory to your son, so that your son may glorify you, [2] just as you gave him authority over all people, so that he may give eternal life to all you gave him. [3] Now this is eternal life, that they should know you, the only true God, and the one whom you sent, Jesus Christ. [4] I glorified you on earth by accomplishing the work that you gave me to do. [5] Now glorify me, Father, with you, with the glory that I had with you before the world began. [6] I revealed your name to those whom you gave me out of the world. They belonged to you, and you gave them to me, and they have kept your word. [7] Now they know that everything you gave me is from you, [8] because the words you gave to me I have given to them, and they accepted them and truly understood that I came from you, and they have believed that you sent me. [9] I pray for them. I do not pray for the world but for the ones you have given me, because they are yours, [10] and everything of mine is yours and everything of yours is mine, and I have been glorified in them. [11] And now I will no longer be in the world, but they are in the world, while I am coming to you. Holy Father, keep them in your name that you have given me, so that they may be one just as we are. [12] When I was with them, I protected them in your name that you gave me, and I guarded them, and none of them was lost except the son of destruction, in order that the scripture might be fulfilled. [13] But now I am coming to you. I speak this in the world so that they may share my joy completely. [14] I gave them your word, and the world hated them, because they do not belong to the world any more than I belong to the world. [15] I do*

449

not ask that you take them out of the world but that you keep them from the evil one. ¹⁶ They do not belong to the world any more than I belong to the world. ¹⁷ Consecrate them in the truth. Your word is truth. ¹⁸ As you sent me into the world, so I sent them into the world. ¹⁹ And I consecrate myself for them, so that they also may be consecrated in truth. ²⁰ I pray not only for them, but also for those who will believe in me through their word, ²¹ so that they may all be one, as you, Father, are in me and I in you, that they also may be in us, that the world may believe that you sent me. ²² And I have given them the glory you gave me, so that they may be one, as we are one, ²³ I in them and you in me, that they may be brought to perfection as one, that the world may know that you sent me, and that you loved them even as you loved me. ²⁴ Father, they are your gift to me. I wish that where I am they also may be with me, that they may see my glory that you gave me, because you loved me before the foundation of the world. ²⁵ Righteous Father, the world also does not know you, but I know you, and they know that you sent me. ²⁶ I made known to them your name and I will make it known that the love with which you loved me may be in them and I in them."

This prayer contains multiple segments that are important to understanding this most wonderful gift that we have received from God. The gift is eternal life. *Now this is eternal life, that they should know you, the only true God, and the one whom you sent, Jesus Christ.* Knowledge of God and His only begotten Son, Jesus Christ, is NOT eternal life.

To "know of" someone and to "know" someone are very different. To truly experience eternal life, we must know God and His Son. We must do more than just study about God. We must get to know Him. We must allow Him to reside in us, to share His will with us, to be His hands, His feet, His heart, His mouth. By studying His Son, Jesus, we can gain some knowledge of Him and His relationship with His Father. We must then strive to let Them in, to allow Them to live in us and we in Them. Only then can we experience eternal life with God. We have to be ready to share the gift of eternal life with Them.

Jesus prays for His disciples and for those who will follow. *I pray for them. I do not pray for the world but for the ones you have given me, because they are yours, and everything of mine is yours and everything of yours is mine, and I have been glorified in them.* Jesus does not want to lose any who truly want to follow Him. His Father knows who they are. He prays that His Father will not let the world overshadow them, to keep them on the right track. If we are to be among "those who will follow," then we must give ourselves to God, the one God, the Triune God.

I do not ask that you take them out of the world but that you keep them from the evil one. They do not belong to the world any more than I belong to the world. Consecrate them in the truth. Here is the tough part that we must accept. Our Lord is not asking His Father to simply take us to heaven. We are to live temporarily in this world. But He is asking His Father to keep us out of the hands of the owner of this world – Satan. He wants us to have the strength to persevere against evil, which only our Father in heaven can grant us. Yet we must still give Him our "fiat." Thy will be done.

Jesus ends this prayer with our mission. *Righteous Father, the world also does not know you, but I know you, and they know that you sent me. I made known to them your name and I will make it known that the love with which you loved me may be in them and I in them.* That is our mission. We are to make the world know that the love of God is in them. Sounds simple! It is not. We have a lot of work to do.

Lord, I hope and pray that I can fulfill all that You expect of me. There is so much, and I am so weak. I need Your help to take each step. I know You are with me, but the world scares me. Hold my hand as I walk through this life. Amen.

Agony in the Garden

Matthew 26:36-46: *³⁶ Then Jesus came with them to a place called Gethsemane, and he said to his disciples, "Sit here while I go over there and pray." ³⁷ He took along Peter and the two sons of Zebedee and began to feel sorrow and distress. ³⁸ Then he said to them, "My soul is sorrowful even to death. Remain here and keep watch with me." ³⁹ He advanced a little and fell prostrate in prayer, saying, "My Father, if it is possible, let this cup pass from me; yet, not as I will, but as you will." ⁴⁰ When he returned to his disciples he found them asleep. He said to Peter, "So you could not keep watch with me for one hour? ⁴¹ Watch and pray that you may not undergo the test. The spirit is willing, but the flesh is weak." ⁴² Withdrawing a second time, he prayed again, "My Father, if it is not possible that this cup pass without my drinking it, your will be done!" ⁴³ Then he returned once more and found them asleep, for they could not keep their eyes open. ⁴⁴ He left them and withdrew again and prayed a third time, saying the same thing again. ⁴⁵ Then he returned to his disciples and said to them, "Are you still sleeping and taking your rest? Behold, the hour is at hand when the Son of Man is to be handed over to sinners. ⁴⁶ Get up, let us go. Look, my betrayer is at hand."*

Mark 14:32-42: *³² Then they came to a place named Gethsemane, and he said to his disciples, "Sit here while I pray." ³³ He took with him Peter, James, and John, and began to be troubled and distressed. ³⁴ Then he said to them, "My soul*

452

is sorrowful even to death. *Remain here and keep watch."* [35] *He advanced a little and fell to the ground and prayed that if it were possible the hour might pass by him;* [36] *he said, "Abba, Father, all things are possible to you. Take this cup away from me, but not what I will but what you will."* [37] *When he returned, he found them asleep. He said to Peter, "Simon, are you asleep? Could you not keep watch for one hour?* [38] *Watch and pray that you may not undergo the test. The spirit is willing, but the flesh is weak."* [39] *Withdrawing again, he prayed, saying the same thing.* [40] *Then he returned once more and found them asleep, for they could not keep their eyes open and did not know what to answer him.* [41] *He returned a third time and said to them, "Are you still sleeping and taking your rest? It is enough. The hour has come. Behold, the Son of Man is to be handed over to sinners.* [42] *Get up, let us go. See, my betrayer is at hand."*

Luke 22:39-46: [39] *Then going out he went, as was his custom, to the Mount of Olives, and the disciples followed him.* [40] *When he arrived at the place he said to them, "Pray that you may not undergo the test."* [41] *After withdrawing about a stone's throw from them and kneeling, he prayed,* [42] *saying, "Father, if you are willing, take this cup away from me; still, not my will but yours be done." [*[43] *And to strengthen him an angel from heaven appeared to him.* [44] *He was in such agony, and he prayed so fervently that his sweat became like drops of blood falling on the ground.]* [45] *When he rose from prayer and returned to his disciples, he found them sleeping from grief.* [46] *He said to them, "Why are you sleeping? Get up and pray that you may not undergo the test."*

John 18:1: *When he had said this, Jesus went out with his disciples across the Kidron valley to where there was a garden, into which he and his disciples entered.*

Many speakers and writers have speculated on what took place during Jesus' agony in the garden. Based on the Gospel passages, we know that He prayed three times a prayer of love for His Father and for mankind. He asked for relief from the burden He was about to endure; but, as was His lifelong commitment, He would follow the will of His Father. He would endure His passion and death so that mankind would be able to enter the Kingdom of Heaven. We must look to this as an example of how our Lord wants us to live. He wants us the endure all that comes before us for the love of God and the love of mankind. It is the will of our Father that we must follow.

Although saddened by the lack of attentiveness of His disciples, Jesus understood their bodily need for sleep. In His love for His disciples, He allowed them to rest until it was time for action. We must also be sensitive to the needs of others and not require more of them than they are capable of doing.

Lord, a horrible story is about to unfold. Out of love for Your Father and all sinners, You continue to do the will of Your Father. You will suffer and die so that we may live. Grant me the graces I need to fulfill the will of our Father in my life. Amen.

Betrayal and Arrest

Matthew 26:47-56: *[47] While he was still speaking, Judas, one of the Twelve, arrived, accompanied by a large crowd, with swords and clubs, who had come from the chief priests and the elders of the people. [48] His betrayer had arranged a sign with them, saying, "The man I shall kiss is the one; arrest him." [49] Immediately he went over to Jesus and said, "Hail,*

Rabbi!" and he kissed him. *⁵⁰ Jesus answered him, "Friend, do what you have come for." Then stepping forward they laid hands on Jesus and arrested him. ⁵¹ And behold, one of those who accompanied Jesus put his hand to his sword, drew it, and struck the high priest's servant, cutting off his ear. ⁵² Then Jesus said to him, "Put your sword back into its sheath, for all who take the sword will perish by the sword. ⁵³ Do you think that I cannot call upon my Father and he will not provide me at this moment with more than twelve legions of angels? ⁵⁴ But then how would the scriptures be fulfilled which say that it must come to pass in this way?" ⁵⁵ At that hour Jesus said to the crowds, "Have you come out as against a robber, with swords and clubs to seize me? Day after day I sat teaching in the temple area, yet you did not arrest me. ⁵⁶ But all this has come to pass that the writings of the prophets may be fulfilled." Then all the disciples left him and fled.*

Mark 14:43-52: *⁴³ Then, while he was still speaking, Judas, one of the Twelve, arrived, accompanied by a crowd with swords and clubs who had come from the chief priests, the scribes, and the elders. ⁴⁴ His betrayer had arranged a signal with them, saying, "The man I shall kiss is the one; arrest him and lead him away securely." ⁴⁵ He came and immediately went over to him and said, "Rabbi." And he kissed him. ⁴⁶ At this they laid hands on him and arrested him. ⁴⁷ One of the bystanders drew his sword, struck the high priest's servant, and cut off his ear. ⁴⁸ Jesus said to them in reply, "Have you come out as against a robber, with swords and clubs, to seize me? ⁴⁹ Day after day I was with you teaching in the temple area, yet you did not arrest me; but that the scriptures may be fulfilled." ⁵⁰ And they all left him and fled. ⁵¹ Now a young man followed him wearing nothing but a linen cloth about his body. They seized him, ⁵² but he left the cloth behind and ran off naked.*

Luke 22:47-53: [47] *While he was still speaking, a crowd approached and in front was one of the Twelve, a man named Judas. He went up to Jesus to kiss him.* [48] *Jesus said to him, "Judas, are you betraying the Son of Man with a kiss?"* [49] *His disciples realized what was about to happen, and they asked, "Lord, shall we strike with a sword?"* [50] *And one of them struck the high priest's servant and cut off his right ear.* [51]*But Jesus said in reply, "Stop, no more of this!" Then he touched the servant's ear and healed him.* [52] *And Jesus said to the chief priests and temple guards and elders who had come for him, "Have you come out as against a robber, with swords and clubs?* [53] *Day after day I was with you in the temple area, and you did not seize me; but this is your hour, the time for the power of darkness."*

John 18:2-12: [2] *Judas his betrayer also knew the place, because Jesus had often met there with his disciples.* [3] *So Judas got a band of soldiers and guards from the chief priests and the Pharisees and went there with lanterns, torches, and weapons.* [4] *Jesus, knowing everything that was going to happen to him, went out and said to them, "Whom are you looking for?"* [5] *They answered him, "Jesus the Nazorean." He said to them, "I AM." Judas his betrayer was also with them.* [6] *When he said to them, "I AM," they turned away and fell to the ground.* [7] *So he again asked them, "Whom are you looking for?" They said, "Jesus the Nazorean."* [8] *Jesus answered, "I told you that I AM. So, if you are looking for me, let these men go."* [9] *This was to fulfill what he had said, "I have not lost any of those you gave me."* [10] *Then Simon Peter, who had a sword, drew it, struck the high priest's slave, and cut off his right ear. The slave's name was Malchus.* [11] *Jesus said to Peter, "Put your sword into its scabbard. Shall I not drink the* *cup that the Father gave me?" [12] So the band of soldiers, the tribune, and the Jewish guards seized Jesus, bound him.*

The Judas Kiss, known throughout the world, sealed the deal. Judas did his part, for which he was paid 30 pieces of silver. Nothing in scriptures says that Judas said he was sorry. He did not repent for his deed. He did not believe that his sin was forgivable. Our Lord deeply loved Judas as He does each of us. And, in that love, He allowed Judas to commit his sin, and scripture prophecies would be fulfilled. Sin does not come out of love, but love allows sin to be committed. The old adage is applicable here: hate the sin but love the sinner. Jesus gave us an example of this.

Poor Peter! Sometimes he not only speaks before thinking things out, but he also acts when he should not. Although, in this case, he believed he was protecting our Lord. Our Lord stopped him before he could make a mess of things and healed the person Peter injured. Out of love, Jesus stopped the aggression and healed the injured.

Then our Lord protected the rest of the disciples. He made sure the attention of the soldiers was focused on Himself, which allowed the others to leave, frightened but unharmed. Again, another act of love, in spite of the fact they were abandoning Him.

Lord, sometimes we look around to see the circumstances without looking deeply to see what is really happening. Open my mind and heart to recognize the love You show in the events I experience or witness and lead me to follow Your example. Amen.

Jesus Before the Sanhedrin

John 18:13-14,19-24: *[13] and brought him to Annas first. He was the father-in-law of Caiaphas, who was high priest that year. [14] It was Caiaphas who had counseled the Jews that it was better that one man should die rather than the people. … [19] The high priest questioned Jesus about his disciples and about his doctrine. [20] Jesus answered him, "I have spoken publicly to the world. I have always taught in a synagogue or in the temple area where all the Jews gather, and in secret I have said nothing. [21] Why ask me? Ask those who heard me what I said to them. They know what I said." [22] When he had said this, one of the temple guards standing there struck Jesus and said, "Is this the way you answer the high priest?" [23] Jesus answered him, "If I have spoken wrongly, testify to the wrong; but if I have spoken rightly, why do you strike me?" [24] Then Annas sent him bound to Caiaphas the high priest.*

Matthew 26:57-68: *[57] Those who had arrested Jesus led him away to Caiaphas the high priest, where the scribes and the elders were assembled. [58] Peter was following him at a distance as far as the high priest's courtyard and going inside he sat down with the servants to see the outcome. [59] The chief priests and the entire Sanhedrin kept trying to obtain false testimony against Jesus in order to put him to death, [60] but they found none, though many false witnesses came forward. Finally, two came forward [61] who stated, "This man said, 'I can destroy the temple of God and within three days rebuild it.'" [62] The high priest rose and addressed him, "Have you no answer? What are these men testifying against you?" [63] But Jesus was silent. Then the high priest said to him, "I order you to tell us under oath before the living God whether you are the Messiah, the Son of God." [64] Jesus said to him in reply, "You have said so. But I tell you: From now on you will see 'the Son of Man* *seated at the right hand of the Power' and 'coming on the clouds of heaven.'" 65 Then the high priest tore his robes and said, "He has blasphemed! What further need have we of witnesses? You have now heard the blasphemy; 66 what is your opinion?" They said in reply, "He deserves to die!" 67 Then they spat in his face and struck him, while some slapped him, 68 saying, "Prophesy for us, Messiah: who is it that struck you?"*

Mark 14:53-65: 53 They led Jesus away to the high priest, and all the chief priests and the elders and the scribes came together. 54 Peter followed him at a distance into the high priest's courtyard and was seated with the guards, warming himself at the fire. 55 The chief priests and the entire Sanhedrin kept trying to obtain testimony against Jesus in order to put him to death, but they found none. 56 Many gave false witness against him, but their testimony did not agree. 57]Some took the stand and testified falsely against him, alleging, 58 "We heard him say, 'I will destroy this temple made with hands and within three days I will build another not made with hands.'" 59 Even so their testimony did not agree. 60 The high priest rose before the assembly and questioned Jesus, saying, "Have you no answer? What are these men testifying against you?" 61 But he was silent and answered nothing. Again the high priest asked him and said to him, "Are you the Messiah, the son of the Blessed One?" 62 Then Jesus answered, "I am; and 'you will see the Son of Man seated at the right hand of the Power and coming with the clouds of heaven.'" 63 At that the high priest tore his garments and said, "What further need have we of witnesses? 64 You have heard the blasphemy. What do you think?" They all condemned him as deserving to die. 65 Some began to spit on him. They blindfolded him and struck him and said to him, "Prophesy!" And the guards greeted him with blows.

Luke 22:54-55,63-71: *[54] After arresting him they led him away and took him into the house of the high priest; Peter was following at a distance. [55] They lit a fire in the middle of the courtyard and sat around it, and Peter sat down with them. ... [63] The men who held Jesus in custody were ridiculing and beating him. [64] They blindfolded him and questioned him, saying, "Prophesy! Who is it that struck you?" [65] And they reviled him in saying many other things against him. [66] When day came the council of elders of the people met, both chief priests and scribes, and they brought him before their Sanhedrin. [67] They said, "If you are the Messiah, tell us," but he replied to them, "If I tell you, you will not believe, [68] and if I question, you will not respond. [69] But from this time on the Son of Man will be seated at the right hand of the power of God." [70] They all asked, "Are you then the Son of God?" He replied to them, "You say that I am." [71] Then they said, "What further need have we for testimony? We have heard it from his own mouth."*

For the most part, Jesus was silent during His questioning. He responded to a couple of things; but only one of His statements made a difference. *But he was silent and answered nothing. Again, the high priest asked him and said to him, "Are you the Messiah, the son of the Blessed One?" Then Jesus answered, "I am; and 'you will see the Son of Man seated at the right hand of the Power and coming with the clouds of heaven.'"* From a Jewish religious standpoint, those words sealed His fate and assured the fulfillment of the scripture prophecy. Caiaphas declared the blasphemy and pronounced the condemnation. Now he would be presented for His condemnation by the world. This is only the beginning.

I often wonder how I would have withstood the pressure of this persecution. But realistically, the trial is easier than the punishment to follow. The only way I could withstand the things that our Lord and the many martyrs who suffered after Him and for Him is out of love. Love is the key.

Lord, I have read the stories of your passion, death, and resurrection many times. I have read the accounts described by many different authors. I believe I understand what You did for us. Help me to always appreciate You gift to us. Amen.

Peter's Denial

John 18:15-18,25-27: [15] *Simon Peter and another disciple followed Jesus. Now the other disciple was known to the high priest, and he entered the courtyard of the high priest with Jesus.* [16] *But Peter stood at the gate outside. So, the other disciple, the acquaintance of the high priest, went out and spoke to the gatekeeper and brought Peter in.* [17] *Then the maid who was the gatekeeper said to Peter, "You are not one of this man's disciples, are you?" He said, "I am not."* [18] *Now the slaves and the guards were standing around a charcoal fire that they had made, because it was cold, and were warming themselves. Peter was also standing there keeping warm. ...* [25] *Now Simon Peter was standing there keeping warm. And they said to him, "You are not one of his disciples, are you?" He denied it and said, "I am not."* [26] *One of the slaves of the high priest, a relative of the one whose ear Peter had cut off, said, "Didn't I see you in the garden with him?"* [27] *Again Peter denied it. And immediately the cock crowed.*

Matthew 26:69-75: [69] *Now Peter was sitting outside in the courtyard. One of the maids came over to him and said, "You* *too were with Jesus the Galilean." ⁷⁰ But he denied it in front of everyone, saying, "I do not know what you are talking about!" ⁷¹ As he went out to the gate, another girl saw him and said to those who were there, "This man was with Jesus the Nazorean." ⁷² Again he denied it with an oath, "I do not know the man!" ⁷³ A little later the bystanders came over and said to Peter, "Surely you too are one of them; even your speech gives you away." ⁷⁴ At that he began to curse and to swear, "I do not know the man." And immediately a cock crowed. ⁷⁵ Then Peter remembered the word that Jesus had spoken: "Before the cock crows you will deny me three times." He went out and began to weep bitterly.*

Mark 14:66-72: *⁶⁶ While Peter was below in the courtyard, one of the high priest's maids came along. ⁶⁷ Seeing Peter warming himself, she looked intently at him and said, "You too were with the Nazarene, Jesus." ⁶⁸ But he denied it saying, "I neither know nor understand what you are talking about." So, he went out into the outer court. [Then the cock crowed.] ⁶⁹ The maid saw him and began again to say to the bystanders, "This man is one of them." ⁷⁰ Once again he denied it. A little later the bystanders said to Peter once more, "Surely you are one of them; for you too are a Galilean." ⁷¹ He began to curse and to swear, "I do not know this man about whom you are talking." ⁷² And immediately a cock crowed a second time. Then Peter remembered the word that Jesus had said to him, "Before the cock crows twice you will deny me three times." He broke down and wept.*

Luke 22:56-62: *⁵⁶ When a maid saw him seated in the light, she looked intently at him and said, "This man too was with him." ⁵⁷ But he denied it saying, "Woman, I do not know him." ⁵⁸ A short while later someone else saw him and said, "You too are one of them"; but Peter answered, "My friend, I am not.*" *⁵⁹ About an hour later, still another insisted, "Assuredly, this man too was with him, for he also is a Galilean." ⁶⁰ But Peter said, "My friend, I do not know what you are talking about." Just as he was saying this, the cock crowed, ⁶¹ and the Lord turned and looked at Peter; and Peter remembered the word of the Lord, how he had said to him, "Before the cock crows today, you will deny me three times." ⁶² He went out and began to weep bitterly.*

Peter had boasted that he would be there for Jesus; then came the denials - three denials before the cock crowed, just as Jesus predicted. The denials accomplished nothing except to show Peter that he was not as strong and fearless as he thought he would be. Our Lord knew Peter and understood His nature, just as He knows and understands each of us. This was a trial Peter had to undergo in order to understand himself better. Peter's denials had no impact on what Jesus was going through for all mankind. The denials were for Peter's benefit.

I do not believe that I would make the same mistake that Peter made. It is not in my nature to act and talk as Peter did. However, I still can learn from Peter's mistakes. The fact is that I am weak in other areas; and, although the ways may be different, I have still failed my Lord and God on many occasions. I can only hope that I will not do so again.

Lord, like Peter, I have a strong ego. It is my pride that has kept me from being Your true disciple. You have shown me on many occasions that I am not living up to Your expectations of me. Grant me the graces I need to speak and act as You would have me do so. Amen.

463

Death of Judas

Matthew 27:3-10: *³ Then Judas, his betrayer, seeing that Jesus had been condemned, deeply regretted what he had done. He returned the thirty pieces of silver to the chief priests and elders, ⁴ saying, "I have sinned in betraying innocent blood." They said, "What is that to us? Look to it yourself." ⁵ Flinging the money into the temple, he departed and went off and hanged himself. ⁶ The chief priests gathered up the money, but said, "It is not lawful to deposit this in the temple treasury, for it is the price of blood." ⁷ After consultation, they used it to buy the potter's field as a burial place for foreigners. ⁸ That is why that field even today is called the Field of Blood. ⁹ Then was fulfilled what had been said through Jeremiah the prophet, "And they took the thirty pieces of silver, the value of a man with a price on his head, a price set by some of the Israelites, ¹⁰ and they paid it out for the potter's field just as the Lord had commanded me."*

The important point that I need to remember in this passage comes from this statement: *Then Judas, his betrayer, seeing that Jesus had been condemned, deeply regretted what he had done.* Judas deeply regretted what he had done. Judas did not get the results he anticipated, so he regretted his action. He did not repent his action. He did not seek forgiveness from Jesus for his action, because he did not believe his sin was forgivable. He was deeply sorry for the decision he made. Judas' action fulfilled the scripture prophecy.

Lord, I know You are a loving God. I know that You are a forgiving and merciful God. Help me to always be confident that I can come to You deeply repentant, and You will forgive me. Amen.

The Trial Before Pilate

John 18:28-38: *[28] Then they brought Jesus from Caiaphas to the praetorium. It was morning. And they themselves did not enter the praetorium, in order not to be defiled so that they could eat the Passover. [29] So Pilate came out to them and said, "What charge do you bring [against] this man?" [30] They answered and said to him, "If he were not a criminal, we would not have handed him over to you." [31] At this, Pilate said to them, "Take him yourselves, and judge him according to your law." The Jews answered him, "We do not have the right to execute anyone," [32] in order that the word of Jesus might be fulfilled that he said indicating the kind of death he would die. [33] So Pilate went back into the praetorium and summoned Jesus and said to him, "Are you the King of the Jews?" [34] Jesus answered, "Do you say this on your own or have others told you about me?" [35] Pilate answered, "I am not a Jew, am I? Your own nation and the chief priests handed you over to me. What have you done?" [36] Jesus answered, "My kingdom does not belong to this world. If my kingdom did belong to this world, my attendants [would] be fighting to keep me from being handed over to the Jews. But as it is, my kingdom is not here." [37] So Pilate said to him, "Then you are a king?" Jesus answered, "You say I am a king. For this I was born and for this I came into the world, to testify to the truth. Everyone who belongs to the truth listens to my voice." [38] Pilate said to him, "What is truth?" When he had said this, he again went out to the Jews and said to them, "I find no guilt in him.*

Matthew 27:1-2,11-14: *[1] When it was morning, all the chief priests and the elders of the people took counsel against Jesus to put him to death. [2] They bound him, led him away, and handed him over to Pilate, the governor. ... [11] Now Jesus stood*

465

before the governor, and he questioned him, "Are you the king of the Jews?" Jesus said, "You say so." [12] And when he was accused by the chief priests and elders, he made no answer. [13] Then Pilate said to him, "Do you not hear how many things they are testifying against you?" [14] But he did not answer him one word, so that the governor was greatly amazed.

Mark 15:1-5: *[1] As soon as morning came, the chief priests with the elders and the scribes, that is, the whole Sanhedrin, held a council. They bound Jesus, led him away, and handed him over to Pilate. [2] Pilate questioned him, "Are you the king of the Jews?" He said to him in reply, "You say so." [3] The chief priests accused him of many things. [4] Again Pilate questioned him, "Have you no answer? See how many things they accuse you of." [5] Jesus gave him no further answer, so that Pilate was amazed.*

Luke 23:1-5: *[1] Then the whole assembly of them arose and brought him before Pilate. [2] They brought charges against him, saying, "We found this man misleading our people; he opposes the payment of taxes to Caesar and maintains that he is the Messiah, a king." [3] Pilate asked him, "Are you the king of the Jews?" He said to him in reply, "You say so." [4] Pilate then addressed the chief priests and the crowds, "I find this man not guilty." [5] But they were adamant and said, "He is inciting the people with his teaching throughout all Judea, from Galilee where he began even to here."*

I am considering Jesus' reaction to what is going on and I see a man with His head clear and answering calmly, in spite of the physical abuse he had received. Pilate evidently was questioning Him calmly. He had been silent for the most part with Caiaphas and the other Jewish leaders because their actions and statements were anything but calm. Jesus knew what to say and how far to go. My lesson from Jesus on this is to face adversity calmly and patiently. I am not to get emotionally charged and try to justify what I do. As Jesus had told His disciples, the advocate will provide the words that need to be spoken at the necessary time.

Lord, our natural reaction to adversity is to defend ourselves. Please help me, when faced with adverse conditions, to be calm and patient. Help me to trust that the Holy Spirit will provide what I need to say and do at the appropriate time. Amen.

Jesus Before Herod

Luke 23:6-12: *⁶ On hearing this Pilate asked if the man was a Galilean; ⁷ and upon learning that he was under Herod's jurisdiction, he sent him to Herod who was in Jerusalem at that time. ⁸ Herod was very glad to see Jesus; he had been wanting to see him for a long time, for he had heard about him and had been hoping to see him perform some sign. ⁹ He questioned him at length, but he gave him no answer. ¹⁰ The chief priests and scribes, meanwhile, stood by accusing him harshly. ¹¹ [Even] Herod and his soldiers treated him contemptuously and mocked him, and after clothing him in resplendent garb, he sent him back to Pilate. ¹² Herod and Pilate became friends that very day, even though they had been enemies formerly.*

Once again, Jesus is placed in front of an excitable Jewish leader, the current token King, the pawn of Rome. Herod is emotionally charged, not because of his belief in the Messiah, but because he had a celebrity in front of him and was looking for a show. Jesus is calm and patient, again facing more abuse. Upset at not being entertained, Herod

467

decides Jesus is a fool rather than a threat. He sends Jesus back to Pilate.

Lord, once again, You know how to deal with those opposed to You. Help me to know what to do if that time comes for me. Amen.

Pilate Declares Jesus Innocent

<u>Luke 23:13-16:</u> *[13] Pilate then summoned the chief priests, the rulers, and the people [14] and said to them, "You brought this man to me and accused him of inciting the people to revolt. I have conducted my investigation in your presence and have not found this man guilty of the charges you have brought against him, [15] nor did Herod, for he sent him back to us. So, no capital crime has been committed by him. [16] Therefore I shall have him flogged and then release him."*

Our Lord remains silent at this point. He knows what is coming. Things have to unfold as they should. Even though Pilate is convinced of Jesus' innocence of a crime against Rome, he is not strong enough to stand by this conviction. Pressure from those around can cause people to do what is wrong in spite of what they believe. It takes extraordinary effort to follow through with what is right.

Lord, knowing what is right and what is wrong does not satisfy a situation. The correct action must be taken. When I know what is right, give me the grace to follow through with the proper action. Amen.

Jesus or Barabbas?

Matthew 27:15-23: *[15] Now on the occasion of the feast the governor was accustomed to release to the crowd one prisoner whom they wished. [16] And at that time they had a notorious prisoner called [Jesus] Barabbas. [17] So when they had assembled, Pilate said to them, "Which one do you want me to release to you, [Jesus] Barabbas, or Jesus called Messiah?" [18] For he knew that it was out of envy that they had handed him over. [19] While he was still seated on the bench, his wife sent him a message, "Have nothing to do with that righteous man. I suffered much in a dream today because of him." [20] The chief priests and the elders persuaded the crowds to ask for Barabbas but to destroy Jesus. [21] The governor said to them in reply, "Which of the two do you want me to release to you?" They answered, "Barabbas!" [22] Pilate said to them, "Then what shall I do with Jesus called Messiah?" They all said, "Let him be crucified!" [23] But he said, "Why? What evil has he done?" They only shouted the louder, "Let him be crucified!"*

Mark 15:6-14: *[6] Now on the occasion of the feast he used to release to them one prisoner whom they requested. [7] A man called Barabbas was then in prison along with the rebels who had committed murder in a rebellion. [8] The crowd came forward and began to ask him to do for them as he was accustomed. [9] Pilate answered, "Do you want me to release to you the king of the Jews?" [10] For he knew that it was out of envy that the chief priests had handed him over. [11] But the chief priests stirred up the crowd to have him release Barabbas for them instead. [12] Pilate again said to them in reply, "Then what [do you want] me to do with [the man you call] the king of the Jews?" [13] They shouted again, "Crucify him." [14] Pilate said to* them, *"Why? What evil has he done?"* They only shouted the louder, *"Crucify him."*

Luke 23:17-23: [18] *But all together they shouted out, "Away with this man! Release Barabbas to us."* [19] *(Now Barabbas had been imprisoned for a rebellion that had taken place in the city and for murder.)* [20] *Again Pilate addressed them, still wishing to release Jesus,* [21] *but they continued their shouting, "Crucify him! Crucify him!"* [22] *Pilate addressed them a third time, "What evil has this man done? I found him guilty of no capital crime. Therefore, I shall have him flogged and then release him."* [23] *With loud shouts, however, they persisted in calling for his crucifixion, and their voices prevailed.*

John 18:39-40: [39] *But you have a custom that I release one prisoner to you at Passover. Do you want me to release to you the King of the Jews?"* [40] *They cried out again, "Not this one but Barabbas!" Now Barabbas was a revolutionary.*

Barabbas was simply a pawn in this game, but he did get his freedom out of the exchange. The fact is that Pilate is finally going to give into the mob.

I enjoy watching western movies. However, the mob scenes were always scary. Was the mob going to get control and hang the innocent victim (or the guilty perpetrator)? Was the marshal going to break up the mob and save the day? Here, Pilate did not have to give into the mob. He had sufficient soldiers to break up the scene and release Jesus. But politics will win. He weighs the cost of the life of one man he had no strong feelings about against the possible trouble he might face with Rome.

To be right before God, we must choose the right rather than the safe. That is not always an easy choice, but it is realistically a choice we make often.

470

Lord, safe or right – they are not always the same answer – even when the mob seems to be my own colleagues or co-workers. Help me to discern what is best for each situation. Amen.

Crucify Him!

John 19:1-16: *¹ Then Pilate took Jesus and had him scourged. ² And the soldiers wove a crown out of thorns and placed it on his head, and clothed him in a purple cloak, ³ and they came to him and said, "Hail, King of the Jews!" And they struck him repeatedly. ⁴ Once more Pilate went out and said to them, "Look, I am bringing him out to you, so that you may know that I find no guilt in him." ⁵ So Jesus came out, wearing the crown of thorns and the purple cloak. And he said to them, "Behold, the man!" ⁶ When the chief priests and the guards saw him, they cried out, "Crucify him, crucify him!" Pilate said to them, "Take him yourselves and crucify him. I find no guilt in him." ⁷ The Jews answered, "We have a law, and according to that law he ought to die, because he made himself the Son of God." ⁸ Now when Pilate heard this statement, he became even more afraid, ⁹ and went back into the praetorium and said to Jesus, "Where are you from?" Jesus did not answer him. ¹⁰ So Pilate said to him, "Do you not speak to me? Do you not know that I have power to release you, and I have power to crucify you?" ¹¹ Jesus answered [him], "You would have no power over me if it had not been given to you from above. For this reason, the one who handed me over to you has the greater sin." ¹² Consequently, Pilate tried to release him; but the Jews cried out, "If you release him, you are not a Friend of Caesar. Everyone who makes himself a king opposes Caesar." ¹³ When Pilate heard these words, he brought Jesus out and seated him on the judge's bench in the place called Stone Pavement,*

in Hebrew, Gabbatha. [14] It was preparation day for Passover,
and it was about noon. And he said to the Jews, "Behold, your
king!" [15] They cried out, "Take him away, take him away!
Crucify him!" Pilate said to them, "Shall I crucify your king?"
The chief priests answered, "We have no king but Caesar."
[16] Then he handed him over to them to be crucified.

Matthew 27:24-31: *[24] When Pilate saw that he was not*
succeeding at all, but that a riot was breaking out instead, he
took water and washed his hands in the sight of the crowd,
saying, "I am innocent of this man's blood. Look to it
yourselves." [25] And the whole people said in reply, "His blood
be upon us and upon our children." [26] Then he released
Barabbas to them, but after he had Jesus scourged, he handed
him over to be crucified. [27] Then the soldiers of the governor
took Jesus inside the praetorium and gathered the whole
cohort around him. [28] They stripped off his clothes and threw
a scarlet military cloak about him. [29] Weaving a crown out of
thorns, they placed it on his head, and a reed in his right hand.
And kneeling before him, they mocked him, saying, "Hail,
King of the Jews!" [30] They spat upon him and took the reed
and kept striking him on the head. [31] And when they had
mocked him, they stripped him of the cloak, dressed him in his
own clothes, and led him off to crucify him.

Mark 15:15-20: *[15] So Pilate, wishing to satisfy the crowd,*
released Barabbas to them and, after he had Jesus scourged,
handed him over to be crucified. [16] The soldiers led him away
inside the palace, that is, the praetorium, and assembled the
whole cohort. [17] They clothed him in purple and, weaving a
crown of thorns, placed it on him. [18] They began to salute him
with, "Hail, King of the Jews!" [19] and kept striking his head
with a reed and spitting upon him. They knelt before him in
homage. [20] And when they had mocked him, they stripped him

of the purple cloak, dressed him in his own clothes, and led him out to crucify him.

Luke 23:24-25: *[24] The verdict of Pilate was that their demand should be granted. [25] So he released the man who had been imprisoned for rebellion and murder, for whom they asked, and he handed Jesus over to them to deal with as they wished.*

Pilate was given a number of opportunities to do the right thing. He admitted to Jesus' innocence. So, the right thing would have been to release Jesus. After all, even Herod agreed that Jesus imposed no danger to Rome. However, there was a larger concern here than just right or wrong. He had to deal with politics; and realistically, that was his job. Right and wrong were only relative to Pilate who had to make his pronouncements based on what was good for Rome. He made the choice to crucify an innocent man to soothe the relations with the local subservient leadership. As time will tell, he ended up losing his job in the long run.

In this part of the gospel passages I chose to focus on Pilate and the decision he made. As has been shown up to this point, our Lord is allowing everyone to mistreat and abuse Him. This was His Father's will. I am not sure that Pilate's decision to scourge Christ really was an alternative to crucifixion or simply a delay of the ultimate decision he would have to make. After all, some writers indicate that scourging was always a preparation for crucifixion.

Pilate is the focal point. Does he give into the mob and take the easy action, or does he continue to press for the release of innocence Himself? He chose to let the mob have its way. "Crucify him!"

473

Lord, only once in my life I had a possibility of being part of a group to decide life or death of an individual. Fortunately, I was released from jury duty on a capital crime trial. I pray, if I am ever in a similar position again, that I will answer Your call and choose the right action. Amen.

The Crucifixion Begins

John 19:17-27: *[17] and carrying the cross himself he went out to what is called the Place of the Skull, in Hebrew, Golgotha. [18] There they crucified him, and with him two others, one on either side, with Jesus in the middle. [19] Pilate also had an inscription written and put on the cross. It read, "Jesus the Nazorean, the King of the Jews." [20] Now many of the Jews read this inscription, because the place where Jesus was crucified was near the city; and it was written in Hebrew, Latin, and Greek. [21] So the chief priests of the Jews said to Pilate, "Do not write 'The King of the Jews,' but that he said, 'I am the King of the Jews.'" [22] Pilate answered, "What I have written, I have written." [23] When the soldiers had crucified Jesus, they took his clothes and divided them into four shares, a share for each soldier. They also took his tunic, but the tunic was seamless, woven in one piece from the top down. [24] So they said to one another, "Let's not tear it, but cast lots for it to see whose it will be," in order that the passage of scripture might be fulfilled [that says]: "They divided my garments among them, and for my vesture they cast lots." This is what the soldiers did. [25] Standing by the cross of Jesus were his mother and his mother's sister, Mary the wife of Clopas, and Mary of Magdala. [26] When Jesus saw his mother and the disciple there whom he loved, he said to his mother, "Woman, behold, your son." [27] Then he said to the disciple, "Behold, your mother." And from that hour the disciple took her into his home.*

Matthew 27:31-37: *[31] And when they had mocked him, they stripped him of the cloak, dressed him in his own clothes, and led him off to crucify him. [32] As they were going out, they met a Cyrenian named Simon; this man they pressed into service to carry his cross. [33] And when they came to a place called Golgotha (which means Place of the Skull), [34] they gave Jesus wine to drink mixed with gall. But when he had tasted it, he refused to drink. [35] After they had crucified him, they divided his garments by casting lots; [36] then they sat down and kept watch over him there. [37] And they placed over his head the written charge against him: This is Jesus, the King of the Jews.*

Mark 15:20-26: *[20] And when they had mocked him, they stripped him of the purple cloak, dressed him in his own clothes, and led him out to crucify him. [21] They pressed into service a passer-by, Simon, a Cyrenian, who was coming in from the country, the father of Alexander and Rufus, to carry his cross. [22] They brought him to the place of Golgotha (which is translated Place of the Skull). [23] They gave him wine drugged with myrrh, but he did not take it. [24] they crucified him and divided his garments by casting lots for them to see what each should take. [25] It was nine o'clock in the morning when they crucified him. [26] The inscription of the charge against him read, "The King of the Jews."*

Luke 23:26-34: *[26] As they led him away they took hold of a certain Simon, a Cyrenian, who was coming in from the country; and after laying the cross on him, they made him carry it behind Jesus. [27] A large crowd of people followed Jesus, including many women who mourned and lamented him. [28] Jesus turned to them and said, "Daughters of Jerusalem, do not weep for me; weep instead for yourselves and for your children, [29] for indeed, the days are coming when people will say, 'Blessed are the barren, the wombs that never* *bore and the breasts that never nursed.' [30] At that time people will say to the mountains, 'Fall upon us!' and to the hills, 'Cover us!' [31] for if these things are done when the wood is green what will happen when it is dry?" [32] Now two others, both criminals, were led away with him to be executed. [33] When they came to the place called the Skull, they crucified him and the criminals there, one on his right, the other on his left. [34] [Then Jesus said, "Father, forgive them, they know not what they do."] They divided his garments by casting lots.*

One thing is certain, the gospel writers cannot be accused of writing with graphic violence. I have read many commentaries on the crucifixion in which the authors tried to describe in detail what Jesus was experiencing. I never felt comfortable in reading those except that they bring a sense of reality to what our Lord experienced in order to bring about our redemption. My wife Martha, in fact, refused to read or listen to any description of the crucifixion, except the gospels at Mass.

As part of my daily spiritual readings, I alternate reading passages of two particular books that cover the time frame from Palm Sunday through the Resurrection. One version is written by Venerable Fulton J. Sheen (*Life of Christ*) and the other contains the apparitions of Blessed Anne Catherine Emmerich (*The Dolorous Passion of Our Lord Jesus Christ*). Both versions cover this time frame in about 300 pages. My goal is not so much to learn the details of Jesus' passion and death as it is to keep His sacrifice in my mind and heart.

It is important that all Christians keep a regular reminder before them of our Lord's sacrifice (passion, death, and resurrection). We cannot allow ourselves to forget this.

I do want to comment further on one part of these verses. Our Lord gave us His Blessed Mother as our mother also.

He gave her a new mission. Originally, her mission was to bring the Christ to mankind. Her new mission is to bring mankind to her son. It is important for us to remember that Mary is our Blessed Mother. We can seek her out and ask for her guidance and assistance. As any mother would, she will place our petitions before the One who could respond properly to them, the Triune God, the Father, His and her Son, and the Holy Spirit. Keep in mind that out of love for His Mother, Jesus will naturally want to please His Mother. She is our best advocate. She will petition her Son on our behalf.

Lord, it is truly important for us to remember always the sacrifice You offered to Our Father in heaven for our redemption. And help me to remember also that our Blessed Mother is our best advocate. Please guide me always to bring these to mind. Amen.

Jesus is Derided on the Cross

Matthew 27:38-43: *[38] Two revolutionaries were crucified with him, one on his right and the other on his left. [39] Those passing by reviled him, shaking their heads [40] and saying, "You who would destroy the temple and rebuild it in three days, save yourself, if you are the Son of God, [and] come down from the cross!" [41] Likewise the chief priests with the scribes and elders mocked him and said, [42] "He saved others; he cannot save himself. So, he is the king of Israel! Let him come down from the cross now, and we will believe in him. [43] He trusted in God; let him deliver him now if he wants him. For he said, 'I am the Son of God.'"*

Mark 15:27-32: *[27] With him they crucified two revolutionaries, one on his right and one on his left. [[28]] [29] Those passing by*

477

reviled him, shaking their heads and saying, "Aha! You who would destroy the temple and rebuild it in three days, ³⁰ save yourself by coming down from the cross." ³¹ Likewise the chief priests, with the scribes, mocked him among themselves and said, "He saved others; he cannot save himself. ³² Let the Messiah, the King of Israel, come down now from the cross that we may see and believe." Those who were crucified with him also kept abusing him.

Luke 23:35-38: *³⁵ The people stood by and watched; the rulers, meanwhile, sneered at him and said, "He saved others, let him save himself if he is the chosen one, the Messiah of God." ³⁶ Even the soldiers jeered at him. As they approached to offer him wine ³⁷ they called out, "If you are King of the Jews, save yourself." ³⁸ Above him there was an inscription that read, "This is the King of the Jews."*

Evil will have its way. To relieve its feeling of guilt, the crowd derides our Lord. This is normal. They want to feel like they are doing the right thing, so they make the victim evil and ridicule him. So, in their minds, evil becomes good, and innocence becomes evil. There is no victory here. It is all about feeling good about what you are doing.

Lord, there were plenty of times in my youth that I followed the crowd; however, I do not believe I have ever participated in something like this. Maybe I have either forgotten or am blocking out the memory. In any case, I pray that you keep me on the right path moving forward. Amen.

The Two Thieves

Luke 23:39-43: *³⁹ Now one of the criminals hanging there reviled Jesus, saying, "Are you not the Messiah? Save yourself* *and us."* [40] *The other, however, rebuking him, said in reply, "Have you no fear of God, for you are subject to the same condemnation?* [41] *And indeed, we have been condemned justly, for the sentence we received corresponds to our crimes, but this man has done nothing criminal."* [42] *Then he said, "Jesus, remember me when you come into your kingdom."* [43] *He replied to him, "Amen, I say to you, today you will be with me in Paradise."*

<u>Matthew 27:44:</u> *The revolutionaries who were crucified with him also kept abusing him in the same way.*

As stated in Psalm 139: "Lord, you have probed me, you know me." God sees what we do. He hears what we say. He knows our innermost thoughts. He knows what is in our hearts. Jesus knew what was in the hearts of the two thieves and He responded. Should we have expected Him to respond differently?

Lord, let me never be so foolish as to believe I can hide anything from You. On the contrary, let me always believe You know me so well that everything You do on my behalf is for my own good. Amen.

The Death of Jesus

<u>Matthew 27:45-54:</u> [45] *From noon onward, darkness came over the whole land until three in the afternoon.* [46] *And about three o'clock Jesus cried out in a loud voice, "Eli, Eli, lema sabachthani?" which means, "My God, my God, why have you forsaken me?"* [47] *Some of the bystanders who heard it said, "This one is calling for Elijah."* [48] *Immediately one of them ran to get a sponge; he soaked it in wine, and putting it on a reed, gave it to him to drink.* [49] *But the rest said, "Wait, let us*

see if Elijah comes to save him." [50] But Jesus cried out again in a loud voice, and gave up his spirit. [51] And behold, the veil of the sanctuary was torn in two from top to bottom. The earth quaked, rocks were split, [52] tombs were opened, and the bodies of many saints who had fallen asleep were raised. [53] And coming forth from their tombs after his resurrection, they entered the holy city and appeared to many. [54] The centurion and the men with him who were keeping watch over Jesus feared greatly when they saw the earthquake and all that was happening, and they said, "Truly, this was the Son of God!"

Mark 15:33-39: *[33] At noon darkness came over the whole land until three in the afternoon. [34] And at three o'clock Jesus cried out in a loud voice, "Eloi, Eloi, lema sabachthani?" which is translated, "My God, my God, why have you forsaken me?" [35] Some of the bystanders who heard it said, "Look, he is calling Elijah." [36] One of them ran, soaked a sponge with wine, put it on a reed, and gave it to him to drink, saying, "Wait, let us see if Elijah comes to take him down." [37] Jesus gave a loud cry and breathed his last. [38] The veil of the sanctuary was torn in two from top to bottom. [39] When the centurion who stood facing him saw how he breathed his last he said, "Truly this man was the Son of God!"*

Luke 23:44-48: *[44] It was now about noon and darkness came over the whole land until three in the afternoon [45] because of an eclipse of the sun. Then the veil of the temple was torn down the middle. [46] Jesus cried out in a loud voice, "Father, into your hands I commend my spirit"; and when he had said this, he breathed his last. [47] The centurion who witnessed what had happened glorified God and said, "This man was innocent beyond doubt." [48] When all the people who had gathered for this spectacle saw what had happened, they returned home beating their breasts;*

480

John 19:28: *After this, aware that everything was now finished, in order that the scripture might be fulfilled, Jesus said, "I thirst."*

Two things come to mind from these passages: compassion and guilt. Then our Lord cried out, *"Eli, Eli, lema sabachthani?"* It was in response to this that some of the crowd, one in particular, were moved with compassion for our suffering Lord. All indications are that He did not drink from the sponge that was offered. However, I believe our Lord felt and understood the compassion from some of the bystanders. It is amazing how a gesture of compassion can be felt and appreciated by the one to whom it is intended.

When all the people who had gathered for this spectacle saw what had happened, they returned home beating their breasts. There were also some in the crowd who actually felt the guilt of the crucifixion of an innocent man. The gesture of beating their breasts is a normal action meaning the acceptance of guilt. We do the same at Mass when we, beating our breasts, say in the Confiteor, "through my fault, through my fault, through my most grievous fault." At that time, they did not know that our Lord had died in reparation for all of their sins and the sins of all mankind. They simply felt the guilt of participating in defiling innocence.

Lord, I have experienced both of the emotions described in these passages. When I read about or view portrayals of Your passion and death, I feel compassion as well as guilt. Help me to both understand those feelings and continue to feel them. You are my all. Amen.

Witnesses of the Crucifixion

Matthew 27:55-56: *[55] There were many women there, looking on from a distance, who had followed Jesus from Galilee, ministering to him. [56] Among them were Mary Magdalene and Mary the mother of James and Joseph, and the mother of the sons of Zebedee.*

Mark 15:40-41: *[40] There were also women looking on from a distance. Among them were Mary Magdalene, Mary the mother of the younger James and of Joses, and Salome. [41] These women had followed him when he was in Galilee and ministered to him. There were also many other women who had come up with him to Jerusalem.*

Luke 23:49: *but all his acquaintances stood at a distance, including the women who had followed him from Galilee and saw these events.*

I do not know (and I have not felt) the draw to follow an individual and just be with him or her over a long period of time. That is what these women, described in these passages, have done. I have experienced something different. There were a couple of times in my life that I have been drawn to be somewhere in particular and I believed that I was being called by God. The difference is that my wife Martha had the same feelings I did. We uprooted our family and went. God calls each of us in different ways. He has different plans for each of us. He called these folks from Galilee to be with His Son, and so they followed and did what they could to serve. He did not lay out a huge plan of action. He simply asked them to be there and to serve as needed.

Lord, keep my mind open to what it is You would have me do. I am Your instrument. Use me as You will. Amen.

The Burial of Jesus

John 19:31-37: *[31] Now since it was preparation day, in order that the bodies might not remain on the cross on the sabbath, for the sabbath day of that week was a solemn one, the Jews asked Pilate that their legs be broken and they be taken down. [32] So the soldiers came and broke the legs of the first and then of the other one who was crucified with Jesus. [33] But when they came to Jesus and saw that he was already dead, they did not break his legs, [34] but one soldier thrust his lance into his side, and immediately blood and water flowed out. [35] An eyewitness has testified, and his testimony is true; he knows that he is speaking the truth, so that you also may [come to] believe. [36] For this happened so that the scripture passage might be fulfilled: "Not a bone of it will be broken." [37] And again another passage says: "They will look upon him whom they have pierced." [38] After this, Joseph of Arimathea, secretly a disciple of Jesus for fear of the Jews, asked Pilate if he could remove the body of Jesus. And Pilate permitted it. So he came and took his body. [39] Nicodemus, the one who had first come to him at night, also came bringing a mixture of myrrh and aloes weighing about one hundred pounds. [40] They took the body of Jesus and bound it with burial cloths along with the spices, according to the Jewish burial custom. [41] Now in the place where he had been crucified there was a garden, and in the garden a new tomb, in which no one had yet been buried. [42] So they laid Jesus there because of the Jewish preparation day; for the tomb was close by.*

Matthew 27:57-61: *[57] When it was evening, there came a rich man from Arimathea named Joseph, who was himself a* disciple of Jesus. [58] He went to Pilate and asked for the body of Jesus; then Pilate ordered it to be handed over. [59] Taking the body, Joseph wrapped it [in] clean linen [60] and laid it in his new tomb that he had hewn in the rock. Then he rolled a huge stone across the entrance to the tomb and departed. [61] But Mary Magdalene and the other Mary remained sitting there, facing the tomb.

Mark 15:42-47: [42] When it was already evening, since it was the day of preparation, the day before the sabbath, [43] Joseph of Arimathea, a distinguished member of the council, who was himself awaiting the kingdom of God, came and courageously went to Pilate and asked for the body of Jesus. [44] Pilate was amazed that he was already dead. He summoned the centurion and asked him if Jesus had already died. [45] And when he learned of it from the centurion, he gave the body to Joseph. [46] Having bought a linen cloth, he took him down, wrapped him in the linen cloth and laid him in a tomb that had been hewn out of the rock. Then he rolled a stone against the entrance to the tomb. [47] Mary Magdalene and Mary the mother of Joses watched where he was laid.

Luke 23:50-56: [50] Now there was a virtuous and righteous man named Joseph who, though he was a member of the council, [51] had not consented to their plan of action. He came from the Jewish town of Arimathea and was awaiting the kingdom of God. [52] He went to Pilate and asked for the body of Jesus. [53] After he had taken the body down, he wrapped it in a linen cloth and laid him in a rock-hewn tomb in which no one had yet been buried. [54] It was the day of preparation, and the sabbath was about to begin. [55] The women who had come from Galilee with him followed behind, and when they had seen the tomb and the way in which his body was laid in it, [56] they

returned and prepared spices and perfumed oils. Then they
rested on the sabbath according to the commandment.

I have discerned two lessons from these passages. The first is that the law must be fulfilled. Anxious as Pilate was for this mess to be over with, he wanted to be sure the rules were followed. The rules said that the perpetrators who were crucified must be dead before their bodies were removed from the crosses. Caiaphas wanted it over as well so that the bodies of the Jews would be removed from the crosses before the feast begins. So, orders were given to ensure this was true. Both the law of men and the law of God were fulfilled with the declared death of the three. The bodies were removed from the crosses.

The second lesson is that some heroes do not show up to save the day; they show up to honor the fallen. This is where Joseph of Arimathea comes in. He stepped out of the shadows and revealed himself to be an admirer of Jesus. He was not openly a follower of our Lord. But he, like Nicodemus, slowly accepted the truth of Jesus teachings. Joseph came forward to honor our Lord by providing Him a place of burial. After getting permission to remove Jesus' body, he gave the body to Jesus' mother until the tomb could be prepared.

Lord, I have failed to acknowledge You openly many times in the past. In saying grace before meals, in saying the rosary or other prayers in public, I tried not to draw attention to myself, when I should have actually been proclaiming my belief. Such a failure! Let me never again be afraid to acknowledge You as my Lord and Savior in public. Amen.

The Guard at the Tomb

Matthew 27:62-66: *[62] The next day, the one following the day of preparation, the chief priests and the Pharisees gathered before Pilate [63] and said, "Sir, we remember that this impostor while still alive said, 'After three days I will be raised up.' [64] Give orders, then, that the grave be secured until the third day, lest his disciples come and steal him and say to the people, 'He has been raised from the dead.' This last imposture would be worse than the first." [65] Pilate said to them, "The guard is yours; go secure it as best you can." [66] So they went and secured the tomb by fixing a seal to the stone and setting the guard.*

People doing evil things usually try to take extra measures to ensure their treachery is not revealed. Sometimes this works and sometimes not. However, evil deeds, treachery, are usually revealed in the long run, no matter how much money, other gifts, or more evil deeds are used to cover it up.

Lord, the day is filled with human activities, some good and some bad. Help me to never be the one to perform or cover up the evil ones. Amen.

Part 15

The Resurrection

The Women at the Tomb

Matthew 28:1-10: *[1] After the sabbath, as the first day of the week was dawning, Mary Magdalene and the other Mary came to see the tomb. [2] And behold, there was a great earthquake; for an angel of the Lord descended from heaven, approached, rolled back the stone, and sat upon it. [3] His appearance was like lightning, and his clothing was white as snow. [4] The guards were shaken with fear of him and became like dead men. [5] Then the angel said to the women in reply, "Do not be afraid! I know that you are seeking Jesus the crucified. [6] He is not here, for he has been raised just as he said. Come and see the place where he lay. [7] Then go quickly and tell his disciples, 'He has been raised from the dead, and he is going before you to Galilee; there you will see him.' Behold, I have told you." [8] Then they went away quickly from the tomb, fearful yet overjoyed, and ran to announce this to his disciples. [9] And behold, Jesus met them on their way and greeted them. They approached, embraced his feet, and did him homage. [10] Then Jesus said to them, "Do not be afraid. Go tell my brothers to go to Galilee, and there they will see me."*

Mark 16:1-11: *[1] When the sabbath was over, Mary Magdalene, Mary, the mother of James, and Salome bought spices so that they might go and anoint him. [2] Very early when the sun had risen, on the first day of the week, they came to the tomb. [3] They were saying to one another, "Who will roll back the stone for us from the entrance to the tomb?" [4] When they looked up, they saw that the stone had been rolled back; it was very large. [5] On entering the tomb they saw a young man sitting on the right side, clothed in a white robe, and they were utterly amazed. [6] He said to them, "Do not be amazed! You seek Jesus of Nazareth, the crucified. He has been raised; he is not here.*

Behold, the place where they laid him. ⁷ But go and tell his disciples and Peter, 'He is going before you to Galilee; there you will see him, as he told you.'" ⁸ Then they went out and fled from the tomb, seized with trembling and bewilderment. They said nothing to anyone, for they were afraid. ⁹ When he had risen, early on the first day of the week, he appeared first to Mary Magdalene, out of whom he had driven seven demons. ¹⁰ She went and told his companions who were mourning and weeping. ¹¹ When they heard that he was alive and had been seen by her, they did not believe.

<u>Luke 24:1-12:</u> *¹ But at daybreak on the first day of the week they took the spices they had prepared and went to the tomb. ² They found the stone rolled away from the tomb; ³ but when they entered, they did not find the body of the Lord Jesus. ⁴ While they were puzzling over this, behold, two men in dazzling garments appeared to them. ⁵ They were terrified and bowed their faces to the ground. They said to them, "Why do you seek the living one among the dead? ⁶ He is not here, but he has been raised. Remember what he said to you while he was still in Galilee, ⁷ that the Son of Man must be handed over to sinners and be crucified, and rise on the third day." ⁸ And they remembered his words. ⁹ Then they returned from the tomb and announced all these things to the eleven and to all the others. ¹⁰ The women were Mary Magdalene, Joanna, and Mary the mother of James; the others who accompanied them also told this to the Apostles, ¹¹ but their story seemed like nonsense, and they did not believe them. ¹² But Peter got up and ran to the tomb, bent down, and saw the burial cloths alone; then he went home amazed at what had happened.*

<u>John 20:1-18:</u> *¹ On the first day of the week, Mary of Magdala came to the tomb early in the morning, while it was still dark, and saw the stone removed from the tomb. ² So she ran and*

went to Simon Peter and to the other disciple whom Jesus loved, and told them, "They have taken the Lord from the tomb, and we don't know where they put him." ³ So Peter and the other disciple went out and came to the tomb. ⁴ They both ran, but the other disciple ran faster than Peter and arrived at the tomb first; ⁵ he bent down and saw the burial cloths there, but did not go in. ⁶ When Simon Peter arrived after him, he went into the tomb and saw the burial cloths there, ⁷ and the cloth that had covered his head, not with the burial cloths but rolled up in a separate place. ⁸ Then the other disciple also went in, the one who had arrived at the tomb first, and he saw and believed. ⁹ For they did not yet understand the scripture that he had to rise from the dead. ¹⁰ Then the disciples returned home. ¹¹ But Mary stayed outside the tomb weeping. And as she wept, she bent over into the tomb ¹² and saw two angels in white sitting there, one at the head and one at the feet where the body of Jesus had been. ¹³ And they said to her, "Woman, why are you weeping?" She said to them, "They have taken my Lord, and I don't know where they laid him." ¹⁴ When she had said this, she turned around and saw Jesus there, but did not know it was Jesus. ¹⁵ Jesus said to her, "Woman, why are you weeping? Whom are you looking for?" She thought it was the gardener and said to him, "Sir, if you carried him away, tell me where you laid him, and I will take him." ¹⁶ Jesus said to her, "Mary!" She turned and said to him in Hebrew, "Rabbouni," which means Teacher. ¹⁷ Jesus said to her, "Stop holding on to me, for I have not yet ascended to the Father. But go to my brothers and tell them, 'I am going to my Father and your Father, to my God and your God.'" ¹⁸ Mary of Magdala went and announced to the disciples, "I have seen the Lord," and what he told her.

Having read and heard these gospel stories many times over the years, I have gotten many insights into what was happening from my own reflections as well as homilies and commentaries, even though the stories do not agree on all of the details. However, today I got three particular messages from these passages.

The women, only some of whom are identified, got up early on the first day of the week to anoint the body of our Lord. This was customary and simply the right thing to do. There is no indication of who organized this effort, only that it was being done. They did not know what to expect when they got there, only that it would be difficult to get to His body because of the heavy stone rolled in front of the opening. The first lesson here is that, if you know that something is the right thing to do in a set of circumstances, then do it; let God take care of the rest.

The second lesson is that, if God wants you to do something specific, He will let you know. This is shown by the message given to the women from the angel(s) in the empty tomb. We probably will not have a visit from angels, but the words may come from someone we know or a total stranger, who is temporarily God's instrument. The words telling us what needs to be done may also come directly from God to us. This is not unheard of. Even though you get the message, you still have a choice to follow through or not.

Then the third lesson I got today is that seeing is not always believing. Simon Peter and John both looked into the empty tomb, but neither one of them attributed the empty tomb to our Lord rising as He said He would do. They went back, amazed, confused, not sure what to make of it.

And finally, after hearing the message brought to them by the women, the Apostles did not believe what they were told. Again, seeing and hearing is not the same as believing.

Lord, to be realistic, to hear Your voice, to understand Your message, I have to want to hear it. Only if I open mind and

heart to You will I be able to grasp what You want me to do.
So, please open both my mind and heart to You. Amen.

The Report of the Guard

Matthew 28:11-15: *[11] While they were going, some of the guard went into the city and told the chief priests all that had happened. [12] They assembled with the elders and took counsel; then they gave a large sum of money to the soldiers, [13] telling them, "You are to say, 'His disciples came by night and stole him while we were asleep.' [14] And if this gets to the ears of the governor, we will satisfy [him] and keep you out of trouble." [15] The soldiers took the money and did as they were instructed. And this story has circulated among the Jews to the present [day].*

Lie upon lie! One deception after another! There will never be an end to it. But there must be a cover-up. The truth cannot be known. As Caiaphas said, one must die for the good of all. The good of all or was it the good of a few? The more the lie is told, the more likely it will become the truth - not in reality, but perceived. *The soldiers took the money and did as they were instructed.* That was easy! It is so much easier to allow evil to flourish than to do good.

Lord, I have always tried to be a man of integrity. Honest I have been and honesty I have looked for. Help me to keep this as a standard of my life. Amen.

On the Way to Emmaus

Luke 24:13-35: *[13] Now that very day two of them were going to a village seven miles from Jerusalem called Emmaus, [14] and* they were conversing about all the things that had occurred. *15 And it happened that while they were conversing and debating, Jesus himself drew near and walked with them, 16 but their eyes were prevented from recognizing him. 17 He asked them, "What are you discussing as you walk along?" They stopped, looking downcast. 18 One of them, named Cleopas, said to him in reply, "Are you the only visitor to Jerusalem who does not know of the things that have taken place there in these days?" 19 And he replied to them, "What sort of things?" They said to him, "The things that happened to Jesus the Nazarene, who was a prophet mighty in deed and word before God and all the people, 20 how our chief priests and rulers both handed him over to a sentence of death and crucified him. 21 But we were hoping that he would be the one to redeem Israel; and besides all this, it is now the third day since this took place. 22 Some women from our group, however, have astounded us: they were at the tomb early in the morning 23 and did not find his body; they came back and reported that they had indeed seen a vision of angels who announced that he was alive. 24 Then some of those with us went to the tomb and found things just as the women had described, but him they did not see." 25 And he said to them, "Oh, how foolish you are! How slow of heart to believe all that the prophets spoke! 26 Was it not necessary that the Messiah should suffer these things and enter into his glory?" 27 Then beginning with Moses and all the prophets, he interpreted to them what referred to him in all the scriptures. 28 As they approached the village to which they were going, he gave the impression that he was going on farther. 29 But they urged him, "Stay with us, for it is nearly evening and the day is almost over." So, he went in to stay with them. 30 And it happened that, while he was with them at table, he took bread, said the blessing, broke it, and gave it to them. 31 With that their eyes were opened, and they recognized him; but he vanished from their sight.* ^{32} *Then they said to each other, "Were not our hearts burning [within us] while he spoke to us on the way and opened the scriptures to us?"* ^{33} *So they set out at once and returned to Jerusalem where they found gathered together the eleven and those with them* ^{34} *who were saying, "The Lord has truly been raised and has appeared to Simon!"* ^{35} *Then the two recounted what had taken place on the way and how he was made known to them in the breaking of the bread.*

Mark 16:12-13: ^{12} *After this he appeared in another form to two of them walking along on their way to the country.* ^{13} *They returned and told the others; but they did not believe them either.*

There are several things that come to mind with this story about the journey to Emmaus.

(One) This has nothing to do with the Resurrection, but my physical and spiritual growth are tied together. Prior to two years ago, I had been doing a three-mile walk each day to help with my physical well-being. I walked at a steady pace, and it took about an hour. According to this passage, the disciples were going about seven miles from Jerusalem; so, my calculation is that it would take them, probably at a relaxed pace, about two and a half to three hours to get to Emmaus. Depending on where Jesus came into the picture, they would have had plenty of time to discuss lots of matters with our Lord.

(Two) The two disciples did not recognize Jesus. Similar statements are made in multiple places in the gospels after the Resurrection. People did not recognize Jesus. Were they simply blinded by sunlight and did not see Him clearly, or did He actually come to them with a different presence. Nothing is explained in the Gospels except that their belief that Jesus was dead would not allow them to recognize Him immediately. However, being with someone for three hours or more would have given them plenty of time to look at Him. My conclusion is that our Lord comes to us in whatever form is necessary to ease us into being comfortable in His presence.

(Three) Jesus interpreted for them what referred to Him in the scriptures. As I indicated above, they probably had plenty of time to talk, listen, and discuss. When you encounter someone who has a comfortable presence, who has a clear way of explaining things, who has an obvious interest and knowledge of something that has been on your mind, then you are going to comfortably discuss matters with this person and easily lose track of time.

(Four) *Stay with us.* Earlier in this book, I wrote about being on a retreat. In the evenings, the retreat master would sit in the common room with everyone who wanted to and discuss whatever was on their minds. We had a good crowd every evening. The two disciples were so fascinated by this stranger and what He was saying, they did not want Him to leave. They wanted to hear and discuss more. When you find something that draws your interest and keeps it, you do not want it to end.

(Five) It was with the blessing of the meal and the breaking of the bread that they finally recognized Him. I am sure they were already suspecting His identity as they were in conversation. However, Jesus' disappearance convinced them that they had been visited by our Lord Himself. They realized the stories they heard about His rising from death were true. In their excitement, they had to go back to Jerusalem and share their story with the Apostles and other disciples. They left immediately and I assume at a faster pace. When you are filled with joy, you want to share it with others as quickly as possible.

495

(Six) Was the bubble burst? They told their story to the Apostles and other disciples who were present and still there was disbelief. In spite of the fact that there were two of them and two credible witnesses were required to assure the truth. On top of that, the Apostles had heard similar statements from Mary of Magdala and the other women who had been at the empty tomb. When things are heard that are contrary to what is expected, especially stories that defy nature, then it takes either first-hand experience or firm desire to believe. We will see this in Thomas.

Lord, there is so much that I can relate to in this story about the two disciples and their journey to Emmaus that I want to cry out to everyone that I believe, just as they did. Help me to share that belief so that others may come to love You as I do. Amen.

Jesus Appears to His Disciples
(Thomas is not Present)

Luke 24:36-43: *³⁶ While they were still speaking about this, he stood in their midst and said to them, "Peace be with you." ³⁷ But they were startled and terrified and thought that they were seeing a ghost. ³⁸ Then he said to them, "Why are you troubled? And why do questions arise in your hearts? ³⁹ Look at my hands and my feet, that it is I myself. Touch me and see, because a ghost does not have flesh and bones as you can see I have." ⁴⁰ And as he said this, he showed them his hands and his feet. ⁴¹ While they were still incredulous for joy and were amazed, he asked them, "Have you anything here to eat?" ⁴² They gave him a piece of baked fish; ⁴³ he took it and ate it in front of them.*

John 20:19-23: *[19] On the evening of that first day of the week, when the doors were locked, where the disciples were, for fear of the Jews, Jesus came and stood in their midst and said to them, "Peace be with you." [20] When he had said this, he showed them his hands and his side. The disciples rejoiced when they saw the Lord. [21] [Jesus] said to them again, "Peace be with you. As the Father has sent me, so I send you." [22] And when he had said this, he breathed on them and said to them, "Receive the holy Spirit. [23] Whose sins you forgive are forgiven them, and whose sins you retain are retained."*

The Apostles (all but Thomas) and some other disciples were gathered together. They were anxious and confused. After all, He was betrayed by one of His closest. All the other Apostles (save one) had abandoned Him. In fact, Peter even publicly denied knowing the man. Then they got these reports about Jesus' body being removed from the tomb and some said He is risen. Then Mary Magdalene and two of the disciples said they actually saw Him and spoke to Him. What were they to believe!?

"Peace be with you." It is likely that some saw Him first and then heard the words. It is also likely that others heard the words and then looked up and saw Him. Was it true; was this really our Lord or was it a ghost? He proved to them He was not a ghost by eating some food. He showed them His wounds. Our Lord wanted them to believe, and they wanted to believe. *They were still incredulous for joy and were amazed.* It is only through Jesus that we can be drawn out of fear, anxiety, and confusion. It is only through Jesus that we can experience true peace.

Lord, there have been plenty of times in my life that I suffered from fear, anxiety, and confusion. It is only in recent years that I have found true peace through You.

Please open my mind and my heart to seek You first when fear, anxiety, and confusion start to make their way into my life. You are my way, my truth, and my life. Amen.

Jesus Appears to His Disciples
(Thomas is Present)

<u>John 20:24-29:</u> *²⁴ Thomas, called Didymus, one of the Twelve, was not with them when Jesus came. ²⁵ So the other disciples said to him, "We have seen the Lord." But he said to them, "Unless I see the mark of the nails in his hands and put my finger into the nail marks and put my hand into his side, I will not believe." ²⁶ Now a week later his disciples were again inside, and Thomas was with them. Jesus came, although the doors were locked, and stood in their midst and said, "Peace be with you." ²⁷ Then he said to Thomas, "Put your finger here and see my hands, and bring your hand and put it into my side, and do not be unbelieving, but believe." ²⁸ Thomas answered and said to him, "My Lord and my God!" ²⁹ Jesus said to him, "Have you come to believe because you have seen me? Blessed are those who have not seen and have believed."*

I recognize two lessons in this passage. First, it might seem obvious. Thomas (or should I say Doubting Thomas as he has come to be known) gets to see our Lord and touch His wounds. This is not remarkable. Thomas is not unlike many people. They require more than words to convince them of the truth of matters. We must be patient with people like this and keep presenting our case. We must also pray that God will open their minds to accept the truth.

Second, *blessed are those who have not seen and have believed.* I am one who has not seen and who believes. And I feel blessed. We, people who say we believe, have not

498

seen. We are blessed. It is important to accept this. Let us face it. Our faith is based on what we have been told, what we have read, things we have experienced. Realistically, our faith is based on love - the love of God. We are blessed.

Lord, I am generally a trusting person, but there are certain things about which I can truly be called a doubting Thomas. Please help me to be trusting in matters of my faith that You will help me discern the truth. Amen.

Jesus Appears to the Eleven

Mark 16:14-18: *[14] [But] later, as the eleven were at table, he appeared to them and rebuked them for their unbelief and hardness of heart because they had not believed those who saw him after he had been raised. [15] He said to them, "Go into the whole world and proclaim the gospel to every creature. [16] Whoever believes and is baptized will be saved; whoever does not believe will be condemned. [17] These signs will accompany those who believe: in my name they will drive out demons, they will speak new languages. [18] They will pick up serpents [with their hands], and if they drink any deadly thing, it will not harm them. They will lay hands on the sick, and they will recover."*

Matthew 28:16-20: *[16] The eleven disciples went to Galilee, to the mountain to which Jesus had ordered them. [17] When they saw him, they worshiped, but they doubted. [18] Then Jesus approached and said to them, "All power in heaven and on earth has been given to me. [19] Go, therefore, and make disciples of all nations, baptizing them in the name of the Father, and of the Son, and of the holy Spirit, [20] teaching them to observe all that I have commanded you. And behold, I am with you always, until the end of the age."*

Matthew and Mark have both described a similar dialogue between Jesus and His Apostles. *Go into the whole world and proclaim the gospel to every creature.* This part of the message is the same in both accounts, although the locations are different. We have to take heart in this particular message. It is a mission given to all of us – not just to the Apostles. This is what we are expected to do. This was not a mission given by God to Abraham, Isaac, Jacob, Moses, or any of the patriarchs and prophets. This is the mission given specifically to all who call themselves Christian.

Signs will accompany those who believe. Mark lists some of these. These are gifts from God. Only He will grant them. It is not for gifted Christians to just do as they please. These signs will be blessings from God, requested by those so gifted in the name of Jesus. We have to keep this in perspective. It is God giving the signs, not mere humans. We are His instruments.

And behold, I am with you always, until the end of the age. This assurance from our Lord is a true blessing to us. He is with us always, spiritually and physically. He gave us the gift of the Eucharist, His Body and Blood, to be present to us always. He is with us, not only to be consumed, but to be present to us in all the tabernacles throughout the world. Come let us adore!

Lord, You have given us our mission in life. And You have assured us that You will accompany us on our journey. Help us to move forward with confidence that, with Your help, nothing is impossible. Amen.

By the Sea of Tiberias

John 21:1-23: *[1] After this, Jesus revealed himself again to his disciples at the Sea of Tiberias. He revealed himself in this way. [2] Together were Simon Peter, Thomas called Didymus, Nathanael from Cana in Galilee, Zebedee's sons[j] and two others of his disciples. [3] Simon Peter said to them, "I am going fishing." They said to him, "We also will come with you." So they went out and got into the boat, but that night they caught nothing. [4] When it was already dawn, Jesus was standing on the shore; but the disciples did not realize that it was Jesus. [5] Jesus said to them, "Children, have you caught anything to eat?" They answered him, "No." [6] So he said to them, "Cast the net over the right side of the boat and you will find something." So they cast it, and were not able to pull it in because of the number of fish. [7] So the disciple whom Jesus loved said to Peter, "It is the Lord." When Simon Peter heard that it was the Lord, he tucked in his garment, for he was lightly clad, and jumped into the sea. [8] The other disciples came in the boat, for they were not far from shore, only about a hundred yards, dragging the net with the fish. [9] When they climbed out on shore, they saw a charcoal fire with fish on it and bread. [10] Jesus said to them, "Bring some of the fish you just caught." [11] So Simon Peter went over and dragged the net ashore full of one hundred fifty-three large fish. Even though there were so many, the net was not torn. [12] Jesus said to them, "Come, have breakfast." And none of the disciples dared to ask him, "Who are you?" because they realized it was the Lord. [13] Jesus came over and took the bread and gave it to them, and in like manner the fish. [14] This was now the third time Jesus was revealed to his disciples after being raised from the dead. [15] When they had finished breakfast, Jesus said to Simon Peter, "Simon, son of John, do you love me more than these?" He said to him, "Yes, Lord, you know that I love you."*

He said to him, "Feed my lambs." [16] He then said to him a second time, "Simon, son of John, do you love me?" He said to him, "Yes, Lord, you know that I love you." He said to him, "Tend my sheep." [17] He said to him the third time, "Simon, son of John, do you love me?" Peter was distressed that he had said to him a third time, "Do you love me?" and he said to him, "Lord, you know everything; you know that I love you." [Jesus] said to him, "Feed my sheep. [18] Amen, amen, I say to you, when you were younger, you used to dress yourself and go where you wanted; but when you grow old, you will stretch out your hands, and someone else will dress you and lead you where you do not want to go." [19] He said this signifying by what kind of death he would glorify God. And when he had said this, he said to him, "Follow me." [20] Peter turned and saw the disciple following whom Jesus loved, the one who had also reclined upon his chest during the supper and had said, "Master, who is the one who will betray you?" [21] When Peter saw him, he said to Jesus, "Lord, what about him?" [22] Jesus said to him, "What if I want him to remain until I come? What concern is it of yours? You follow me." [23] So the word spread among the brothers that that disciple would not die. But Jesus had not told him that he would not die, just "What if I want him to remain until I come? [What concern is it of yours?]"

This passage is slightly out of sequence. It is identified as an appendix to the Gospel of John, placed after what is accepted as the close of the Gospel. There are two basic stories embedded here.

The first is the recognition of Jesus by the Apostles. Once again, they do not immediately recognize Him. We do not know what physical form Jesus took after His resurrection. Obviously, it must have been different from what were His features before His passion and death. It could simply have been that He was clean shaven rather than bearded. And maybe His hair was shorter. He had the wounds. But He was different enough that Jesus' closest friends did a double take to recognize Him. So why is this significant? It is because it relates back to what Jesus told Thomas, "Blessed are those who have not seen and have believed." No one who was born after Jesus ascended to His Father has ever seen Him. Yes, we have portraits (portrayals of what He might have looked like), but we have never actually seen Him. We have plenty of words that tell us what He said and did. And a few words that describe Him generally. So, could we recognize Him if He chose to stand before us and talk to us? What form would He take? To truly recognize Him before us would be a blessing. It would be a gift only He could give us.

The second is a story of second chances. A second chance is being given by our Lord to Peter. He denied even knowing our Lord three times, openly to public inquiry. Peter was repentant, not like the remorse of Judas. Now Jesus is giving Him a chance to say how much he loves Him. Even here, Peter is stumbling. Referring back to this story as presented by Venerable Fulton J. Sheen in his book "Life of Christ," the actual word (love) used by Peter and Jesus were not the same. Jesus had to coax Peter into using the right word to describe how He was feeling. If Jesus asks me the question, "Do you love me?" Would I use the right word? Would I love Him the way He wants me to love Him?

My sister just walked into my room and showed me an apple she was peeling (one we bought yesterday). On the outside, the apple looked and felt like it would be great to eat. On the inside, the apple was rotten. Sometimes, all we have to go by are outward appearances; we never really know what is inside. But our Lord does.

Lord, I feel like there is so much I still need to learn. Help me, guide me, so that I may never be a disappointment to You. Amen.

Endings

<u>Mark 16:19-20:</u> *[19] So then the Lord Jesus, after he spoke to them, was taken up into heaven and took his seat at the right hand of God. [20] But they went forth and preached everywhere, while the Lord worked with them and confirmed the word through accompanying signs.*

<u>Luke 24:44-53:</u> *[44] He said to them, "These are my words that I spoke to you while I was still with you, that everything written about me in the law of Moses and in the prophets and psalms must be fulfilled." [45] Then he opened their minds to understand the scriptures. [46] And he said to them, "Thus it is written that the Messiah would suffer and rise from the dead on the third day [47] and that repentance, for the forgiveness of sins, would be preached in his name to all the nations, beginning from Jerusalem. [48] You are witnesses of these things. [49] And [behold] I am sending the promise of my Father upon you; but stay in the city until you are clothed with power from on high." [50] Then he led them [out] as far as Bethany, raised his hands, and blessed them. [51] As he blessed them, he parted from them and was taken up to heaven. [52] They did him homage and then returned to Jerusalem with great joy, [53] and they were continually in the temple praising God.*

<u>John 20:30-31:</u> *[30] Now Jesus did many other signs in the presence of [his] disciples that are not written in this book. [31] But these are written that you may [come to] believe that Jesus is the Messiah, the Son of God, and that through this belief you may have life in his name.*

504

John 21:24-25: *²⁴ It is this disciple who testifies to these things and has written them, and we know that his testimony is true. ²⁵ There are also many other things that Jesus did, but if these were to be described individually, I do not think the whole world would contain the books that would be written.*

Endings intrigue me. Every writer wants to say something meaningful at the end of his or her article or book. Hopefully, it will be something that will stay in the minds of the readers. Our Gospel writers had a purpose in writing their stories about Jesus, the Christ. Hopefully each was satisfied that he fulfilled the task he set out to do. So, the ending would have to be appropriate to each Gospel.

- Matthew ended his with the final mission to go out and baptize all nations. Jesus' words ended Matthew's Gospel: *And behold, I am with you always, until the end of the age.* Jesus assured them He would always be with them.
- Mark ended his with the ascension and the disciples going out on their mission: *they went forth and preached everywhere, while the Lord worked with them and confirmed the word through accompanying signs.*
- Luke's ending included more specific training to the disciples, and the disciples stayed close to the temple waiting for the advocate that was promised: *They did him homage and then returned to Jerusalem with great joy, and they were continually in the temple praising God.*
- John actually had two endings: the first showed that he completed what he set out to do and the second was the last verse of the appendix story.

As a writer and one who has devoted the last ten years of his life to understanding Jesus, what He taught, and how He

505

lived, I appreciate the last sentence of John's Gospel: *There are also many other things that Jesus did, but if these were to be described individually, I do not think the whole world would contain the books that would be written.* What I have written is nowhere near the billions of words that have been published over the last two thousand years.

However, I do get one lesson from the gospel endings. It is obvious that our Lord loved His disciples, especially His Apostles and those helpers who were part of His close family group. They all loved Him also. Love is what He offered to them, and it was love they returned to Him. It is all about love.

Lord, endings of books are not endings of life. The endings of the Gospels were the beginnings of the faith journeys of Your followers. I look forward to the rest of my journey, for it will bring me closer to You. Amen.

Part 16
My Conclusion

Have I Fulfilled My Mission?

Let us go back to the introduction and recap what my goal was in starting this project. I wrote, "God sent us His only begotten Son to redeem us and to show us how He expects us to live. Jesus' life is a clear example that the way God, our Father, expects us to live is possible. ... Jesus is our everything. It is Jesus whom we should imitate in all we say and do. ... We should be imitating His life and following His teachings. That is what you do when you truly love and respect someone. ... If I truly love our Lord, if I truly want to walk like Him, talk like Him, do things in the way He would do them, then I must study Him, how He lived, what he taught. Then and only then could I answer the question: what *would* Jesus do?"

In his book "Just Like Jesus," Max Lucado wrote: "God rewards those who seek *Him*. Not those who seek doctrine or religions or systems or creeds. Many settle for the lesser passions, but the reward goes to those who settle for nothing less than Jesus Himself. And what is the reward? What awaits those who seek Jesus? Nothing short of the heart of Jesus. 'And as the Spirit of the Lord works within us, we become more and more like Him' (2 Corinthians 3:18). Can you think of a greater gift than to be like Jesus?"

While reflecting on what I have read in the Gospels, I jotted down some notes about what I believe Jesus was telling me in the stories I was reading. Some are related to what Jesus said or did. Some are related to the circumstances and conditions present during those stories that help me to better understand what Jesus said and did. In all, I came up with more than 300 notes. These are all part of the treasure that I discovered during my study. I have included these notes in an appendix. They are my Pearls of Great Value.

There are various themes that I presented throughout the Gospels and quite a number of those themes are repeated often.

There is no problem with repetition, it represents emphasis on important topics. Below are 30 topics that are repeated often:

1. Will of God
2. Presence of God
3. Word of God
4. Fidelity of God
5. Humility
6. Healings/Miracles
7. Fulfillment of the law/Commandments
8. Acceptance
9. Gifts/Talents
10. Prayer
11. Trust
12. Truth/Honesty
13. Relationships
14. Courage/Perseverance
15. Forgiveness and Mercy
16. Unconditional love
17. Choices/Decisions
18. Faith/Hope/Love
19. Judgment and Motivations
20. Discernment
21. Eternal Life/Eternal Punishment
22. Conversion
23. Right/Wrong - Good/Evil
24. Understanding/Wisdom
25. Repentance/Reconciliation
26. Power/Control
27. Punishments/Consequences
28. Guidance
29. Mission/Goals/Objectives
30. Patience/Silence

There is one thing I am reminded of on a regular basis. St. Vincent de Paul said that he has only one sermon to preach, but he tells it in a thousand different ways. The repetition in the Gospels reflects that very idea. Jesus spent about three (3) years wandering about the Holy Land preaching. It is only logical to believe He repeated his message many times in many different ways.

When I reflect on all of the above and try to summarize this briefly, I find I cannot do better than what our Lord gave us in the two great commandments: love God above all things and love everyone else as He loves them. Do this and it fulfills the law. It is all about love.

Recently, I read Psalm 78 (not the first time). It has a message that fits with my particular study.

Psalm 78

Give heed, my people, to my teaching;
Turn your ear to the words of my mouth.
I will open my mouth in a parable
and reveal hidden lessons of the past.

The things we have heard and understood,
The things our fathers have told us,
These we will not hide from their children,
but will tell them to the next generation:

the glories of the Lord and His might
and the marvelous deeds He has done,
the witness He gave to Jacob,
the law he established in Israel.

If we truly believe that Jesus is God, if we truly believe that Jesus is present in the Eucharist, then as soon as we walk into church, we would fall on our knees in adoration, in joy to be close to Him. Yes, there would be times when we would fear if we were burdened with sins we had committed; but we should also be confident that, out of His love for us, we will be forgiven. I think we all have yet to grow in our faith – and that includes me. This study has been one step in growing my faith – my faith in Jesus Christ, the Son of God. My next step is to start living what I have learned.

I truly believe that, if I do so, then I can easily and legitimately picture myself as walking side by side with my Lord Jesus.

From Our Lord's Prayer:
Fiat Voluntas Tua!
Thy Will Be Done!

Appendix

The Pearls of

Great Value in

My Treasure

The Pearls of Great Value in My Treasure

Two saints provide us with good advice related to the study of Holy Scriptures. St. Basil the Great wrote: *Studying inspired Scripture is the most important way of finding out what we should do. There we find both instructions for our conduct and the lives of blessed men, given to us in writing as living examples of godly life, so that we may imitate their good deeds.* In addition, St. Cyril of Alaxandria wrote: *If you wish to explore the Holy Scripture, and you overcome your laziness and apply yourself, thirsting for the knowledge, then every good thing will be yours. ... Then you will rejoice as much in having the knowledge you desire as others who are worldly do when they insatiably accumulate Indian gems and gold. In fact, you will rejoice even more, "for wisdom is better than jewels, and all that you may desire cannot compare with her," as it is written (proverbs 8:11).*

My studies over the years have provided me with a great treasure (wisdom). My treasure consists of many pearls of great value:

    A. The actions and teachings of our Lord Jesus;

    B. The teachings and interpretations of the Apostles and other scripture authors;

    C. The teachings and interpretations of other spiritual writers and speakers; and

    D. My own interpretations of what I have learned.

This study of the Gospels has provided me with the following Pearls of Great value. I share them here. There are definitely some that seem to be repeats of others. That is all right. Important messages need to be repeated.

    1. Like me, all the Gospel writers were not eye witnesses of Jesus life. However, like me they all believed that Jesus was both human and divine.

    2. Sometimes faith has to be drawn out of us by physical

means.

3. Mankind would not and could not reconcile their sins with God, so God had to take the steps necessary for our reconciliation.

4. Next to Jesus, Mary is set before us as a true example of a life to be followed and imitated.

5. Mary's willingness to do God's Will, like Jesus' willingness to do the Will of His Father in heaven, is the key to gaining eternal life.

6. Praise and thanksgiving should be our regular greetings to God for all of the blessings He showers on us.

7. God is always faithful to His promises (covenants).

8. God works in His time frame – not ours.

9. A humble birth was Jesus' first experience as a human.

10. The shepherds may have been the first to be in visitation and adoration of our Lord.

11. Even though God's will and plan can be temporarily impacted by the wills of humans, He always has a way to brings us back in line.

12. God does not always call believers to be instruments of His plan.

13. Joseph learned to recognize God's messages; this is something we must do as well.

14. Our faith calls for us to believe Jesus was fully human; so, it only makes sense that He was raised fully human.

15. Jesus did not come to change the law, but to fulfill it.

16. Obedience was an important virtue that Jesus practiced.

17. Like John the Baptist, do not be afraid to do the right thing and challenge evil.

18. God has called all of us to fulfill His will even though

we may not see it to completion.

19. If you are to follow what you believe to be the Will of God, then you must be willing to accept the consequences, whatever they may be.

20. We must humble ourselves before God and mankind.

21. We must not blow our own horn, telling the world how good or important we are.

22. The special gifts that we have been given are to be used in service to others. We can use them to benefit ourselves, but we must always keep in mind how we can be of service to others.

23. You may pray to God seeking His help in some way, but do not expect His answer to be what you are asking for. Expect Him to respond to what is your need.

24. Only God is to be worshipped.

25. The more we give in to the temptations to commit little sins, the easier it is to give in to temptations to commit bigger sins.

26. Jesus is always delving deep and inviting people to see what is ahead. Examination: "What are you looking for?" Invitation: "Come and see..." Explanation: "You believe because..." Enticement: "You will see greater things..."

27. Sometimes it only takes a little trust to say "yes" to Jesus; but in the long run, staying the course takes more.

28. Jesus honored His Mother and father by obedience.

29. It was out of love that He performed miracles for people in their need.

30. Jesus was a faithful Jew. He honored the Sabbath and the Feasts.

31. Acting out of zeal or fervor is not the same as anger, but it may appear to be so. Actions made out of love

are not always seen for what they are.

32. Always keep an open mind and listen for the truth spoken out of love.

33. Jesus is available to those who need Him.

34. Being "born again" is not instantaneous, we must learn to be followers of Christ.

35. When speaking with Jesus, expect to have something to mull over.

36. Those who choose to not acknowledge Jesus as the Son of God and follow what He says will be condemned.

37. We must reject the call of the world and live by God's Will.

38. Jesus spent many hours walking and talking with His Apostles and disciples, a time of friendship.

39. We must all humble ourselves before God; we must decrease, He must increase.

40. We must accept Jesus' words as truth and obey the will of Him who sent Jesus.

41. Learning is one thing. At some point, we must start to live what we have learned.

42. Jesus was always looking for someone to invite to grow closer to Him and His Father.

43. Our food is to do the will of the one who sent us.

44. Wherever Jesus went, He drew followers.

45. Jesus' message to the people was: "The kingdom of God is at hand. Repent, and believe in the gospel." It is a message that people today still need to hear.

46. Before His public life, Jesus did not make known who He is. He was simply another boy grown to adulthood – no one special.

47. There is a time to speak and a time to be silent. Knowing the difference can save a lot of heartaches.

48. Once you know what God is asking of you, it takes

courage and perseverance to move forward.

49. They dropped everything and followed Him. Could I do the same? No matter how strong your faith is, it still takes courage to move forward.

50. Jesus spoke with authority.

51. There are many people in this world who have learned to tell lies and leave people believing it is the truth. It is not always easy to recognize the difference.

52. Our Lord does not always have to be asked to be healed. Out of love, He will act.

53. Jesus always found time and a place to keep prayer in His life.

54. The mission of all Christians is "catching men" for God.

55. Jesus' love is unconditional.

56. Jesus was not a showman. He did not require a lot of fanfare.

57. Jesus knows what we need and, in His love for us, he grants what we need.

58. Even if annoyed, Jesus responded to Pharisees and other groups calmly and sincerely.

59. People become set in their ways. It is difficult for those set in their ways to accept new ideas. It is not impossible, but difficult.

60. Jesus came to fulfill the Law, not change it.

61. The sabbath was made for man, not man for the sabbath.

62. The son of Man is Lord of the sabbath.

63. Jesus is never intimidated by those spying on Him.

64. We will never know the Mind of God, how He makes decisions and who He chooses as His Instrument.

65. We tend to jump to conclusions of black and white, good and bad. The gray areas only show up after some thought.

66. The greatest gift God has given us is hope, but hope always requires something from us.

67. In order to be poor in spirit, we have to develop the attitude of detachment from the things of this world.

68. Every bad thing that happens is an opportunity for someone to love another. Because that is what comfort is.

69. It is easier to accept accusations of wrong doing when they are true. It is harder when they are not true; but even these our Lord asks us to accept meekly and humbly. We are not to fight back because that gives-in to pride.

70. Righteousness wants everyone to do what is right in the eyes of God. If everyone does what is right in the eyes of God, then the world will change. We are in control.

71. We can only change how we react to people and things around us. We cannot change what other people do or think, but we can influence them.

72. God expects us to do what is right at this moment in time. Period.

73. Mercy says that, even though the person who committed the act is deserving of the consequence, we will forego the consequence and move forward in life.

74. Our Lord has given us the way; forgiveness of our sins and living a good life is the way to purity of heart.

75. Anyone who can calm a situation and bring peace to a conflict (without causing more conflict) is blessed.

76. Blessed are all of us who use our gifts to help others for we will be called children of God.

77. In the United States, our beliefs are being ridiculed. This persecution is not because of what we individually have said or done, but for who we are and

what we say we believe.

78. We must keep in mind that God expects us to be always faithful to Him, because He is always faithful to us.

79. With God, anything is possible.

80. We must do more than talk about our faith, we must live it.

81. It is easier for heaven and earth to pass away than for the smallest part of a letter of the law to become invalid.

82. Our emotions can be sinful depending on how we act upon them.

83. Our thoughts can be just as sinful as our actions.

84. The only way for a marriage to really work is for God to be part of it and for both parties to want it to work and are willing to do what it takes.

85. If we kept our answers to "yes," "no," and simple explanations, life would be better for everyone.

86. Those who experience the good things in life will, over time, experience the opposite. That is life in this world. We will never be totally happy in this world.

87. Jesus does not want us to be abused and He does not want us to be further abused, but He certainly does not want us to become the abuser either.

88. Love everyone, no matter who they are.

89. Reaching perfection may be out of reach, but I should strive to be a better version of myself.

90. God judges us based on the motives behind our actions.

91. Jesus tells us to pray quietly and on our own where only God can hear us. Then our reward will be from Him.

92. When Jesus gave us the Lord's Prayer, it was the first time we were encouraged to call God "our Father;"

and so, we are His adopted children.

93. The measure with which you measure will be measured back to you.

94. The things you value most are the things that will capture your mind and heart.

95. Jesus gives us His teachings in many different ways.

96. I must always keep in mind that God is my master.

97. Our Lord wants us to be concerned with those things that are under our control and how we act or react in response to them.

98. God knows what we need, and He will provide for those needs.

99. Be discerning to those to whom you spread the good news.

100. God, like any loving father, will give you only what is good for you, regardless of what it is you have asked for.

101. Do to others whatever you would have them do to you.

102. Entering through the wide gate satisfies temporarily, but you will never find fulfillment.

103. Entering through the narrow gate requires obedience and perseverance.

104. A bad person can become good and produce good fruit.

105. Change is a necessary part of growth, and growth is necessary for every human being.

106. To enter the kingdom of heaven, we must do the Will of God.

107. To study our Lord's teaching requires an effort on our part.

108. Jesus spoke with authority as no one else could, simply because He is the authority.

109. Jesus' love for us is not to satisfy the current need but

to also prepare us to move forward.

110. Jesus always understands how much we actually believe; and He does not hold weak faith against us. The healings He performs are a gift out of His compassion and love for us.

111. Jesus always was concerned about others. His love and compassion were unlimited. He helped. He never sought recompense or praise. He was here to do His Father's will.

112. God wants me – 100% of me – and will not be satisfied with less.

113. In spite of His disciples' lack of faith, Jesus helped them and encouraged them to depend on Him, especially when the going gets tough.

114. I may not always understand God's reasons for doing what He does, but it is important that I accept what He decides.

115. God loves all His creation, including the pagans and gentiles; all receive His blessings as He chooses to dispense them.

116. When it comes to seeking healing from God, the faith of the person to be healed or the faith of the person requesting the healing is a strong factor.

117. Jesus was always honest and up front with His Apostles, even if that honesty was something they did not want to hear.

118. Whoever acknowledges Jesus before others, He will acknowledge before His heavenly Father. But whoever denies Him before others, He will deny before His heavenly Father.

119. Jesus wants His followers to be at peace, to accept what is to come. He will be with them.

120. Jesus' way will cause controversy – even within families.

121. If you spend your time in search of the world, you may or may not gain it; but you will lose your chance for eternal life.

122. Jesus tells us here that we will be rewarded for following Him and His teachings.

123. Jesus expects us to observe, learn, and reason out what the answers are and not expect God to present the answers word for word.

124. Jesus was open and honest in His statements. The statements were not always easy to understand; but in the long run, the truth became clear.

125. No matter how much we would want it otherwise, there will be lost souls.

126. No matter what the circumstances are, we must be grateful to God for what He has given us.

127. When people unload themselves to our Lord, the load does not disappear; our Lord shares the load – not bears the load.

128. Jesus looks at what we do and why we did it, then He judges based on that.

129. We all need to adjust our value systems and place God and His will above all else.

130. It is our role as Christians, as humans, as servants of the poor to give aid wherever and whenever we can to make life easier for those in need.

131. Jesus continued to do the will of His Father in spite of what others may have thought.

132. Jesus always had the right thing to say for the situation and He promised us that, if we live as His Father wants us to, then the Holy Spirit will provide us with the words we need when we need them.

133. The words about good fruit coming from good people and bad fruit coming from bad people must be accepted along with the belief that this is not a

permanent condition. Bad people can change and can start to produce good fruit. Just as the opposite is true.

134. Jesus does not perform miracles to prove His abilities or His power. He is not presenting a show.

135. The healings Jesus performs, the demons He drives out, all of His miracles, are not guarantees of future safety and health. Everything He has done is for the moment. It is up to us to do what is necessary to keep ourselves clean.

136. Those baptized, who believed in Jesus and followed His will, are the adopted children of His Father and, therefore, members of His family.

137. Jesus tells His Apostles that not everyone will understand His parables. The parables are really intended for His Apostles to understand and to explain the meaning to others.

138. At times, Jesus did get frustrated with His Apostles; but He loved them anyway.

139. It surprises me how many people who call themselves Christians and say they believe Christ is God; and yet, they refuse to acknowledge the existence of Satan. Jesus Himself speaks of Him. They refer to Satan as a fairy tale character. Why would God, who is the God of truth, speak of Satan if he does not exist?

140. Jesus is telling us that unless we strive to understand, we will lose what we have. The more we strive to understand, and the more we share what we know, the more will be revealed to us.

141. One thing we need to realize is that we will never know how everything exists and works. It is up to us to accept what is, to observe and to question, but always to accept.

142. Our Lord allows us to live and grow among the worldly. We have to choose to live rightly.

143. Faith, hope, and love will fill us with the drive to learn more and to do more, to be part of our Lord's body – His Kingdom.

144. Jesus spent time privately with His Apostles and other disciples, explaining His teachings, things He did not share with the crowds.

145. We are more likely to come across treasures of knowledge and wisdom rather than of material value. We need to be able to store those up and call upon them as we need them.

146. When God heals someone, the healing is real; not just a relief of symptoms that will return later.

147. Jesus follows what His Father does, just as sons generally model their lives after what they see in their fathers.

148. As the Son of God, Jesus can do what He chooses: healing whoever He wants, giving life to whoever He chooses. And He can pass this power on to whoever he chooses.

149. I should not be trying to analyze shoulda, woulda, coulda moments. I need to accept what is and focus on what is God's will for me.

150. Semantics are important when dealing with any ages-old document. You have to understand the words used and why. Simply replacing them with today's words do not always paint the same picture.

151. After exerting Himself to help the crowds, Jesus goes off to be by Himself (probably to pray and recuperate).

152. Our faith is the key to our relationship with God, so we can expect to have our faith tested over and over again.

153. Even if we fail our test, God loves us so much that He will give us other opportunities to prove our faith.

154. Jesus was always honest with the people He encountered. It was not only scribes and Pharisees that He challenged, He also challenged the common folk.

155. What Jesus is present to us in the Eucharist, His living example and all of His teachings are the way to live this life and prepare ourselves for our heavenly journey.

156. Jesus wants us to understand the reality of what we are told to do. We have to make the right decision and not follow hollow or false precepts.

157. Jesus' compassion was not restricted to Jews alone.

158. Jesus affirmed what the scriptures and prophets of old taught about the way people should live.

159. Our Lord was ever thoughtful of the people who came to Him.

160. I will not always understand everything our Lord says and does.

161. Faith is a gift – a gift from God. God has to select us and grant us this gift if we ever hope to grow close to Him and spend eternal life with Him.

162. Not everyone hears and understands what is said in the same way. Further explanations are normally required.

163. In reading these passages from the bible, we have to try to place ourselves in the mindset of both sides of the conversation.

164. We must live in this world and make the best of it; but we must not let the world control us. We must place our trust in God and live as He wants us to. It is all a matter of choice.

165. My natural human curiosity drives me to know everything about everything. However, I resign

myself to the belief that You will reveal to me what I need to know when I need to know it.

166. Everything is possible to one who has faith. We must all strive to strengthen our faith.

167. There are times when we will hear things we don't want to hear, but we cannot change them simply by ignoring them. We have to discern the truth and act on it.

168. There are times when we will be required to do things we are not really obligated to do, and we will do them to avoid offending others or causing conflict.

169. We are to humble ourselves before God and man. We are also to love each other with the love that Jesus taught us.

170. As long as we accept what Jesus is teaching us, then we are also accepting the will of His Father in Heaven. For Jesus came to fulfill the will of His Father.

171. Regardless of "religious" affiliation, if the person doing the mighty deed is Christian and does the deed in Jesus' name, then we should accept it as something good.

172. We are all tempted in many different ways. But we still have the choice to give in to the temptation or to push it aside. The choice is ours. But the punishment is severe for the ones who cause others to sin.

173. Our passion, our fervor, our zeal is what keeps our faith strong and keeps us growing. If we lose that zeal, there is no simple solution to bringing it back. We must strive to keep our passion alive.

174. I must never lose sight of the fact that I am important to God. I must never forget that I need to keep my focus on Him and understand and follow the guidance provided by my Guardian Angels.

175. If your brother sins, rebuke him; and if he repents, forgive him. If he does not repent, treat him as an outsider, because he may someday cause you to sin.

176. If what we pray for (in spite of two or more praying with us) is deemed by our heavenly Father to be inappropriate or inopportune at this time, then the answer can be "no."

177. The fact is that we should be willing to forgive our brother whether it is seven times, seven times seven times, seventy-seven times, on to infinity.

178. I must keep love, forgiveness, and mercy at the forefront of any actions I take.

179. We cannot always assume that people reject Jesus because He is God or because of His teachings and miracles. Personal agendas often come into play.

180. When going out to do the Will of God, it is best to always go in pairs, as Jesus taught.

181. There are so many people in this world who would welcome the Word of God, but we have so few people to bring it to them.

182. The more we use the gifts we are given, the more confidence we have in our ability to use them.

183. This life is about growing close to God, doing His will, and spending eternity with Him.

184. Why would any men, women, or children follow Jesus if He did not smile and laugh and enjoy life?

185. We know from Gospel passages that Jesus often prayed to, talked with His Father. He prayed on behalf of the people who came to hear His words. He prayed for those He healed. He prayed for those who hated Him. And He rejoiced with them as well.

186. The two great commandments are truly come from God regardless of who actually pronounced the words.

187. Both passages of the two great commandments and the parable of the Good Samaritan confirm the fact that Jesus came to fulfill the law, not to change it.

188. There are times when we need to ensure that our priorities are set with God first.

189. If our Lord places someone in need in our path, we should strongly consider helping our Lord in the person of the one in need.

190. Jesus came down hard on the Pharisees and scholars of the law. They could not deny His accusations. That is why they plotted against Him.

191. Jesus did not go out of His way to pick a fight. The fight always came to Him.

192. Greed is never satisfied. Our lives should be bringing us closer to God rather than building walls between us. The more we are focused on our treasures, the less we are able to keep God in our lives.

193. We will never know when our Lord is going to call us to account for what we have been doing. So, do things according to God's will; and, when God calls on us, all will be well.

194. We should fear offending God by our disobedience; otherwise, we are no better than Pavlov's dog.

195. Jesus is calling for all to repent of their sins and be reconciled with God. If we do, we may be fruitful in the future.

196. Jesus made it clear that acts of compassion are good regardless of the day of the week.

197. The first shall be last and the last shall be first. Jesus' warning was for all sinners. Following the law, living the will of the Father, as Jesus showed us the way, will lead us through the narrow gate.

198. I am not very different from Jesus' other disciples. I suppose that, if I were there with them at that time,

Jesus' words would fly over my head as well. It is only after the fact that I know the truth.

199. Even though Jesus' mission is to the Israelites, the whole world needs to accept Him as Lord.

200. Humbling ourselves before others is at the same time humbling ourselves before God. Humility is a virtue we should all practice.

201. The ones who value the gift of faith will follow the precepts of the faith and spend time and resources to grow it. They will be welcomed to the feast and enjoy it.

202. There will be more joy in heaven over one sinner who repents than over ninety-nine righteous people who have no need of repentance. God will make every effort to find sinners and bring them back to the fold.

203. Forgiveness and mercy are part of God's expression of love for all of us.

204. Trust is only gained by doing things in the manner expected. Being trustworthy in some things will gain you more opportunities to show your worth.

205. You cannot serve both God and the world, at least not to the expectation of both.

206. The law is the law, and it will be until the end of time.

207. The law is meant to apply to everyone, not just men and not just women.

208. The homeless, the poor, the people in need are real and their needs are real, so we should not simply look or walk the other way.

209. Jesus forewarned us that, even though He foretold His passion, death, and resurrection, all people would not believe and repent of their sins. His disciples would have a lot of work ahead of them.

210. We are called to humble ourselves before God.

211. Sometimes it is the one you least expect to respond who actually does.

212. The kingdom of God began with the Incarnation of Jesus. It was Jesus' taking on His human nature that made it possible for the Church to be formed.

213. When Jesus comes, it will be too late to start preparing ourselves. The things of this world will have no meaning. It is only us and God, and our state of being at that time.

214. We have to be persistent in the things we pray for, at least the things that are really important to us. God will answer our prayers out of love for us, not because we are nagging Him.

215. We all need to admit our failings and humble ourselves before our Lord and Creator.

216. I need to be as faithful to the Will of God as Jesus is.

217. I must follow God's will completely, or else it becomes my will, not His.

218. If I am to imitate the life of Jesus, then I must not fear; I must have courage to follow the will of Him who sent me.

219. In spite of the amount of time I spend in prayer, I believe my prayer life is lacking. I must develop this to improve my spiritual life.

220. There are times when our Lord is merciful, even when we do not ask for mercy.

221. Those who follow Jesus will not walk in darkness.

222. If we choose to not believe that Jesus is God, then we cannot go with Him to His heavenly kingdom.

223. Following our faith frees us from conflict. We are free. All we need is the courage to do so.

224. It is important that I recognize God's voice in the promptings that I get, because it is He that I want to follow.

225. We should never allow others to intimidate us into doing or saying what is not right and good.
226. God does not punish anyone for someone else's sin.
227. In reading Jesus' life and teachings, it is up to us to reach an understanding of the lessons He wants us to learn. Sometimes this can only be done over time and much investigation.
228. Although we humans tire from the routines and burdens of life, God does not. He is always ready to listen to us and love us as only He can.
229. The type of relationship that we should have with our Father in heaven is like the innocence of children as well as their ultimate love and dependence on their parents and others to care for and protect them.
230. It is the will of our Father in heaven that we live by His commandments and do His will throughout our lives, not just at certain times or for a period of time.
231. The wealthy will find it difficult to enter the kingdom of heaven because they will be dedicated too much to acquiring and keeping the treasures of this world. However, some of the wealthy will be saved. All things are possible with God.
232. The rewards that come from following the Will of God are the intangibles that come with love, friendship and service to each other. And these rewards will continue on through all eternity.
233. Even the evilest person who ever lived, who experiences a conversion, may be invited to enter the kingdom of heaven. Let us pray that we will be there to rejoice with him.
234. No amount of reasoning will open a closed mind.
235. Jesus' love for others can still be manifested in following the will of His Father even when that is not apparent to us.

236. Love of our Lord can inspire us to have the courage necessary to face our fears.

237. Our faith, like that of Martha, can help us to acknowledge that Jesus is not just a friend and loved one; but He is the Messiah, the Son of God.

238. A sad truth is that evildoers normally can find the words to unify and instigate the crowd.

239. God does not always say things we want to hear; but we must listen, and act based on what He says.

240. What we must learn is to be humble before God and each other. We must seek to serve rather than be served.

241. If the request for forgiveness is sincere, reconciliation for the sin committed should be given, if at all possible.

242. God expects each of us to use the gifts we are given to bear fruit. If we are not fruitful, what we have will be taken from us.

243. Those who are non-believers or opposed to God and His will shall face eternal punishment.

244. God knows what is in our hearts and gives us what we most need.

245. Miracles are not always needed. When God chooses to meet the need of an individual, He will move whatever hearts are necessary to accommodate the need.

246. It is sad but true that the mob can be moved to do both good and bad, depending on the influence and mood. Only God knows what is in the hearts of those in the mob.

247. Jesus, and therefore the Father and the Holy Spirit, can feel all the emotions that any human can feel.

248. Jesus says, "believe that you will receive it, and it shall be yours." I still have to work on this.

249. Jesus is able to read the hearts of those who approach Him and always has an appropriate answer for those who challenge Him.

250. Following the Will of God is what is important; but, just as important is the timing. Following God's will now, at the present time, is what God wants. Who you are and what you do today is what is important to God.

251. My life must be lived in such a way that I keep the Presence of God ever before me, which means I must continue to study and pray.

252. I must have confidence that the Holy Spirit will provide me with the words I need to say when I need them. I, however, should never expect a particular result, such as conversion, from what I say.

253. We are expected by God to accept the situation we are in and fulfill the requirements of that situation. We may not be happy about it, and we may work at changing that situation; but, in the meantime, we must follow the rules of life as they exist.

254. When our physical bodies expire, our souls will still live on for all eternity. We will transition (whatever that means and whatever form that takes) either to eternal life ultimately with God in heaven or eternal damnation in hell. However, in either case it will still be life.

255. My life is based on what I believe (faith). It should also be based on what I know (reason).

256. Thou shalt not preach one thing and practice another.

257. Thou shalt not lay heavy burdens on people's shoulders but not lift a finger to help them.

258. Thou shalt not boast of how good a person you are. Thou shalt not seek honors in public gatherings. Thou shalt not seek titles of prestige. Thou shalt not seek greatness but humble yourself.

259. Thou shalt not close the gates of heaven to all who wish to enter.

260. Thou shalt not place higher value on the things of this world rather than on God and all He sends us.

261. Thou shalt not place higher value on the things of this world but ignore judgment, mercy, and fidelity.

262. Thou shalt not cleanse the outside but ignore the evil within.

263. Therefore, do and observe all things whatsoever hypocrites tell you, but do not follow their example.

264. When the value of the gift we offer is higher than "making room for more" or something we "will not miss," then it will have meaning to God. Our gift must be a sacrifice.

265. Knowing what the future will bring is not always good news. It is only important for us to know what God wants to reveal to us.

266. Only God knows what the future holds in store for us. May our daily prayers be in gratitude for all of God's blessings, and an appeal for His forgiveness and mercy for all of our sins.

267. All the world will know when Jesus comes again. Until that time, we should not speculate about His coming.

268. We should live our lives in such a way that we will be ready for our Lord when He does come.

269. It is in how we treat others that we tell our Lord how we feel about Him.

270. We can choose to grant favors to one and not to others. We choose to forgive wrongs done to us. We choose to be merciful or not. The reason behind our choice, our motivation, is what is really important.

271. God will treat us as we treat others: loving, caring, forgiving, ignoring, harming, abandoning. In the end,

we will face the consequences of our own choices: eternal life or eternal punishment.

272. God speaks to each of us, but we are not always tuned into Him and hear what He is saying to us.

273. Jesus ascended into heaven, but He left His physical presence here with us in the form of bread and wine, His Body and Blood, His Eucharistic presence.

274. Our Lord wants us to trust His word and follow Him, in spite of the potential consequences from those in "authority."

275. What Jesus wants is for us to accept what He says as the words of His Father in heaven; and to realize that, if we reject Him and His words, we are also rejecting His Father.

276. Discerning the truth about what happened in history helps us to avoid making similar mistakes. However, the judging of individuals must be left in the hands of God.

277. The plans to do evil are normally done in the shadows.

278. That is the way of faith. You must persevere in your studies in order for your faith to grow. His disciples had the best teacher.

279. Being a leader is about responsibility to those who are followers. The leader has to consider the needs of those who follow because it is about their welfare as well as the cause they are promoting.

280. If we accept the message Jesus gives us, then we accept the message of the one who sent Him. If we follow Jesus, then we follow His Father. If we follow Jesus, we follow the Triune God.

281. There are no secrets I can keep from my Lord. In spite of that fact, He allows me to proceed with the choices I make, even if it saddens Him to do so.

282. I must partake in His body and blood, not just acknowledge it. This gift has no meaning for us if we do not accept it. And, it has more meaning for us if we accept it often.

283. Our Lord is with us always. He comes to us through the Mass and is present to us in tabernacles throughout the world. I have spent time visiting Him in the tabernacle, but not nearly as often as I could have. This is something I must change.

284. Jesus' love for us is unconditional. He loves us in spite of who we are, what we say, or what we do. He is willing to forgive every sin we commit if we truly repent. He is willing to be merciful to us, sinners. That is what He is asking of us: do the same.

285. If ever I am in circumstances that are similar to Peter in the Passion narratives, I can only hope I will do better.

286. Jesus wanted His disciples to know that they would face much opposition to what He taught and what they believe.

287. Jesus told us more than once that He came to do His Father's will, and He has been doing so in word and deed. It is trust He is asking for from us.

288. If we ask anything in Jesus' name, He will do it. He will answer our requests based on His Father's will.

289. It is in following God's will that we show our love for Him. It is in following God's will that we will find Jesus, because He will reveal Himself to us.

290. Our Father in heaven will send the Holy Spirit to be with us always, to teach us what to say, to guide us in what we do. The Holy Spirit will be our guiding light.

291. If we do what Jesus does and follow the will of our Father in heaven, then we will be at peace, in spite of what the world throws our way.

292. Jesus is the one who calls us, we are His chosen ones. We do what we can to follow Him, to bear good fruit. But His Father, our Father in heaven is the one who judges us.

293. As friends of Jesus, we are friends of His Father. And as would be expected, friends treat each other with love.

294. It is the acknowledgement and assurance of our Lord that His followers, His disciples, will suffer for belief in Him and His teachings. Our Lord does not set a time limit on this.

295. This is the work of the Holy Spirit: to guide us to glorifying God through the works we do.

296. If we live as the Father wants us to live, we will be with Jesus at the end of our earthly lives.

297. The truth of the matter is that whatever we ask for in the name of Jesus will be given by the Father if it fits into His plans for us or for the one we are praying for.

298. Jesus wants His disciples (and us) to love His Father as He loves us, as His Father loves us.

299. Running away in the face of danger is a natural reaction. We need to pray that we will react as God wants us to.

300. We must strive to let God in, to allow Him to live in us and we in Him. Only then can we experience eternal life with God. We have to be ready to share the gift of eternal life with Him.

301. If we are to be counted among the disciples of God, then we must give ourselves to God, the one God, the Triune God.

302. Jesus wants us to have the strength to persevere against evil, which only our Father in heaven can grant us. Yet we must still give Him our "fiat."

303. Our mission, given us by Jesus, is to make the world know that the love of God is in them.

304. Jesus wants us to endure all that comes before us for the love of God and the love of mankind. It is the will of our Father we must follow.

305. We must also be sensitive to the needs of others and not require more of them than they are capable of doing.

306. Hate the sin but love the sinner.

307. Protect the innocent.

308. The only way I could withstand the things that our Lord and the many martyrs who suffered after Him and for Him is out of love. Love is the key.

309. God has shown me on many occasions that my pride is keeping me from living up to His expectations of me. I pray He will grant me the graces I need to speak and act as He would have me do so.

310. I know God is a loving, forgiving, and merciful God. I must always be confident that I can come to God deeply repentant, and He will forgive me.

311. Face adversity calmly and patiently. I am not to get emotionally charged and try to justify what I do. As Jesus had told His disciples, the advocate will provide the words that need to be spoken at the necessary time.

312. Pressure from those around can cause people to do what is wrong in spite of what they believe. It takes extraordinary effort to follow through with what is right.

313. To be right before God, we must choose the right rather than the safe. That is not always an easy choice, but it is realistically a choice we make often.

314. The decisions I make in the future may not always be simply based on right or wrong. The world always

tends to complicate our decision making. I need to discern and choose what our Father will have me do.

315. It is important that all Christians keep a regular reminder before them of our Lord's sacrifice (passion, death, and resurrection). We cannot allow ourselves to forget this.

316. Keep in mind that out of love for His Mother, Jesus will naturally want to please His Mother. Our Blessed Mother Mary is our best advocate. She will petition her Son on our behalf.

317. Evil wants to portray itself as doing the right thing, so it makes the victim evil and ridicules him. So, in their minds, evil becomes good, and innocence becomes evil.

318. God sees what we do. He hears what we say. He knows our innermost thoughts. He knows what is in our hearts. He knows us.

319. It is amazing how a gesture of compassion can be felt and appreciated by the one to whom it is intended.

320. The crowd did not know that our Lord had died in reparation for all of their sins and the sins of all mankind. They simply felt the guilt of participating in defiling innocence.

321. God calls each of us in different ways. He has different plans for each of us. He called these folks from Galilee to be with His Son and so they followed and did what they could to serve.

322. The law must be fulfilled.

323. Some heroes do not show up to save the day; they show up to honor the fallen.

324. Evil deeds are usually revealed in the long run, no matter how much money, other gifts, or more evil deeds are used to cover it up.

325. If you know that something is the right thing to do in a set of circumstances, then do it; let God take care of the rest.

326. If God wants you to do something specific, He will let you know.

327. Seeing and hearing is not the same as believing.

328. The more the lie is told, the more likely it will become the truth – not in reality, but perceived.

329. It is so much easier to allow evil to flourish than to do good.

330. Our Lord comes to us in whatever form is necessary to ease us into being comfortable in His presence.

331. When you encounter someone who has a comfortable presence, who has a clear way of explaining things, who has an obvious interest and knowledge of something that has been on your mind, then you are going to comfortably discuss matters with this person and easily lose track of time.

332. When you find something that draws your interest and keeps it, you do not want it to end.

333. When you are filled with joy, you want to share it with others as quickly as possible.

334. When things are heard that are contrary to what is expected, especially stories that defy nature, then it takes either first-hand experience or firm desire to believe.

335. It is only through Jesus that we can be drawn out of fear, anxiety, and confusion. It is only through Jesus that we can experience true peace.

336. Some people require more than words to convince them of the truth of matters. We must be patient with people like this and keep presenting our case. We must also pray that God will open their minds to accept the truth.

337. Our faith is based on what we have been told, what we have read, things we have experienced. Realistically, our faith is based on love. – the love of God. We are blessed.

338. *Go into the whole world and proclaim the gospel to every creature.* It is a mission given to all of us – not just to the Apostles. This is what we are expected to do. This is the mission given specifically to all who call themselves Christian.

339. Signs will accompany those who believe. It is God giving the signs, not mere humans. We are His instruments.

340. Jesus is with us always, not only to be consumed, but to be present to us in all the tabernacles throughout the world. Come let us adore!

341. Could we recognize Jesus if He chose to stand before us and talk to us? What form would He take? To truly recognize Him before us would be a blessing. It would be a gift only He could give us.

342. If Jesus asks me the question, "Do you love me?" Would I use the right word? Would I love Him the way He wants me to love Him?

343. Sometimes, all we have to go by are outward appearances; we never really know what is inside. But our Lord does.

344. It is obvious that our Lord loved His disciples, especially His Apostles and those helpers who were part of His close family group. They all loved Him also. Love is what He offered to them, and it was love they returned to Him. It is all about love.

Topical Index

Index of My Reflections

544

Made in USA - Kendallville, IN
54746_9798218602871
02.11.2025 2017